W9-ACV-582

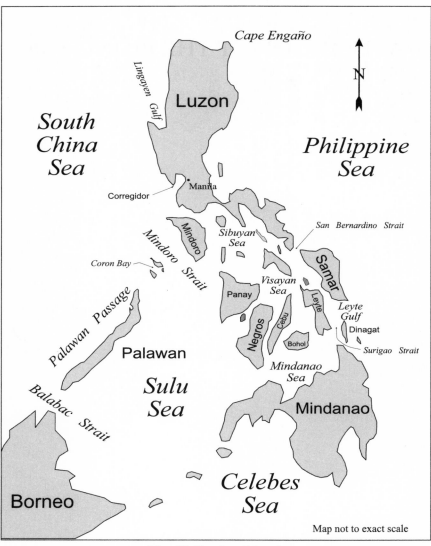

The Philippine Islands

AFTERNOON OF THE
RISING SUN

The Battle of Leyte Gulf

Kenneth I. Friedman

PRESIDIO

Published by Presidio Press, Inc.
505 B San Marin Drive, Suite 160
Novato, CA 94945-1340

Library of Congress Cataloging-in-Publication Data

Friedman, Kenneth I.
    Afternoon of the Rising Sun : the Battle of Leyte Gulf / Kenneth I. Friedman.
      p. cm.
    Includes bibliographical references (p. 402) and index.
    ISBN 0-89141-756-7
      1. Philippine Sea, Battles of the, 1944 I. Title.

D774.P5F75 2001
940.54'25—dc21

                    2001036633

Unless otherwise noted, all photos courtesy U.S. Naval Historical Center

Printed in the United States of America

I dedicate this book to several wonderful people. My wife, Lydia, spent many hours in editing this work and was unflagging in her constructive criticism and support. My three children—Hilary, David, and Marla—were generous with their ongoing encouragement, suggestions, and time.

A special thanks goes to the editor I hired to redact this book, Jennifer McDowell, Ph.D. She provided an indispensable service by helping me structure this book and by giving me a more effective way of stating what I wanted to say.

I also wish to dedicate this book to the veterans' organization, the Tin Can Sailors, who helped in contacting the veterans I interviewed to gather invaluable primary material. Also, the veterans who served aboard the light carrier USS Cabot deserve my appreciation for the help they gave me while doing the research for this book.

Lastly, I dedicate this book to all the veterans of World War II, who saved the world from impending disaster and gave everything they had so my country's citizens can live in peace and freedom.

Contents

Maps

Preface

Leyte Gulf is not the best known of all the battles in World War II, and no noted historian considers it to be a battle that dramatically altered the course of the war in the way Midway, El Alamein, or Stalingrad did. So why did this particular battle draw me in, causing me to dedicate more than three years of my life to this exacting challenge?

First, this naval battle was the largest ever fought in terms of ships and men. Second, the stakes involved were extremely high for both sides. The Philippines were a prize well worth fighting for, one the Japanese had snatched from the Americans in 1942 by cunning and daring. So, the Americans had to drive the invaders out in order to defeat their insatiable territorial ambitions. Third, and most important, in this confrontation between the two greatest fleets in World War II, some of the most talented and most controversial individuals in both navies were set against one another in a contest of wit, will, and resources. Finally, the incredible bravery of the sailors who waged this battle inspires respect, admiration, and awe, and so a detailed account of their activities will add to the literature on World War II naval history.

In researching this book, I have drawn on primary and secondary sources. The primary sources include oral recollections via personal documents (memoirs and letters) and personal interviews with several American naval veterans who served in that battle. Secondary sources consist of books and articles.

All the veterans interviewed were contacted through the veterans' organization named the Tin Can Sailors. This group kindly allowed me to attend their 1996 annual convention in Las Vegas, where I met some of the men and spent very gratifying moments with them. The Tin Can Sailors allowed me to place, without charge, a notice in their quarterly publication, and this brought a deluge of letters, diaries, and other materials that I have incorporated into the narrative. Words cannot express my gratitude to this group for its practical assistance and support. It is an honor to include this organization in the book's dedication.

The views that I express on the Battle of Leyte Gulf are entirely my own, however, and I take full responsibility for them. Throughout this book, the reader will encounter many unfamiliar naval and military terms, and jargon. For this reason, I have included a glossary of technical terms that the reader can use to make the reading experience more enjoyable.

In choosing the title of this work, my purpose was to highlight the position of Japanese naval power after almost three years of bloody struggle against the ever more powerful United States Navy. When the Japanese bombed Pearl Harbor, the Japanese empire was at the peak of its power—like a scorching, scourging sun that had risen from the depths of centuries of obscurity. After winning victory after victory, the Japanese navy reached the zenith of its power at Midway and at the great naval battles around the Solomon Islands.

However, from that time forward, Japan's sun began to wane, and, by the time the Battle of Leyte Gulf was waged, Japan's naval power was like a sun ripe to sink below the rim of the Pacific Ocean. Still, this sun had not yet lost all its luster. Japan still had the will to fight and the dogged hope of not merely enduring, but of winning and turning the tide of war in its favor. But Leyte Gulf proved instead to be late afternoon in the sundial of Japanese sea power. And so, when this battle closed, the Japanese empire's sun was about to sink forever below the western horizon.

Kenneth I. Friedman

Glossary

ACI: Air Combat Intelligence.

Avenger: American torpedo plane with a large round body and a gun turret that could fire to its rear. The Avenger could be modified to carry bombs.

B-29: American heavy bomber used in the bombing campaign of Japan.

battery: A group of similar artillery pieces, for example, guns or missile launchers, that function as a single tactical unit. Also, a unit in the artillery branch of an army corresponding to a company in an infantry regiment.

battle line: Naval battle formation in which heavily armed naval ships form a line from which they deliver maximum firepower against an approaching enemy.

catapult: Apparatus used to accelerate an airplane's takeoff from a carrier's deck.

chart house: Room on board a ship where maps and navigational charts are stored.

chief of naval operations: American naval officer in command of the entire United States Navy.

CIC: Combat Information Center: a place on board a ship in which all information concerning a tactical situation is collected, analyzed, and disseminated to naval commanders to aid them in making decisions. This center was developed in the latter stages of World War II as naval battles became more complex and fast-moving.

CINCPAC: Commander in Chief, Pacific Fleet.

Combat Air Patrol: A group of naval fighter aircraft flying over a carrier task force to protect it from enemy air attacks.

CVE: Navy designation for escort carriers. Also called "jeep carriers," they are far smaller than the fast carriers that have a displacement of more than 30,000 tons.

DE: Navy designation for a destroyer escort, a smaller version of the destroyers that had been built for convoy duty in the North Atlantic.

displacement ton: Equivalent to 2,240 pounds of sea water. A term used to indicate the size of a ship.

dreadnought: Type of warship, named for the British battleship *Dreadnought*, built in the early twentieth century, the first of its kind in which the caliber of all its main guns was the same.

ensign: The lowest rank of commissioned officers in most of the world's navies. Also, the flag flown by a nation's warship in battle.

fall of shot: Naval term used to designate the process of observing where shells from naval gunfire impact the water around an intended target.

flag plot: Designated location on an admiral's flagship where the total battle's situation is plotted and analyzed.

general quarters: The command used by the United States Navy to send a ship's crew to their assigned battle stations and prepare for duty.

Grumman fighter: *See* Wildcat fighter.

Hellcat fighter: *See* Wildcat fighter.

Helldiver: An American naval dive-bomber.

JANAC: Joint Army-Navy Assessment Committee.

home islands: Japan's main islands: Honshu, Hokkaido, Kyushu, and Shikoku.

JCS: United States Joint Chiefs of Staff.

Judys: An American term for a type of Japanese navy dive-bomber.

kamikaze: A Japanese word that means "divine wind." The word was immortalized into Japanese culture when typhoons all but destroyed two invading Mongolian fleets in 1274 and 1281, thus saving Japan from invasion.

LCI: Landing craft, infantry.

LCT: Landing craft, tank.

lee: Side of a ship that is shielded from the wind.

lose way: A nautical term meaning that a ship has slowed to such an extent that steering becomes difficult to maintain.

LST: Landing ship, tank.

LVT: Landing vehicle, tracked. Amphibious personnel carriers that also were known as "alligators." They had special tracks that provided traction in the water as well as on the land.

MAGIC: The American effort to break both the Japanese military and diplomatic codes.

NROTC: Naval Reserve Officer Training Corps.

OCTAGON: Combined Chiefs of Staff Conference held in Quebec during September 1944.

order of battle: The way military forces are organized when preparing for battle.

PBY: An American patrol bomber in wide use at the beginning of World War II. Also called the *Catalina.* Although slow and cumbersome, it was an effective patrol bomber because of its long range of approximately 1,500 miles.

PB4Y: A modified B-24 bomber with superior range and speed to the PBY.

pointer: Person in a gun crew responsible for directing the aim of a gun.

port: Seagoing nomenclature for the left-hand side of a ship.

PT boats: American motor torpedo boats. Used extensively during World War II as scouting vessels and light attack craft.

PURPLE: American code name for the machine to which the Japanese diplomatic code was entrusted during World War II. The machine's movements were such as to create a near-random sequence. It was built in the late 1930s and was operational between Tokyo and Washington, D.C., in 1939. William F. Friedman, in charge of some of America's code-breaking efforts, and his staff broke the code in October 1940.

screws: A nautical term for a ship's propellers and the shafts to which they are attached and turned by the ship's engines.

SHO-GO: The Japanese plan to counter America's next move following the Battle of the Philippine Sea and prior to the Battle of Leyte Gulf. "Sho" is the Japanese word for victory.

sound-powered phone system: Telephone system used aboard naval vessels that did not require electricity to operate. Needed to maintain shipboard communication if electrical power were to fail during battle.

starboard: Seagoing nomenclature for the right-hand side of a ship.

star shell: Shell fired that, when ignited, delivers a bright light so that artillery or naval spotters can see their target in darkness.

Station HYPO: Code name for the American naval intelligence center located on Oahu, Hawaii. One of several centers that engaged in intercepting and analyzing Japanese military radio traffic. Other centers included Station CAST in the Philippines and Station NEGAT in Washington, D.C. After the Japanese captured the Philippines in 1942, the Americans relocated CAST to Australia.

Taffy: Radio call sign given to the American escort carrier groups at the Battle of Leyte Gulf.

TBS: Abbreviation for "talk between ships." It is a radio telephone that relies on line-of-sight communication.

TDC: Abbreviation for a torpedo data computer—an analog computer on board American World War II submarines that calculated the settings needed for accurate firing of the ships' torpedoes.

torpedo director: A set of machinery used for the controlling and firing of a ship's torpedoes.

UDT: Underwater demolition team.

ULTRA: A name used to cover all high-level military or other intelligence (for example, SIGINT) obtained by intercepting electronic signals (radio, radar, wire).

Visayan Islands: A group of islands within the Philippine Islands that includes Bohol, Cebu, Negros, Panay, Leyte, Masbate, and Samar. Also known as the Visayans or Visayan Island Group.

wardroom: A place used by the officers serving on board a ship for dining and other meetings.

Wildcat fighter: American carrier fighter plane that served as the primary naval fighter aircraft throughout World War II. Succeeded by the Hellcat fighter. Primarily manufactured by the Grumman Aircraft Company.

windward: The side of a ship that faces the direction of an oncoming wind.

Zekes, Zeroes: Japanese planes that were the primary fighter aircraft that served throughout the Japanese armed forces, including aboard Japanese aircraft carriers.

zigzag: A maneuver used by ships that makes a series of "z" movements through the water to avoid attacks by submarines or aircraft.

Prologue

The First Blow

The klaxon horn blared, piercing the comfortable silence of a calm Sunday morning, and shook Cmdr. Clifton Albert Frederick Sprague awake. Scrambling into his clothes, he ran out the door of his quarters and sprinted as fast he could to the bridge, where he screamed into the speakers, "Quarters! Quarters! Dammit! Hurry!" Explosions like rolling thunder filled the Hawaiian morning air. The first bombs fell from attacking Japanese planes on December 7, 1941, at 7:50 A.M.

Sprague's ship, the seaplane tender *Tangier,* was anchored next to the dock at Ford Island. The old battleship and target ship *Utah* and the cruisers *Raleigh* and *Detroit* were tethered forward of the *Tangier.* Battleship Row, which included the battleships *Arizona, Maryland, California, Pennsylvania, Tennessee, Oklahoma, West Virginia,* and *Nevada,* the oiler *Neosho,* and the ammunition ship *Vestal,* was on the other side of Ford Island.[1] Vibrations from the bombs exploding all around Ford Island rumbled through the *Tangier.* A seaman rushed from the mess hall, yelling, "They're bombing us! They're bombing us!" All around Pearl Harbor, Schofield Barracks, Hickam Field, Wheeler Field, Bellows Field, flame and smoke shot up as the missiles found their targets.

By 8:00 A.M., the official alarm came from the Ford Island control tower commander: "Air raid, Pearl Harbor. This is no drill!" This message echoed around the world and changed the course of history.

But the pandemonium outside the *Tangier* did not touch the organized, purposeful spirit prevailing within it—a by-product of the many drills

Sprague had ordered since taking command in July 1940. The *Tangier*'s gunners opened fire almost immediately on the attacking airplanes. Shell casings clanked loudly as they fell to the metal deck from the breeches of the ship's 3-inch guns. Every man aboard the seaplane tender knew his job and went to it the moment the horn sounded. Such exactitude was normal on any ship Sprague commanded. His know-how and quiet, self-assured manner inspired confidence and discipline in his crew, winning the kind of respect that ensured wholehearted cooperation.

Sprague watched silently from the *Tangier*'s bridge, a characteristically unemotional look on his face as the Japanese planes streaked over the *Tangier*'s port side, attacking the Ford Island Naval Air Station. Plumes of fire and smoke filled the air. A string of bombs hit a hangar packed with PBY patrol planes, extinguishing it in a pyre of fire and smoke. Sprague estimated that about forty or fifty planes had attacked Ford Island and the ships anchored in the surrounding water.

As Sprague's crew filled the sky with antiaircraft fire, Japanese torpedo bombers released a rain of destruction. Two torpedoes slammed against the side of the old battleship *Utah,* sinking it in just eight minutes.

Shortly after that, the cruisers' *Raleigh* and *Detroit* were hit. The *Raleigh* soon sank by its stern. Then, as if a torrent of turmoil had been turned off abruptly, the attacking airplanes, their cargo of torpedoes spent, wheeled away northeastward toward Pearl City, flying over the nearby mountains and returning to their carriers some 200 miles to the north.

On the southeastern side of Ford Island, the same spell of destruction reigned. A pillar of black-red smoke shot into the air directly above the mortally wounded *Arizona.* This once-proud queen of the U.S. Pacific Fleet lay in the oil-covered, flaming water—a twisted mass of red-hot steel. More than 1,000 men had perished in her decks below. The battleships *Utah* and *Oklahoma* were also total losses. Meanwhile, smoke enveloped the *Tangier* in a cloak of invisibility, and this invisibility became a shield, helping her escape any significant damage. Had she been hit, the inevitable explosions from the many stored torpedoes below her main deck could have wiped out half of Ford Island.

Meanwhile, columns of black smoke rushed skyward from the other battleships lining Battleship Row, and in this massive stockpile of destruction lay the demise of the Pacific Fleet's battle line. It was now on Pearl Harbor's muddy bottom.

Cliff Sprague issued few orders on that fateful day. Instead, he watched quietly as his crew went about their duties. One crewman remembered:

"But then, he always was cool. At Pearl Harbor, he acted like he'd thought everything out. Sprague knew just what to do, like he was born to command during a crisis."

Another reason also kept Sprague on the bridge. His inexperienced crew had never been through an enemy attack, and since they were not battle tested, they needed to see their commander facing the enemy along with them. An officer on the *Tangier* remembers: "All those men on the main deck and above it, at one time or another as they fought, could see Sprague calmly standing there throughout the battle. That impressed us officers and encouraged the men."

During a lull in the bombing, between 8:25 and 8:40 A.M., the *Tangier*'s crew had time to check the watertight doors, hatches, ports, ammunition supplies, and hoses. As they moved about the ship with calmness and efficiency, their demanding training schedules reaped enormous rewards.[2]

The second Japanese attack struck as suddenly as the first. At 8:40, its lead-off bomb landed just short of the *Tangier*. Sprague, as 300-pound bombs fell from the sky, was certain his ship would be hit; yet luck or fate were with him, for only dull thuds reverberated through his seaplane tender, and the bombs did little damage. He guessed later these bombs had burrowed into the harbor's mud before exploding harmlessly.[3]

Pearl Harbor naval headquarters, in the meanwhile, sent out a bewildering array of confusing, contradictory commands. During one five-minute span, Sprague received the following sequence of befuddling orders:

1. Commence firing at reported enemy aircraft.
2. Cease firing.
3. Disregard the order to cease fire.
4. "Fire at will" at a different but unnamed group of presumed enemy aircraft.

Panic acted as a free-floating enemy all its own as the unprepared Americans tried to cope with this brazen challenge. Needless to say, the gunfire from Sprague's ship accomplished little in the way of damage to the Japanese aircraft overhead, but several of Sprague's men were forced to take refuge near the *Tangier*'s bow to escape the friendly fire of errant American bullets, a frequent and painful hazard in warfare.[4]

Nonetheless, the converted seaplane tender's crew performed their duties well. Despite the fact that the *Tangier* had only seven guns, her crew's performance was one of the few bright spots on that tragic day. Her guns had kept right on firing while many other ships fired not a single shot. Her crew stopped only when they ran out of ammunition.[5]

Sprague was satisfied with his crew's performance. America was in a shooting war now, for the first time in more than twenty years, and his skills would, he knew, be sorely needed. Whatever his role might be, he was determined to do his job and let his work speak for itself.

The American public did not learn much about Sprague until later in the war, as his name was not mentioned in the aftermath of Pearl Harbor. Nonetheless, he merits more attention than he has received in naval histories up to now.

Clifton Sprague was the only major U.S. naval commander to participate in both the Pearl Harbor disaster and the American victory at Leyte Gulf. In both these events, he performed with distinction. Douglas MacArthur, William F. Halsey, and Chester W. Nimitz received the lion's share of publicity after October 1944, and Adm. Thomas Kinkaid, Sprague's Seventh Fleet commander, also became better known.

Nevertheless, it was Sprague who would make the critical difference between defeat and victory at the Battle of Leyte Gulf. All his coolness and correct decision making under fire he applied so well at Pearl Harbor would be seen again in the waters off Samar Island. But before his and his command's heroism could manifest itself, the Pacific war would expand in scope and ferocity. Many important battles needed to be fought and won by the Americans.

The Americans Strike

After World War I, Japan was rewarded with the Gilbert and Marshall Islands in the Central Pacific for fighting against the Central Powers. During the years between the world wars, they extended their empire by fortifying these islands and creating a string of almost impenetrable fortresses. During 1943 and the first eight months of 1944, the Americans made significant progress in pushing the Japanese back toward their home islands as United States naval forces and marines took the Gilbert and Marshall Islands. The perimeter of the Japanese empire had been penetrated and now was dramatically shrinking. The Americans were drawing nearer to the Japanese shipping lanes between the home islands and Southeast Asia. The tremendous battles for Tarawa, Kwajalein, and Eniwetok pushed the Japanese back toward their naval base at Truk.

In June 1944, the Japanese navy suffered a painful defeat in the Battle of the Philippine Sea, in which the Japanese lost over 200 planes. The bulk of the Japanese fleet, however, including most of its remaining carriers, escaped serious damage. But the loss of aircraft and, more important, the loss of irreplaceable pilots and crews, left the Japanese navy crippled, without essential air cover to protect it at Leyte. The Japanese carrier fleet now was but a shell of its former self.

Although the Battle of the Philippine Sea was not the significant strategic naval defeat some American admirals had hoped for, it nonetheless allowed the Americans to capture the Marianas. With this critical island group in their possession, the Americans now had bases located near enough to the Japanese home islands to bomb them around the clock. The flying distance to Japan had been reduced by more than 1,200 miles. For the first time in the Pacific war, the Japanese people would begin to feel the same sting, agony, and death their citizen counterparts in Nazi Germany had been feeling since 1943.

MacArthur's Southwest Pacific command had its share of successes, too. American and Australian military and naval forces under the general's leadership moved rapidly up New Guinea's northern coast. Using what the Americans called the "hit-them-where-they're-not" strategy, successful landings on New Guinea made possible the capture of the important harbors at Wakde, Biak, Noemfoor, and Sansapor. This string of victories along the thousand-mile advance culminated in the capture of Hollandia in Dutch New Guinea and placed MacArthur's forces at New Guinea's westernmost point by mid-1944, ready to invade the Philippines.[6]

This was a heady time for the Allies. So many victories had been won in Europe and the Pacific that rumors ran rampant through all levels of command predicting the war would end by Christmas 1944. Other more sensible people were less optimistic, however. Despite having sustained severe losses in France, Italy, and the Soviet Union, the Third Reich was not yet finished.

The Japanese military establishment, for its part, remained a viable fighting force, too, with its primary supply lines between the East Indies and the home islands intact, although diminished. But American submarines made their presence felt there by inflicting enormous losses on

the Japanese merchant fleet, so that by August 1944, the Japanese merchant navy had lost over 2,800,000 tons of merchant shipping.[7]

Japan's near-fanatical defense of the Central Pacific islands showed
that the Japanese were still ready to fight anyone, anywhere, and ready
to die for their emperor. The Americans' next objective, meanwhile, became a subject of considerable debate. General MacArthur and the navy
could not agree on a target. Where would they strike next? The answer
to this question would dictate how, when, and where the Pacific war
would go, and how it would end.

Chapter 1: American Strategy

By the end of 1943, the idea of a dual Allied advance across the Pacific had been firmly established. With the blessings of the combined chiefs of staff, President Franklin D. Roosevelt and British Prime Minister Winston Churchill's strategy was to have MacArthur's Southwest Pacific Force advance to New Guinea's northern coast, and from there invade the southernmost Philippine island of Mindanao. Nimitz's Central Force, using the Fifth Fleet, would take the Marshalls, Truk, possibly one more of the Caroline Islands, and the Marianas, including Saipan, Tinian, and Guam. Both lines of advance would converge on the Luzon-Formosa-China triangle, from which Japan would be bombed, blockaded, and possibly invaded.[1]

Nimitz traveled to Brisbane on March 25, 1944, to meet with MacArthur. During their conference, the differences between the two commanders became clear regarding the attack strategy in retaking the Philippines. MacArthur was dedicated to returning to the Philippines for a variety of reasons. He had given his word in 1942. While he had political concerns about the Philippine people and Asians in general, he was also sensitive to American public opinion.

Nimitz disagreed with MacArthur because he thought MacArthur's position did not rest on military considerations. The admiral's sole goal was to find the shortest route to the Luzon-Formosa-China triangle. MacArthur had criticized those he called the "gentlemen in Washington," but Nimitz defended them, stating they were merely, like himself, trying to do what was best for the country.[2]

1

By July 1944, the major question of which Japanese-held territory to attack next was still unresolved. Plans were in place to occupy the Palau Islands in September and to invade Mindanao in December. But both Nimitz and MacArthur were uncertain what to do after these plans were achieved.

The Joint Chiefs of Staff (JCS) believed Formosa (now Taiwan), Luzon, and various places on the Chinese coast were good candidates for bases from which to invade the Japanese homeland. The United States Navy, supporting Adm. Ernest J. King and Admiral Nimitz's position, strongly recommended the Bonin Islands and Formosa as the key points of conquest. The navy felt a Philippine invasion would require too much time and cost too many casualties, compared with what they believed would be the relatively easy conquest of Formosa. Their main argument was that a Formosan invasion was the boldest, most direct means of accelerating Japan's defeat.

In countering these arguments, MacArthur noted that a Formosa invasion would leave the flank of the American supply lines exposed to the still powerful Japanese naval and air forces currently occupying the Philippines. Furthermore, the abandonment of the Philippine people to continued Japanese oppression would validate Japanese propaganda that Caucasian Americans would not risk a single white American life to rescue Filipinos.

Whatever option the Allies ultimately chose, however, there was general agreement on the idea that the option should include the element of surprise.

Meanwhile, the Japanese made two strategic moves that influenced Allied strategy. In February 1944, they repositioned a major portion of their fleet, taking it from the Inland Sea in Japan to Lingga Roads near Singapore. The major reason for this shift was for closer proximity to reliable fuel oil sources. According to the British, this movement of such a large Japanese naval force increased the threat to India. At the end of May 1944, the Japanese army completed a southerly advance from Hankow, China, to Hanoi in French Indochina (now Vietnam). This maneuver threatened American B-29 bases in China and forced Generalissimo Chiang Kai-shek away from the Chinese coast. Therefore, any friendly places that might have existed for Allied bases on the Chinese coast were now gone. Allied plans for a Formosa–Bonin Islands strategy now appeared to be far less viable.

The debate over which strategy should prevail therefore intensified. MacArthur made one proposal that included the invasion of Mindanao on October 15, 1944, followed by the rapid capture of that island's Japanese air bases. This approach would provide air cover for an attack on Leyte by mid-November. With Leyte secure, the invasion of Luzon could begin in January 1945. The navy's response disparaged MacArthur's proposition, which Admiral King described as impractical. A deadlock took place when the Joint Chiefs of Staff proposed an operation called Granite II, a plan to continue the war against Japan by attacking Formosa, competing directly with MacArthur's proposal. The navy generally favored Granite II over MacArthur's approach, despite the fact that it left intact the Japanese occupation of key Chinese coastal port cities.

The South Pacific campaigns were completed successfully in May 1944, and the Solomon Islands were captured as well. The once powerful Japanese base of Rabaul was now isolated and impotent. Admiral Halsey, who had led the American successes, met with Admirals King and Nimitz in San Francisco, where he learned he would be given a new assignment. By June 1944, Halsey would no longer be South Pacific Area commander, but, following the Marianas campaign, he would go to sea again as commander of the Third Fleet, relieving Adm. Raymond Spruance. He would command in an alternate manner this robust collection of American sea power that had achieved so much success in the Central Pacific operations under the direction of Admiral Spruance.

Under Spruance, the fleet would be referred to as the Fifth Fleet. When Halsey assumed command, it would be called the Third Fleet. Admiral King introduced these numerical fleet designations in March 1943, with the Third Fleet being Halsey's South Pacific naval units, the Fifth being Spruance's Central Pacific forces, and the Seventh being the American naval units in the Southwest Pacific, led by Adm. Arthur S. Carpender and later Admiral Kinkaid.

The former Third Fleet of the South Pacific, however, had significantly fewer ships when compared to the Third Fleet of which Halsey took command in August 1944 for the operations in the Palaus and the Philippines. This new force had more than 500 combat ships that had been part of the Central and South Pacific units, as well as many new vessels that had joined the Central Pacific armada from the American mainland.

An officer in the Joint Intelligence Center at Pearl Harbor observed, "The chameleonlike ability of the fleet to take on the color of its commander was remarkable." Under Spruance's leadership, the fleet "re-

fused to be distracted from its objectives, and we could read its schedules and confidently plot the locality of all its forces at any hour." On the
other hand, when it "went to sea under Halsey, whose staff was splendid
opportunists, neither the Japanese nor the Estimate Section [at Pearl
Harbor] knew what to expect."[3]

Meanwhile, General MacArthur was by no means standing still. Ever
since the Allies had successfully landed on New Guinea's northern
shore in early 1943, MacArthur's staff had been kept busy developing a
plan called RENO—a master plan for winning the war in the Far East.
Following the normal military planning process, RENO evolved over
time. As the Allies leapfrogged westward along the New Guinean northern coast, the plan's revisions became known as RENO II, III, IV, and V.
One overriding principle common to all of RENO's revisions was that
the capture of the Philippines would sever the main north-south supply
artery to Japanese factories, thus ending the war with minimum risk and
losses.

In all of RENO's various phases, MacArthur insisted on one guiding
principle: the Philippine invasion should take place under cover of his
own land-based bombers. This meant there would be a landing on Mindanao with Lt. Gen. George C. Kenney's air force providing air cover
from Morotai in the Halmaheras, an archipelago 300 miles away from
the Philippines across the Celebes Sea. There were other good reasons
for landing on Mindanao. The island was large, it did not have strong
Japanese occupying forces, and it had active and well-organized guerrilla
forces.

MacArthur's experience in New Guinea had shown him that air superiority was an essential part of successful invasions. The RENO plan
provided the safe assurance of air cover for the invasion troops. Of
course, if Mindanao could not be taken, the required air support would
have to come from another source—the United States Navy. MacArthur
did not want to rely on the navy, however, but instead wanted his triumphant return to the Philippines to be his show alone.

Despite MacArthur's arguments, the Philippines seemed to the navy
to be a distraction from the navy's own Central Pacific axis of advance.
In mid-1944, after the great carrier raids on Palau and Truk and the capture of Saipan by the marines, the navy pressed its plan on the White
House to bypass the Philippines entirely in favor of a landing on Formosa.

When he discovered the contents of the navy's plan in early 1944,
MacArthur adamantly rejected them. Nimitz had written a letter to Ad-

miral King about his March 25–27 Brisbane meeting with MacArthur. In it, Nimitz said:

> Everything was lovely and harmonious until the last day of our conference when I called attention to the last part of the . . . directive which required of him and me to prepare alternate plans for moving faster and along shorter routes towards the Luzon-Formosa-China triangle . . . he [MacArthur] then blew up and made an oration of some length on the impossibility of bypassing the Philippines, his sacred obligations there—redemption of the 17 million people—blood on his soul, deserted by the American people, etc., etc."[4]

While Nimitz accused MacArthur of emotionalism in his report to King, any good geopolitician looking at the map of the Pacific could not ignore MacArthur's arguments. The Philippines did indeed represent a large and powerful land mass that could not be safely bypassed, while Formosa had few good landing beaches. A more important reason was the fact that the Formosa plan did not consider the feelings of the 17 million Filipino allies who would play an important political role in Asia after the war had been won. MacArthur continued to argue his own views by sending a barrage of cables to the War Department. According to MacArthur, these were greeted either with silence or, even worse, indifference. MacArthur grew increasingly frustrated over his lack of progress with the War Department. The navy, meanwhile, was only a phone call away from the president, with MacArthur thousands of miles away. It was well known that the president favored the navy, because he had served as assistant secretary of the navy during World War I, so the navy's superior communications with the president gave MacArthur good reason to be concerned.[5]

As the clock ticked down, the debate intensified. Reaching an agreement seemed impossible. The president would have to break the deadlock, or the Pacific war effort would languish. He had to act soon, asserting his obligations as commander in chief.

The Summit at Pearl Harbor, July 1944

The train slowly approached the San Diego train station. Franklin Delano Roosevelt, thirty-second president of the United States, was tired. He had been president since March 4, 1933, and had faced many problems. The Great Depression had resisted almost all governmental efforts to resolve it. When Adolf Hitler threatened world peace by occupying Austria and Czechoslovakia and by invading Poland, thus igniting World War II, Roosevelt tried in vain to convince Americans that the United States needed to enter the war in order to save Western civilization. It was not until the Japanese surprise attack on Pearl Harbor, however, that American passions were inflamed enough to seek the defeat of the Axis powers. The war in its turn awakened American industrial power, which tugged the American economy out of its economic depression and positioned the country to become the world's dominant economic power. When the war was over, the American economy would have no peer.

However, these events had taken a terrible toll on the president's health. He had contracted polio while vacationing on the Canadian island of Campobello in 1921, and he was never again healthy. The daily demands of work had made him look like a frail old man. Roosevelt made history when he became the first president of the United States to serve a third term, and he had seriously considered not running for a fourth term. But when the Democratic Party had conferred the nomination on him for an unprecedented fourth term, Roosevelt realized there was much work still to be done and accepted the challenge.

Although Italy had capitulated in 1943, the Germans and Japanese were not yet ready to surrender, even though the tide had turned in the Allies' favor. The Germans were now defending the Third Reich on many fronts. The Americans, British, and Canadians had landed successfully in France, where they were engaged in dramatic battles in the fields and hedgerows of Normandy. The Americans and British were slugging their way up the Italian boot, inflicting serious casualties on the Germans. The critical Battle of the Atlantic was being won by the Allies. Nazi U-boats no longer roamed the oceans without fear of ending up on the Atlantic Ocean's bottom. Allied convoys now sailed the Atlantic in safety to fuel the war in France and to supply the Russians over the still treacherous voyage to Murmansk and Archangel. The mighty American industrial base was making its presence felt all over the world. American and British bombers were reducing the German industrial heartland to rubble with daily, large-scale bombing raids. The Russians were driving the Wehrmacht from Russian soil while killing and capturing many German soldiers. Stalin's demands for a second front had been satisfied. The Third Reich's days were numbered. It would never see its thousandth year.

The Pacific War, in the meanwhile, had turned in the Americans' favor, with Japanese defeats at the Coral Sea, Midway, the Solomons, and New Guinea. The Japanese navy had lost almost all its irreplaceable pilots in the Marianas Turkey Shoot. After that debacle, the Imperial Japanese Fleet had but thirty-five aircraft left.[6]

American submarines inflicted crippling losses on the Japanese merchant fleet. The flow of supplies between Southeast Asia and the Japanese home islands slowed to a trickle, but it had not been stopped. A debate between the navy and MacArthur now grew extremely heated with no decision forthcoming about where to go next. Roosevelt knew he had to meet with MacArthur and Nimitz in order to iron out an agreement. On July 20, 1944, he boarded the heavy cruiser *Baltimore* and headed for the Hawaiian Islands.[7]

The warm, bright Hawaiian sunlight shimmered on the water's surface as the heavy cruiser *Baltimore* rounded Diamond Head. The president's arrival was supposed to be a military secret, but, nonetheless, there were many soldiers and sailors lining the docks as the cruiser gracefully headed for Pearl Harbor.

The cruiser stopped off Fort Kamehameha to allow a tugboat to come alongside. Admiral Nimitz's party, which included Lt. Gen. Robert C. Richardson, the senior army commander in the Hawaiian Islands, climbed up the stairs suspended down the cruiser's side and came aboard. The presidential flag flew on the main mast to honor the former assistant secretary of the navy and now commander in chief.

As the *Baltimore* moved slowly up the channel into Pearl Harbor, thousands of eyes gazed at her, hoping to catch a glimpse of their president. Sailors dressed in gleaming white dress uniforms lined the rails of the ships in the harbor as the bands played. The sound of work stopped temporarily as silence descended. The only noise came from aircraft formations flying overhead.

When the ship carrying its notable cargo moved across the world's most famous harbor, Adm. William D. Leahy, Roosevelt's closest naval adviser, observed that there was "no striking evidence remaining of the frightful damage inflicted in the sneak attack by the Japanese on our fleet as it rode easily at anchor on Sunday, December 7, 1941."

Twenty-six admirals and generals in dress whites paid their respects to the president. Every man in the harbor lined the rails of each ship as the cruiser advanced up the channel and approached the docking pier.

The bright, white uniforms contrasted sharply with the gray ships' paint, creating an impressive occasion few would forget. It had been a long journey since the dark day of December 7, 1941. As notes from the boatswain's pipe pierced the air, ruffles, pipings, and flourishes resounded. At the center of this impressive sight was Roosevelt, who was in his element.

The boarding party then departed from the *Baltimore* by boat while Roosevelt and Nimitz remained on board. The graceful cruiser slowly approached the pier where several senior officers waited in a row, their silver and gold shoulder boards shining in the afternoon sun. Several lines were thrown from the dock as the ship was tugged snugly against the pier.

A bit of humor lightened the occasion when the group's senior admiral ordered a "right face" so they could board the ship. It had been a long time since these men, upon whose shoulders rested not only ornamental gold but the responsibility for deciding the course of a world war, had last practiced close-order drill. Two of the admirals mistakenly turned left. The *Baltimore*'s sailors cheered lustily to see their superior officers show a bit of disarming human frailty.

It was a funny, ironic moment. No German sailor would ever have been permitted to laugh at a German officer as the men of the *Baltimore* did. It would have been unthinkable, too, for any Japanese sailor to chuckle at his officers in this way. Any sailors foolish enough even to grin at his superiors most certainly would have faced severe punishment and, in some cases, death. If two Japanese admirals had been so careless to face the wrong way, they probably would have killed themselves for their inexcusable loss of face.

This casual attitude toward their superiors by the American sailors was, in fact, not a sign of weakness in the American military establishment. Instead, it was a natural outgrowth of America's freedom to criticize its government and government officials, and thus was a major strength. For it was not just the vast production capacity of the United States that had caused the sting of Axis defeats. Those sailors who had just chuckled at their superiors were the same sort of people who had defiantly thrown wrenches at strafing Japanese fighters when Pearl Harbor was attacked over two years ago. They were the same kind of men who made samurai-like sacrifices at Midway. They were like the marines on Guadalcanal who had repeatedly beaten back Japanese suicide attacks. And they would be the same kind of men who would fight against seemingly in-surmountable odds and amaze the world with their selfless sacrifice a few months later off a little-known island called Samar.[8]

General MacArthur stared out the plane's window over Oahu. He had not seen Hawaii in many years and had not set foot on American soil since leaving for his assignment as commander of the Philippine forces in 1937. As his plane circled to head east into the prevailing trade winds for a landing at Hickam Field, he glanced over the left side at Pearl Harbor. No evidence of damage from the December 7 attack was visible.

After disembarking from the aircraft, the general walked along the tarmac, slid into a car bearing flags with his four-star insignia on each fender, and proceeded to Fort Shafter, where he would be housed during his stay in Hawaii. A note awaited him there from the president directing him to come to the *Baltimore* as soon as possible. There he was to meet with the president and Nimitz. As he approached the dock where the *Baltimore* was moored, his concerns over the meeting's purpose mounted.

The general's car sped down the pier, then screeched to a halt. MacArthur stepped out of the car clad in familiar khaki trousers, a brown leather air force jacket, and a Philippine field marshal's cap. He briskly climbed up the *Baltimore*'s gangplank to a chorus of boatswains' pipes, smartly saluted the flag at the stern, and disappeared inside for the meeting.

Roosevelt warmly greeted MacArthur. Although the general had met Nimitz before, Roosevelt reintroduced the two men. At first they posed for press pictures and talked casually. An important decision was waiting to be made, so the group retired to a private residence near Waikiki to refresh themselves after their long journeys.

The general was not happy. He suspected that he was ordered to this meeting to provide Roosevelt with a photo opportunity to bolster his chances for reelection. MacArthur's suspicions were at least partially confirmed when he posed for pictures with Nimitz, Leahy, and the president on the *Baltimore*'s main deck. That evening, MacArthur's gloomy mood remained unchanged when a message arrived from President Roosevelt asking MacArthur to accompany him and Admirals Leahy and Nimitz on an inspection tour of Oahu's military installations the next morning. MacArthur felt he was too busy to waste time on such niceties.

General Richardson, the senior army officer in Hawaii before MacArthur arrived, made the arrangements for the presidential inspection tour. He had trouble finding a suitable car for the president and his party, because the only cars available were a bright red, five-passenger beauty belonging to Honolulu's fire chief and a larger, less colorful sedan whose owner was the madam of one of Honolulu's better-known brothels. Fearing the latter vehicle would be recognized, Richardson picked the smaller fire chief's car.[9]

During the tour that took place the next day, MacArthur reflected on some reports he had read from the guerrilla forces in the Philippines who were now fighting a difficult campaign of sabotage and disruption. These reports supported his contention that the Japanese were unyielding, dedicated, ruthless occupiers. Stories of brutal reprisals against innocent civilians and of harsh, inhuman treatment of American and Philippine prisoners of war haunted his thoughts.

Opposition to his plan of liberation had powerful supporters. The Joint Chiefs of Staff in Washington, prodded by Admiral King and supported by Gen. George C. Marshall, opposed the invasion of the Philippines and favored the invasion of Formosa and the Bonin Islands. The general had a difficult selling job before him. But he had reasons for optimism.

Admiral King and General Marshall were back in Washington. MacArthur would be meeting only with the president, Admiral Nimitz, and Roosevelt's naval adviser, Admiral Leahy. The charismatic general had persuasive powers at his disposal, having engaged in, and won, many difficult arguments. Even more important, he knew that the arguments he had at his disposal were more powerful, from a political point of view, than those held by Nimitz.

If the United States reneged on its promise to liberate the Philippines, the Japanese would gain a tremendous propaganda victory. MacArthur hoped the president would grasp this potential for political disaster. The general was convinced he would win the day if he imbedded his military strategy in a robe made of political cloth.

That evening, Roosevelt, MacArthur, Nimitz, and Leahy sat down to dinner in a cream-colored stucco mansion on Waikiki Beach made available for the occasion by the millionaire Christopher Holmes. No record of the dinner conversation is available. Either the talks were classified or else too mundane to be recorded for posterity. What was said after dinner *was* recorded. No longer classified, it cannot be considered mundane from a historical point of view.

After dinner, the men moved into the large living room. Huge maps of the Pacific hung on the walls. Roosevelt pushed his wheelchair past a map, pointed to Mindanao, and asked, "Douglas, where do we go from here?" MacArthur responded, "Leyte, Mr. President, then Luzon!" Nimitz and MacArthur made alternate presentations, using a bamboo pointer to illustrate their arguments.

Nimitz urged bypassing the Philippines and invading Formosa. Although Nimitz supported the Joint Chiefs of Staff's position of a Formosan invasion, MacArthur sensed he was not committed to it in full. The president nodded his head noncommittally as Nimitz listed the reasons for capturing Formosa.

The admiral's arguments made good strategic sense. Formosa provided a choice location from which to block the flow of oil to Japan. It was close to China, so America could establish air bases there for bombing the Japanese home islands. Formosa would also provide a solid base of operations for the invasion of Japan, just as the British Isles had served that purpose for the D-day invasion of Western Europe at Normandy on June 6, 1944.

MacArthur silently respected Nimitz's arguments, for they proved the admiral had a sound military mind. But MacArthur knew Nimitz was wrong and waited his turn. Nimitz finished, then sat down.

With his pipe tucked firmly between his teeth, MacArthur slowly rose to his feet. Removing his pipe from his mouth, he began to speak:

> I have listened to Admiral Nimitz's presentation and have been heartened by the thorough and complete analysis that formed his position. There are sound military arguments for this alternative. But, Mr. President, this plan is fraught with disaster. The invasion of Formosa would leave a very powerful Japanese naval and military based in the Philippines in the American rear. These forces could inflict severe losses on the long American supply lines based in the Marianas and Ulithi. American forces would be exposed to formidable Japanese attacks on Luzon and Leyte. The potential for a humiliating Allied defeat that would rival Bataan and Corregidor is too great to make this step.
>
> More importantly, Mr. President, I made a promise to return to the Philippines. This had the force of the government of the

United States behind it. To go back on this promise would reinforce Japanese arguments that white America will never risk lives to rescue yellow-skinned Asians.[10]

The President, in turn, set aside his familiar long cigarette holder and addressed MacArthur: "Douglas, that promise was made by you, not me. Besides, we have to think of the big picture. We cannot waste American lives invading the Philippines when they will be ultimately needed for the invasion of the Japanese homeland."[11]

MacArthur replied: "With all due respect, Mr. President, the political costs are too high not to invade the Philippines. That promise I made had the force of committing you as commander in chief. You are running for reelection this fall. Can you afford the accusation by your opposition that you would renege on a promise by one of your senior commanders? The integrity of the force of the argument that America is the bastion of freedom and liberty for all the world's peoples would be in jeopardy. This would call into question not only your honor, Mr. President, but the honor of the American people."[12]

MacArthur made further forceful humanitarian arguments when he said, "You cannot abandon seventeen million loyal Filipino Christians to the Japanese in favor of first liberating Formosa and then returning it to China. American public opinion will condemn you, Mr. President, and it will be justified."

The general continued the argument by observing that 3,700 American prisoners of war waited to be liberated, and while MacArthur agreed that Japanese supply lines would be cut if the Americans captured Formosa to the north and Mindanao to the south, the occupying Japanese would strip the Philippines of all food and supplies, thereby starving the Filipino population and the American prisoners.

He argued, further, that a serious military problem existed, because Mindanao was too far away to reach the Japanese airfields on Luzon using land-based aircraft. However, if the Americans could establish airfields on Leyte or Mindoro or both, the Japanese airfields on Luzon could be destroyed. Thus, MacArthur's forces could land in the Lingayen Gulf off Luzon and be in Manila in five weeks.

The president noted he had reports of powerful Japanese air and ground reinforcements in Manila: "Douglas, to take Luzon would demand heavier losses than we can stand. It seems to me we must bypass it."

Sensing his arguments were affecting the president, MacArthur pointed out that if the Americans landed in Formosa, they could not rely on help from the local populace, because the Japanese had occupied the island for almost fifty years. But if the Americans landed in the Philippines, they could expect extensive help from the Philippine underground. In some areas, several guerrilla units had made progress in removing the conqueror. He had been receiving information from Filipino guerrillas ever since the Japanese occupation, keeping in close touch with what was going on there.

MacArthur insisted that the United States had a moral obligation to the Philippine people to set them free as soon as possible, and he reopened the old wounds of Bataan and Corregidor, stating that America had abandoned not only the loyal Filipinos, but thousands of Americans as well. There were, at that very moment, hundreds, if not thousands, of American men, women, and children deteriorating in Japanese concentration camps where they lived wretched lives, suffering terrible privations.

He stated that the Filipinos would be able to forgive us for failing to protect them from the Japanese in 1941. They would even be able to forgive any particular failures in trying to rescue them. But they would never be able to forgive America if it did not *even try* to free them. And if the Philippines alone were not incentive enough, MacArthur warned that America's postwar image in that part of the world would be at stake.

MacArthur was never in better form than he was on that evening. He used no notes, no prepared maps of his own, and never doubted the correctness of his views. He applied his considerable persuasive skills and charismatic personality with full force, and Roosevelt appeared to be moved by his chain of reasoning. Nimitz's counterarguments, on the other hand, became less frequent and grew less forceful. Leahy seemed to agree with MacArthur.

Roosevelt thought a bit, smiled, then remarked. "Douglas, you should have been a politician. We will look at your plan when we get back to Washington and let you know."

The discussions ended at midnight. The men agreed to meet the next morning. MacArthur's arguments had won the day. He had persuaded not only the president, but Nimitz too.[13]

Leahy, who observed the discussions rather than participated in them, wrote later:

After so much loose talk in Washington, where the mention of the name MacArthur seemed to generate more heat than light, it was both pleasant and very informative to have these two men who had been pictured as antagonists calmly present their differing views to the Commander-in-Chief. For Roosevelt it was an excellent lesson in geography, one of his favorite subjects. The President was at his best as he tactfully steered the discussion from one point to another and narrowed down the area of disagreement between MacArthur and Nimitz.

MacArthur agreed with Leahy, later writing that Roosevelt "was entirely neutral in handling the discussion." Leahy noted that both Nimitz and MacArthur had told the president they could execute their particular plans using the forces then available in the Pacific, adding that it was "highly pleasing and unusual to find two commanders who were not demanding reinforcements."[14]

The next day MacArthur met privately with the president. If any doubts remained in Roosevelt's mind, they soon would be dispelled. The general took this priceless opportunity to look Roosevelt in the eye and say that if the Philippines were not taken, "I daresay that the American people would be so aroused that they would register most complete resentment against you at the polls this fall."

MacArthur had convinced Roosevelt he was right, and now had a formidable ally. The general knew he needed all the help he could get. Many influential, high-ranking officers still did not support him, and many obstacles remained. But MacArthur had won an important victory in Hawaii, bringing him a giant step closer to his promised return to the Philippines.[15]

In a later note, Nimitz remarked that the decision to invade the Philippines was sound military strategy. He never had been convinced that invading Formosa was the right move. Furthermore, General Marshall now also supported the plan. Two factors MacArthur had brought up appealed to him most particularly. The first was the summons to national honor; the second was the relative ease of capturing Luzon rather than Formosa.

Finally, MacArthur had three important men on his side.[16]

The Honolulu summit produced a degree of consensus on an overall American Pacific strategy. Nonetheless, the Joint Chiefs were not impressed by the events in Hawaii, and among them the arguments continued, pro and con, over "Luzon, Formosa, or what?"

Nimitz's chief planner, RAdm. Forrest P. Sherman, met with the Joint Chiefs of Staff on September 1, 1944, and forcefully argued that a decision must be made soon. Nimitz's forces had no mission following the Palau operation, which was to begin no later than September 15. Admiral King still opposed a Luzon operation. King argued that the "sentimental reasons" that presumably underlay the liberation of the Philippines were going to extend the date of the Japanese surrender. Admiral King's opinions on invading the Philippines were more negative than those of any other members of the Joint Chiefs of Staff. Nonetheless, General Marshall had been won over to MacArthur's side.

At this time, the only point of agreement was a directive ordering MacArthur to occupy Leyte on December 20, 1944—six weeks after the target invasion date for Mindanao. Admiral King still insisted Formosa should be captured before the Japanese had time to reinforce it. However, an equally stubborn Marshall asked, "Where should we go after Formosa?"

Despite the lack of a firm consensus, MacArthur's staff nonetheless worked persistently to complete the Philippine invasion plans. They put in many long hours with certain members of the Joint Chiefs of Staff in Washington and created an operational timetable that ended on March 1, 1945.

The presentation of the plan to the OCTAGON (Combined Chiefs of Staff) conference took place in Quebec on September 11, 1944. Roosevelt and Churchill attended the conference and reviewed the plan. Although it was changed yet again about a week later, it nonetheless showed that the Joint Chiefs of Staff agreed with MacArthur. While the plan did not reflect MacArthur's strategy in full, it suggested that a massive joint operation between Nimitz and MacArthur's forces would land troops either on Luzon to secure Manila by February 20, 1945, or on Formosa and Amoy off the Chinese coast by March 1, 1945.[17]

Changing the Plan

Admiral Halsey stood on the command bridge of the battleship *New Jersey* in August 1944. An impressive sight filled his binoculars as the imposing ships of the Third Fleet sailed from Eniwetok. Much had changed since that fateful day at Pearl Harbor. The industrial might of the United

States had built a powerful navy from the ashes and ruins of the calamitous attack. Halsey thought it would be a long time before a force of this magnitude would appear in the world again.

The Third Fleet was on its way to bomb Yap, the Palaus, and Mindanao to prepare for the invasions of these islands now planned for some time. The Third Fleet also planned diversionary air strikes at the Bonins. The objective was to destroy Japanese air forces that might oppose the upcoming landings on Morotai and Peleliu and deceive the enemy as to the Allies' next move.

Halsey's planes proceeded to attack the air defenses on Mindanao on September 9 and 10, 1944. Because the Japanese endeavored to conserve their short supply of aircraft, they did not send patrols into the sky to fight off the Americans. They had decided not to commit their aircraft until the moment of the actual invasion. Thus, the attacking American aircraft were virtually unopposed, and at the same time they caught the Japanese completely by surprise. Subsequent American attacks two days later on Cebu, Negros, and Mindanao inflicted further damage. As before, few Japanese aircraft rose to meet the Americans, and those that did were shot down. The Japanese aircraft being held in reserve, however, proved to be sitting ducks instead of offensive weapons, because they were destroyed on the ground. Furthermore, the Third Fleet's air assaults wrecked Japanese installations and burned supplies. These attacks thoroughly disrupted training and Japanese morale sank lower and lower.[18]

Not facing any Japanese opposition, the Third Fleet successfully completed air operations in the Palaus and Mindanao. Surprised by the weak, or at times nonexistent, Japanese response, Halsey canceled further air attacks. He met with his staff and decided the Japanese air forces had ceased to exist as a fighting power. Halsey knew what he had to do next: advance the date of the current plan to invade the Philippines planned for December.

On September 13, Halsey sent an urgent message to Nimitz in Hawaii, which Nimitz forwarded at once to the OCTAGON conference in Quebec. Halsey offered two suggestions: (1) postpone the projected assault on Yap, and (2) advance the Philippine invasion's target date from December so that the attack on Leyte would take place in October. This second suggestion was fraught with far-reaching effects. If the Americans rescheduled the Leyte invasion date to October, the troops that would have been used for the Palaus, Yap, Morotai, and Mindanao invasions could now be diverted to General MacArthur for an immediate landing on Leyte.

Later that evening in Quebec, Admiral King's aide, Alexander S. McDill, entered the admiral's suite with a message in hand. King, attired in his dressing gown, was preparing for dinner. The message McDill handed to King was from Nimitz and addressed to MacArthur. It stated Nimitz still wanted to capture the Palaus and was willing to bypass Yap. Nimitz proposed releasing the XXIV Corps and its associated amphibious assault shipping to other duties. These troops were currently loading at Pearl Harbor and could be diverted for an early attack on Leyte. It was King's habit to write action notes in the margins of a message and then return the message to his aide. This time, however, he stuffed the message in his pocket and proceeded on to dinner.

Meanwhile, the cruiser *Nashville* maintained radio silence while making rapid progress to Morotai. General MacArthur's deputy, Lt. Gen. Richard K. Sutherland, read a message from Halsey, which he received on the *Nashville*. After due reflection, he realized that Halsey's message was a heaven-sent opportunity. Halsey's idea was, in fact, brilliant. Sutherland knew all the careful planning MacArthur had put into the upcoming Philippine operation. This plan called for establishing a series of airfields as MacArthur's forces went about the business of taking the islands back from the Japanese. However, this plan had not taken into account the problem of the monsoons.

A solution to this problem existed, of course. The development of fast carrier forces had changed the traditional view about the use of airpower. These carrier task forces had the capacity to deliver powerful blows while operating hundreds of miles away from any land area. The surviving Japanese defenders on the Gilberts, Marshalls, and Marianas most definitely could testify as to the validity of this statement.

The Battle of the Philippine Sea had shown that powerful naval air forces could turn away enemy attempts to defeat large troop landing operations. If Halsey's task force could be diverted earlier than planned, the feasibility of landing troops on Leyte would be very real indeed. Airfields would not be needed immediately on Leyte. Halsey's fleet would be able to supply sufficient support to invading troops until land bases could be established after the monsoons had ended.

Sutherland believed that MacArthur would immediately agree with

Halsey's idea. Acting for MacArthur, Sutherland quickly sent messages to Halsey, Nimitz, and the Joint Chiefs of Staff in support of the basic framework of Halsey's proposal. Nimitz agreed, with the proviso that the Palau Islands operation go on as planned in order to secure an air base and an anchorage in the rear of the Leyte operation. MacArthur, meanwhile, would invade Leyte on October 20, 1944—a two-month advance in the planned invasion of the Philippines. Halsey's fleet would provide the tactical naval and air support for the landings, along with the naval forces that were under MacArthur's command.

The next evening, September 14, as the Joint Chiefs of Staff dined with their Canadian hosts, an American staff officer came into the room carrying a message from MacArthur's headquarters that accepted Nimitz's offer. Because of the recently discovered Japanese weaknesses in the defense of the Philippines, MacArthur also proposed moving the Leyte invasion date from December 20 to October 20. Anticipating immediate approval, the American planners in Quebec already had drafted a message. The circumstances were such now that the Joint Chiefs moved faster than ever and completed their deliberations in less than an hour.

Later, the Joint Chiefs sent an order instructing MacArthur and Nimitz to attack Leyte immediately and to bypass Yap. The Joint Chiefs also agreed with Nimitz on attacking the Palau Islands, but this proved to be an unfortunate decision. The value of these islands would not, in the end, justify the ensuing heavy American casualties in that costly operation.

The president, Churchill, and the Canadian prime minister were attending meetings when a message arrived on September 15 stating that MacArthur, Nimitz, and Halsey had agreed to the proposal. General Marshall, representing the Joint Chiefs of Staff, now fully supported the new proposal. Ninety minutes later, a dispatch arrived at Nimitz and MacArthur's headquarters approving the new Leyte operation now planned for October 20, 1944. Additional orders included the following:

1. A diversion of the attack forces from the Yap invasion to Leyte.

2. After unloading at the Palau operation, all shipping would proceed to Southwest Pacific ports to be used for landing troops and matériel at Leyte.

3. All naval fire support ships and escort carriers employed in the Palaus would be assigned temporarily to the Seventh Fleet com-

mander, Admiral Kinkaid, to provide naval and air support for the
landings at Leyte.

4. Ulithi would be captured immediately to serve as the site of
an advanced fleet base.

The Americans now had set the stage for the invasion of Leyte, an operation that showed bold, decisive, original, and far-reaching thinking
on the part of the senior American commanders. The rapid change in
plans demonstrated that the Americans could nimbly modify their plans
to take advantage of rapidly changing, strategic conditions. Practically
every American military force not currently fighting in the Pacific theater would be used at Leyte. No Australian troops would be brought in;
several Royal Australian Navy ships, however, would take part, along with
one ship from the Royal Navy, the HMS *Ariadne*. The sheer size of the
operation would be overwhelming and would be equal to, if not surpass,
the invasion of France in terms of the number of vessels and aircraft involved.

When the OCTAGON conference adjourned on September 16, no decision had been made as to what operations would follow the Leyte invasion. Admiral King, however, initiated a process for future operations
when he ordered that such planning would begin by the end of September.[19]

MacArthur and Halsey can share the credit for the switch from Mindanao to Leyte. Invading the Visayas allowed MacArthur to flank and divide both sides of the Japanese occupation forces on Luzon to the north
and Mindanao to the south. But Leyte's capture would not be an easy
task. MacArthur's men now faced their most desperate fight since Buna.
The Japanese, forced to make a belated decision once American intentions were known, would throw in everything they had: Army, Air Force,
and the remnants of the still mighty Imperial Fleet with its monster battleships, the 68,000-ton *Yamato* and the *Musashi*.

The Japanese knew the Americans were coming to Leyte. Lieutenant
General Shuichi Miyazaki of the Japanese Imperial General Headquarters observed:

> Viewed from the standpoint of political and operational strategy,
> holding the Philippines was the one essential [sic]. . . . With the
> loss of these islands, Japanese communications with the Southern
> region would be severely threatened. The loss of the Philippines

would greatly affect civilian morale in Japan. The islands were essential as a strategic base for the enemy advance on Japan. After their recapture, the advantage would be two to one in favor of the Americans.[20]

General MacArthur emerged victorious from the debate, and, therefore, the two-pronged attack that would issue from the Southwest Pacific and from the Central Pacific now converged at Leyte.

Prelude to Disaster

The American command structure was simple; uniting it for action was a complex task. The two principal commanders were General MacArthur and Admiral Nimitz. They split responsibilities in what would prove to be the greatest invasion effort since D-day. Leyte was a combined operation joining the forces of the Southwest Pacific under General MacArthur and the Central Pacific command under Admiral Nimitz. The command structure defining these two commands was as follows:

> Gen. Douglas MacArthur: Southwest Pacific Forces
> VAdm. Thomas C. Kinkaid: Central Philippines Attack Force,
> Seventh Fleet
> RAdm. Thomas L. Sprague: Providing air support for the
> Leyte landings
> Adm. Daniel E. Barbey: Northern Attack Force
> VAdm. Theodore S. Wilkinson: Southern Attack Force
> RAdm. Jesse B. Oldendorf: Fire Support Unit South
> Lt. Gen. Walter Krueger: Commanding General, Expeditionary Force
> Adm. Chester Nimitz: Central Pacific Forces
> Adm. William F. Halsey: Third Fleet

General MacArthur assigned the following tasks for the Leyte invasion to Admiral Kinkaid:

1. Transport and establish landing forces ashore in the Leyte Gulf–Surigao Strait area by coordinating with the Commanding General, Expeditionary Force, Lt. Gen. Walter Krueger.
2. Support the operation by:

    a. Providing air protection for convoys and direct air support for landings and subsequent operations, including antisubmarine patrol of the gulf and combat air patrol over the amphibious ships and craft, using Kinkaid's escort carriers.

    b. Lifting reinforcements and supplies to Leyte in naval assault shipping.

    c. Stopping Japanese reinforcements, by sea, of its Leyte garrison.

    d. Opening the Surigao Strait for Allied use; sending naval forces into Visayan waters to support current and future operations.

    e. Providing submarine reconnaissance, lifeguard service, and the escort of convoys.

The duties of the Nimitz-Halsey command were the following:

    1. Cover the Leyte amphibious landings.

    2. Strike Okinawa, Formosa, and northern Leyte on October 10–13.

    3. Strike Leyte, Cebu, and Negros islands; support Leyte landings from October 16–20.

    4. Operate in strategic support of the Leyte operation by destroying Japanese naval and air forces threatening the Philippines area, on and after October 21.

If one examines, literally, each commander's orders, no conflicts appear. However, Nimitz's orders to Halsey generated the seeds of what would set the stage for one of the greatest controversies in World War II. The orders in question were the following:

    1. Cover and support the Southwest Pacific Forces in order to assist in seizing and occupying the Central Philippines.

    2. Destroy enemy naval and air forces in, or threatening, the Philippines area.

These orders are straightforward and direct. However, it was an additional directive that became the source of controversy, one that would be debated for decades to come. This controversial addition stated, "In case opportunity for destruction of major portions of the enemy fleet is offered or can be created, such destruction becomes the primary task."[21]

• • •

No one knows the origin of this additional order. When the eminent United States Naval Academy professor emeritus Edwin B. Potter interviewed Admiral King after the war, King stated he had instructed Nimitz to include it. However, a later letter from King to Potter suggests that King was not as positive as he had earlier claimed to be as regards issuing this order. Potter noted in his biography of Halsey that the sentence was not written in either King's or Nimitz's style, suggesting by this that a staff member may have added the order. The two other sentences in the operational order were either numbered or lettered in outline form, but this one sentence had neither a number nor a letter before it. This fact reinforces the idea that the sentence may have been added as an afterthought. However, the originator's identity remains either unknown or, at best, unclear.

As far as Halsey was concerned, though, all this speculation about from where the order came mattered not a whit. There it was, on paper, in black and white, and Halsey never hesitated to make use of it. In his opinion, the Seventh Fleet had a defensive role, while his own Third Fleet's role was offensive. His intentions for the upcoming battle were never clearer than when he wrote a letter to Nimitz at the end of September 1944:

> I intend, if possible, to deny the enemy a chance to outrange me in an air duel and also to deny him an opportunity to employ an air shuttle (carrier-to-target-to-land) against me.
>
> Inasmuch as the destruction of the enemy fleet is the principal task, every weapon must be brought into play and the general coordination of these weapons should be in the hands of the tactical commander responsible for the outcome of the battle. . . . My goal is the same as yours—to completely annihilate the Jap fleet if the opportunity offers.[22]

Nimitz never said anything intended to change Halsey's mind. In fact, it was Nimitz who had put Halsey into this command position precisely because of the volatile admiral's natural aggressiveness. Halsey's superior wanted him to be free to pursue the Japanese fleet if it should show up at Leyte. All previous operations for the Fifth Fleet had been Spruance's responsibility. The Fifth Fleet, which included the landing forces, directed its own amphibious landings, while its carrier striking forces did two jobs. They were to directly support the landings *and* to defend against any of the Japanese fleet's counterattacks. However, the amphibious forces had been assigned from the Third Fleet to the Seventh Fleet, and Vice Admiral Kinkaid had the responsibility for the landings on the Philippine beaches. Thus, Halsey in reality had a free hand to go after the Japanese fleet if it should appear.

Twelve days prior to the Leyte landings, Nimitz wrote a letter to Halsey in which he clearly stated that Halsey was free to use his own judgment if the tactical situation so justified:

> You are always free to make local decisions in connection with the handling of the forces placed under your command. Often it will be necessary for you to take action not previously contemplated because of local situations which may develop quickly and in light of information which has come to you and which may not yet be available to me. My only requirement in such cases is that I be informed as fully and as early as the situation permits.[23]

Halsey had been given the opportunity to interpret his mission in any way he wished. He could support MacArthur's troops with all the resources at his disposal. However, should an opportunity present itself to destroy the Japanese Imperial Fleet, he could pursue it with every ounce of aggressiveness in his soul.

Given what happened at the Battle of Leyte Gulf, the question naturally arises: Why would a respected and experienced American naval commander, such as Halsey was, take the bit between his teeth and run with it? The reason may lie in American naval doctrine. All American naval officers had been trained with a primary objective in mind: the destruction of the enemy's fleet. The British Royal Navy's officers also had been trained in this way since Admiral Nelson's time. The philosophy of the American naval strategist Alfred Thayer Mahan had carried on this principle. A certain symmetry exists here as regards the army's basic canon of destroying the enemy's army. However, a leading British writer on naval strategy, Sir Julian Corbett, wrote in 1911 that the "paramount function of a covering force in an amphibious operation is to prevent interference with the . . . landing, support and supply of the Army."[24]

Until the Leyte invasion, American naval operations in the Pacific had functioned under the aegis of Corbett's principle. His idea is based on the precept "that destruction of the enemy force is not an end in itself, but merely one possible means to victory. It follows that the main and overriding objective of a naval force supporting or covering an amphibious operation is to support and cover, unless it is expressly ordered to do something different."[25]

During the Saipan operation in June 1944, Admiral Spruance behaved cautiously when pursuing the Japanese fleet. However, when no Japanese threat existed to the landing operations off the Marianas, he then went after the enemy fleet. Halsey criticized Spruance for showing insufficiently aggressive behavior in the Battle of the Philippine Sea. For his part, he did not intend to repeat what he considered to be a serious mistake on Spruance's part.

Nimitz's added order to Halsey's operational tasks did indeed effectively relieve him from providing continuous support to MacArthur's main mission of seizing and controlling Leyte Island if the situation called for a change, and thus freed the admiral to decide what his primary duty was. His orders contained no directives that required him to coordinate with or to obtain agreement from MacArthur for any action he might take.

Halsey and MacArthur were both aggressive and accustomed to getting their own ways. It may have been too much to expect that these two strong-willed men would surrender to the other if or when a conflict arose between their objectives.

Because no single commander was in charge of the entire Leyte operation, the command structure was unstable. MacArthur's command philosophy was that he did not wish to interfere with naval operations, which meant he would leave Admiral Kinkaid to make naval command decisions.[26]

Given these facts, it is clear that the seeds of disaster had been planted, and, if circumstances permitted, these seeds would grow and flower.

Chapter 2: The Japanese Get Ready

Since the beginnings of the Japanese navy, and particularly since Adm. Heihachiro Togo's 1905 victory over Czarist Russia's naval forces at Tsushima Strait, the reigning Japanese doctrine was to lure the enemy fleet into one great naval battle and defeat it by overwhelming force. This concept guided the attack on Pearl Harbor, the Battle of Midway, and the Battle of the Philippine Sea. However, contrary to expectations, the American fleets were not destroyed. At Pearl Harbor, the Japanese negligently had left intact the American naval repair facilities and dry docks, the fueling and fuel storage facilities, the submarine base, and the aircraft carriers. Thus, the American navy had a foundation on which to build the largest naval force the world had ever seen. This naval force then proceeded to win the Battle of the Coral Sea, Midway, the naval battles of Guadalcanal, and the Battle of the Philippine Sea. The cumulative effect of these crushing defeats crippled Japan's sea power and airpower. Nonetheless, their fleet remained a formidable fighting force.

After the Philippine Sea debacle, the Japanese naval staff began designing a plan for the next battle, one they initially assumed would take place in July or August 1944. The overall plan was named SHO-GO (or Victory Operation). It assumed that Allied attacks could occur in a number of places over a wide area. Their plan, therefore, contained options to cover the possible locales. The range of alternatives included the Kuriles in northern Japan through the main islands of Kyushu and Honshu, Okinawa, and on to the Philippines. The SHO-GO plan was based on the assumption of an air force reserve present either on Formosa or

Luzon that was able to shift to the diverse locales according to need. The fleet, anchored at Lingga Roads near Singapore and at the home islands, would steam to the chosen battle sites. Naval forces near the home islands would engage in operational exercises so as to be ready to move at a moment's notice.

The planning activity's outcome was a joint Japanese army-navy paper that appeared just after Hideki Tojo's cabinet was replaced on July 18, 1944.[1] This paper moved the original planned date of July or August 1944 ahead, stating:

> When the enemy attacks in one of the decisive battle areas, maximum air, sea, and ground strengths would be assembled. The enemy carriers and transport convoys will be sought out and annihilated on the spot. And if a landing is affected, the enemy forces would be destroyed as they land.[2]

On the eve of Roosevelt's Pearl Harbor meetings with MacArthur and Nimitz in July 1944, the Japanese assembled a set of specific alternatives labeled SHO-1 through SHO-4, depending on the strike location. SHO-1 covered the Philippines; SHO-2 centered on Formosa and the Ryukyu Islands; SHO-3 focused on the Japanese Home Islands of Honshu, Kyushu, and Shikoku; and SHO-4 defended Hokkaido and the Kuriles. For the first time, Japanese army units were to be placed under naval operational control. This decision reflected a determination to avoid the jurisdictional mistakes made in defending Guadalcanal.[3]

However, the Japanese realized that in continuing the war, their military resources were limited. An operations planner in the Japanese army wrote:

> No matter how much effort Japan may exert, and although she may be able to engage in a decisive battle before the end of this year, it will hardly be possible for her to counter any powerful attack during and after this year. The only way out of this difficulty is to check the enemy's advance.[4, 5]

Despite all the difficulties facing them, Japanese planners were determined to recover from the disastrous defeat in the Marianas Islands and further modified the SHO-GO plan so as to be ready for battle by again postponing the plan's execution time frame to the early spring of

1945. The Americans, however, had an agenda of their own. They were set to invade the Philippines well before the Japanese were ready.[6]

Following the defeat of the Japanese navy in the Marianas, Japanese planners guessed that the Imperial Navy needed about eight months, until about mid-February 1945, to once again be a viable fighting force. However, as matters turned out, the Combined Fleet had to move into battle with everything it had in only four months, beginning Operation SHO-1 on October 18. Because of this earlier-than-planned start, the fleet had only three months of training at Lingga Roads. And they were lucky to have this time, given the fact that the Americans had made so much rapid progress in the third year of the war.

Operation SHO-1's design was supposed to stop any American invasion of the Philippine Islands by implementing the following tasks:

1. Land-based naval air forces:
     a. Meet the American invasion forces at a distance of 700 miles from the home islands.
     b. Reduce the Americans' strength by attacking with aircraft, using bombs and torpedoes.
     c. Cooperate with the Army Air Force to destroy the remaining enemy force on the invasion beaches.
2. Combined Fleet:
     a. Assemble at Brunei Bay, north of Borneo.
     b. Sortie to intercept the enemy's convoys and escorts at the most opportune time.
     c. Defeat the Americans overwhelmingly at the invasion point using superior naval strength after the Americans have begun landing troops on the Philippine beaches.
     d. Lure the American carrier forces northward by moving Vice Admiral Ozawa's carrier force southward from Japan.

The Fifth Base Air Force, land-based air forces in the Philippines under the command of VAdm. Takujiro Ohnishi, and the Sixth Base Air Force, land-based air forces on Formosa with VAdm. Shigeru Fukudome in command, were responsible for the first task. The Combined Fleet was responsible for the second, with the exception that the aircraft carriers under the command of Vice Admiral Ozawa were placed under VAdm. Takeo Kurita's command.[7]

Meanwhile, Halsey's carrier aircraft began the Formosa Air Battle on October 12, 1944. This battle resulted in disastrous Japanese aircraft losses for the Sixth Base Air Force. Still in denial, however, the Japanese propaganda machine reported to the Japanese citizens at home that this air battle was a great victory. However, the truth was otherwise, because the Japanese Formosa air forces lost so many planes in this battle that it became utterly useless for the SHO-1 plan. These losses would significantly influence the role of Ozawa's carriers during the Battle of Leyte Gulf, which will be described in a later chapter.

However, let us now consider what Japanese air strength remained for SHO-1 following the Formosa debacle.

When Vice Admiral Ohnishi arrived in the Philippines on October 17 to take command, the Japanese Fifth Base Air Force had no more than 150 operable planes of limited capability. Meanwhile, attacks by American carriers on Japanese matériel at Truk and at Palau in the Caroline Islands—325 planes had been lost at Truk and 203 at Palau—only made matters worse.

Ohnishi was Japan's leading authority on naval aviation. He had been a chief adviser to Adm. Isoroku Yamamoto on this specialty. Due to the lack of aircraft and trained crews, he realized at once that his command could not perform its SHO-1 assignment using traditional air force tactics. The only chance his forces had was to adopt a far more drastic method so as to make maximum use of the few planes he had left.

It was in this manner, then, that the idea of the "suicide attack aircraft" was born. Because of the desperate conditions he faced in taking command of the Philippines, Ohnishi formed the Kamikaze Special Attack Corps.

Naval historians and analysts have justifiably criticized Ohnishi's decision, asserting that the Kamikaze Corps's attacks had no major effect on the Leyte Gulf naval battles. Furthermore, the formation of the Kamikaze Corps can be viewed as an outgrowth of the samurai ethic of *Bushido*, which teaches the military to regard self-sacrifice as an honor and a public duty. However, one major factor should not be forgotten: The few Japanese planes left in the Philippines in October 1944 could not accomplish anything at all by using conventional attack methods. Had the kamikaze attacks been able to cripple the flight decks of American carriers, Kurita's force could have possibly met and defeated the Americans in a decisive surface engagement. But, the suicide effort implemented did indeed fail at Leyte. Kurita's surface ships, as a result, were deprived of vital air support and so had to face long odds.

The Japanese did not successfully overcome the devastating aircraft and aircrew deficiencies that existed prior to the engagement at Leyte Gulf. As an example, consider the fact that since their Philippine-based planes could fly no more than approximately 700 miles, the Japanese could not attack the oncoming American fleet, or even detect its presence. Attempting to overcome this deficiency, Adm. Soemu Toyoda, commander in chief of the Japanese navy, ordered all of Kurita's thirty-two float planes moved from his battleships and cruisers to a field on Mindoro Island. However, an agreement was made to the effect that Admiral Kurita could recall these planes at any time.

The Japanese had other factors to consider in deciding what to do with their battleship and cruiser scout planes. The range of Admiral Ohnishi's own planes was too short to be able to search for the approaching American fleet. However, the ships' scout planes did have sufficient range to perform this vital function. But if the planes had remained with the fleet, they might have been lost, because the waters between Brunei and Leyte, through which the Imperial Fleet had to steam, were so full of American submarines that their mother ships could not safely retrieve the planes if they went down.

The Japanese military endlessly and bitterly debated the disposition of its naval planes for SHO-1. It must be acknowledged that at that point in the war naval planners knew that to send a fleet into battle without adequate air cover was a foolish decision. As planes from Kurita's ships were sent off to Mindoro, one staff officer prophetically remarked in disgust, "I'd hate to be responsible for this decision when enemy submarines attack."

Most of SHO-1's tasks had a certain desperate logic to them, as did the overall plan for the Combined Fleet. Interception of an enemy fleet was a proper function of the main surface force. Specific fleet training exercises had been enacted for this purpose. In addition, the fleet had been trained for nighttime operations, including lightning attacks into enemy-held harbors. The 18-inch guns of the *Yamato* and the *Musashi* had the ability to blast many a ship out of the water and, given the training and practice the crews had undergone, had a fair chance of escaping unharmed. The decision to bet on the ability of Ozawa and his carriers to lure the American fast carriers away from the Leyte beaches was chancy, at best, yet this desperate gamble would prove to be a highly effective one. Stranger things had happened before in the annals of warfare.

Great dissatisfaction arose in the Japanese Combined Fleet over the order to destroy the Americans on the invasion beaches. Kurita's fleet was supposed to steam rapidly into Leyte Gulf in broad daylight and attack and destroy as many American ships in the harbor as possible. The Japanese had some success in executing this maneuver in the nighttime battles for Guadalcanal two years earlier. However, they had never attempted an undertaking of this kind in daylight.

For twenty years prior to World War II, Japanese naval training emphasized gunnery practice for its capital ships and hit-and-run tactics for its destroyers. During that period, the firepower and range of the larger ships had increased, while the speed and maneuverability of the smaller ones had improved significantly. The Japanese considered that a proper role for the heavy ships was to bombard targets from long range by attacking enemy harbors at night. They viewed the specific roles of destroyers or submarines to attack enemy harbors in daylight. Destroyers and submarines, not cruisers or battleships, should attack enemy convoys. Many officers in the Combined Fleet considered any daytime attacks by battleships and heavy cruisers as foolhardy and risky. But this was exactly what Kurita's force was expected to do.

The men of the Japanese Combined Fleet accepted the fact that Operation SHO-1 was a final, all-out attempt to meet the Americans in that long-sought-after, decisive naval battle. They expected to be able to depend on their experience and training in implementing the tactics called for in the SHO-1 plan. When they learned that they would have to make an unprecedented, untried daylight attack into Leyte Gulf, their anger mounted. In the view of many of them, this operation was impossible and suicidal.[8]

Allied objectives were no secret to the planners in Tokyo. Since the capture of Saipan in the Marianas and Hollandia in the Southwest Pacific, the Japanese navy's planners believed that America's next logical objective was the Philippines, to be followed by attacks on the Ryukyu Islands. The Japanese strategists' top priority now became to put in place a plan for a decisive battle in the Philippines. Imperial General Headquarters had already anticipated that the Palau and Morotai operations would occur in mid-September.

The Japanese considered the Philippines to be a critically important strategic possession. They relied almost totally on oil, minerals, and other raw matériel from Southeast Asia to keep their war machine functioning. The Japanese merchant marine plied their ships from the south through the South China Sea and passed within air-attack range of Philippine-based planes, a fact of major importance should the Americans secure air bases there. Since American submarines had taken a terrible toll on Japanese shipping along these vital trade routes, the Japanese were just barely holding their own in providing critical supplies to their industrial base in the home islands. If the Americans did succeed in capturing the Philippines, the supply lines between the home islands and the Japanese-held possessions in Malaysia and the Netherlands East Indies would be cut, hastening the war's end and Japan's defeat.

The Philippines were also extremely valuable to the Japanese as a base for troops and as a staging area for ships. When they captured the islands from the Americans in 1942, the Japanese had hoped to gain the cooperation of the natives, but had little or no success. Instead, Filipino guerrilla operations forced the Japanese army to expend precious resources that could have been used elsewhere. Because of the strategic importance of the Philippines to the Japanese, they then had to strengthen their considerable military force in the Philippine Islands in order to meet the Americans' next move. While the exact location of the initial American landings was unknown, the Japanese strategy was to emphasize the defense of Luzon Island as the last bastion of their presence in the Philippines.

After the Battle of the Philippine Sea, the principal Japanese surface forces moved to Lingga Roads to be near their primary fuel supply and to conduct training exercises. The aircraft carriers returned to the Inland Sea for the purpose of training new air groups. However, this task was a daunting one. The severe losses they had sustained in the Marianas Turkey Shoot cried out for trained replacements, but the Japanese did not have an organized training program for naval air crews as did the Americans. Almost all the experienced pilots who could have provided training based on actual combat experience had lost their lives. Furthermore, all the training that was going to be done had to be accomplished while the carrier fleet was anchored in the Inland Sea. Given the fact that America was pushing the Japanese as rapidly and as hard as it could, the Japanese had neither the time nor the battle-tested trainers to give the new crews the training they needed. And these green air crews were going to face the combat-wise American veteran air crews fresh from recent victories.

Japanese intelligence was not sure where the first landing would take place. As noted earlier, four separate plans had been designed to anticipate landings in the Philippines, Formosa-Ryukyus, Honshu-Kyushu, and Hokkaido-Kuriles. Imperial General Headquarters would have to wait for the Americans to move before deciding which plan to implement. Despite all the possibilities, it seemed to Japanese strategists that the Philippines would be the most likely American target of attack.

Other sources confirmed this assessment. A loose-talking American official at a cocktail party in the Soviet Union had stated that the American air forces now based in China soon would be attacking Japanese bases to isolate the Philippines. This report was immediately transmitted to the Japanese. Nonetheless, it was sound military thinking and intuition that led the Japanese to believe that an attack on the Philippines was indeed the next American move in the Pacific.

Admiral Soemu Toyoda traveled to Manila on October 7, 1944. He felt certain that Halsey's Third Fleet might launch large-scale air attacks on Okinawa, Formosa, or the Philippines in preparation for an invasion. His intelligence personnel had informed him that there was indeed a heavy concentration of transport ships in Hollandia and Wadke in New Guinea. The navy section of the Imperial General Headquarters predicted that the landings needed in the upcoming American invasion would occur somewhere in the Philippines during the last ten days of October, with the most likely location being Leyte.

Thus, Japanese intelligence had guessed correctly the general location and approximate time of the next major attack by the Americans. Despite all the agonizing debates, arguments, and discussions by the American commanders, the Japanese in fact had figured out, in a general way, what would happen next. They made a fatal error, however, by not guessing accurately the precise location of the landings. Admiral Toyoda, therefore, did not alert his forces until Allied ships were actually seen in Leyte Gulf.

The landings occurred on October 20, and they continued with only local opposition. Four days would go by before the Japanese navy would respond. By then, however, it would be too late to stop the Americans.

Allied Intelligence Mistakes

Allied intelligence was less accurate than the Japanese with regard to positive predictions. Southwest Pacific intelligence guesses as to Japanese intentions came the closest with regard to what the Japanese were not doing than with respect to what they were going to do. Lieutenant General George C. Kenney, commander of the Allied Air Forces Southwest Pacific, predicted on September 24, 1944: "The objective [Philippines] is relatively undefended—the Japanese will not offer strong resistance to the operation."

On October 4, General Kenney thought that a fleet action was "less likely than ever." As A-day—the day designated by the Americans for the opening of the Leyte landings—approached, Allied intelligence estimates became increasingly inaccurate. On October 19 (A-day minus one), Halsey told MacArthur that the Japanese fleet would be deployed into small groups and make "Tokyo Express"–like runs at Leyte.

On A-day, MacArthur's headquarters circulated a paper called "Enemy Capabilities of Naval Reaction to Allied Landings on the Philippines." It confidently declared that any approach by the Japanese fleet through either the Surigao or the San Bernardino Straits was "impractical because of navigational hazards and lack of maneuvering space."

On A-day plus one, the Southwest Pacific Intelligence Summary expressed the opinion that there was "no apparent intent" on the part of the Japanese navy "to interfere with our Leyte landings."

Admiral Kinkaid declared that the Japanese would approach Leyte using a strategy similar to the Tokyo Express runs used in the Solomons. He also stated that there was a distinct possibility that enemy planes would operate west of the Palawan Passage.[9]

Kenney, MacArthur, and Kinkaid made incorrect assessments in that they grossly underestimated the willingness of the Japanese to defend the Philippines, the type of defense they would offer, and the size of the naval force the Japanese would deploy. These misconceptions could have been the cornerstone of an Allied tragedy.

Air Battle over Formosa

Formosa is an island near Mainland China, about 200 miles north of the Philippine island of Luzon, forming the division between the East and South China Seas. The body of water between Luzon and Formosa is the Luzon Strait. As noted earlier, Formosa had been a subject of vitriolic debate among American commanders as to its suitability as the next American target of attack. When the Joint Chiefs of Staff sent an order to Nimitz and MacArthur on October 4, 1944, authorizing the invasion of the Philippines, the decision had been made that the next step for the advance on Japan would proceed through these islands.[10]

Therefore, Formosa was not to be invaded. But, this did not mean that this island would escape military action. Quite the contrary. The most important and influential struggle that occurred prior to the Battle of Leyte Gulf was the vast air battle that took place over and near that much-discussed island.

The Third Fleet left Ulithi Atoll over the two-day period of October 3–4, 1944. The gargantuan fleet required two days to leave the atoll's huge lagoon, because it took that much time for all these ships to pass through the harbor's entrance. Just before dark on October 7, the entire fleet rendezvoused about 375 miles west of the Marianas Islands. The fleet's previous assignments had demanded much from their planes, ships, and men. Despite the fatigue that permeated this vast armada, the duties that lay before the men were absolutely essential to the success of the upcoming Leyte operation.

Such a large gathering of warships must have been an impressive sight. The fast carrier forces of the Pacific Fleet had the greatest assemblage of Essex-class carriers ever gathered together and the most modern, fastest battleships ever built.

Wanting to deceive the Japanese into believing his ships were going to attack the Bonin Islands just southwest of the Japanese home islands, Halsey sent a task group commanded by RAdm. Alan E. Smith to pursue a separate course from the main fleet and head toward Marcus Island. This force included the heavy cruisers *Chester*, *Pensacola*, and *Salt Lake City*, as well as six destroyers.

They attacked Marcus Island on October 9 and made a great show of bravado to ensure that the Japanese knew they were there. Smith's diversionary force approached the island behind a heavy weather front and stood off Marcus Island just below the horizon. The force created dummy radar targets and shot off numerous fireworks hoping to deceive the Japanese into believing a very large force was about to attack and invade. Although they bombarded the island from dawn to dusk, they failed to impress the Japanese.

Just after the beginning of this bombardment, an American patrol bomber shot down a Japanese patrol plane flying along the Tropic of Cancer on October 9. The Japanese pilot did not report that his plane had been attacked, so the commandant at the Sasebo Naval District in Japan knew only that the aircraft had disappeared. He immediately jumped to the conclusion that the patrol plane had been shot down by American carrier-based aircraft. Thus, he alerted all naval forces in the southern Japanese home island area, while the Third Fleet operated about 225 miles southwest of where the airplane disappeared. This incident nearly triggered an early activation of the Japanese SHO plan. For the Japanese, it was fortunate that this did not come to pass.

Because of these two incidents, the first strikes on Okinawa and the smaller Ryukyu Islands on October 10 came as no surprise to the Japanese, yet this proved to be of no help to them. The Third Fleet attacked the Japanese air bases and anchorages with 1,396 aircraft sorties from dawn to dusk that October 10. The American air attacks sank many ships, including one submarine tender, twelve torpedo boats, two midget submarines, four cargo ships, and a large number of auxiliary sampans. The Japanese never revealed how many of their aircraft were destroyed, but American intelligence estimated a loss of approximately 100 Japanese aircraft. This operation cost the Americans twenty-one aircraft, five pilots, and four crewmen. The submarine *Sterlet*, on rescue duty off Okinawa, picked up six downed American aircrews. This was the first time since Doolittle's raid in 1942 that large American task forces had approached so closely to the Japanese home islands.

Hearing of the American attack on Okinawa while in Formosa, Admiral Toyoda guessed correctly that these attacks were the beginning of large-scale American operations. Toyoda's chief of staff, RAdm. Ryunosuke Kusaka, alerted the Japanese navy's Base Air Forces (land-based air forces) to begin the SHO-1 (Leyte) and the SHO-2 (Formosa) operations. He also issued orders to VAdm. Shigeru Fukudome, commander of the Sixth Base Air Force, to "attack and destroy the enemy."[11] An additional order, which later proved to be vitally important, directed the carriers *Zuikaku, Zuiho, Chitose,* and *Chiyoda* and the converted battleship-carriers *Ise* and *Hyuga* to stand by and transfer all their functional planes to land bases.

Stranded in Formosa, Toyoda realized that the start of American air operations signaled the beginning of the "general decisive battle" and decided to remain in Formosa to direct operations. In an almost uncanny way, VAdm. Gunichi Mikawa in Manila guessed that the next American air attack would be on Formosa, where Admiral Fukudome depended

on about 230 fighter planes to defend the island. In this defense, Fukudome would rely on his elite "T" force based on Kyushu to attack the
American carriers.

Meanwhile, the fast carriers of the Third Fleet, Task Force 38, planned
to strike the Aparri airfield on Luzon's northern coast. After taking on
fuel from twelve oilers, two carrier groups launched sixty-one planes,
twenty-two of them armed with rockets, to attack the Luzon airfield on
October 11 at 12:40 P.M., from a range of 323 miles. As they arrived over
Luzon, no Japanese opposition rose to meet them. They attacked and
destroyed approximately fifteen Japanese aircraft on the ground, losing
only seven planes in the process. The American Combat Air Patrol shot
down three Japanese aircraft, one of which came as near as 25 miles to
the task force. Overall, the attack on the Aparri airfield did not accomplish much, but it gave the Japanese defenders on Formosa another day
to prepare for the coming onslaught.

The Formosa Air Battle began the next day, October 12. It lasted three
days and had two objectives. The first was to destroy all Japanese air
strength on Formosa; the second was to prevent the island from being
used as a staging base for aircraft to attack the Philippines.

Just as the eastern sky was changing from dark to light, Task Force 38
arrived 50 to 90 miles east of Formosa, and in position to launch its
planes. The American carriers were prepared for attacks by Japanese aircraft, yet nothing happened that morning. Then, just before sunrise at
5:44 A.M., the carriers launched a fighter strike for the purpose of establishing air superiority over Formosa and the Pescadores. The pilots
had superb flying weather with enough wind to easily launch and land
the aircraft. There was just enough cloud cover to help the American pilots begin their attacks while providing excellent visibility over the target area.

American pilots flew 1,378 sorties that day from all four Task Force
38 carrier groups and vigorously attacked the Formosa airfields and shipping. The one additional day of preparation had availed the Japanese
nothing.

Admiral Fukudome described the combat immediately above his
command post as he saw many aircraft falling from the sky in flames.
Thinking these planes were American, the Japanese admiral clapped his
hands, shouting, "Well done! Tremendous success!" However, after taking a second look, he discovered that the falling planes were not American but Japanese. Later, he gave a poetic and powerful description of

the air battle: "Our fighters were nothing but so many eggs thrown at a stone wall of the indomitable enemy formation."[12]

American aircraft severely damaged Japanese ground installations and destroyed Fukudome's base headquarters. Only sixty operational Japanese fighters remained when the second American attack came over. None were left on the ground to intercept the third wave. Despite losing forty-eight planes, the American carriers remained near Formosa the rest of the day.

But the Japanese were by no means ready to give up. When Task Force 38 had attacked Okinawa on October 10, Japanese resistance had been light. However, during the three-day battle over Formosa, the Japanese attacked the American fleet with a resolve and ferocity the Americans had not seen since Midway and the Solomons.

At 7:00 P.M. on October 12, Japanese bombers armed with torpedoes raided the American fleet and inflicted considerable damage on Task Force 38 in an attack that lasted until midnight. These aircraft were from the elite "T" force based on Kyushu—Fukudome's best hope for destroying the American fleet. Fukudome admitted losing forty-two aircraft during these raids. Planes of the American Combat Air Patrol from the carriers *Cabot* and *Independence* shot down several Japanese planes and caused other losses by antiaircraft fire.

The next day, October 13, Task Force 38 moved into a new launching position off Formosa. At 6:14 A.M., a half hour before sunrise, a large wave of American aircraft took off. The strike pattern approximated that of the first day but with fewer sorties—974—all of which took place before noon. Several airfields whose existence was unknown before the attacks began were pummeled by American pilots. It had been assumed that about four airfields were operational, yet these pilots discovered at least fifteen.

During the twilight hours of October 13, four Japanese bombers came in at low levels, escaping radar detection and attacked the carrier *Franklin*. Antiaircraft fire shot down the first two aircraft; a third Japanese plane dropped its torpedo, just missing the *Franklin*'s bow before being destroyed. A fourth aircraft dropped its torpedo and just missed the *Franklin*'s fantail. Hit by intense antiaircraft fire, the plane caught fire and crashed on the carrier's flight deck, slid across it, then burst into flames and careened overboard.

The *Franklin*'s damage was light. The heavy cruiser *Canberra*, however, sustained serious torpedo damage. Because of this damage, the third day's assault on Formosa on October 14 was smaller than the attacks of the previous two days. One strike made up of 146 fighters and 100 bombers hit the island, with seventeen fighters and six bombers lost. In addition, a series of fighter planes from the carriers took off at dawn, destined for Luzon. They destroyed a few Japanese planes on the ground. The Twentieth Bomber Command of the United States Army Air Corps sent 109 B-29s from China to attack Formosa. That day the Japanese attacked again, and the carrier *Hancock* took several hits and was left smoking. The light cruiser *Reno* took a hit from an apparent suicide plane and caught fire. However, the Americans did not lose a single ship, even though the heavily damaged cruisers *Canberra* and *Houston* needed towing.[13]

During the three-day Formosa Air Battle, the largest battle since the Marianas Turkey Shoot, the Japanese lost more than 500 planes. Most of these planes were from Vice Admiral Ozawa's already dwindling carrier striking force. About forty freighters and other small craft were sunk, and many others were damaged. The Japanese sustained tremendous losses in the form of ammunition dumps, hangars, barracks, machine and other repair shops, and industrial plants.[14]

The American navy in the Pacific, for its part, had not been so seriously damaged since Midway and the Solomons. The suddenness and ferocity of the Japanese's opposition worried Halsey and the Task Force 38 commander, VAdm. Marc Mitscher. They talked over the short-range radio and decided they faced two choices: (1) The cruisers *Houston* and *Canberra* could be abandoned and sunk, or (2) the fleet could withdraw and take the cruisers with them in tow. They quickly chose the second alternative.

The downed American planes burned furiously in the water and shot up large plumes of smoke that could be seen for miles. Japanese pilots, observing this evidence of destruction, made a crucial mistake, for they assumed the smoke plumes came from burning American ships. Therefore, they reported that a large number of American ships were on fire, and this misinformation caused great rejoicing in a Tokyo hungry for good news; Japanese propaganda went right to work. On October 17, a radio broadcast proclaiming a tremendous Japanese victory filled Japanese airwaves:

October 17 (Domei)—The name of Vice Admiral Mitscher . . . together with the name Saipan, is indelibly stamped in the hearts of us, the one hundred million people of Japan, as a name to be remembered for vengeance. He was one of the planners of the Doolittle raid . . . participated in the Battle of Midway . . . was made air force commander in the Solomons. His ability was recognized [and] he became commander of the jewel of the Pacific fleet, the 58th Task Force, and invaded Saipan. The pitiful end of [the 58th Task Force] must have been vividly witnessed by him from his watery grave.

An American radioman listening to this broadcast, commented with both insightfulness and vision: "It's a socko finish for the scenario, boys, but it's going to leave you in a tight spot when you have to write the sequel."[15] Bitter experience had taught American sailors to take Japanese propaganda claims with a grain of salt.

On October 16, an American search plane reported sighting Japanese fleet units moving southward. As late afternoon approached, for a few tense moments the American pilots thought they would be attacking these Japanese ships as darkness approached, then returning to their ships at night. Mitscher, contradicting Japanese propaganda claims and very much alive, weighed the reports of the search plane's pilot. He met with his staff, and decided the movement was a feint, and this guess turned out to be correct. He decided to keep his armor-piercing bombs for another day. Mitscher's decision was based on the fact that he vividly recalled how American pilots had landed in the water after running out of fuel on June 20 in the Philippine Sea, so he was determined not to make the same mistake twice.

However, there was strong evidence the Japanese were considering another fleet action. Halsey guessed Admiral Toyoda might very well believe the highly exaggerated reports by his sources, given the fact that the radio broadcast had proclaimed a Japanese victory over the American navy. Therefore, Halsey ordered Mitscher to send two task groups eastward to surprise the Japanese should they steam out from behind the Philippines.[16]

Since the Japanese pilots had reported the burning American ships in conjunction with the retreat of the American fleet from Formosa, the Japanese naval high command thought this situation offered them an opportunity too good to ignore. They, therefore, ordered VAdm. Kiyohide Shima's fleet to hunt for the supposedly heavily damaged American fleet south of Formosa. Tokyo chose Shima's force because it was fast, mobile, and endowed with the fast heavy cruisers *Nachi* and *Ashigara*, the light cruiser *Abukuma*, and seven destroyers. After participating in fleet exercises with the Japanese carriers in Tokyo Bay, Shima had left Hiroshima in early October. His fleet made good progress through the Bungo Strait, arriving near Formosa in mid-October close to the last-reported American position.

Shima's men had high hopes for their upcoming mission, believing they would find the American fleet in a badly crippled condition. They expected easy pickings ripe for the taking. But as Shima neared the scene of his intended "mop-up operation," he peered into his binoculars and beheld an astonishing sight. Two gigantic naval forces steamed in perfect battle order before him. If he attacked as commanded, his small force would be overwhelmed in less than five minutes. Prudently, he reversed course, and headed for safety at a flank speed of 34 knots.[17]

Shima's failed mission is yet another classic example of poor Japanese battle planning. The lesson it teaches is that seemingly competent commanders can be misled if they do not carefully evaluate optimistic reports made by their own personnel. Furthermore, the Japanese could ill spare the fuel wasted by Shima's vain journey. This was by no means the last time the Japanese would experience frustration and suffer defeat as a result of faulty intelligence. It had happened at Midway, the Solomons, and in the Philippine Sea. It would happen again in Leyte Gulf.

Although there is no universal agreement as to how many aircraft the Japanese lost during this huge air battle, most scholars estimate that the Japanese forfeited the availability of over 600 aircraft of all kinds, almost 60 percent of the aircraft that the Japanese had committed. Japanese land-based air strength was now crippled on Formosa and in the Philippines. Ozawa's carriers had no chance at all to rebuild their air strength before the Battle of Leyte Gulf. Only a few hundred planes were now operational. As a result, they could not execute an integral portion of the SHO-1 plan, which required the application of overwhelming air strength against the American invasion force in the Philippine Islands.

Adding insult to injury, Shima's futile chase after the supposedly damaged American ships not only wasted scarce fuel, but his ships were now too far away from Ozawa's main body to be able to join his command for the upcoming SHO-1 operation. On the American side, Halsey lost fewer than 100 aircraft. The damage to the three American cruisers and one carrier did not diminish the Third Fleet's overwhelming strength.

Shima's force was now off in limbo, with no clear mission. This lack
of clarity of purpose would continue into the Battle of Leyte Gulf and
was the first in a series of Japanese tactical blunders. It was the Imperial
Navy and Imperial General Headquarters in Tokyo that had set in motion the premature execution of the SHO plan on October 12 by not
properly coordinating their actions. Had the Japanese planes attacked
the Americans one day earlier, while the American pilots were attacking
Luzon, several American ships could have been sunk or heavily damaged
because of their lack of air defense. However, this lack of coordination,
combined with faulty tactics, kept Japanese aircraft on the ground in Formosa and gave American pilots the opportunity to demolish them on October 12.

The Japanese had gambled that their aircraft would be able to sink
or to severely damage the American task force and thus interfere with,
or perhaps stop, the American invasion plans, but it was a gamble they
lost. The tactics of the Japanese naval staff resulted instead in the point-
less destruction of Japanese airpower, making it virtually unfit for the upcoming battles. Compared to this fiasco, the order to send Shima's fleet
south to search hopelessly for "crippled" American ships was just bad
planning.

And the blunders did not end there. The Japanese army's inflated
claims of inflicted damage on American ships led them to form the mistaken belief that the Americans would postpone their invasion plans because their ships had been too severely damaged, thus affecting Japanese
plans regarding troop placements on the individual islands. As a result,
the Japanese delayed the defensive planning they would need for the upcoming invasion. For these and other reasons, the Americans would meet
no appreciable opposition when they landed on the Leyte beaches.[18]

The Formosa Air Battle was now over. Halsey would say it had been a
"knock-down, drag-out fight between carrier-based and shore-based air."
Its effects on future Japanese operations off and around Leyte Gulf would
become known only when the needed aircraft would not be there to support their fleet operations. The aircraft would not be there because they
did not exist.

The Japanese Navy Plans Its Next Move

Since the Japanese were in the dark as to the precise locations of the
American landings, the SHO-GO operational plan called for four dif-

ferent scenarios. As mentioned earlier, these contingency plans concerned Allied attacks on the Philippines, Formosa-Ryukyus, Honshu-Kyushu, and Hokkaido-Kuriles. (While the latter three scenarios are interesting from an academic point of view, I will concentrate on the Japanese plan for the first battle location, the Philippines.) This SHO-1 plan for the attack on the Philippines called for three naval forces to converge on the landing area. The first one was the main body and called the Northern Force by the Americans. It was under the command of VAdm. Jisaburo Ozawa and consisted of almost all of the remaining Japanese carriers. This force would advance on Leyte from the north in an attempt to lure the powerful American Third Fleet away from the landing areas. The ships in this force included the large carrier *Zuikaku*, the last carrier afloat from the Pearl Harbor attack, and the light carriers *Zuiho, Chitose*, and *Chiyoda*.

The second collection of ships was the formidable First Striking Force, with VAdm. Takeo Kurita as its commander. The largest part of the First Striking Force, called the Center Force by the Americans, had the largest and newest battleships in the Japanese fleet, the *Yamato* and the *Musashi*. Completed in 1942, these two giants were the world's largest fighting ships. Each had a displacement of 68,000 tons, carried nine 18.1-inch guns, and bristled with a generous array of smaller caliber guns. These ships were more powerful than the largest American Iowa-class battleships. The Center Force also had three older battleships, the *Nagato, Kongo*, and *Haruna*, ten heavy cruisers, two light cruisers, and fifteen destroyers.

The *Kongo, Haruna*, and *Nagato* had main armaments of 14-inch guns and were in the same class as the American battleship *Maryland*. But all three of these Japanese battleships were faster than the *Maryland*. However, the naval treaties that Japan signed prior to World War II had forced Japan to reduce the main armament in all new battleships from 16-inch to 14-inch guns. Therefore, on their new battleships, the guns were smaller than those on the American battleships *Tennessee* and *California*, which had 16-inch guns since they had been built prior to the signing of the naval treaties. But all Kongo-class ships were faster than their American counterparts.

The remaining ships belonged to Force C—part of the Southern Force as designated by the Americans—and were under the command of VAdm. Shoji Nishimura. Force C had two older battleships, the *Fuso* and the *Yamashiro*, which had top speeds of 24 knots and each mounted twelve 14-inch guns; one heavy cruiser, the *Mogami;* and four destroyers. This force would be joined by ships from Vice Admiral Shima's Second Striking Force, following its abortive attempt to attack Halsey's Third Fleet after the Formosa Air Battle, thus forming the Southern Force. It would come up from the south and follow Nishimura's force as he steamed through the Surigao Strait. The Second Striking Force contributed two heavy cruisers, one light cruiser, and seven destroyers. In another display of uncoordinated planning, Shima's command was kept separate from Nishimura's.

The Japanese senior commanders that fought at Leyte Gulf gave every appearance of attracting problems. Vice Admiral Shoji Nishimura was no exception to this pattern.

Nishimura's Japanese naval service revealed a record replete with misfortune. During the Japanese invasion of the Philippines in December 1941, his first assignment was to convoy an invasion force to Luzon. In carrying out his mission, he was the only one who experienced any losses. Although the loss consisted of a minesweeper that succumbed to bad weather, the Imperial Navy took considerable pride in being able to guide ships through rough weather. In a similar vein, when he commanded the Fourth Destroyer Flotilla, he was escorting invasion units for the main Luzon landing that took place in December 1941. However, American submarines torpedoed and sank several transports under his command.

His bad luck continued into 1942. When the Americans were vastly overpowered and outnumbered by the Japanese navy during the invasion of the Philippines in early 1942, he managed to humble a destroyer escort off Balikpapan. In February 1942, when the destroyers under his command failed to challenge American ships, they thereby ensured an American victory in the Makassar Strait. Later in 1942, during the Battle of the Java Sea, he aggressively and prematurely shot his torpedoes, which failed to inflict any damage.

Despite these blunders, he was promoted to the command of a cruiser division that bombarded Henderson Field on Guadalcanal after the American marines landed on that island in August 1942. The ensuing shelling by Nishimura was so ineffective that American planes took off the next day and sank six of his seven transports and a light cruiser. In July 1943, he proceeded down the Solomons' "slot" to attack Vella Lavella. Whereas he discovered no ships, American planes attacked his force, sank a destroyer, and crippled the cruiser *Kumano*. Several Japanese naval officers thought he had a death wish, but his onetime superior, Admiral Ozawa, had a high opinion of him.[19]

Nishimura was a typical seagoing officer who, unlike other Japanese admirals, had risen to the rank of vice admiral without ever having held a staff assignment in the navy ministry. Thus, his experience was not as balanced as it should have been. He was appointed to the command of the Force C only one month prior to the decisive battle at Leyte Gulf. While the assignment was considered to be a second- or third-rate command, he did not complain or grumble. When ordered to join in the Leyte battle, he responded with typical samurai-like enthusiasm. Yet Nishimura's feelings sheltered an inappropriate death wish, for he saw in this assignment an honorable opportunity to die.

Nishimura had lost his beloved only son, Teiji, in the Philippines. A graduate from Etijima, the Japanese equivalent of America's Annapolis, Teiji was at the top of his class. The young man perished when his float plane blew up on takeoff. Although he never revealed his feelings about his son's death, Nishimura probably welcomed an assignment that would give him the opportunity to join his son by dying nobly—forever true to the samurai code.

During the evening before leaving Lingga Roads, Nishimura exchanged toasts and greetings with the commanders of each ship and squadron. Although he betrayed no hint of his feeling of anticipating death on this mission, Admiral Kurita and his chief of staff, RAdm. Tomiji Koyanagi, noticed that Nishimura was animated by a sense of resolve and determination. A few days later, this star-crossed officer met his fate by going down with his ship in the Surigao Strait.[20]

The Japanese strategy was to lure the American fleet into one, final, winner-take-all battle. However, the Japanese fleet had taken significant losses at Midway and the Battle of the Philippine Sea, particularly in the critical areas of aircraft carriers and experienced air crews, the odds for success were much lower than fifty-fifty.

The plan was that the Northern Force would approach the Leyte landing area from the north, its primary goal being to entice Halsey's Third Fleet away from Leyte. If this deception worked, no significant American naval airpower would be on hand to protect the landings. If this part of the plan worked, the Japanese would be able to catch the American landing forces in a pincer movement between the Center Force and the Southern Force.

The northern pincer, the Center Force, would approach the Leyte landing areas from the Palawan Passage through the Sibuyan Sea and the San Bernardino Strait between Luzon and Samar Island and attack Allied naval shipping in Leyte Gulf from the north. The southern pincer, the Southern Force, would enter the Surigao Strait from the Mindanao Sea and attack the Allied naval force from the south. The overall objective was to prevent Allied landings in the Philippines. This, the Japanese hoped, would slow, or perhaps stop, the seemingly relentless American advance on its home islands, thus ending the war. The Japanese military leadership hoped that if the SHO-1 plan succeeded, the Americans would tire of the war and sue for peace.

The once magnificent Japanese fleet had been reduced to a position of inferiority. Nonetheless, the upcoming battle was viewed with real optimism, and Imperial General Headquarters considered it to be the one that would decide the fate of the Japanese empire. In many respects, this assessment turned out to be a valid one.[21]

Japanese Fleet Movements

On October 18 at 1:00 A.M., Kurita's Center Force left Lingga Roads. The ships had so little fuel to spare that the escorting destroyers did not sweep for American submarines outside the harbor's mouth. Only the float planes on the ships could be spared to patrol for enemy submarines. While at sea later that afternoon, a message arrived from Imperial Fleet headquarters in Tokyo ordering Kurita to execute the SHO-1 battle plan. Thus, Japanese naval forces were now steaming toward the Philippines before the first American soldier had set foot on the Leyte beaches.[22]

When the fleet sailed from Lingga Roads, a line of proud ships sailed to their destiny. Almost every Japanese capital ship was in this procession. It included the giant battleships *Yamato* and *Musashi,* followed by the powerfully armed, 39,000-ton battleship *Nagato.* The fast 32,000-ton former battle cruisers *Kongo* and *Haruna,* remodeled into battleships with their now well-recognized pagoda-shaped masts, majestically followed their larger, faster partners. The older 35,000-ton battleships *Fuso* and *Yamashiro* followed in line. Accompanying these battleships were eleven fast heavy cruisers, each carrying 8-inch guns, and led by Kurita's flagship, the *Atago.* Two modern 6-inch-gunned light cruisers led nineteen destroyers, each having four 5-inch guns, eight 24-inch "long lance" torpedo tubes, and up to twenty-eight 25mm antiaircraft guns. Any lay observer could not help but be impressed by such a monumental sight.[23]

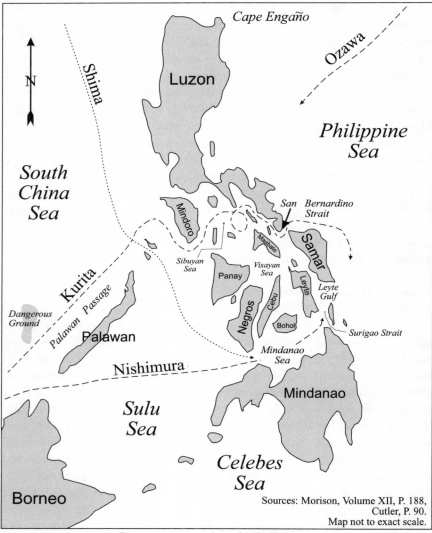

Japanese approach to the Philippines

Kurita planned to reach Brunei on October 20. At midnight on the 19th, his fleet was 165 miles west-northwest of Brunei, at which point it changed course to enter its harbor. At this location, the Americans first discovered Kurita's fleet. The Seventh Fleet's intelligence officer, Capt. Arthur H. McCollum, was troubled over the Japanese surface fleet's movements from Singapore. Knowing that the Japanese fleet was anchored in Lingga Roads, and that it was experiencing critical fuel shortages, he guessed correctly that these ships would need to refuel at Brunei before proceeding to Philippine waters. The Borneo harbor was the only logical choice for the refueling. Located on Borneo's northern shore, Brunei's large harbor had a water depth sufficient to protect a large fleet of big capital ships. More important, it was close to the Miri oil fields.

On the morning of October 20, McCollum's appraisal proved to be correct. Patrolling off the northern New Guinea coast, an American search plane observed a large fleet of Japanese ships, noting that it had at least one battleship, three light cruisers, three destroyers, and six other warships. The plane's pilot radioed a report to Pearl Harbor.

However, the naval communications center in Honolulu essentially ignored the sighting since they knew Kurita had many more ships than those seen by the plane's crew. McCollum was skeptical, too, about the sighting, and after the war, he told an interviewer that planes in that area had never reported ships before. Nonetheless, the search plane's crew was right: a large Japanese naval force had passed under their noses.

Although the Americans doubted that Japanese ships were near the New Guinea coast, the Japanese knew the Americans had seen them. Japanese radio operators aboard the *Yamato* picked up strong American radio transmissions from the aircraft overhead and knew these constituted a sighting report. One Japanese destroyer squadron heard several sighting messages from noon until late in that day. Japanese radio intercepting stations also heard the messages repeated at American radio relay stations in the Admiralty Islands and at Honolulu. From that time forward, the Japanese assumed the Americans knew what they were doing. In reality, however, the Americans found out about Kurita only from ULTRA and not from these perfectly valid sighting reports.[24]

On October 20, 1944, Vice Admiral Kurita surveyed his fleet lying at anchor in Brunei's harbor in Borneo. After completing rigorous fleet training exercises in the heat and humidity of Southeast Asia, they had steamed from Lingga Roads near Singapore to take part in the execution of the Japanese SHO-GO plan.

Born in 1899, Takeo Kurita was an aloof man thoroughly schooled in traditional Japanese naval officer values. He had successfully entered the Japanese Naval Academy at Etijima after passing a demanding oral interview, enduring a difficult series of academic and physical tests, and passing a thorough character check of himself and his entire family. At Etijima, located on the Inland Sea, he adopted its rules of conduct: loyalty, discipline, and absolute conformity. Despite intensive military training at Etijima, graduates were imbued with several weaknesses, including (1) a need for precise orders before executing them, (2) an inability to adapt to unexpected events during battle, (3) a weakness for not envisioning the entire strategic picture but rather focusing on the immediate situation, and (4) an extreme aversion to taking risks during the heat of battle.

His training at Etijima stressed the attainment of victory through a single, decisive battle with the enemy. No better example of the narrow fanaticism he learned at Etijima can be found than in the intramural sports promoted at the academy. In these activities, cadets who were able to win with a single, powerful blow or movement were rewarded. In the martial-arts contest of kendo, for example, victory was awarded to the man who succeeded in knocking down his opponent with a single blow from a four-foot bamboo club. In the sport called otaoshi, the object is to capture the other team's flagpole using every means possible.

Japanese naval strategy employed highly intricate maneuvers that relied on deception, diversion, and division of the enemy's forces for the purpose of opening a path to deliver one decisively powerful and victorious blow. The plan for the Battle of Midway is an excellent example of such a strategy. In this battle, the Japanese tried to lure the American carriers into a position that would enable the Japanese fleet to destroy the entire American fleet in a single battle. No consideration was ever given to the strategy of wearing down an opponent using a series of confrontations that would, in the end, dissipate its resources. The Imperial Japanese Navy did not deviate from this single-minded strategy throughout the entire war.

After graduation from Etijima, Kurita served on both destroyers and cruisers, and after achieving flag rank in 1938, he eventually commanded a force protecting invasion transports in the Dutch East Indies in the early days of World War II. When he was fifty-five years old, he led the bombardment group assigned to protect the Japanese invasion forces at Midway. On October 14, 1942, that force bombarded the American marines on Guadalcanal. Later, Kurita received a promotion and was awarded a command with the Second Fleet at the Battle of the Philippine Sea.

During his naval service, Kurita adopted the predictable Japanese weakness for ultraconservative tactics combined with a disturbing tendency to perpetually doubt the potential success of any mission. Trepidation, uncertainty, and vacillation clung to his command style. This helps explain why his Seventh Cruiser Division suffered heavy damage at Midway, where several of his ships collided with one another. During the campaign at Guadalcanal, he had retreated in the face of four charging American torpedo boats. In succeeding Adm. Nobutake Kondo, who had been in charge of the landing forces at Midway, Kurita commanded a support force of two fast battleships and six destroyers that had seen action at the Battle of Santa Cruz. But this proved to be yet another Japanese defeat. Then, when at Rabaul, he assumed command of the Japanese Fifth Fleet, which had seven of the Imperial Fleet's fastest and most modern heavy cruisers, but these ships sustained heavy damage due to incessant American and Australian air raids that ultimately led to Rabaul's total isolation as a viable naval and air base in the South Pacific.

At the Battle of the Philippine Sea, he was one of the first senior Japanese naval officers to advocate retreat. His combat record could not claim a single victory. A highly tentative officer, Kurita was often overwhelmed with vacillation. It should come as no surprise, therefore, that even as he and his staff were briefed by Tokyo officers who had come especially to see them at Brunei, he doubted his chances of success in executing the SHO-1 plan at Leyte Gulf. Complicating his situation was the fact that his force was ordered to attack enemy transports without the benefit of substantive air cover. So, even before he left Brunei, he was mentally prepared to retreat when confronted by daring attacks, though he did not underestimate the importance of defending the Philippines from an American invasion.[25]

After suffering the disastrous defeat at the Formosa Air Battle, Vice Admiral Ozawa had only 137 aircraft left to allocate among the remaining aircraft carriers. Ozawa's forces, for their part, were skeletal and unusable for effective combat operations. Faced with terrible losses such as these, the Japanese needed to adopt a change of plans. Any hope of victory depended on the surface forces in the south.

Because of his seniority and combat experience, Ozawa easily could have been awarded the overall command of the entire SHO-1 operation. However, since the carriers had been rendered impotent with only a few aircraft aboard, after most of their aircraft had been moved to land bases, Ozawa relinquished tactical command to Kurita, since Kurita's fleet was the primary attacking force.

We can only speculate as to what would have happened if there hadn't been a change in commanders. Would Ozawa have acted any differently than Kurita did at Leyte Gulf?

Like Kurita, Ozawa had accumulated a good service record since the war began. A dignified, physically impressive man, Ozawa was taller than the average Japanese man. His record revealed a balance between sea duty and several important staff assignments. He had been chief of staff to the commander of the Combined Fleet. Just before the war began, he commanded both battleship and carrier divisions. Experience such as this would have been invaluable in the coming battle at Leyte. Furthermore, Ozawa's performance as commander of Japanese forces at the Battle of the Philippine Sea merited high marks. Even though the Japanese had been thoroughly defeated by a vastly superior American force, he conducted himself well. His performance compares favorably with that of his opponent, Raymond Spruance, who had displayed extraordinary capabilities at that battle, just as he had at Midway.

Kurita and Ozawa had few similarities and many differences. Ozawa's presence was tall and commanding; Kurita was shorter with a quiet, weathered, and stern countenance. Ozawa's manner was more relaxed. When Kurita had a rare shore assignment, he both taught and was a student of tactics at the Naval Torpedo School. When Japan went to war with the United States, Kurita spent most of his assignments at sea, gaining experience in destroyers, cruisers, battleships, and torpedo warfare. While Ozawa specialized in naval aviation and commanded carriers and their associated task groups, Kurita's commands included a cruiser division, followed by a battleship division, and, finally, the First Striking Force. He also had direct combat experience in the bloody Solomons' campaign.

Despite the importance of aircraft carriers and aviation in deciding the outcomes of the Pacific war's major naval battles, Kurita lacked experience in these fields. Nonetheless, it was his destiny to carry the fate of the Japanese empire in his hands. Ozawa's thankless task was to use his carrier group as a sacrificial lamb to be slaughtered by the Americans. Still, with plentiful luck and clever planning, a real chance of success existed for the Japanese.

Kurita's actions would become the subject of much heated debate for decades, as naval historians sought to decipher not what happened at Leyte Gulf but rather *why* it happened. In the end, Ozawa's conduct at Leyte Gulf received positive reviews because he had fulfilled the strategic task assigned to him.[26]

If one compares the records of the two men before Leyte Gulf, Ozawa's was the more promising. Yet both men had been inculcated with Japanese naval battle methods, meaning that they had never been trained to adapt battle tactics to rapidly changing conditions. The Americans, on the other hand, had been schooled in adaptive tactical battle behavior. The most likely outcome, therefore, is that even if Ozawa had been in charge of the Center Force, the result would have remained the same.

Nestled in Brunei's large harbor, many Japanese ships filled their fuel tanks. The lush, green Borneo mountains, some more than 12,000 feet high, encircled the bay, protecting Kurita's force from visual, radio, and radar detection. The only American sighting of his fleet had been ignored, and no Allied submarines or aircraft were nearby to detect the presence of his ships. As of the early evening of October 21, 1944, the Americans had no firm intelligence as to where the Japanese fleet was or its intentions.

Had any reconnaissance flight crew overflown the harbor on that day, they would have seen the mighty *Musashi* and *Yamato*, along with five other battleships, five cruisers, and nineteen destroyers dotting the water. They also would have seen several small craft assembled near Kurita's flagship, the cruiser *Atago*. Other boats brought Kurita's subordinate commanders to the cruiser for a presail briefing.

Vice Admiral Matome Ugaki, commander of Kurita's battleship forces, and the other officers aboard the *Atago*, listened attentively. The SHO-1 plan ordered Kurita's fleet to stop the American Philippine invasion by attacking their troop transports. Several officers in the room privately objected to this attack on "lowly," unarmed transports instead of on the American fleet's power center. Some officers still hoped to pursue a "decisive engagement." Others strongly felt this was the Imperial Japanese Navy's last chance to die an honorable death for the glory of the empire. One such patriot was RAdm. Tasuku Nakazawa. He believed attacking troop transports was no way for the Imperial Fleet to "bloom as flowers of death."[27] Some officers put the matter less poetically: "We do not mind death, but we are very concerned for the honor of the Japanese Navy. If the final effort of our great Navy should be spent in engaging a group of empty cargo ships, surely Admirals Togo and Yamamoto would weep in their graves."[28]

Kurita, consistent in his attitude of vacillation, skepticism, and tentativeness, and his chief of staff, RAdm. Koyanagi, also did not agree with the SHO-1 plan. When Kurita conducted training exercises off Lingga Roads, Koyanagi met with representatives of the Combined Fleet staff in Manila, and while he did not try openly to convince the Tokyo planners of the need for a complete change in the plan, he asked, "According to this order, the primary targets of First Striking Force are enemy transports, but if by chance carriers come within range of our force, may we, in cooperation with shore-based air, engage the carriers and then return to annihilate the transports?"

Koyanagi's cautious approach brought success. Combined Fleet headquarters in Tokyo did indeed modify the SHO-1 plan so Kurita could go after the American carriers should they appear. Although Kurita still had doubts that the SHO-1 plan could succeed, he nonetheless hoped he would have the opportunity to attack the American carriers instead of the troop transports. Consequently, his staff began the hard work of preparing for the coming battle. He and his staff met frequently, studied nautical and topographical charts, all the while examining tactical doctrines. They also focused their efforts on the three possible sites for the American landings: Lamon Bay in the north, Davao Gulf in the south, and Leyte Gulf in the center.

On October 20, however, their decision was made for them when news arrived that the Americans had sailed into Leyte Gulf and landed on Leyte's beaches. Kurita and his staff's plan was in readiness. Kurita would split the fleet into two forces that, in turn, would form a pincer attack from the north and south of Leyte Gulf, catching the American landing ships in the middle.

The Center Force, which included Ugaki's Battleship Division One, would move from Brunei to the north through the Philippine archipelago by way of the Sibuyan Sea. After passing through this narrow inland waterway, his force would pass through the San Bernardino Strait, head southward along the island of Samar's eastern coast, and attack the American landing forces at Leyte Gulf from the north.

Force C would leave Brunei after Kurita's force had sailed. While its journey was shorter, it faced many more hazards. The route would pass through the Sulu and Mindanao Seas. The Japanese knew American submarines patrolled this passage and that American airplanes could attack from bases in Hollandia. If Nishimura remained on schedule, Force C would pass through the Surigao Strait, enter Leyte Gulf from the south, and attack the American transports at about the same time that Kurita's force attacked from the north.

Any commander assumes a higher risk by dividing his forces. Each of the elements created are of necessity weaker than the whole. Furthermore, the operation becomes more complex, because it is harder to coordinate each of the divided forces over greater distances. However, if conditions are right, some advantages accrue that counterbalance these problems. A pincer offensive attacks an enemy force simultaneously from two directions, which compels the enemy to divide his forces. If both of the pincer forces do not attack precisely at the same time, the enemy would then react to the first force. But when the second force arrives, the enemy must respond by splitting his forces again. This splitting makes him more vulnerable to the first attacking force.

The array of American forces in Leyte Gulf were indeed vulnerable to a pincer maneuver. One Japanese force could draw away the defending American warships, and this would leave the highly vulnerable, lightly armed American amphibious forces undefended. The second Japanese force could then attack and destroy the defenseless Americans without interference.

The risks for the Americans were great. An amphibious landing increases the risk of an opposing naval attack, because it is a static operation. While in the process of landing its troops on the shore, it cannot respond to a naval attack, because it must cover the landings with a naval bombardment of enemy shore installations and defenses. One naval historian and analyst has described an amphibious operation like having "one leg ashore, one leg afloat."[29] A navy guarding a beachhead is in a defensive posture and cannot be as mobile as when pursuing an offensive operation.

This was a refreshing change for the Japanese, for now they could go on the offensive. They had been in a defensive mode for so long while enduring the devastating attacks of Halsey's highly mobile Third Fleet that they could now cling to a slim hope of grabbing the tactical advantage for a change.

Nonetheless, the Japanese faced an inescapable fact: the Americans outnumbered and outgunned them. Although they did not have perfect intelligence reports, they knew what awaited them at Leyte. The American invasion force (Kinkaid's Seventh Fleet) had more than 700 ships, including a mighty force of warships and several battleships. If this was the only force the Japanese had to contend with, their pincer attack plan had an excellent chance of success.

But Halsey's Third Fleet introduced a formidable player into the mix.

It had just completed a series of successful operations, attacking and destroying large numbers of Japanese land-based aircraft. The Japanese knew Halsey's personality only too well. His arrival in the Southwest Pacific had helped turn the tide in the Solomons. The losses Halsey inflicted on Japanese aircraft wrecked their chances of providing effective support to the SHO-1 operation.

The Third Fleet consisted of aircraft carriers, battleships, cruisers, and countless destroyers. Should the Japanese meet Halsey, they knew they would lose their fleet, for his fleet, combined with Kinkaid's Seventh Fleet, would overwhelm them, sending every Japanese warship to the bottom. In such an eventuality, it would not matter what the Japanese plan was or what maneuvers they executed. Facing both American fleets simultaneously could have but one outcome: the total destruction of the Imperial Fleet.

Facing such insurmountable odds, how could the Japanese plan succeed? Warfare throughout the ages has offered an answer to this thorny question—through deception. Military history is filled with stories in which an inferior force has defeated an overwhelmingly superior force by deceiving its enemy. A successful deception by the Japanese could indeed overcome the numerical advantages of the Americans, and the Japanese plan was sound. The Japanese knew that their losses of trained and experienced naval pilots had, in effect, rendered their carriers useless. However, the Japanese had good intelligence, which informed them that the Americans were not privy to this fact. Thus, the Americans could very well believe that the remaining Japanese carriers posed a serious threat.

Ozawa's carriers therefore would approach the Philippines from the north, making every effort to be discovered by the Americans. They would fill the airwaves with fake radio message traffic so American listening posts would be able to fix the carriers' positions. If luck was on the Japanese side, the American carrier forces would withdraw from the Leyte Gulf area, leaving Kurita's Center Force with a wide-open path to the defenseless American transports off the Leyte beaches. The plan's success relied upon how many American carrier planes could be lured away from Leyte Gulf.

The SHO-1 operation's odds for success were slim, but if everything went Japan's way, the Japanese fleet could inflict a devastating defeat on the American navy. They knew by now that they could not win the war, but if the Americans could be turned back at Leyte Gulf, then the upcoming American presidential elections might take a surprising turn. At best, Roosevelt could be defeated at the polls. At worst, the Japanese victory at Leyte Gulf could force a change in American policy. The Americans could then be persuaded to come to the negotiation table rather than continue the war. Clearly, for the Japanese, this was an alternative highly preferable to unconditional surrender.

The briefing aboard the *Atago* drew to a close. Kurita rose to his feet and spoke to his subordinates, delivering a pragmatic, fatalistic message, one inspired by the long history of the samurai warrior. Vice Admiral Ugaki, standing a few feet away, shared Kurita's sentiments. Kurita's words hid any apprehensions he may have felt about the coming operation:

> I know that many of you are strongly opposed to this assignment. But the war situation is far more critical than any of you can possibly know. Would it not be a shame to have the fleet remain intact while our nation perishes? I believe that Imperial General Headquarters is giving us a glorious opportunity. Because I realize how very serious the war situation actually is, I am willing to accept even this ultimate assignment to storm into Leyte Gulf.
>
> You must all remember that there are such things as miracles. What man can say that there is no chance for our fleet to turn the tide of war in a decisive battle? We shall have a chance to meet our enemies. We shall engage his task forces. I hope that you will not carry your responsibilities lightly. I know that you will act faithfully and well.[30]

The men in the room sat silently for a few seconds. As emotion welled up inside them, knowing the nearly impossible task they faced, they leaped to their feet and shouted in unison, *"Banzai! Banzai! Banzai!"* Exiting the room, they climbed into their boats and returned to their ships. Soon they would depart from Brunei and try, once more, to save the Japanese empire.[31]

Kurita had done all he could to prepare his command for the battle that was to come, but doubts remained deep within him. As his fleet topped its fuel tanks and strengthened its resolve to get under way, he mulled over the problems facing him. He did not know the kind of air defense he could expect from the land-based air forces. He knew a strong American surface fleet would face him, even if Ozawa succeeded in luring the Third Fleet northward. He might very well lose half his force. But he could not dwell on such misgivings now.

Kurita reviewed three possible routes to Leyte Gulf. The first was the southern route that passed from Borneo and came near Morotai. It would bring him within range of American land-based air forces and potentially subject his fleet to air attacks. The second route was to proceed north of Luzon Island, around the Philippines, and continue southward toward Leyte. This course was the longest one, so Kurita rejected it. By October 1944, Japanese merchant navy losses had been so catastrophic that the Imperial Fleet was experiencing severe oil shortages. Fuel availability now dominated all other considerations in Japanese naval operations. The third route was through the Palawan Passage and was the only viable alternative left. Although it was a more dangerous route, because American submarines operated in that area, when stacked against the other alternatives, it offered the lowest risk and the greatest opportunity.

So, Kurita issued orders for his ships to proceed through the narrow body of water between Palawan Island and an area known as Dangerous Ground. Appropriately named, Dangerous Ground contained many reefs and shallows that extended well into the South China Sea. Many ships had been lost over the centuries in this treacherous body of water.

Kurita's assumptions about American subs operating in Palawan Passage were correct. Submarines from the American Seventh Fleet had received full alert orders on October 20 to look out for Japanese ships.[32]

On October 22 at 8:00 A.M., Kurita's fleet left Brunei as thick clouds hung over the bay. Whitecaps dotted the water as a stiff breeze blew. Although these were the last remnants of the Imperial Fleet, they could evoke admiration in anyone able to see such great ships moving majestically out of Brunei Bay. Caught up in the drama of the moment, some of Kurita's officers were inspired to be optimistic about the upcoming struggle.

Leading the way like elegant and stately dowagers at a fancy dress ball were the *Yamato*, *Musashi*, and *Nagato*. They were followed by the older battleships *Kongo* and *Haruna*. The heavy cruisers stirred the water—the *Atago*, *Takao*, *Maya*, *Chokai*, *Myoko*, *Haguro*, *Kumano*, *Suzuya*, *Tone*, and *Chikuma*. The light cruisers *Yahagi* and *Noshiro* fell behind, and fifteen destroyers brought up the rear.

But foul weather was afoot and increased the difficulty of searching out submarines. However, the big ships were equipped with radar and sound gear capable of ferreting out these underwater denizens. The fleet swept through the bay's broad mouth at an easy 18 knots. To reduce harm from potential submarine attacks, the fleet began independent zigzagging maneuvers after reaching the open sea.[33]

As the impressive fleet slid out of Brunei Bay, Kurita transmitted a message to his commanders: "Penetrating through San Bernardino Strait at sunset on 24 October, I will destroy the enemy surface forces in a night battle east of Samar and then proceed to the Tacloban area at daybreak on 25 October to destroy the enemy transport and convoy and landing forces."

Seven hours after the main sections of the fleet departed from Brunei, Nishimura's smaller Force C also pulled out of Brunei Bay. The two groups planned to enter Leyte Gulf together and attack the American landing transports. If this did not prove feasible, each would attack their prey alone.[34]

Ozawa assembled his force from ships and aircraft located in and around the home islands. Japan had a rich store of carriers, including new 17,000-ton light ones. Unfortunately for Japan, however, she had almost no carrier-based aircraft and few trained air crews. Therefore, Ozawa was able to scrape together only 137 aircraft. The only fleet carrier in the force, the *Zuikaku,* had twenty-four fighters, sixteen fighter-bombers, seven dive-bombers, and a dozen torpedo-bombers. The light carriers *Zuiho, Chiyoda,* and *Chitose* would convey about forty fighters and fighter-bombers, seventeen attack aircraft, and seventeen torpedo-bombers. Ozawa also had two old 35,000-ton battleships, the *Ise* and *Hyuga,* which had been converted into hybrid battleship-carriers by replacing their two aftermost 14-inch gun turrets with a flight deck and hangar for seaplanes. There were now no aircraft available for these ships, so they were crammed with more than a hundred light antiaircraft guns and six antiaircraft rocket launchers to defend the carriers against American air attacks.[35]

For good reason, Ozawa was not comfortable with his new command. After the Japanese fleet had been resoundingly defeated at the Battle of the Philippine Sea, his chief of staff, RAdm. Keizo Komura, was to claim, in postwar interviews, that Ozawa and he knew then that the Imperial Fleet was no longer a viable fighting force. While one can argue that this assertion did not apply to the entire fleet, it is certainly the case that the small naval air force on Ozawa's carriers was too insignificant to mount either an offense or a defense.

As the doomed force's ships gathered in the Inland Sea on October 19, Ozawa realized painfully how far the once-dominant Imperial Fleet had fallen. The *Zuikaku* was the only large carrier left to send into battle. It was the last surviving fleet carrier from the great Pearl Harbor victory. When the Japanese were giddy with victory after victory in late 1941 and early 1942, Japan's carrier force was the world's largest and most powerful. But the crushing defeats inflicted at Midway, Santa Cruz, and the Philippine Sea had reduced the once mighty Japanese carrier force to the *Zuikaku* and the light carriers *Chitose, Chiyoda,* and *Zuiho.* The *Zuiho,* which had been considered too small to send into battle, had been used for training naval air crews, escorting convoys, ferrying aircraft, and providing combat air patrol. Now, however, she was pressed into service for this most inauspicious of missions.

Just two years earlier, Japanese naval aircraft had filled the skies, terrorizing the entire Pacific region. Now the Japanese had been reduced to mustering a pitiful 137 aircraft. Two float planes from the light cruiser *Oyodo* were to serve as scouts. For Ozawa, it must have been stinging to realize that he had at his disposal such a beggarly collection of aircraft for the upcoming battle.

As the Northern Force departed empire waters, Ozawa knew his pitiful collection of 137 planes could not inflict appreciable damage or provide air cover for anyone. All Japanese surface vessels entering the Battle of Leyte Gulf were, in effect, like warriors without shields.[36]

On October 21, Vice Admiral Shima received orders to "support and cooperate" with Nishimura's Force C. Instead of providing precise plans and orders, Shima's instructions gave him total discretion. Orders such as these must have produced confusion and consternation in his mind, and he must have sensed that they were a reflection of the total lack of communication and coordination that characterized Japanese naval planning in the latter stages of the war.

Left to his own devices, Shima actually made no attempt to rendezvous with Nishimura. Their forces, in fact, would meet only when Shima's cruiser *Nachi* collided with Nishimura's cruiser *Mogami* during the Battle of Surigao Strait. It is evident that the Japanese naval high command had never thought of Shima's mission as more than an exercise in futility. Their wish inevitably was fulfilled.[37]

• • •

Meanwhile, Kurita's Center Force headed for the open sea in a northeasterly direction through the Palawan Passage and soon was beyond the range of American land-based patrol aircraft. His lookouts reported several periscope sightings, which made Kurita increasingly nervous. The American submarines tracked Kurita's Center Force and soon would form part of the opening gambit in the upcoming giant naval battle.

The American and Japanese navies were on the move toward Leyte Gulf. Many surprises awaited them. The Americans had committed a huge force to recapture the Philippine Islands, returning freedom to the oppressed Filipinos and cutting Japanese supply lines. Tying together their force in order to cover the greatest landing of the Pacific theater, with supply lines stretching over 1,000 miles, was an enterprise fraught with disastrous possibilities. The Japanese's situation was so desperate, on the other hand, that they were willing to sacrifice every ship they had. The Japanese empire had not faced a situation this dire since Kublai Khan had tried to invade their homeland in the thirteenth century. A divine wind had saved them then. Perhaps a stroke of luck would save them yet again.

Chapter 3: A Promise Kept

Before the invasion of Leyte Island could get under way, the waterways leading into Leyte Gulf and the beaches had to be swept clean of mines and other obstacles. All Japanese troops and artillery had to be cleared off the islands of Dinagat, Homonhon, and Suluan before the invasion fleet could enter the gulf and land troops on the Leyte beaches. The battleship *Pennsylvania* and the cruisers *Denver*, *Columbia*, and *Minneapolis* were slated to shell the beaches with heavy caliber fire. Many smaller ships traversed the entrance to Leyte Gulf to assist in the minesweeping effort.

The force used for these varied assignments, under the overall command of RAdm. Jesse B. Oldendorf, was divided into three groups. The first, called the Minesweeping and Hydrographic Group, was led by Cmdr. Wayne R. Loud and consisted of forty small ships of various sizes. It left Manus Island on October 10 and was due to arrive on October 17 at the rendezvous site, Point Fin, outside Leyte Gulf about 17 miles east of Dinagat's northern tip. Its mission was to sweep all mines from Leyte Gulf's entrances and destroy underwater obstacles that could interfere with the landings on the Leyte beaches.

The second group, called the Dinagat Attack Group, consisted of ten ships (two destroyers, five destroyer-transports, two frigates, and a fleet tug) and was commanded by RAdm. Arthur D. Struble. It left Hollandia on October 12 and was estimated to arrive at Point Fin on October 17. This group had the responsibility of bombarding and invading Dinagat, Suluan, Homonhon, and Calicoan Islands and destroying all radar in-

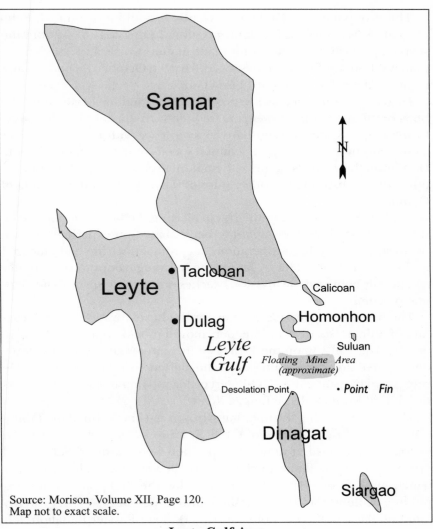

Leyte Gulf Area

On the map:
Samar

Leyte

• Tacloban

Calicoan

• Dulag

Homonhon

Leyte Gulf

Suluan

Floating   Mine   Area
(approximate)

Desolation Point

• *Point   Fin*

Dinagat

Siargao

N

Source: Morison, Volume XII, Page 120.
Map not to exact scale.

stallations there that had been reported by air reconnaissance. These radar stations had to be taken out, because they could give an early warning to Japanese defenses of the approaching Seventh Fleet. Struble also commanded the army's 500-man Sixth Ranger Infantry Battalion lodged on eight destroyer-transports ready to storm the islands' beaches.

This group met Loud's ships on October 15 and took on fuel. Refueling at sea is always a difficult proposition. In this case, a 30-knot wind stirred up a heavy sea, which only made matters worse, and it took more than two hours to fill their tanks. By 5:00 P.M. on October 15, both groups resumed their journey toward Leyte Gulf.

Heavy seas continued as the two groups headed for Leyte Gulf. The bows of the smaller minesweepers frequently disappeared under large, frothy waves as they worked hard to keep pace with the larger, faster ships. Only by maintaining a maximum speed could they stay on station. Despite all their efforts, some of them nonetheless straggled behind the other vessels, meeting the other ships off Leyte Gulf on the evening of October 16.

While this operation ran the risk of alerting the Japanese that the invasion of Leyte Island was about to begin, based on experience drawn from earlier amphibious operations, a cardinal doctrine had emerged in the Pacific. It was safer by far for the invading troops to reconnoiter and heavily bombard the invasion beaches rather than worry about alerting the enemy.

The first step in clearing the way for the Leyte invasion was the capture of Suluan Island. Minesweepers moved in and approached the little island at 6:30 A.M. on the 17th. Twenty minutes later, Japanese lookouts spotted the approaching ships and alerted Toyoda on Formosa. He responded by issuing the SHO-1 alert order and immediately sent orders to Admiral Kurita to leave Lingga Roads.

The honor of firing the opening salvos in the liberation of the Philippines was given to the crew of the light cruiser *Denver*. At 8:00 A.M. on October 17, the cruiser moved to a position 6,500 yards off Suluan and opened fire. Yellow flame and brownish-yellow smoke belched from her 6-inch guns as powerful shells headed for the Philippine shore, exploding violently as they smashed into their targets. After twenty minutes elapsed, the men of Company D, Sixth Ranger Battalion, left their destroyer-transports and stepped on Philippine soil, keeping MacArthur's promise to return. Once ashore, the well-trained soldiers wasted no time in relishing the honor bestowed on them. They headed for the lighthouse, in which the light had already been smashed by one of the *Denver*'s shells, looking for Japanese troops. They destroyed the thirty-two-man Japanese garrison on the island and received a royal welcome from the natives. There were only three American casualties.

Dinagat was the next island to be invaded. The Rangers on Suluan were picked up by their transports and taken to a place off the northern tip of Dinagat, called Desolation Point. They had a rough trip, because the wind blew hard, whipping up the seas. Admiral Struble had selected a beach about 450 yards wide on Dinagat's western coast just south of Desolation Point. When the soldiers landed on an empty beach, the Ranger's unit commander reported that the Japanese apparently had abandoned the island. The soldiers found valuable Japanese hydrographic charts, which proved indispensable for the later Okinawa invasion.

Meanwhile, the third group in Oldendorf's force moved into action. The heavily armed Bombardment and Fire Support Group, consisting of twenty-six ships and under Oldendorf's direct command, and RAdm. Thomas Sprague's escort carriers cruised slowly outside Leyte Gulf. The wind had freshened and the seas had become rougher, matching the prediction of Sprague's weather experts of rougher weather over the next two days. Accordingly, Sprague urged that A-day be postponed. But Oldendorf's weather people had a more optimistic forecast. Sure enough, by mid-watch on October 18, the winds had died down and the seas had moderated, but not enough for the smaller minesweepers. These smaller ships still had a tough time clearing the waters around Homonhon Island, yet in the end they successfully completed this important mission with their usual efficiency, thus allowing the Rangers to land. This time, too, the Americans found no Japanese and no artillery on Homonhon.

A large Japanese minefield lay between Dinagat and Homonhon, a threat that had to be removed before the Seventh Fleet could enter Leyte Gulf. The strong winds and high seas increased the minesweeping ships' difficulties as they tried to sweep the mines, even though most of the mines lay on the surface. An inaccurate message arrived on Oldendorf's flagship, the cruiser *Louisville,* saying that the minefield had been cleared, but on October 18, at 6:57 A.M., Commander Loud reported that only one-fifth of the minefield had been swept. Twenty-six mines had been recovered, but a line of them remained floating on the surface, still blocking the path into Leyte Gulf between Dinagat and Homonhon.

A normally cautious commander would have stopped the larger capital ships from entering Leyte Gulf because of the still-active minefield.

However, Oldendorf felt further delay could force a one day's slippage for A-day. Using his prerogative as senior commander in the immediate area, he ordered the battleship *Pennsylvania,* the cruisers *Minneapolis, Louisville,* and *Denver,* and supporting destroyers into Leyte Gulf. Homonhon Island was close to starboard as several minesweepers led the way. Despite the threat posed by the presence of undisclosed mines, the ships were in position by 2:00 P.M. off Dulag, a town on Leyte Island.

The American heavy naval guns then opened fire and continued their bombardment for over an hour. The Japanese guns remained silent. Underwater demolition teams (UDTs) moved off the destroyer-transports into the landing craft, and, unlike the invasions carried out on the smaller islands at Leyte Gulf's entrance, the Americans discovered that these landings were going to be violently opposed. As the UDT sailors left their landing craft, the Japanese defenders opened up with 75mm artillery, machine guns and mortars.

The destroyer-transport *Goldsborough* moved within one mile of the beach and opened fire with her 4-inch guns. Dense jungle vegetation completely concealed the Japanese gun emplacements. The Americans had no idea what, if anything, they were hitting. Apparently, the American counterfire was unsuccessful, as a 75mm shell hit the *Goldsborough's* forward smokestack, killing two sailors. The ship sustained relatively minor damage, while one landing craft took a hit and sank.

At 3:50 P.M., the UDTs returned to their ships, reporting no further obstacles. The Leyte beaches were now ready for the upcoming landings. Oldendorf, however, had not completed his task of demolishing any possible Japanese positions on the beaches. Since a risk of mine damage no longer existed, Oldendorf ordered the remaining ships in his bombardment group into Leyte Gulf.

The next day, October 19, Oldendorf's Bombardment Group relentlessly pounded the Leyte beaches. However, the Americans suffered another naval loss at Leyte Gulf. As darkness fell on October 19, the destroyer *Ross,* occupied with covering the minesweepers about 8 miles off Homonhon Island, struck a floating mine and lost all power. To prevent capsizing, her crew threw all loose weight from her topside decks into the water. But then she hit a second mine and listed at a 14-degree angle, placing the hapless ship in deep trouble.

Displaying the outstanding seamanship the Americans had repeatedly shown throughout the war, the crew kept the destroyer afloat. As dawn came up over the gulf on October 20, the tug *Chickasaw* came alongside and towed the crippled *Ross* to safety into an anchorage. Heavily damaged, this destroyer was out of the fight. Twenty-three men lost their lives or were missing, and nine had sustained wounds as a result of their ship hitting those two mines. The *Ross* would be the only destroyer in World War II to strike two mines and survive to fight again.[1]

The removal of the *Ross* proved to be what Patrick Keane, a seaman serving aboard the destroyer *Halford*, discovered was a stroke of good fortune. The *Halford* was part of Admiral Sprague's escort carrier group, Taffy 3. When the *Ross* left the Gulf, the *Halford* received orders to take the damaged destroyer's place in Oldendorf's Bombardment and Fire Support Group. This meant that she would not be among Sprague's Taffy 3 group of destroyers to face Kurita's powerful force off Samar on the 25th. If the *Halford* had been with Taffy 3, she likely would have suffered the same fate as her companion ships, the destroyers *Johnston* and *Hoel* and the destroyer escort *Samuel B. Roberts*. One could say with absolute certainty that the *Halford*'s crew were very, very lucky sailors.

While the *Chickasaw* towed the *Ross* to safety, Oldendorf split his force into southern and northern groups. The southern group remained off Dulag and resumed their bombardment of that town at 8:35 A.M., and the northern group moved into position off Tacloban. Twenty-five minutes later, their guns opened fire with sound and fury. The UDTs found the Tacloban beaches to be good places to land troops, with no obstacles to block their way.

As the American shells slammed into the Japanese positions, the entrenched Japanese did not hesitate to fight back. Three shells struck the destroyer *Aulick*, and her power train failed. Quickly, her crew restored power, and she continued shelling the beaches while suffering only minor damage.

The dense undergrowth on the Leyte beaches made the problem of assessing damage difficult and made aerial reconnaissance troublesome. There was no way to see whether the shells hurled on the beaches were destroying any Japanese installations, weapons, or personnel. For this reason, the ships did not have specific targets assigned to them. Instead, each ship had an area of responsibility. When it had shelled its area sufficiently, spotters were then used either to find new targets or to wipe camouflage away from existing ones. Admiral Oldendorf observed: "Some ships took the scarcity of targets to indicate a license to spray their assigned areas with shells."[2] As a consequence, the bombardment ships wasted too much ammunition and destroyed much Philippine private property. This ammunition misuse would later play an important part in the Battle of Surigao Strait.[3]

As Oldendorf visualized the geography surrounding Leyte Gulf, it became apparent to him that the Japanese would attempt to enter the gulf from the south through Surigao Strait, and might approach Leyte Gulf from the north around Samar Island, after navigating the San Bernardino Strait. He ordered his ships to move into a position nearer to the northern entrance of Surigao Strait, where they could oppose both attack paths from either direction. From this location, Oldendorf could move rapidly to defend against a Japanese naval attack as soon as reconnaissance and intelligence reports provided the location of the Japanese. However, Oldendorf believed the Japanese would come up the Surigao Strait, because this narrow body of water was closest to their bases in the Netherlands East Indies bases.[4]

As the sun set on October 19, Oldendorf moved his force to the assigned position. As it turned out, this was a highly advantageous maneuver.[5]

By the afternoon of October 19, the Japanese were convinced that the Americans were landing on Leyte. Lieutenant General Sosaku Suzuki, commanding general of the Thirty-Fifth Army, with its headquarters on Cebu, gave orders to carry out the defense of the island. Earlier Japanese defensive schemes had depended on annihilating the Americans on the beaches. But the success of defense-in-depth techniques used on Peleliu had convinced the Japanese of the need to apply a combination of two defensive techniques.

They had not built a complicated system of concrete pillboxes and other permanent defensive structures on Leyte, because such devices had proven to be ineffective against heavy naval bombardment. Instead, strong defensive positions had been created off the beaches in several layers so that advancing American units would encounter continuous Japanese resistance as they moved inland. The intent was to delay American ground forces until the Imperial Fleet could arrive and deal a devastating blow. Furthermore, since the Japanese had only one division on Leyte, they could not mount any effective resistance given such a small number of troops.

Meanwhile, offshore, RAdm. Thomas Sprague's escort carrier force launched their planes on the morning of October 19. Sprague commanded three carrier groups, each of which had the call signs Taffy 1, Taffy 2, and Taffy 3. Each group had six escort carriers—sometimes called "Jeep" carriers because of their dwarfed size when compared with their larger cousins, the 30,000-ton-plus Essex-class fast carriers.

When Halsey announced that he was moving his fast carriers north nearer to Luzon, Sprague had to change his attack plans. Instead of supporting the landings as originally planned, Halsey wanted to attack air bases on Luzon so the Japanese could not shuttle aircraft to them from their Formosa bases. Halsey justified this change of plans further by saying that the Third Fleet could act as "bait" for any Japanese naval units that might come southward from the home islands. Thus, the task of supporting the landings fell directly on Sprague's Taffy units.

Perfect weather greeted Sprague's planes as they lifted off the Jeep carriers' decks. For the two-day period of October 18–19, they attacked and destroyed Japanese defensive installations, and any Japanese ships or barges that moved into Leyte Gulf. After returning to their ships to rearm and refuel, the planes resumed their attacks on airfields on Cebu, Negros, Panay, and Mindanao. These bases had been clobbered previously by Halsey's aircraft in September. Now, it was the Seventh Fleet's turn. Sprague's pilots found many aircraft on the ground and wrecked them where they stood. There was virtually no air opposition.

Flushed with success, the American pilots wondered why the Japanese did not rise to meet them and defend their bases. The reason was actually a simple one. They were saving their aircraft to attack the massive American landing force now approaching Leyte Gulf. With the SHO-1 plan under way, the Japanese expected their ships to appear and destroy the vulnerable American landing ships in Leyte Gulf in five more days, on October 24. Then Japanese aircraft would swoop down and finish off the Americans with telling, hammering blows from the sky. There was another reason, too. The Japanese had lost 500 planes in the Formosa Air Battle of October 12–14 and had to conserve their resources.

The Seventh Fleet began air searches of Leyte Gulf's western approaches. The newer Privateer patrol plane (PB4Y), which had been replacing the venerable PBY patrol aircraft, flew from a newly captured airfield on Mindanao. These air searches included ocean areas west of Palawan Island up to a point north of Manila Bay off the west coast of Luzon Island. However, Kurita's and Nishimura's approaching forces remained undiscovered. But, on October 23, at 12:20 P.M., the American patrol aircraft managed to find Shima's force north of Palawan Island.

As already noted, Rear Admiral Oldendorf's ships had cleared the way into Leyte Gulf and then bombarded the Leyte beaches into oblivion (or so they thought). Rear Admiral Thomas Sprague's escort carrier aircrews did an outstanding job of destroying all targets of opportunity on and around Leyte Island, executing their assigned plan perfectly. Many Japanese aircraft had yet to enter the fray, Japanese troops had not put in an appearance, and the Imperial Fleet had not yet appeared. These first units from the Seventh Fleet had paved the way for what would become the greatest onslaught from the sea since the invasion of France on June 6, 1944.[6] The American invasion armada was on its way.[7]

First Lieutenant Carlos Keasler, serving with MacArthur's intelligence unit, saw the bombardment and remembered how that operation had affected him:

> In the early morning the day of the landing, October 20, 1944, the skies were clear and the sea was calm. The Japanese shore batteries opened up on us. Then our battlewagons, heavy cruisers and aircraft from carriers began their work of softening these positions. The 16-inch shells from the ships and the bombs raining from our planes soon had the desired effect of silencing most of the gun emplacements. An exploding 16-inch shell from a battlewagon is an awesome sight, and you wondered why the island did not sink. When they lifted their fire, surprisingly some gun emplacements started firing at us.
>
> The destroyers now had their turn. They went in close and engaged the holdouts. After they had reduced the remaining resistance, the LSTs and troop ships moved in and landed the infantry and field artillery units who engaged the enemy ground troops who were in the jungle.[8]

The American armada reached Point Fin at 11:00 P.M. on the 19th. As in previous invasions, every man slated to board a landing craft the next day and head for the beaches prepared in his own way for what lay ahead. A light breeze blew on deck. Few men caught much sleep. Homonhon Island presented a faint blur to starboard.

The tides off the Leyte beaches varied only two and one-half feet. High tides would arrive just after 10:00 A.M. Therefore, the soldiers would hit the beach at ten o'clock on the morning of October 20 so the landing craft could draw as near to the beach as possible, leaving a minimal distance for the troops to reach the cover of the jungle's undergrowth.

One invasion force, commanded by Adm. Daniel E. Barbey, headed north toward San Pedro Bay off Tacloban. The other force, commanded by VAdm. Theodore S. Wilkinson, steamed toward Dulag.

Dawn on the 20th approached slowly. Those men who had the good fortune to be on deck and to enjoy whatever breeze there was, saw Samar Island's vague outlines off the starboard quarter. Heavy clouds appeared in the east. As the sun rose, the breeze stopped. Hot, muggy weather was in store. Below decks, the men sweated profusely. Leyte Island was unknown to many of them; its features grew clearer in the advancing light as its gray, irregular shape took visible form. The stillness was shattered when a Japanese patrol plane appeared and was destroyed on the spot.

As the Filipinos on Leyte Island caught sight of the great fleet approaching their homeland, their hearts filled with joy on realizing that their hour of deliverance had come. The few Americans who had survived with them were now looking freedom in the eye.[9]

President Roosevelt sent a message to the Philippine people at this momentous hour:

> The suffering, humiliation and mental torture that you have endured since the barbarous, unprovoked and treacherous attack upon the Philippines nearly three years ago have aroused in the hearts of the American people a righteous anger, a stern determination to punish the guilty and a fixed resolve to restore peace and order and decency to an outraged world. . . .
>
> On this occasion of the return of General MacArthur to Philippine soil with our airmen, our soldiers and our sailors, we renew our pledge. We and Philippine brothers in arms—with the Almighty God—will drive out the invader; we will destroy his power to wage war again, and we will restore a world of dignity and freedom—a world of confidence and honesty and peace.[10]

Hitting the Beach at Tacloban

A yellow haze formed just as the sun's rays hit Leyte Island. But as the ships slowly assumed their positions, Samar Island's features became clearer. The mists disappeared as the sun burned away the moisture. Palm-fringed beaches, behind which the Japanese lay in wait, were now clearly visible.

At 6:45 A.M. on October 20, a signal to begin the troop landings was flashed from the bridge of Admiral Barbey's flagship, the *Blue Ridge.* Carefully, the ships moved through the gray water, avoiding the reefs dotting the gulf's bottom, and eventually reaching the launching point about 7 miles from the beach. At 8:00 A.M., the landing boats, hanging from their davits, swung out over the water and descended to the water's surface. While the coxswains kept the boats close to the ships' sides, the men climbed down the hanging landing nets into the boats. As the boats filled up, they moved away from the landing ships and circled around in predetermined patterns.

Certain boats, called control boats, directed the landing boats' journey to the beaches as they moved into preassigned positions. Signalmen on each control boat hoisted colored flags and flashed messages from blinker lamps and searchlights. Each signal routinely and efficiently moved the craft from the circles to assigned landing areas on the beaches. Orders issued from bullhorns while the boats' engines made dull, whirring noises that grew louder in the soldiers' ears as they descended the rope ladders and got into the boats bouncing in the water's swells. Anyone unfamiliar with the intricacies of modern amphibious landings might have seen this movement as chaotic. However, each maneuver was designed to make the attacking troops' movement from ship to beach as precise as possible. The timing was critical because troops had to be on the beaches by 10:00 A.M. to take maximum advantage of the high tides.[11]

Shells from the American ships offshore whined, snarled, and whooshed toward Leyte Island, hitting Japanese positions behind the beaches. At about 7:00 A.M., three pre–World War II battleships—the *Mississippi, Maryland,* and *West Virginia*—along with three destroyers, moved into position just south of Samar. By 9:00 A.M., each ship had fired its quota of thirty shells per large-caliber gun. These ships then moved southward as RAdm. Russell S. Berkey's group took their places to continue the shelling of the Japanese positions. Eight destroyers drew closer to Tacloban to concentrate their fire on positions nearer the town.

As the shells pounded shore positions, aircraft from Halsey's fleet and Kinkaid's escort carriers added to the rising crescendo of explosions.

Halsey's aircraft supplied air support to the troops and conducted strikes on airfields in northern Mindanao, Cebu, Negros, Panay, and Leyte. Two other fast carrier groups maintained positions east of Leyte where they conducted patrols. The *Independence*, the only carrier with trained aircrews able to conduct dangerous night patrols, contributed to the effort as well. The Jeep carriers provided sixteen fighters and six torpedo-bombers over Leyte Gulf.

The naval bombardment reached a climax at 9:30 A.M., setting the stage for the landing craft to head for the shore. Waves of these craft formed up as the boats' coxswain moved them into position, awaiting the signal flag. At 9:43 A.M., the landing craft began a 5,000-yard race to the shore. Eleven LCIs (landing craft, infantry) with rockets on board moved within 1,200 yards of the beaches and began launching their rockets. A few minutes later, 5,500 4.5-inch rockets were hurled toward the beaches while the cruisers and destroyers ceased firing. The Japanese were by no means silent however. At 9:40 A.M., they fired mortar shells from positions hidden in the nearby hills and continued firing for the next two hours.

The landing craft arrived on schedule as planned. As their bottoms crunched down on the sand, the soldiers rushed into the water and headed for the beaches. Men of the 24th Infantry Regiment pushed 300 yards inland in the first seven minutes. Three waves of boats reached the beaches unharmed. The Japanese began firing at the landing troops, but no Japanese shells came near them. But, at 10:16 A.M., the Japanese fired mortar shells as the fourth wave of boats hit the shore. This time their fire was extremely accurate, and their shells killed three men and wounded fifteen others. Carlos Keasler's startling recollection probably reflects how the soldiers felt as they hit the beach with Japanese mortar shells falling all about them: "It was here I discovered that . . . I could hit the dirt . . . crawl into my helmet and be safe as at home in bed."[12]

It could have been much worse. When the marines landed on Tarawa and tried to wade across its death-plagued lagoon, they were torn to pieces. Here at Leyte, the American soldiers were not subjected to that level of danger. Compared to most amphibious landings in World War II, these landings were nearly perfect. The Americans had everything going for them—perfect weather, no surf, no mines in the water or on the beaches, no underwater obstacles, and relatively light Japanese resistance. One problem the Americans did face, despite landing at high tide, the LSTs (landing ships, tank) could not draw nearer the shore due to

the beaches' flat terrain. Therefore, unloading the tanks and other vehicles took longer than expected, which gave the Japanese more time
to increase the accuracy of their fire and to inflict more damage on the
landing craft. The cruisers *Phoenix* and *Boise* tried to help when they fired
200 rounds at Mount Guinhandang, but their fire came too late to be
of any assistance to the landing ships.

Another problem that increased the damage toll was the lack of pon-
toon causeway units. American commanders had thought they would not
be needed, but they were.

Meanwhile, American landings to the north, nearer to Tacloban, pro-
voked no Japanese opposition. The LSTs located there moved easily to
the beaches. At 11:22 A.M., a Japanese battery opened fire on the oncoming landing craft but was silenced by the *Boise*. By midafternoon,
troops, vehicles, and matériel had been unloaded. The invasion was now
in full swing, a fact most pleasing to General MacArthur.

Now it was time for the general to make his grand entrance.[13]

Chapter 4: A Historic Event

Aboard the light cruiser *Nashville* on October 20, General MacArthur was finishing a pleasant lunch with his staff. Reports had reached him that the initial landings in San Pedro Bay in the northern part of Leyte Gulf had gone well. In addition, the opening naval bombardment by Vice Admiral Kinkaid had delivered a devastating barrage in the beach area near Tacloban.

Lunch done, MacArthur stood on the bridge, dressed in a fresh, smoothly pressed, suntan-colored uniform and wearing his familiar braided hat and sunglasses. As he gazed out at the landing beaches, a smile of satisfaction crossed his face. His mind took him back to the last time he had been in Leyte Gulf. It was in 1903, and he was a young second lieutenant in the army engineers. His West Point education, with top marks and a top ranking in his graduating class, lay behind him, and a promising military career and an unknown future lay ahead.

The sound of firing from the beaches shook him from his reverie. Glancing around at the people on the *Nashville*'s bridge, he saw some members of the press. Smiling broadly, he turned to his chief of staff, Lt. Gen. Richard K. Sutherland, and remarked, "Well, believe it or not, we are here." It was time to go ashore.

The general let himself down a ladder into a barge that also carried Philippine president Sergio Osmeña, members of his cabinet, staff officers, and press people. The barge pulled away from the cruiser, and, as it neared the beach, the coxswain slowed the engine. The barge's bow ground onto the sand. The coxswain released the lever that dropped the ramp, and MacArthur walked calmly down it into the knee-deep water. He had performed this ritual many times before, yet this occasion was different.

MacArthur led the procession of dignitaries up the beach's gentle sandy slope. A sudden rain squall deluged the party, but as MacArthur surveyed the scene, he and the others present knew this was a truly historic occasion. Filled with the drama of the moment, MacArthur stepped over to a Jeep, ignored the beating rain, grasped a radio microphone in his hands, and addressed the Philippine people and the world:

> I have returned. By the grace of Almighty God our forces stand again on Philippine soil—soil consecrated in the blood of our two peoples. We have come, dedicated and committed, to the task of destroying every vestige of enemy control over your daily lives, and of restoring, upon a foundation of indestructible strength, the liberties of your people.
>
> At my side is your president, Sergio Osmeña, worthy successor to that great patriot Manuel Quezon, with members of his cabinet. The seat of your government is now therefore firmly reestablished on Philippine soil.
>
> The hour of your redemption is here. Your patriots have demonstrated an unswerving and resolute devotion to the principles of freedom that challenges the best that is written on the pages of human history. I now call upon your supreme effort that the enemy may know from the temper of an aroused and outraged people within that he has a force there to contend with no less violent than is the force committed from without.
>
> Rally to me. Let the indomitable spirit of Bataan and Corregidor lead on. As the lines of battle roll forward to bring you within the zone of operations, rise and strike. Strike at every favorable opportunity. For your homes and hearths, strike! For future generations of your sons and daughters, strike! In the name of your sacred dead, strike! Let no heart be faint. Let every arm be steeled. The guidance of divine God points the way. Follow in His Name to the Holy Grail of righteous victory.[1]

MacArthur's stirring words were a fitting tribute to the trial by fire that his listeners had undergone in body and soul and that was not yet over.

MacArthur had shown brilliant military leadership and a sterling resolve in order to reach this historic moment, this great milestone in the progress of this bloody, brutal war. He had led a mighty military force through the Solomon Islands and up the northern coast of New Guinea, defeating large Japanese forces without getting trapped in long, protracted battles that could have created calamitous Allied casualties. And MacArthur was more than a general; he also was a symbol of the resolve of the millions of people determined to defend not only their homeland, but their values and ways of life. Pride filled his heart as he reflected on these things and on what had been accomplished. This day was his. After enduring a long, hard journey, he had returned. Completing his historic address, he got aboard the landing craft and returned to the *Nashville*.[2]

Naturally, President Roosevelt read MacArthur's speech. He had always found MacArthur irritating because of his pompous attitude and sense of superiority. It was undeniable, though, that MacArthur knew how to motivate his troops. Roosevelt, however, was cognizant of the fact that the navy had made just as large a contribution to the success of this day as had MacArthur's forces, and so he wanted to make sure that the navy would not be forgotten. Taking pen to paper, Roosevelt composed the following note to Nimitz and Halsey:

> The country has followed with pride the magnificent sweep of your fleet into enemy waters. In addition to the gallant fighting of your fliers, we appreciate the endurance and super seamanship of your forces. Your fine cooperation with General MacArthur furnishes another example of teamwork and the effective and intelligent use of all weapons.[3]

The ground battle had gone well thus far. Landings near Tacloban ended with the town's capture on October 23. Vice Admiral Kinkaid requested that the general move his operations ashore so the *Nashville* could be used to add firepower to the landing force. While MacArthur wished to remain on board, Kinkaid did not want to jeopardize the general's life as the cruiser embarked on its new mission. Kinkaid's request was right. MacArthur moved his headquarters to Tacloban, freeing the *Nashville* to join Oldendorf's force in the upcoming battle in the Surigao Strait.

Meanwhile, the Twenty-fourth Infantry Division was fighting a difficult battle alone trying to capture Mount Guinhandang, a hill north of
the town of Palo, which was about 5 miles south of Tacloban. It was the
invasion day's primary objective and had proven to be a formidable ob-
stacle. The Japanese had placed automatic weapons in camouflaged
caves, emplacements, and trenches along the slopes. However, these positions were vulnerable to naval gunfire. With the help of ships offshore,
the troops of the Twenty-fourth took the mountain, secured it, and successfully defended it against a Japanese counterattack. In this way, the
hill was secured.

While the northern landings had gone well, with few American casualties, this rosy scenario was not to be repeated for the landings near the
town of Dulag, about 16 miles south of Tacloban.

The Americans at Dulag

The Dulag landings began on schedule on October 20. One of the attack's objectives was to capture and secure Japanese-held airfields behind
the beaches. The Seventh and Ninety-sixth Infantry Divisions landed on
a 5,000-yard stretch of sandy beach that was nearly perfect for large-scale
amphibious operations. The attack plan was to meet the troops in the
north near Tacloban. If the operation proved successful, the Americans
could form a 13-mile-wide front that would allow for a broad advance
into Leyte Island's interior.

Waves of landing craft began to form at the line of departure at 9:15
A.M., as air strikes came in from the escort carriers. A devastating, loud
naval bombardment commenced, increasing in volume until it sounded
like a thunderous orchestra reaching a crescendo in a tempestuous sym-
phony. The crack of 5-inch guns, the rattle of 40mm repeating automatic
weapons, the deep boom from the battleships' large caliber rifles, and
the weird noises of the rockets were nightmarish, as if drawn from
Dante's *Inferno*. By 9:30 A.M., as the LCI (landing craft, infantry) boats
surged toward the beaches, the din reached a maximum. LVTs (landing
vehicles, tracked) then followed the LCIs toward the shore.

The coastal plain on this part of Leyte Island was much wider than
the one in the north. By October 1944, it was a green, level area covered
with rice and corn fields and coconut groves. At 9:15 A.M., planes from
the escort carriers and mortars in the LCIs began pounding the area.
The high trajectory mortar shells and bombs dropped from the attack-

ing aircraft inflicted much heavier damage than the flat trajectory of the missiles from the offshore naval bombardment ships. Thirty minutes after the initial shelling began, rocket-equipped LCIs preceded the LVTs onto the beach and began their own bombardment.

An American observation plane dropped so many flares that the light grew as bright as the sun at midday. The landing craft carrying the infantry were now almost on the beaches. All ships had begun aiming their fire a mile inland and at the flanks of the landing beaches. Their firing continued until 10:20 A.M., as their shells hit targets 1,000 yards farther inland. Shells from a Japanese 75mm battery, which offered the only significant opposition, struck the water on both sides of the American destroyer *Bennion*, straddling the ship and wounding five sailors. The continuous and cataclysmic ships' fire permanently silenced it.

Facing light Japanese opposition, the Seventh Division captured Dulag around noon. The Japanese rapidly withdrew when faced with superior American force. Dulag was not much of a town, and after the intense shelling, little was left of it. A stone Spanish church, partially destroyed by gunfire, became a field hospital. The rest of the town was made up of wooden thatched houses that would collapse if leaned on. The narrow streets were strewn with papers, clothing, and the possessions of Filipinos who willingly paid for their freedom with the destruction of their property. The town's natives enthusiastically greeted their liberators, and not many tears were shed for what was lost. The Japanese, who had oppressed their country for nearly three years, had been conquered and expelled from their town. The people who had evacuated the town prior to the invasion now began returning from their places of refuge in nearby hills. Filipinos in boats came out to the ships for food, at the same time providing valuable intelligence about Japanese positions farther inland.

The Ninety-sixth Division had an easier time than their comrades from the Seventh. Japanese guns on a small hill fired on the landing area. They were easily overwhelmed, and the Ninety-sixth secured its position.

A moving, flag-raising ceremony, though not as famous as the later flag-raising on Iwo Jima, began around 10:30 A.M. It held a far greater significance, however, for the Filipinos and Americans gathered around the flagpole. Only forty-two minutes had elapsed since the first American troops had landed. As the soldiers looked up at the flag, they knew there would be many more months of difficult fighting, with severe

Japanese opposition. Many of these men were seasoned veterans in the Pacific campaign and knew the Japanese were an implacable, resolute, committed foe. The war in the Pacific was by no means over.

However, at that communal moment, they and their Filipino comrades had good reason to feel an overwhelming sense of pride in and satisfaction at what had been achieved. Their thoughts of comrades left behind in the jungles of Guadalcanal, Bougainville, New Guinea, Peleliu, and on the beaches of Tarawa, Kwajalein, Eniwetok, and Saipan filled their minds. They had come a long way since the dark days of Pearl Harbor, Bataan, Corregidor, and Wake Island. The sight of the Stars and Stripes flapping in the crisp Philippine breeze demonstrated dramatically what had happened before and what was to come. A hard fight for the rest of Leyte, the conquest of Luzon, and the bloody battle for Okinawa still lay ahead. Many of the men alive on that day would not return home. They would be left behind here and in nameless places. There were not many dry eyes at this historic celebration of freedom and liberation, a liberation that had begun and would continue well into 1945. The Americans had kept their promise.

No one standing near that flagpole could have foreseen that their success on that day was still in jeopardy. A powerful Japanese naval force was on its way to destroy the Americans, and the largest naval battle in history would have to be fought to keep the victory won on this day.

Chapter 5: Landing the First Punch

After departing Brunei on October 22, Kurita navigated his fleet toward the Palawan Passage, where Dangerous Ground would be on his port side and Palawan Island on his starboard side on his way to the San Bernardino Strait. As darkness fell, his ships zigzagged in a course parallel to the Palawan coast in a northeasterly direction at a speed of 16 knots. Zigzag course changes decreased the risk of successful submarine attacks, and because his destroyers were not leading the fleet, early submarine detection was nearly impossible.

Furthermore, because the fleet could steam only as fast as its slowest ship and maintain a zigzag course, its speed was 4 knots slower than an American submarine's top surface speed. Because no Japanese aircraft patrolled the skies, American submarines could move with relative safety on the surface. The reefs, the narrow passage, and the shoals all forced the fleet to abandon its zigzag course at the Palawan Passage and steam in a straight line. Any submarine in the area could easily strike the Japanese fleet in this vulnerable position. The fleet's radio interception operators did indeed detect a number of radio transmissions and plotted their location as being in Kurita's path. Some two hours later, another interception located a submarine parallel to and west of the fleet.

Twelve American submarines were close enough to the Philippine Islands to report all Japanese ship movements. Among them were the *Darter* and the *Dace*, which had taken up stations off Palawan Island's southern tip. The *Darter*'s captain was Cmdr. David H. McClintock. His submarine's sound-detection gear had picked up high-speed propeller

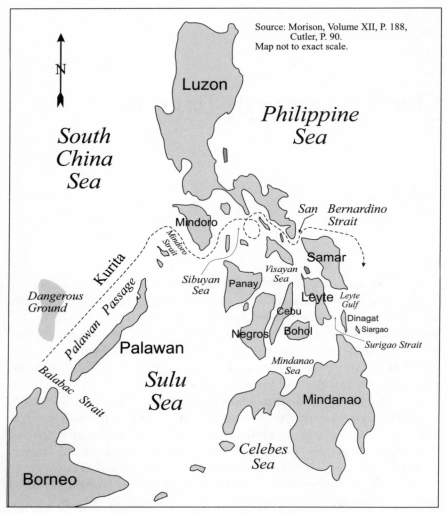

Kurita's approach to the Philippines

sounds from several Japanese warships. The *Darter* tried to catch up with these ships but wasn't fast enough. Later, however, both boats caught up with Kurita's fleet and followed it off Palawan Island, relaying continuous reports about their sightings of Japanese warships to American senior commanders.

McClintock's patrol report recorded a vivid narrative of the two submarines' stalking of the Japanese ships:

[We] sent out three contact reports, giving final estimate task force of eleven heavy ships. Tracking party said that gaining attack position was hopeless due to high speed (initial estimate, 15 knots). We managed to average about 19 knots. Estimates of enemy speed began to drop until finally it was fifteen knots. We had them now! Did not attack in darkness, as it was considered vital to see and identify the force which was probably on its way to interfere with the Leyte landing. It was felt there could be no radical dawn zig due to size of force and narrowness of Palawan Passage. Targets did not zig during night.

As the sun rose over the Palawan Passage, the American submarines had moved into a position advantageous for an attack.[1]

The *Darter* and the *Dace* had left their Brisbane, Australia base on September 1. Although they had been at sea for more than three weeks, they had accomplished little. Their assignment to search north of Celebes Island during the Palau and Morotai landings had yielded not a single Japanese ship. By the end of September, their fuel nearly spent, they refueled at a base near New Guinea and received minor repairs from the submarine tender *Orion*. Replenished and refueled, the two boats then resumed patrolling their assigned areas.

By late 1944, American naval and air forces were roaming all over the Western Pacific. To avoid being attacked by "friendly" forces, American submarines had to make use of "safety lanes," which were marked out in longitude and latitude on the charts used by Allied ships, planes, and submarines. Cautious submarine skippers made certain they stayed within these lanes as they operated around American bases or within range of land-based aircraft. Sometimes eager crews of American planes and ships would mistakenly attack American submarines due to navigational errors on the part of the submarine commanders, or because American submarines were incorrectly identified as Japanese.

For example, on October 3, the *Darter* was occupying a safety lane but was attacked by an American hunter-killer group of planes and destroyer escorts. The *Darter* gave all the proper signals, but still had a difficult time convincing its erstwhile attackers that it was friendly. That same day another American submarine, the *Seawolf*, occupying that same safety lane, disappeared. The *Darter*, however, stayed on the surface, left the area at top speed, and slipped away from any and all friendly ships. McClintock breathed a sigh of relief.

A few days later, the *Darter* was in its assigned patrol area, which extended approximately 100 miles west of the southern half of Palawan Island, to the northwest coast of Borneo, and then as far as Brunei Bay. Given the *Darter*'s position, any large Japanese fleet coming from the southwest along Borneo's western coast would be within her attack range. In effect, the *Darter* was right in Kurita's path. The *Dace*, commanded by Cmdr. Bladen D. Claggett, joined McClintock's boat on October 10, and the two submarines formed a two-boat wolf pack.

Relentlessly pursuing one convoy that had escaped them in shallow water, they found that their perseverance paid dividends when the two subs sank two ships and damaged two more inside the Borneo barrier reef. Both boats' radio operators received a message on the 14th ordering them to cover the Balabac Strait and the Palawan Passage. After a four-day wait, another radio message reported a southbound convoy about halfway up Palawan Island's west coast.

The *Darter* raced north to join the *Dace*. On the morning of October 19, the two captains moved their boats into position for speaking via megaphones. As they conversed, two Japanese destroyers approached them suddenly and at high speed, causing the submarines to dive hastily. Each submarine fired four torpedoes: all missed.

The two Japanese destroyers dropped a few depth charges, then left the area. Apparently, the destroyers' captains had more important matters on their minds. This action was reported to Admiral Kurita, and he became more nervous, realizing the high risk posed by moving into the Palawan Passage.

The *Darter* and the *Dace* spent a quiet day on October 20. On a news broadcast, they heard about the invasion of the Philippines. They then headed for the Balabac Strait, a location on a line the shortest distance between Singapore and Leyte. McClintock and Claggett were unaware that Kurita had moved to Brunei Bay.[2]

Pursuit in Palawan Passage

The moon shone brightly on the water in the early morning of October 22. The water's hissing sound moving past the *Darter*'s hull was a familiar one to McClintock. He was on the bridge scanning the horizon. The skipper usually did not stand watch at this early morning hour. He enjoyed this misleadingly peaceful time on submarines. Although thoroughly trained in boats, the crews of these killing vessels invariably needed respite from the tension and bone-rattling din that sprang to life during depth-charge attacks. McClintock was no exception. As the lookouts in position above him scanned the horizon, McClintock heard the familiar whirring sound of the whirling radar antenna atop the *Darter's* highest point.

Since the attack on Pearl Harbor, American submarines had shouldered the offensive operational load against the Japanese merchant navy. The number of submarines had grown steadily, wreaking havoc on the Japanese merchant marine. Ton for ton, the submarine was the most deadly warship in the world. Borrowing the successful tactics used by the Germans, American submarines had sunk more than 2 million tons of merchant shipping.

Japan, an island nation, relied almost solely on merchant shipping to feed its war machine. The success of American submarines had reduced the flow of vital war matériel to a trickle. After all, the primary reason Japan had waged war on the United States in the first place was to secure a free flow of raw material to the home islands. Japanese naval commanders would later cite the success of American submarine warfare as one of the major factors contributing to their defeat.

The *Darter* and *Dace* patrol had been a successful one thus far. Two Japanese merchant ships had been sunk by the hunter-killer group on October 12. Their conning towers would have two more miniature flags painted on them. Ten days then passed with no action. The crews had become restless, but they were a disciplined group, hungry for action. All their hard training would pay off soon, for the tranquility of the last ten days was about to be broken.[3]

The two submarines moved carefully southward through the Dangerous Ground shoals toward Balabac Strait. Around midnight, the two submarines moved near enough to one another so their captains could converse via megaphone. Claggett noted he was low on fuel and so should leave the area for refueling. The two boats were approximately 50 yards apart and moved slowly at 5 knots using battery power. They had received two reports showing two separate convoys, and both submarine skippers had agreed to attack. The captains were about ready to go their own way when the *Darter's* conning tower speaker suddenly squawked: "Radar contact, 130 degrees T[rue], 30,000 yards—contact doubtful—probably rain."

The radar contact appeared on the bridge's repeater screen, catching McClintock by surprise. A single thought flashed through his mind: the Japanese fleet. The *Darter*'s radar operator immediately reported that the contacts were ships. McClintock gave the *Dace* the contact's range and bearing by megaphone. Claggett answered immediately: "Let's go get them." At 12:23 A.M., on October 23, the *Darter* and the *Dace* increased their speed to flank so they could quickly close the distance and pursue the contact. The radar contact was heading on a northward course in Palawan Passage.

The American submarines were on the contact's left flank. As they drew nearer, a formidable, tantalizing target took form on the horizon. McClintock quickly surmised they were not chasing merchant ship convoys but a Japanese warship task force. He sent three contact reports to American naval headquarters. His final estimate of the number of ships in the Japanese force was that it had at least eleven heavy ships. McClintock hoped this was the Japanese fleet's main body and decided it was vital to know the force's actual composition before attacking.

The Japanese ships steamed on a course of 039 degrees at a speed of 16 knots. The *Darter* and the *Dace* moved at 19 knots, closing the distance at their fastest speed. By 5:20 A.M., the Americans confirmed the contact as five battleships, ten heavy cruisers, and two light cruisers. Twelve to fourteen destroyers screened the convoy on the formation's flanks and center.

McClintock noted that, for some strange reason, the Japanese were not zigzagging while negotiating the passage, reasoning they might be trying to avoid the Dangerous Ground's shoals to the west. The submarines' radars swept ahead while they moved slowly forward at 15 knots. McClintock ordered the *Darter* to increase speed and close the range.

The Japanese formation consisted of five parallel lines of ships as it moved up the Palawan Passage on an approximate northeasterly course. The far left line had the light cruiser *Noshiro* and two destroyers, each about 500 meters apart, followed by a 3-kilometer space with two more destroyers in line. The next line to the right consisted of heavy ships, led by the heavy cruiser and Kurita's fleet flagship *Atago*. The heavy cruisers *Takao* and *Chokai* and the battleship *Nagato* followed, each about 500 meters apart. The heavy cruisers *Kumano* and *Suzuya* and the battleship *Haruna* followed about 3 kilometers behind. Three more destroyers were in a line in the formation's center, about 2 kilometers to the right. To the right of these destroyers came the longest line of ships, led by the heavy cruiser *Myoko*, which was followed by the *Haguro* and *Maya* and the

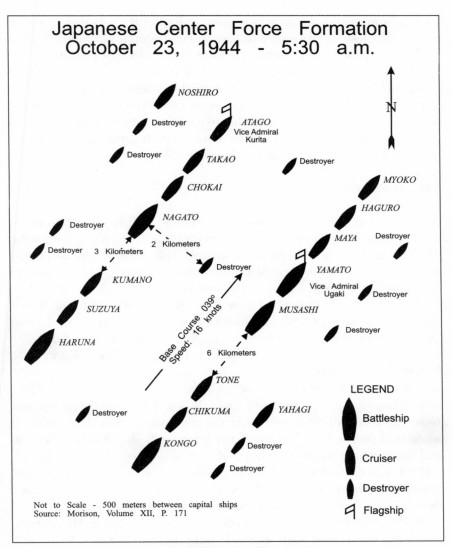

Japanese Center Force Formation October 23, 1944 - 5:30 a.m.

N

NOSHIRO

Destroyer   ATAGO
                        Vice Admiral
                        Kurita

Destroyer   TAKAO   Destroyer

                CHOKAI   MYOKO

        NAGATO   HAGURO

Destroyer   MAYA   Destroyer

Destroyer   3 Kilometers   2   Kilometers   YAMATO

                        Destroyer   Vice Admiral
        KUMANO   Ugaki   Destroyer

    SUZUYA   MUSASHI

                        Base Course 039°
HARUNA   Speed: 16 knots   Destroyer

                        6   Kilometers

                TONE   LEGEND

Destroyer   CHIKUMA   YAHAGI   ▉ Battleship

        KONGO   Destroyer   ▉ Cruiser

                Destroyer   ▌ Destroyer

Not to Scale - 500 meters between capital ships   ⌐ Flagship
Source: Morison, Volume XII, P. 171

Kurita in Palawan Passage

mighty battleships *Yamato* and *Musashi*. The commander of the battleships, Vice Admiral Ugaki, was in his flagship, the *Yamato*. At a distance
of 6 kilometers behind these ships, the heavy cruisers *Tone* and *Chikuma*
and the battleship *Kongo* followed. The outside and easternmost line had
three destroyers, the light cruiser *Yahagi*, and two more destroyers.[4]

The American submariners were surprised at the position assumed by the Japanese destroyers. No destroyers had been positioned ahead of the fleet to provide early submarine warnings. This lack of a proper antisubmarine screen in combination with the clear weather would make the attack all that much easier. McClintock immediately signaled headquarters, which relayed the sighting report to Admiral Halsey. The Center Force's whereabouts had remained a mystery since it had left Lingga Roads. Now, the mystery had been solved. The beginning of the Battle of Leyte Gulf was but moments away.[5]

Moving in for the Attack

McClintock shifted his attention to the second column of capital ships. He could not see the destroyer column on his left. From the sizes of the blips on the radar screen, the last ship looked like a battleship. He moved the *Darter* into position to attack this column of ships from the port side and asked the *Dace* to attack from starboard.

By 4:25 A.M., the *Darter* had moved 10 miles ahead and to the left of the Japanese ship column. McClintock waited for the Japanese ships to come to him. The *Darter* slowed so it matched the targets' speed. He would wait for first light to attack. The *Dace* passed the *Darter*'s bow, headed for the Japanese formation's right, and waited for enough light so it could attack using the periscope.

McClintock left the conning tower to study the radio reports and found that most of the men were in the mess room. They were skeptical when told they would soon attack the Japanese fleet. Thus far, their patrol had not been as lucky as they had wanted it to be. Later, McClintock said, "I didn't blame them. I wasn't absolutely sure myself. I had a small fear that the ships might be high-speed transports and not the [Japanese] fleet." He continued matching the Japanese fleet's speed.

At about 4:30 A.M., all hands retired to the mess for coffee. Twenty minutes later, he ordered them to battle stations. At 5:10 A.M., McClintock reversed course and headed for the column of big ships. He ordered "up periscope" and peered in. The dawn's eastern light began to change the sea's color, and the sky stood clear without a trace of clouds. After lowering the periscope, he dove to 300 feet in order to check the water's depth and density, then returned to periscope depth. McClintock ordered the periscope raised again and peeked through the lens.

He saw one long gray shape with its entire column bearing down on him. The periscope's image, however, was unclear. What kind of ships were coming at him? Cruisers? Battleships? He swung the periscope around to the southeast where the light was brighter and better, and there they were. It seemed to McClintock that the entire Japanese navy was right before him: battleships, cruisers, and destroyers! And the unmistakable pagoda-shaped superstructures on the battleships clearly identified them as Japanese.

Interestingly, the submarine's sound gear did not pick up any evidence that the ships were out there, because they were too far away to "ping" with the submarine's sonar. McClintock swung the periscope around. His executive officer, Lt. Ernie Schwab, wanted to know what McClintock saw. The skipper kept swinging the periscope and muttering to himself.

"What's there?" Schwab asked.

McClintock replied, "Battleships." The periscope swung again.

"What's there?"

"Cruisers." McClintock turned the periscope yet again and continued speaking in barely audible tones.

"What's there?"

"Battleships."

All doubt about what those ships were evaporated. The object of every submariner's dream lay in front of the two American boats—a large, powerful fleet of capital warships headed straight toward them.

The gray ships loomed larger in the periscope with the *Darter* and the *Dace* slightly east of the column's track. The ships were almost on a course parallel with the submarines. At 5:25 A.M., the huge bow waves raised by the formation's leading ships identified them as those made by heavy cruisers. Sighs of frustration surged through the conning tower of the *Darter*, as the men realized the targets were not all battleships. Still, it was a beautiful sight indeed to any submariner's eyes. As the Japanese ships steamed in a close column, the Americans imagined the Japanese captains calling their crews to general quarters, closing watertight doors, with the officers pacing the bridge dressed in white uniforms.

McClintock hoped the first ship in the column was the flagship. And it was! An admiral's flag flew on her main mast. At 5:27 A.M., the leading cruiser's range was under 3,000 yards. McClintock ordered all tubes loaded, flooded, and made ready to fire.

The course of the Japanese ships then changed, so their sides now faced the submarine's torpedo tubes. No "bow shot" would be needed here. The cruiser's range from the *Darter* shortened to just under 1,000 yards. McClintock could clearly make out the ship's profile.

But the target's new course forced the conning tower's crew to prepare for a different shot, while in the *Darter*'s periscope, which stayed up for what seemed like several minutes, the leading cruiser loomed huge, looking like a large, vicious dog with a bone in its teeth. As her bow wave flew high past her prow, her bridge's rearward slant emphasized her speed. McClintock knew without any doubt she was an Atago-class heavy cruiser; he had become familiar with her silhouette in submarine school when he practiced attack tactics. From the models, he had learned to recognize the characteristic flat bridge's angle and remembered it well.

The real thing now was looming in his periscope's crosshairs. As the Japanese ships turned, the cruiser's angle on her bow increased; her beam's image grew larger—55 degrees, 60 degrees, 65 degrees. She moved closer to the *Darter*. There was no better time to attack than at this moment.

McClintock's commands reeled out with staccato-like rapidity:

"Shooting bearing."

"Mark."

"Fire One!" McClintock shouted, identifying the firing of a torpedo from torpedo tube number one.

As McClintock ordered the firing of five more torpedoes from the bow tubes, the missiles whooshed from the submarine's forward tubes into the water as he watched through the periscope. The cruiser had stopped turning now and was straightening its course. A searchlight on the cruiser's bridge pointed eastward as it flashed signals to the rest of the fleet. Evidently the doomed ship was sending some routine message, totally oblivious of her fate. The Americans had achieved total surprise.

But the *Darter* had more targets to attack in this truly target-rich environment.

"Shift targets to second cruiser," ordered the captain.

The periscope turned in the direction of the new target.

"Bearing mark."

Lieutenant Dennis Wilkinson, the target data computer (TDC) operator, yelled, "Give me a range! Give me a range! Give me a range! You can't shoot without a range."

McClintock adjusted the periscope's range finder and said, "1,500 yards." All Wilkinson needed was the final bearing.

"TDC ready."

"Bearing mark."

"Fire Seven!" McClintock yelled, ordering a torpedo fired from torpedo tube number seven in the *Darter*'s stern.

Just as the first torpedo left the stern tubes, a heavy explosion erupted.

"Depth charge!" Schwab yelled.

"Depth charges, hell," shouted McClintock. "Torpedoes!"

Walter Price, another conning tower sailor, punched the torpedo firing keys, jumping up and down at each explosion, yelling, "Christ, we're hitting them, we're hitting them!"

Three more torpedoes hissed from the stern tubes, heading for the second cruiser. The six "fish" from the bow tubes left a characteristic small wake as they sped toward the first cruiser. As four torpedoes from the stern tubes sped toward the second, five explosions sent geysers of water flying on the first target's side. McClintock swung the periscope around for another look. His words vividly describe the wild scene on the water's boiling surface: "She was belching flame from the base of her forward turret to the stern; the dense black smoke of burning oil covered her from forward turret to stern. She was still plowing ahead, but she was also going down by the bow. Number One turret was cutting the water. She was finished."

McClintock expected the destroyers to come after him seeking vengeance. Knowing they would crisscross his position and drop a series of depth charges, he plunged the *Darter* into deep water. Four more torpedo explosions boomed as the submarine's bow dipped down. Luck was with him, for the depth charging was ineffective and sketchy. For safety's sake, the *Darter* stayed deep.[6]

Now it was the *Dace*'s turn. Claggett had been watching the carnage through his periscope, and as thick black smoke engulfed the first cruiser, he could not make out the ship's sinking. Black smoke belched from the second cruiser as well, and he saw the Japanese destroyers riveting their attention on the spot where the *Darter* had submerged.

So, Claggett now took up his attack, because at this point the Japanese were unaware of his presence. He expected the Japanese ships to disperse into a defensive formation because its two leading members had been hit. Much to his surprise, nothing happened, possibly because the Japanese ships were operating in highly confined waters. His best guess was that fear of running aground outweighed the fear of submarines.

The Japanese ships turned slightly to the right, reducing their distance to the *Dace*. Picking his target—a large cruiser leading the capital ships' starboard column—Claggett began his approach.

As the dawn's light grew brighter, the cruiser moved closer to the *Dace*. As Claggett waited for the range to close, he turned the periscope in a circle, awestruck by the enormous fleet approaching his boat. With so many ships from which to choose, he grew greedy and decided to change his target. It was the third ship in the starboard line that he wanted to sink. She looked like a Kongo-class battleship, so he let the first two ships pass by.

"I never thought the time would come when I would let two heavy cruisers go by," he would say later, but the third ship definitely had a larger superstructure.

As the column moved toward the *Dace*, Claggett launched six torpedoes, then dove deep to avoid a battleship that was drawing too close for comfort. As the boat dove deeper, the *Dace*'s crew heard four explosions which could only come from detonating torpedoes.

A tremendous blast ripped the waters as the torpedoes found their target. Doubtless the ship's magazine had blown up. Gruesome noises from the ship's death throes continued for twenty-five minutes. Claggett remembered them as the most horrific sounds he had experienced in all his patrols, and he feared for his command's safety. His engineering officer, Lieutenant Jones, cried, "Let's get the hell out of here."[7]

Jones and Claggett were of one mind, but it was not an easy task to avoid the sinking ship and the vicious depth charge attack that would most certainly come from the destroyers that they expected to descend upon them. The submarine remained submerged in deep water for several hours, and its crew heard two destroyers charge down on them, for the whine of their high-speed propellers was unmistakable. But, for whatever reason, the destroyers dropped no depth charges; instead, they headed away from the *Dace*.

The First Japanese Losses

The *Atago*, the Japanese fleet's flagship, was the first ship the *Darter* attacked. Her silhouette was easily recognizable. The first funnel had a sharp backward rake; her second stood perfectly vertical. The main mast was situated just ahead of the first funnel. Her bridge slanted backward, giving a distinctly streamlined look. A large ship, the *Atago* was more than 203 meters long, had a nearly 15,000-ton displacement, was powered by four turbines with twelve boilers, and had a maximum speed of more than 34 knots. Her armament ranged from five 200mm (about 8 inches) guns to forty-two 25mm antiaircraft guns. The big cruiser carried twenty-four torpedoes and had the capability of carrying three airplanes, but her planes had been taken to strengthen the thin Japanese air defenses around the Philippines.

The Japanese knew that the American submarines had been stalking them all evening. At 2:50 A.M., a report reached Admiral Ugaki that Japanese radiomen had intercepted a strong signal from a submarine on a frequency of 8,470 kilocycles. This signal confirmed that the Americans knew where Kurita's fleet was.

Ugaki worried increasingly about the trouble on its way as he stood on the *Yamato*'s bridge. The world's largest battleship was the fourth in the starboard line of heavy ships. One hour before sunrise, the ships had moved into a shortened formation, one designed to defend against submarine attacks. Dawn's light had just appeared in the eastern sky. Despite McClintock's observations that the Japanese fleet was not following a zigzag pattern, in fact, these ships were engaged in longer, less drastic maneuvers. Following this plan, Kurita ordered all ships to make a simultaneous port turn just before 5:30 A.M.

Suddenly an explosion ripped the air followed by a glow near the port column. Ugaki later recalled, "I suddenly spied off the port bow on the dawning horizon the flames from an explosion and what appeared to be a widening water spout."

He ordered a brisk, emergency turn to starboard.

A few moments later, Ugaki saw that two ships had been hit. Two destroyers moved rapidly to come to the damaged ships' aid and to rescue the survivors.

Explosions, one after the other, hit the *Atago* and mortally wounded her. Huge shocks shook the big cruiser from bow to stern. The Japanese mistakenly thought the attack had come from nearly 2,000 yards away, but their estimate of the submarine's position was wrong. The American submarine was less than 1,000 yards away. Four torpedoes hit the heavy cruiser's starboard side just as she had begun her port zigzag. They hit along the ship's entire length, the blows almost evenly spaced from forward to amidships to aft. Water flooded her below decks, and she immediately began to list to starboard by nearly 8 degrees. The captain ordered the flooding of the port engine and boiler rooms to bring the ship to a level keel, but it was already too late to save the ship. The starboard side's watertight compartments had been blown away, leaving a huge hole open to the sea. It was not long before her list increased to 18 degrees and then to 25 degrees.

The captain ordered "all hands on deck," and men tried to rush to the main deck from the compartments below. Many couldn't make it and drowned when the *Atago* sank.

The exploding torpedoes had a deadly impact on the now-doomed cruiser. The first one had struck the bow near the bread lockers and damaged all the forward, starboard side's storerooms. Although the officers ordered the men to start the pumps, it was futile.

The second torpedo struck the number one boiler room's side, bathing the room in steam. Steam and flames gushed from the bridge's port side air intake and the middle deck's port and starboard air intakes. Cracks in the hull opened suddenly, and water rushed into the junior officers' quarters near the main battery control station. Rapidly falling steam pressure caused the lights to flicker, dim, and die. The electrical power died as well. The bridge's telephone and, later, the entire telephone system ceased operating.

The captain ordered "full right rudder," but there was no response because the cruiser's electrical system failed. The *Atago*'s list increased.

The third torpedo crashed into the number six boiler room so swiftly that the voice tube whistled. Cracks appeared in the number six and number seven boiler rooms' center bulkhead, and flames shot through into number seven. Meanwhile, water and oil spray showered the number three torpedo mount, located directly above the number six boiler room. The mount's crew was blown from their posts to the after-control station. Because of the severe damage, the torpedo officer ordered the torpedoes and other heavy objects on the starboard side thrown overboard. Seven of the cruiser's torpedoes followed the other debris into the water. The eighth was unmovable.

The fourth torpedo thrust a hole in the starboard after-engine room's rear bulkhead, wreaking horrific damage. Water flooded the aft generator room. Cracks opened in the control boardroom bulkhead, and the flooding could not be stemmed. The starboard shaft alley and after-transformer room filled with water; fuel oil and water gushed up through the seamen's aft compartments; water flooded into the number five turret powder magazine. Five magazine crewmen drowned.

The ship's list increased to 32 degrees. Kurita assessed the situation, concluding he would have to abandon the hapless cruiser as his flagship. The admiral and his staff thereupon left the flag plot and slid overboard into the water. The destroyer *Kishinami*, now standing by, pulled the wet officers aboard. The staff's assistant medical officer and chief clerk rescued the emperor's picture and carried it to the destroyer. The *Atago* now had a 42 degree starboard list.

The order went out to the *Kishinami*, "Approach the side."

"Prepare to lower the ensign," cried the cruiser's captain.

Water filled the number five turret, and the list increased to 54 degrees. The bridge lost all communications with the exception of the voice tube, and the sea lapped only a few feet below the number two turret dome.

The officers on the bridge destroyed classified materials, code machines, and books by placing them in weighted sacks or locking them in the code rooms. They had moved quickly to lock up the map room and wardroom's cabinet. Therefore, there was no way these secret materials could float up to the water's surface as flotsam and be picked up by the Americans. The captain ordered "abandon ship," and the *Kishinami* and the destroyer *Asahimo* rescued any men able to make it over the side.

Men floundered in the water as the big cruiser disappeared beneath the waves. The destroyers rescued the captain, 43 officers, and 667 petty officers and men, but the chief engineer, 18 officers, and 340 petty officers and men went down with the ship.

The destroyers remained in the area, searching through the flotsam littering the water's surface, but nothing important was found. The emperor's secrets, one of his ships, and 359 of his men now lay entombed deep on the ocean floor.

The *Darter*'s second target was the *Atago*'s sister ship, the heavy cruiser *Takao*. About a minute after torpedoes hit the *Atago*, two torpedoes struck the *Takao*. Executing a maneuver that would ultimately save the big cruiser from sinking, her captain alertly ordered a left full rudder seconds before the American torpedoes struck.

The first torpedo struck the starboard side below the bridge, and a second hit below the aft deck, damaging both her seaplanes still on board. A nearly 12-by-24-foot hole opened in the hull, as did a second one 12 feet high and nearly 50 feet long. The physical damage inside the cruiser was devastating. Nonetheless, only thirty-three men lost their lives and about thirty were injured. The ship began to list about 10 degrees to starboard. After the torpedoes crashed into the *Takao*, the steering became inoperable. The engines slowed and stopped, and she was dead in the water. At this point, the captain ordered counterflooding, so her list decreased and she stabilized. The crew began making an emergency rudder. As the repairs continued, the destroyers *Asahimo* and *Naganami* moved to her side and began to protect the cruiser from further submarine attacks.

The heavy cruiser *Maya*, part of the capital ships' starboard column, had been torpedoed by the *Dace*. Like her sister ships, the *Atago* and the *Takao*, she was a fast, modern, dangerous weapon, but American torpedoes soon ended this sea tiger's life. The first struck her on the port side near the chain locker, the second opposite the number one gun turret, the third in the number seven boiler room, and the last in the port after-engine room. The big cruiser immediately listed sharply to port, exploded, and broke into several pieces.

As she slipped beneath the waves, the destroyers *Akishimo* and *Shimakaze* tried to rescue the survivors struggling to stay alive in the water. Although the *Maya* sank quickly, her crew was very lucky. Although the captain went down with the *Maya*, the destroyers saved 769 men, including the executive officer, out of a crew of 1,000 officers and men in only four short minutes.

Despite the disastrous losses, the Japanese sailors kept their discipline. Although Ugaki had not formally taken command, when he ordered his course change, the other ships followed. Confusion reigned, however, when the *Maya* exploded. Kurita and his staff, now aboard a destroyer, were trying to recover from their ordeal in the water. Vice Admiral Ugaki was the second most senior officer in the Center Force and temporarily assumed command, because Kurita was no longer on his flagship. Ugaki later described the situation: "If other submarines are present, not only would it be dangerous to effect a radical retirement. But as the senior commander present, a radical separation would not be feasible from the standpoint of visibility."

When the *Maya* blew up, the explosion caused Ugaki to tremble. The cruiser was directly ahead of his flagship, the *Yamato*. If the battleship had not been in the position she was, three or four torpedoes might have hit her. Turning to starboard and maneuvering ahead to evade the *Dace* was a dangerous tactic. However, it forced the *Dace* to dive and perhaps saved the rest of the fleet from further attacks.

Periscopes appeared to be everywhere, though in reality both American submarines were now deep in safe water. Ugaki saw a periscope to port and reversed course. Pandemonium permeated the normally calm Japanese naval force. Although the *Darter* and the *Dace* were the only submarines in the area, Ugaki was absolutely certain he saw at least four periscopes slicing through the water. He remarked later: "It is no exaggeration to say that for a time the first section was in utter confusion."[8]

But the confusion gradually gave way to calm as no further shocks befell. Because the *Atago* was lost, Ugaki received a visual signal that he was to take command of the fleet's communications at 7:00 A.M. After breathing a sigh of relief on learning Vice Admiral Kurita was safely aboard the *Kishinami*, Ugaki learned that he was to take command of the entire fleet at 8:30 A.M. In effect, he had already done so.

Ugaki could now reset his position when he saw the mountains of southern Palawan Island looming in the eastern sky. He had only a 20-mile-wide path available to him between the island's shallows and reefs and the still uncharted Dangerous Ground shoals. These narrow waters increased the fleet's vulnerability to further submarine attacks. Realizing that time was running out and that daylight was increasing, he had no choice but to try and extricate the fleet from this perilous situation as quickly as possible.

He ordered the Center Force's speed increased from 16 to 24 knots. Signal flags shot up the *Yamato*'s mast, and blinker lights flashed the orders. By 9:15 A.M., the fleet knew Ugaki was in temporary command. Messages were sent to the Combined Fleet Headquarters asking for rescue forces to tow the *Takao* to safety. Ugaki assured his superiors that the fleet's mission would continue despite the disastrous losses.

The *Takao*'s busy crew did what they could to restore their ship. Ugaki ordered the destroyers *Naganami* and *Asahimo* to stay with the helpless cruiser. By 10:50 A.M., the cruiser's engineers got the engines started, but it was of little use. Soon the engines refused to run at all. At 11:00 A.M., the *Asahimo* returned five of the *Takao*'s crewmen who had been blown overboard by the torpedo explosions. Then, forty minutes later, radio signals arrived from the Combined Fleet that help was on its way from Brunei.

At noon, the *Takao's* nervous crew thought they had sighted a submarine, but the destroyers found nothing. Two hours later, damage-control parties made the optimistic assessment that they could bring the ship into port under her own power. Although they needed a temporary, jury-rigged rudder, the engineers thought it could be done. By 9:00 P.M., the *Takao* was moving under her own power. By midnight, she was able to head for Brunei at a speed of 6 knots and expected to reach port in two days.

Meanwhile, Vice Admiral Ugaki continued commanding the fleet. The Center Force had few Japanese officers able to take command responsibility in an emergency. By virtue of having the most experience in the fleet, he was the most qualified and next in seniority to Kurita. He had shown excellent judgment at Midway in June 1942, when as Admiral Yamamoto's chief of staff he persuaded him to return to Japan after they had lost four big carriers—an action that probably saved the fleet.

However, the events of this day, and the fleet's reduced resources, placed Ugaki in a defensive posture. The best course would have been to increase the fleet's speed, yet a critical fuel shortage made this impossible. If the fleet increased its speed, many ships, particularly the destroyers, would run out of fuel, so Ugaki reduced the fleet's speed to 20 knots.

The specter of fuel shortages once again had pushed the Japanese naval commanders into making less-than-optimum decisions. Fuel shortages had forced Kurita to select the more dangerous Palawan Passage because it shortened the distance between Brunei and Leyte Gulf. Then, while steaming west of Palawan Island, the fleet had no choice but to steam in a simpler zigzag course instead of a more protective, complex zigzag pattern, because the latter would have consumed more fuel. Under normal conditions, a prudent naval commander would have sent his destroyers ahead of the fleet to screen against submarine attacks. But the chronic fuel shortages prevented Kurita from doing that, too.

Three more groundless submarine scares shook the fleet as Ugaki led it through the Palawan Passage's narrow waters. After safely navigating the fleet through these treacherous waters, he changed course in a northward direction. At 3:40 P.M., the destroyer *Kishinami* came alongside the *Yamato,* and Kurita and his staff began moving his flag command aboard the big battleship. One-half hour later, Kurita raised his pennant above the battleship and resumed command of the Center Force. Being a loyal officer, Ugaki passed all the fleet's obligations to his superior and ordered his staff to help Kurita and his men in any way they could. The fleet then resumed their original course for the San Bernardino Strait.

On the morning of October 24, Kurita issued new orders stating that the force would use sonar searches from sundown until thirty minutes before sunrise. His force maintained a speed of 20 knots as it moved toward the big battle its men hoped would take place in less than forty-eight hours. Meanwhile, after wreaking so much havoc on the Japanese, the American submarines had serious problems of their own.[9]

The Americans Lose the *Darter*

By 8:00 A.M. on October 24 the depth charge attacks had ceased, and the Japanese destroyers had moved away from the *Darter*. It was now safe enough for McClintock to bring his boat up to periscope depth where he could survey the surrounding area. He saw that the *Takao*, his second target, was dead in the water. Planes circled around her, and a strong, three-destroyer screen stood by, obviously lending assistance to the damaged cruiser. He tried approaching her twice to sink her, but the destroyers stopped him each time, so McClintock temporarily gave up and decided to wait for the safety of darkness. Also, his exhausted crew needed a much-deserved rest as they had been in constant contact with the Japanese force for two consecutive nights.

After sunset, the sky darkened into a dense blackness. The *Darter* surfaced while still within sight of the *Takao*. McClintock radioed a report to his Brisbane base describing the morning's battle—the sinking of the *Atago* and reporting, to the best of his knowledge, what other ships remained in the Japanese force.

When the crippled *Takao* began her southwesterly journey toward Brunei, the *Darter* and the *Dace* separated and tried to sink her. The *Dace* moved eastward around the Japanese force's rear. The *Darter* headed west and passed through a large pool of fuel oil, a pool so large it took an hour to get through it.[10]

The waters in the Palawan Passage are dangerous enough to navigate in daytime, but in darkness, they are more treacherous still. The channel between the reefs along Palawan Island to the east and Dangerous Ground to the west is only 25 miles wide, but it is pockmarked with pinnacles and shoals named for past ill-fated sailing ships. One of these is an underwater promontory called Bombay Shoal, a treacherous coral reef on the passage's eastern side named after an East Indian trading ship that had run aground there about a century ago. At high tide, it was invisible when the *Darter* approached it.

The two submarines had been maneuvering for twenty-four hours in these misleadingly safe waters using only dead-reckoning navigating techniques—compass readings and speed estimates—to learn where they were. To protect themselves against Japanese air attacks, the two boats remained submerged throughout the day and thus could not take any sightings on Palawan Island's mountains. When they surfaced at dusk, heavy cloud cover made it impossible to make star sightings. To avoid the destroyers and move into an attack position similar to the one they had used to bushwhack the Japanese fleet earlier that morning, the *Darter* steamed on a westward roundabout course.

McClintock had taken a calculated risk. He knew the course he had chosen to avoid the Japanese destroyers was fraught with hazards. The more the *Darter* relied on navigating by dead reckoning, the greater the risks. Only a quarter-knot of miscalculation in speed would put the *Darter* in danger.

At 12:05 A.M., the *Darter*'s keel scraped and crunched against the coral of Bombay Shoal, making a tremendous crash. The sound was so loud a Japanese destroyer picked it up on its sound gear and closed to 12,000 yards, but, for some unknown reason, the destroyer turned away. Obviously, the destroyer's captain was unable to evaluate what had happened.[11]

Meanwhile, the *Darter*'s situation grew desperate. The tide was low; water barely covered the reef. Moving in the gloomy darkness at a speed of 17 knots when she crashed, the *Darter*'s hull was now stuck hard and fast high on the reef. All efforts to clear her were unsuccessful. Therefore, McClintock ordered all classified papers burned and secret equipment destroyed as Japanese aircraft roared overhead in the dark evening sky. At any moment a Japanese warship might come swooping down on the helpless submarine. She was trapped as surely as a fly in amber.

McClintock radioed for help, so the *Dace* broke off stalking the *Takao* and answered the *Darter*'s pleas for assistance. The *Dace* slowly and carefully edged as near the *Darter* as possible. A line was thrown to the stranded boat. Waiting for high tide at 2:46 A.M., they tried detaching the boat using all available means. But nothing worked. By 3:45 A.M., the *Dace* was almost 50 yards from the *Darter*'s stern, and threw over yet another line, but they could not pull the boat free. Defeated, the two submarines launched their rubber boats and began moving the grounded submarine's crew to the *Dace*.

McClintock knew it was almost a certainty that the Japanese would board his boat soon after he abandoned it. He glanced at a Japanese ship model of the *Atago* on the wardroom's wall, which the crew had used for recognition drills. Grabbing a sheet of paper, he scrawled, "Was this the one?" and leaned the paper against the model. Then, in keeping with the time-honored tradition that the captain is the last to leave his ship, McClintock climbed into a rubber boat and paddled across the water to the *Dace*.

Before the *Darter*'s men took their leave, they set some demolition charges to detonate the torpedoes' warheads. The fuses were set to blow up the warheads at 4:55 A.M. The *Dace*'s log had a 4:50 A.M. entry noting, "Heard slight explosion but could see no damage."[12]

The first attempt to destroy the *Darter* had failed. Claggett tried to sink her by firing four torpedoes into the hull, but they exploded harmlessly on the reef. The *Dace* fired thirty 4-inch shells into the *Darter* along its waterline, but the doomed submarine was too high on the reef so the shells had no effect at all.

Dawn was appearing in the eastern skies on October 24, and daylight provided a clearer view of the scene. As a Japanese aircraft flew overhead, the *Dace*'s gunners dropped their ammunition and scrambled into the conning tower. The hatch closed briskly, and the boat crash-dived. The *Dace* was not hit because the plane bombed the *Darter* instead.

But the hapless American submarine was not easily destroyed. By midmorning, a Japanese destroyer had moved near the reef and remained nearby. Although planes hovered above in an effort to protect the destroyer, the *Dace* had no more torpedoes and could not attack the tempting target. Looking through the periscope's eyepiece, Claggett and McClintock watched as Japanese sailors boarded the stranded submarine. For safety's sake, Claggett kept the *Dace* at a safe distance from the Japanese ship. Although they were not certain, they believed the Japanese removed some communications equipment.

When it was safe after dark, Claggett surfaced the *Dace* and moved toward the grounded submarine. He wanted to use his own demolition supplies to apply the coup de grâce; but, his sound men heard Japanese "pinging" as the *Dace* moved close to the *Darter*. It sounded like a Japanese submarine, and the Americans turned to meet the new threat.

Then the sea suddenly became silent. Later that night, the *Dace* sent a radio message asking for help in destroying the *Darter* and for authorization to head for Fremantle in Australia. Permission to leave the area arrived shortly afterward.

The *Dace* was a crowded boat when the *Darter*'s crew came aboard. The addition of eighty-one passengers included an officer for whom Claggett had been best man at his wedding and the brother of a *Dace* crewman. The *Dace* now was carrying almost double her normal complement with 165 officers and men on board. All Claggett could do was tell the *Darter*'s men to pick one place and remain there—except when they had to use the head.

Because the *Dace*'s mess had only enough space for her crew, the *Darter*'s crew's meals were brought to them where they were. Some of the *Dace*'s men shared the available bunks, but other newcomers had to sleep on empty torpedo skids and other makeshift arrangements to pass the time. The *Darter*'s officers played poker continuously. Lieutenant Wilkinson of the *Darter*, and the biggest winner aboard, had brought with him a little book in which he kept score. If an officer stayed in the game, he could have a seat, and Ernie Schwab noted later, "The only way I can get a seat in the damned boat is to buy it, and I intend to sit on a cushion from here to Australia no matter how much it hurts my pocketbook." By the end of the eleven-day trip, everyone had to eat mushroom soup and peanut-butter sandwiches, as food supplies had been almost exhausted. Still the men kept in good spirits.

Claggett remarked, "I couldn't get Commander McClintock out of my bunk for the rest of the trip except for poker." However, Lt. R. C. (Mike) Benitez, the *Dace*'s executive officer, said later, "We were happy. Few submarines had done what we had done." The *Dace* and *Darter* together had sunk two Japanese heavy cruisers and heavily damaged another. A severe crimp had been put in the Japanese plan to storm the Leyte beaches and to wreak havoc on the American invasion.

While the *Dace* continued to Fremantle, the Americans sent the submarine *Rock* to Bombay Shoal to destroy the grounded *Darter*. Futilely, she fired ten torpedoes at her, but they exploded against the intervening reef. On October 31, the navy's largest submarine, the *Nautilus*, arrived on the scene with orders to destroy the *Darter*. Its gunners fired fifty-five 6-inch shells at point-blank range into the *Darter*. The *Nautilus*'s commanding officer stated in his patrol report, "It is doubtful that any equipment in *Darter* would be of value to Japan—except as scrap."[13]

A gallant submarine's life had ended. However, she did not lie alone in these dangerous waters off Palawan Island. The *Darter* had plenty of company. Not too far from the submarine's shallow grave were the remains of Kurita's former flagship, the *Atago*, and the Japanese heavy cruiser, the *Maya*. The *Takao*, meanwhile, after receiving repairs enough to continue without towing, returned to Lingga Roads, permanently out of the war with a wrecked engine. On the other side of the equation, the Americans had been truly fortunate during the Battle of Leyte Gulf's opening gambit. Not one American submariner lost his life. All hands arrived safely in Fremantle with the earned right to jubilantly celebrate their great victory over the Japanese's Center Force.[14]

The *Darter*'s and the *Dace*'s crews had set the stage for the Battle of Leyte Gulf. Vice Admiral Kurita had much to face in the Sibuyan Sea. However, the Americans were about to experience some misfortune of their own, when, for a while, Japanese airpower would make its presence felt in the eastern waters off the Philippines.

Chapter 6: The Americans Lose a Great Lady

While Kurita's Center Force steamed through the Sibuyan Sea, other air attacks took place on October 24, one of which inflicted the heaviest loss the Americans sustained during the Battle of Leyte Gulf.

Planes from RAdm. Forrest Sherman's Task Group 38.3's carriers commenced air attacks against the Japanese airfields on Luzon. As the American planes attacked the Japanese, they defended themselves with determination and grit. However, the Japanese were not strictly on the defensive.

While the Americans attacked Japanese targets on Luzon, Japanese land-based aircraft launched a counterattack on Sherman's force. Executing their part of the SHO-1 plan that included the use of land-based aircraft against the American fleet, they launched three separate air attacks, each having fifty to sixty aircraft. However, the Americans intercepted the incoming planes in such a way as to again prove their mastery of the air surrounding the Philippine Islands.

The first American planes to intercept the attacking Japanese were seven Hellcat fighters launched from the fleet carrier *Essex*, led by Cmdr. David McCampbell, the *Essex*'s Air Group commander. As his flight group conducted Combat Air Patrol operations, McCampbell spied a formation of at least sixty Japanese fighters, bombers, and torpedo-bombers at 8:33 A.M. From a position high above the approaching Japanese, his relatively small force had the altitude advantage and was able to dive down on the unsuspecting Japanese pilots. McClintock and his fellow pilots, flying in sections of two and five planes, attacked the highest-flying Japanese fighters first and shot them down. The Japanese bombers then retreated through an overcast cloud cover and escaped, while the Japanese fighters began revolving in a small, tight circle.

McCampbell and his wingman, Lt. (jg) Kenneth Rushing, maintained their altitude advantage and waited for the orbiting Japanese fighters to cease circling. When they did, the two American pilots attacked, inflicting heavy losses. McCampbell later recalled the action:

> In the next hour or so, we followed the formation of the weaving fighters, taking advantage of every opportunity to knock off those who attempted to climb to our altitude, scissored outside, straggled or became too eager and came to us singly. In all we made 18 or 20 passes, being very careful not to expose ourselves and to conserve ammunition by withholding our fire until within very close range. After following the decimated formation nearly all the way to Manila—there were 18 enemy planes left in the formation when we broke off—we returned, nearly exhausted of ammunition and so near fuel exhaustion we had barely enough gas to taxi out of the arresting gear.[1]

McCampbell shot down at least nine planes, Rushing got six, and the other five pilots destroyed at least two aircraft apiece, which did not include some they failed to see splash into the ocean. McCampbell's group continued their attack for ninety-five minutes but had to stop when their fuel ran low. They broke off their assaults and returned instead to the safety of the carrier *Langley*, rather than the *Essex*.

The light carrier *Princeton*'s Air Group had a similar success, taking a heavy toll on attacking Japanese aircraft. Just as the American planes were landing on the carrier's deck, however, a single Japanese bomber pilot circled above the low overcast and waited for his chance. At 9:38 A.M., he saw a break in the clouds, dove his plane through it, and skillfully released a single 550-pound bomb. The missile crashed into the *Princeton*'s flight deck on the port side amidships, penetrated three decks, and exploded in the ship's bakery, instantly killing three bakers. A massive blast set off a dangerous gasoline fire in the hangar deck. The flames entered the open bomb bay doors of six Avenger bombers that were waiting to rearm and refuel. One by one, several torpedoes in the planes' bomb bays exploded, tossing the 25-foot forward elevator nearly mast high. The elevator fell back into the hole left by the explosion. The concussion caused by the falling hunk of steel blew the after elevator onto the flight deck. The *Princeton*'s skipper, Capt. William H. Buracker, ordered damage control parties to try to save the ship and ordered all but 490 men to abandon ship.

The sun came out from behind some clouds as a 15-to-20-knot breeze stirred the water's surface. A ground swell began while the *Princeton* floated almost dead in the water, heading into the wind. Hundreds of men assembled on the flight deck's forward end, the site farthest from the explosions. At 9:53 A.M., Admiral Sherman ordered the destroyers *Gatling, Irwin,* and *Cassin Young* to stand by while the rest of the carrier group left the immediate area. The *Irwin* tried to draw near the *Princeton*'s forecastle, but the overhang of the carrier's guns stopped its approach. Lieutenant Richard M. Jackson, responsible for the maintenance of the *Princeton*'s aircraft, witnessed the impending tragedy and described the transfer of some of the men:

> Many men jumped or went down lines from the flight deck into the water and swam the narrow path to the cargo nets hanging on the destroyer's side. The eccentric wave action between the ships made this, for some, a nightmare of swimming the gap, many times only to be thrown back just as fingers clutched for the nets. Equally disconcerting was the site of five to ten men slopped together in a single wave, catching the net simultaneously, and then the stronger climbing over the weaker. A number drowned in this mess, although most climbed the nets successfully with the help of the destroyer's crew. Others drifted aft of ships and with the help of machine-gun fire from the destroyers fantail eluded sharks and were picked up by their boats.

The *Irwin* finally closed the distance to the hapless carrier so men could actually jump from the pitching carrier's decks to the even worse pitching destroyer's decks. Jackson continues his recollections of this point in the transfer:

> Badly burned members of the "black gang" had felt their way up to the forecastle, and several of us assisted in tossing them across the momentarily narrow gap to waiting hands on the destroyer's

bow. This was much more difficult than it sounds, because the two bows were rising and falling at different rates, causing a constantly changing vertical depth from minus 3 feet to plus 10 feet. Also, the bow of the destroyer at that point was only about 3 feet wide.[2]

At 10:04 A.M., the light cruiser *Birmingham* also joined the crippled carrier, making her commanding officer, Capt. Thomas B. Inglis, the senior officer on the scene. After carefully considering the best way to rescue the *Princeton*'s men, he ordered the light cruiser *Reno* to provide protection against any aircraft attack and directed the destroyers to remove as many men from the water as possible. Inglis used his own ship to fight the raging fires on the carrier because the cruiser was the best equipped ship for this hazardous task.

The *Birmingham* replaced the *Irwin* and the *Cassin Young* on the carrier's weather bow. At 10:55 A.M., a line was thrown from the *Birmingham* to the burning carrier. Hoses immediately followed. A volunteer firefighting party of thirty-eight men, under the command of Lt. Alan Reed, went aboard the carrier to help with salvage operations. Lieutenant Commander H. B. Stebbings, the *Princeton*'s first lieutenant, and the air operations officer, Lt. Cmdr. J. M. Large, directed the damage-control party in its valiant efforts to bring the roaring fires under control. The destroyer *Morrison*, which had picked up about 400 survivors, also came to the *Princeton*'s lee side to send engineers aboard to help fight the fires. The destroyer's foremast and stack were crushed when they became wedged between two of the carrier's air uptakes, located about halfway between the carrier's bow and stern. Heavy debris, including some vehicles, plummeted onto the destroyer's decks. A jeep and an electric airplane tractor fell on her bridge, then bounced off the main deck. Meanwhile, the *Irwin* moved in closer and came to the *Morrison*'s rescue. Several towlines broke while attempting to remove the *Morrison* from the chaos, but the *Irwin* managed to move the *Morrison*'s bow a few feet so that the damaged destroyer could clear itself under her own power.

The cruiser *Reno*, after providing protection against aircraft attack, also spent an hour trying to help the *Princeton* fight the raging fires, but now Japanese aircraft attacked again. The *Reno* left the *Princeton*'s side at 12:12 P.M. to resume defending against the oncoming Japanese airplanes. The *Birmingham* had been battered while assisting the *Princeton* in putting out the raging flames. After more than two and a half hours of struggle in a rough sea, it appeared that the fires were under control.

At 1:30 the *Birmingham*'s sonar reported a submarine contact, and Inglis reluctantly ordered his cruiser to leave the carrier's side.

The Japanese air attack utterly failed, however. It originated from Ozawa's carriers and was the only air attack Ozawa attempted that day. The Japanese planes split into groups. Hellcat fighters from the fleet carrier *Lexington*, positioned 45 miles northeast of Admiral Sherman's main body, intercepted one group. Radar detected the other large group of approaching Japanese airplanes about 90 miles to the northeast. Only a few of these planes penetrated the American Combat Air Patrol, and six to eight aircraft made ineffective attacks on the *Lexington*, *Essex*, and *Langley*.

By 2:45 P.M., the air attack came to an end. In the meanwhile, the sound contact reported by the *Birmingham* turned out to be nothing at all.

The *Birmingham* then moved back to the *Princeton*'s weather beam and sent some of her firefighters aboard again. While the cruiser defended the damaged carrier against the Japanese air attack, the carrier's firefighting parties made good progress in bringing the fires under control. However, there was one blaze the fire crews could not douse. It approached the torpedo storage compartment to the rear of the hangar, where extra bombs were stored, making the *Princeton*'s skipper apprehensive.

The wind's velocity increased to 20 knots and the sea's swell increased also. Captain Buracker asked the *Reno* to tow the *Princeton*, but the cruiser had no towing gear on board. After some discussion between Captains Inglis and Buracker over the TBS (talk between ships), the two captains decided to move the *Birmingham* closer to the *Princeton* to give as much aid as possible until the fires could be extinguished. The plan was for the *Reno* to act as a tugboat to push the *Princeton* to safety. As the *Reno* closed at 3:23 P.M., a colossal explosion from the carrier's torpedo stowage struck, blowing off most of the carrier's stern and an entire section of its rear flight deck. Steel debris poured all over the *Birmingham* while her topside was crowded with firefighters, antiaircraft gunners, and sailors trying to pass lines in preparation for towing the carrier.

It is difficult to reconstruct the destructive, terrifying effects this tremendous explosion had on the men who experienced it, but an eyewitness account conveys the ship's agony, an agony met with equal measures of courage:

The spectacle which greeted the human eye was horrible to behold. . . . Dead, dying and wounded, many of them badly, horribly covered the decks. The communication platform was no better. Blood ran freely down the waterways, and continued to run for some time.

Said our executive officer, who inspected the ship immediately, "I really have no words at my command that can adequately describe the veritable splendor of the conduct of all hands, wounded and unwounded. Men with legs off, with arms off, with gaping wounds in their sides, with the tops of their heads furrowed with fragments, would insist, 'I'm all right. Take care of Joe over there,' or 'don't waste morphine on me, Commander; just hit me over the head.'"[3]

Amazingly, the *Birmingham* suffered only slight damage, but many of her men were either killed or wounded. After her crew buried the dead at sea, she steamed under her own power to the American West Coast, where she was repaired in time to participate in the Okinawa invasion the following March. Her fire-fighting crews had broken new paths for fire fighting on the high seas, and this hard-won experience was useful later on the carriers *Bunker Hill* and *Franklin*.

However, the *Princeton* suffered a fate far worse than that of her rescuers. Although she was still seaworthy, no more ships were available to tow her. The fires started by the massive explosion in the torpedo storage burned toward the aircraft gasoline tanks and main magazines, unflooded because of the loss of water pressure. By 4:00 P.M., the carrier's skipper, Captain Buracker, was reluctantly forced to order the damage control party to abandon ship. The destroyer *Gatling* took the remaining crew on board, and, at 4:38 P.M., Buracker left the *Princeton*. To prevent the carrier from becoming a derelict and navigational hazard and to prevent the Japanese from capturing her, Admiral Sherman ordered her torpedoed and sunk.

The *Irwin*, brimful with about 600 survivors, was given the job of performing the coup de grâce on the *Princeton*. Unfortunately, her torpedo director had been so badly damaged in the efforts to aid the *Princeton* that any attempt to fire torpedoes accurately was futile. The destroyer moved about one mile away from the dead carrier's beam and fired several torpedoes manually. The first one hit the *Princeton*'s bow. The second missed astern. A third porpoised, broached, and headed directly back toward the *Irwin*. Its Captain ordered flank speed and hard left rudder. The wayward "fish" passed about 30 feet away on a parallel course. The fourth and fifth torpedoes missed as well. A sixth torpedo followed the same path as the third, missing the *Irwin* by an even narrower distance. The *Reno* sent two torpedoes toward the carrier approximately one minute apart. The first hit just below the forward gasoline tank, and about 100 thousand gallons exploded into a roaring flame, blowing the *Princeton* to bits. At 6:00 P.M., all that remained of the gallant carrier was an enormous cloud.

An unfortunate series of events ended the saga of this valiant carrier and her crew. An opportunistic blow by a single Japanese pilot had caused the carrier's demise. This would be the only major loss the Americans would suffer at the Battle of Leyte Gulf. The same could not be said for the oncoming Japanese ships now approaching Leyte by way of the Sibuyan Sea.[4]

USS *Essex*. Among planes on deck are SBDs, F6Fs, and TBMs.

Grumman F4F Wildcat Fighters fly in tactical formation of four-plane divisions. The planes are wearing the red-outlined national insignia briefly employed at that time.

Japanese battleships *Nagato* (right), *Yamato* (center), and *Musashi* (left), at Brunei, Borneo, in October 1944, just before the start of the Battle of Leyte Gulf.

Japanese fleet leaves Brunei on 22 October 1944 to take part in the Battle of Leyte Gulf.

Japanese battleship *Yamato* hit by a bomb during the Battle of the Sibuyan Sea, 24 October 1944.

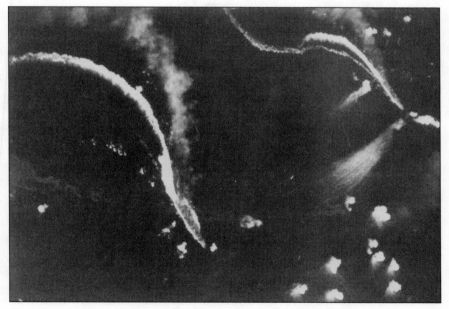

Two Japanese aircraft carriers (probably *Zuikaku* and *Zuiho*) under attack during the Battle off Cape Engaño, 24 October 1944.

A U.S. Navy ship rescues American survivors of the Battle off Samar on 26 October 1944. Some 1200 American survivors were rescued during the days following the battle. (U.S. Army photograph)

USS *Cabot*. American light carrier that took part in the Battle of Leyte Gulf.

Japanese battleship *Musashi* during the Battle of the Sibuyan Sea, 24 October 1944. The ship appears to be down at the bow and may be sinking.

Japanese battleship *Musashi* and other ships under attack during the Battle of the Sibuyan Sea, 24 October 1944.

Crewmembers of the sinking Japanese aircraft carrier *Zuikaku* salute as the naval ensign is lowered during the Battle off Cape Engaño, 25 October 1944.

Transferring Admiral Ozawa's headquarters from the sinking aircraft carrier *Zuikaku* to the light cruiser *Oyodo*, during the Battle off Cape Engaño, 25 October 1944.

Crewmembers of the sinking Japanese aircraft carrier *Zuikaku* throwing explosives over the side during the Battle off Cape Engaño.

USS *West Virginia*. American battleship sunk at Pearl Harbor and resurrected to fight at Leyte Gulf. (National Archives)

Zuikaku (Japanese aircraft carrier).

USS *Tangier*.

Japanese battleship *Musashi*, leaving Brunei in 1944, possibly just before the Battle of Leyte Gulf.

USS *Samuel B. Roberts* in October 1944, a week or two before she was lost in the Battle off Samar, 25 October 1944.

USS *Johnston*. American destroyer sunk in Battle off Samar.

Lieutenant Commander Ernest E. Evans at the commissioning ceremonies of the USS *Johnston*. Evans was *Johnston's* commanding officer from 27 October 1943 until she was sunk on 25 October 1944.

Rear Admiral David M. LeBreton presents the Navy Cross to Lt. Cmdr. Robert W. Copeland at Norfolk, Va., 16 July 1945. Lieutenant Commander Copeland received the Navy Cross for heroism while in command of the USS *Samuel B. Roberts* during the Battle off Samar, 25 October 1944.

President Franklin Delano Roosevelt, thirty-second president of the United States and commander-in-chief during almost all of World War II. (Library of Congress)

Admiral Chester Nimitz, commander-in-chief Pacific Fleet. (U.S. Naval Institute)

Vice Admiral Takeo Kurita, commander of Japanese Center Force at Leyte Gulf. (U.S. Naval Institute)

Rear Admiral Clifton A. F. Sprague, commander of Taffy 3 in Battle off Samar. (U.S. Naval Institute)

Vice Admiral Jisaburo Ozawa, commander of Japanese Northern Force at Leyte Gulf. (U.S. Naval Institute)

Rear Admiral Shoji Nishimura, commander of Force C at Battle of Surigao Strait. (U.S. Naval Institute)

General Douglas MacArthur, commander of American landing forces at Leyte. (Library of Congress)

Admiral Thomas C. Kinkaid, commander of Seventh Fleet at Leyte Gulf. (U.S. Naval Institute)

Admiral William Halsey, commander of Third Fleet at Leyte Gulf. (U.S. Naval Institute)

Chapter 7: Struggle in the Sibuyan Sea

Kurita's Center Force had survived the first attack by American submarines, but it had lost three heavy cruisers—two lay on the bottom of the Palawan Passage, the other was limping back to Brunei. But his fleet still faced a long journey, and their next milestone was the Sibuyan Sea on their way to the San Bernardino Strait. If Kurita imagined the Americans had given up their assault on his fleet, he was sadly mistaken. As the Center Force rounded Palawan Island, heading in a southeasterly direction through the Mindoro Strait, Kurita could not guess he and his command would soon experience the full fury of six American carrier-based aircraft attacks.

Where Were the Japanese Going?

Admiral Kinkaid's primary mission was to support the Leyte landings. His force had made significant strides on the way to achieving this objective, and Kinkaid was ready to transfer the responsibility for the landings to the army. However, the admiral could not make a permanent transfer of full responsibility to General MacArthur until the landings were completely successful. Meanwhile, MacArthur remained on the cruiser *Nashville*. Kinkaid was concerned about Japanese fleet movements around the Philippines. Although he knew Halsey's Third Fleet had many planes that could conduct search missions, he decided to rely on his own resources to find the Japanese. Orders went out to all submarines

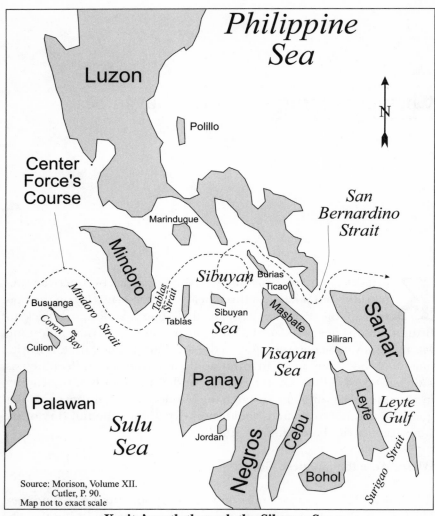

Kurita's path through the Sibuyan Sea

and other units in his command to learn the whereabouts of the Japanese navy.

Obeying Kinkaid's order, all of the Seventh Fleet's submarines assumed positions around the Philippine Islands to give early warnings of Japanese naval movements. Since major Japanese naval units were concentrated in the Brunei Bay area, Kinkaid paid particular attention to what was happening there. In cooperation with the Pacific Fleet's submarine command, he sent submarines to places off the Makassar Strait, to the entrances to the Celebes and Sulu Seas, and off Hainan and Luzon Islands. While the *Darter* and the *Dace* had considerable success in attacking Kurita's force, the Pacific Fleet's submarines pursued other targets, but failed to find Ozawa's Northern Force. Halsey was with his Third Fleet carriers east of the Philippines and intensely interested in locating the Japanese carriers and sinking them. He was supposed to receive help from land-based planes on Palau and Saipan.

The *Darter*'s message of October 23 at 2:00 A.M. reported three large ships off Palawan Passage's southern entrance and alerted American naval commanders. The submarine's first message was sent to RAdm. Ralph W. Christie in Australia. Halsey received a copy on the battleship *New Jersey* at 6:20 A.M. The mystery over the location of the Japanese heavy ships was a mystery no longer. McClintock's message is one of the most significant of the Pacific War:

> SECRET. URGENT. 108-S FOX 4253 from Task Unit 71.1.4 [*Darter*] to CTF 71: *Darter's* No. 6. Three probable battleships 0100/H [Hour] [1:00 a.m.] 23rd 08 [degrees] 28N [North] 116 [degrees] 30 [minutes] E [East], c. [course] 040 [degrees], speed 18 [knots]. Radar pips 34,000 yards. Closing.[1]

Halsey immediately launched night-flying aircraft to find the Japanese, but the ensuing air search turned up nothing.

The next morning, a continuous stream of messages flooded the radio room on Kinkaid's flagship. Another message from the *Darter* reported eleven Japanese warships. A later message from the *Darter* reported the *Atago*'s sinking and the successful torpedo hits on the *Takao*. Then the *Dace* reported sinking another big ship. Its identity was unknown; the ship was later identified as the *Maya*. The submarine *Angler* also reported a sighting of several large capital ships.

As he reviewed these events, Kinkaid grew more concerned about the Japanese fleet's movements. Although the army apparently controlled Leyte, Kinkaid had doubts about the outcome of the developing situation. The crews of the cargo ships had worked quickly to unload the massive amount of matériel the troops needed to continue with their capture of Leyte Island. Yet a dangerous scenario loomed as even more likely—an attack by strong Japanese naval units on the helpless landing ships pouring supplies onto the Leyte beaches. If some of those powerful Japanese battleships and cruisers should catch the ships where they were, the Leyte invasion could end in disaster.

However, the Americans had brought to this invasion the most powerful naval force the world had ever seen in order to ensure the success of these landings. If the Japanese fleet should appear, it was reasonable to expect its utter destruction. From Kinkaid's point of view, everything on the afternoon of October 23 was going according to plan. He had placed his three escort carrier groups along Leyte Gulf, from north to south. Halsey's four carrier groups, fast battleships, and the other supporting ships of the Third Fleet patrolled to the east. As Kinkaid examined the locations of the Third Fleet, his worries lessened. He mused, "Well, that's exactly what I would do if I were stationing these carriers myself," and he relaxed slightly.

As the evening of October 23 approached, Kinkaid became more convinced than ever that the Japanese navy planned to approach Leyte Gulf from the west to try to stop the Leyte landings. So, he sent warning messages to MacArthur, Halsey, Nimitz, and King.

However, Halsey's fleet had been at sea for a long time. They had battled Japanese air forces at Formosa, Okinawa, and Luzon, and the fleet's ships needed to replenish their supplies and give their men some rest and relaxation. Although he could not spare all his task groups at one time, Halsey could spare one group. If the Japanese should turn up, he had force enough to stop them. His chief of staff, RAdm. Robert B. (Mick) Carney, recalled some of the concerns confronting his commanding officer:

> If you will remember, beginning with the 10th of October at Okinawa, these carriers and their air groups had been fighting almost continuously for fourteen days. They needed replenishment and they needed rest in the worst way. Nevertheless, this was no time to give too great consideration to that sort of thing.[2]

Just like Kinkaid, Halsey and his men also monitored the situation carefully. On the morning and afternoon of October 22, his carrier force—Task Force 38—launched aircraft in search of the reported Japanese force covering an area from the southwest to the northeast of Leyte Gulf. The search planes soared over the Sibuyan Sea in the northwest and the waters west of Luzon for a distance of at least 100 miles. In

an effort to give relief to some of his ships, Halsey ordered Admiral Mc-
Cain's task group to proceed to Ulithi for replenishment while the three
remaining carrier groups searched nonstop for the elusive Japanese. By
the next day, the searchers had found nothing.

By October 23, more sightings by aircraft and submarines in the South
China Sea showed that the Japanese ships were west of Leyte Gulf, thus
increasing the possibility of a large-scale Japanese counterattack. However, from an American point of view, the risks to the Japanese of such
an attack were so great that it seemed hard to believe they would try it.
But by the night of the 23rd, the Americans were forced to revise this
conclusion, because it became apparent that a massive Japanese attack
was in the making. Halsey and Kinkaid decided to move closer to the
Philippines's east coast and reinforce the search across the Philippines
and into the South China Sea to find out just what were the Japanese
doing.[3]

However, Halsey had problems of his own, and these were not
known to key men serving in the Third Fleet who would have benefited
from having the information. One concerned a key commander in the
Third Fleet—VAdm. Marc Mitscher, Halsey's Task Force 38 carrier commanding officer. Mitscher had recently suffered a heart attack but was
still with the fleet. Had Nimitz and King known of Mitscher's condition,
Mitscher would have been placed on sick leave. In fact, Commodore
Arleigh Burke, Mitscher's chief of staff, tried to relieve his commander of as much detail and trouble as possible by performing much of
his work.

Halsey's staff sat around the *New Jersey*'s flag plot, contemplating the
alternatives. One thing they knew for sure was that the Japanese would
try to surprise them. By now, this was a familiar Japanese tactic. Halsey
recalled bitterly how the Japanese had surprised the Americans during
the chaotic days in the South Pacific. He was certain the Japanese would
try to use their carriers and the Luzon airfields as intermediate refueling points for shuttling aircraft to and from their land bases. Such a scenario was particularly likely because, as Mitscher recalled from the Formosa Air Battle, the Japanese air forces must have had severe logistical
problems because they were using so many different types of planes. All
these different aircraft types meant the Japanese had to keep a great variety of parts on hand near their battle locations. But their carrier
strength had been so depleted in previous battles with the Americans

that they had lost much of their supplies, which meant these aircraft had to be at Japanese land bases.

This would by no means be the first time the Japanese had launched aircraft from their carriers, touched down at land bases, and attacked American ships from there. They had done this at the battle for the Marianas Islands in June 1944. Since the Pearl Harbor debacle, the Americans had rebuilt their fleet with new big carriers, improved light carriers, and supplementary escort carriers that could guard convoys and supply planes to the carrier fleet. Thus, the fight had become a carrier war. The only hope for a Japanese victory was to sink the now seemingly omnipotent American Pacific Fleet. The only way of having a chance to do this was to throw in all the aircraft they had. If this meant stripping all aircraft from their carriers in order to attack the Americans, and thereby leave their carriers more vulnerable to attack, so be it.

Although the concerns of Halsey's staff were similar to those of Kinkaid, Halsey's staff had to focus more on strategy, evaluating what the Japanese were going to do, then make the appropriate plans. Commander Gilvin M. Slonim, Halsey's assistant intelligence officer, commented after the war:

> The normal reaction of the Japanese commander faced with an emergency was to send an operation order to his command saying, "Attack with all forces available and destroy the enemy!" Frequently such stereotyped operation orders were intercepted. When analyzed in the light of available forces many were meaningless, because the commander did not have sufficient forces to come anywhere near destroying the enemy.[4]

The time for a decision was rapidly approaching, but by October 22, Halsey's staff needed more information. Messages concerning the Japanese fleet began reaching the Third Fleet's communications centers. The first one, sent on October 23 at 2:00 A.M., was from the *Darter*, reporting its first sighting of three ships.

Even in this time of modern warfare and high-speed radio communications, it was common practice for messages to pile up in code and radio rooms, so sometimes it would take many hours before messages reached their destinations. During the Battle of Leyte Gulf, this situation was made worse because of the split command responsibility between MacArthur and Nimitz. The main decoding and retransmission facility was located on Manus Island, under MacArthur's command. The volume of American and Japanese radio traffic had grown to such an extent that it overwhelmed the communications staff on Manus. Furthermore, subconsciously, the staff would give priority to messages meant for MacArthur's command. Thus, some messages between the two command structures were subject to longer than normal delays. These delays played an important part in the upcoming battles in Leyte Gulf.

Based on the *Darter's* message, Halsey expanded the next day's air search into the Sibuyan Sea. On the morning of October 24, RAdm. Gerald F. Bogan received a message ordering his Task Group 38.2 to probe westward, including the area around Coron Bay, near the eastern approaches to the Sibuyan Sea. Halsey reasoned that the reported ships might already be in Coron Bay and ready to execute the Tokyo Express–like attacks that both Halsey and Kinkaid expected.[5]

Enemy Contacted

Many cynical American naval commanders doubted the Japanese would make an aggressive move. The *Darter's* report quickly disposed of this notion on October 23, however. Intelligence personnel decoded several dispatches that led to an inescapable conclusion. Three sizable enemy naval fleets were on their way to the Philippines. Two closed on Leyte from the west (Kurita and Shima), while a third (Ozawa) approached from the northwest. Their mission was clear: destroy the American landings and make the Americans sue for peace. Anxiously, the Americans swiftly planned their response. Who would be the victor and who the vanquished would be decided in the execution of these plans.

At sunrise of October 24, an American Helldiver dive-bomber took off from the *Intrepid,* an aircraft carrier attached to Halsey's Third Fleet and part of Admiral Bogan's Task Group 38.2. The pilot flew at 10,000 feet over the southern cape of Mindoro Island. Daylight dawned with almost unlimited visibility. The sun shown from the aircraft's rear as the pilot and the rest of his crew scanned the ocean. Islands dotted what seemed to be an almost glasslike sea. The pilot searched for what seemed to be an eternity. But then, as his eyes moved carefully across the horizon, they abruptly encountered an awesome spectacle. It was

Admiral Kurita's Center Force with the world's largest battleships, moving at a north-by-northeast heading, rounding Mindoro Island's southern tip, and entering the Tablas Strait. The large formation appeared to be on course for the Sibuyan Sea and heading for the San Bernardino Strait.

The American pilot glanced down at his watch, which registered 8:22 A.M. He picked up his radio's microphone, making the plane's radio crackle to life: "The force consists of 4 BB [battleships], 8 CA [cruisers], 13 DD [destroyers]. Location is south of southern tip Mindoro, course 050, speed 10–12 knots. No transports in the group, in all a total of 25 warships."[6]

The sighting report immediately reached Halsey's headquarters, where Halsey's first impulse was to direct the Third Fleet through the San Bernardino Strait and engage the Japanese in a surface action. However, naval intelligence had predicted that these waters were heavily mined, and Halsey knew that Admiral Nimitz's orders did not allow him to take such an action. The next logical alternative was to attack the approaching Japanese fleet by deploying aircraft from the Third Fleet's powerful carriers.[7]

Halsey's tendency to take immediate action would not be denied, however. Only five minutes after receiving the sighting, he sent orders directly to his task group commanders. He had four stalwart, fast carrier task groups under his command, but one of them (McCain's Task Group 38.1) was on its way to the Ulithi Atoll, an island group many hundreds of miles to the south and east of the Philippines.

As of October 24, the number of ships and ship types for each task group in Halsey's Third Fleet was as follows:[8]

Commander Task Group	Fleet Carriers	Light Carriers	Battleships	Heavy Cruisers	Light Cruisers	Destroyers	Totals
McCain (38.1)	3	2	0	4	2	21	32
Bogan (38.2)	1	2	2	0	3	18	26
Sherman (38.3)	2	1	3	0	3	10	19
Davison (38.4)	2	2	1	2	0	12	19
TOTALS	8	7	6	6	8	61	96

The appearance of the Japanese force apparently came as a surprise to Halsey, and it caused him to make a swift change of tactics. He realized at once that the only possible explanation for these ships in this location was that they were on course to enter the Sibuyan Sea, steam through the San Bernardino Strait, and attack the American landings from the north. Halsey ordered the sighting report to be forwarded immediately to his commanders. Admirals Sherman and Davison received orders to rapidly cut their task groups' distance to the San Bernardino Strait.[9]

By noon on October 24, three fast carrier groups were deployed on a broad front: one group (Sherman) to the north, the second (Bogan) off the San Bernardino Strait, and the third (Davison) 60 miles south of Samar. The Americans readied themselves for the first of four major engagements in the struggle for Leyte Gulf: an air-surface battle called the Battle of the Sibuyan Sea.[10]

The Sibuyan Sea Starts to Boil

October 23 was a miserable day for Admiral Kurita. His force had lost three heavy cruisers to American submarine attacks. Then, as though fate had pierced him with an arrow, one of the lost ships, the *Atago*, was his flagship. Because of this loss, he had suffered the indignity of spending time in a lifeboat in the waters of the Palawan Passage before being rescued by one of his destroyers. It then took some time for him to make his way to the battleship *Yamato* and transfer his flag there.

His fleet had traveled north, then northeast, and steamed southwest through the Mindoro Strait between Coron Bay and Mindoro Island. After midnight, Kurita ordered a change of course to the southeast. On October 24, at 6:25 A.M., the Center Force was rounding Mindoro Island's southern tip on course toward the Sibuyan Sea on its way to the San Bernardino Strait. Despite the problems he had encountered up to this time, he had orders to keep going, because the life of the empire was at stake.

The disastrous submarine attacks on Admiral Kurita's force on October 23 had obliged Admiral Toyoda's Combined Fleet headquarters in Japan to reexamine the beleaguered admiral's situation. After assembling the information fragments that came in from a number of sources, Toyoda's staff sent out a restatement of Kurita's orders, which read as follows:

It is very probable that the enemy is aware of the fact that we have concentrated our forces. He will probably act in the following manner:

1. Concentrate submarines in great strength in the San Bernardino and Surigao Straits areas.

2. Plan attacks on our surface forces, using large type planes and task forces, after tomorrow morning [October 24].

3. Plan decisive action by concentrating his surface strength in the area east of San Bernardino Strait and Tacloban where he has his transport group. He should be able to dispose himself in this manner by afternoon of 24th.

Our plans:

1. Carry through our original plans.

2. In effecting the operations, the following points are specially emphasized:

(a) Make up for our inferior surface strength by making every effort to direct the enemy to the north toward the Main Body of the Mobile Force [Northern Force].

(b) Maintain an even stricter alert against submarines and aircraft. Utilize every possible trick to keep enemy submarines under control, particularly while breaking through the narrow strait.

(c) Destroy enemy task force carriers with our shore-based planes, while his carrier-based planes are engaging our surface forces.

On the afternoon of October 23, the Japanese feared American submarines more than American airpower because their Center Force had already lost three heavy cruisers to these deadly denizens of the deep. The Combined Fleet now placed the utmost emphasis on luring the American Third Fleet to the north, a deception that would bring the American carriers within range of the potent Japanese air forces on Luzon Island.

The Japanese Second Air Fleet flew from Formosa to Manila bearing its orders. The Second Air Fleet's operations officer, Cmdr. Mariyoshi Yamaguchi, reiterated: "The first mission [of the Second Air Fleet] was to attack the Task Force [Halsey's Third Fleet] and wipe out the American

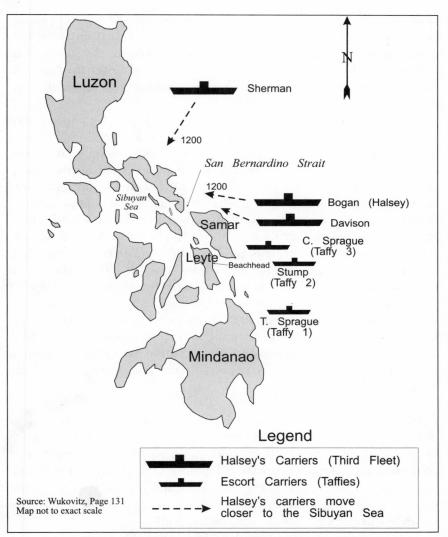

Luzon

Sherman

N

1200

San Bernardino Strait

1200

Sibuyan
Sea

Bogan (Halsey)

Davison

Samar

C. Sprague
(Taffy 3)

Leyte — Beachhead

Stump
(Taffy 2)

T. Sprague
(Taffy 1)

Mindanao

Legend

Halsey's Carriers (Third Fleet)

Escort Carriers (Taffies)

Halsey's carriers move
closer to the Sibuyan Sea

Source: Wukovitz, Page 131
Map not to exact scale

Placement of American carriers, Oct. 24, 1944

landing force in Leyte Gulf. The second mission would be to fight back the Army Landing Force."[11]

These orders did not specifically mention providing Kurita's force with protection, and there were not enough planes to both protect the approaching Japanese naval forces and to attack the Third Fleet. Conceptually, the Japanese air attack plan did not differ from what its air-power advocates had promoted in the past. Yet, at this stage of the war, a large gap now existed between what was feasible for the Japanese to achieve and what its planners wanted. At a conceptual level, the Japanese plan to destroy the American carriers was sound only as long as sufficient airpower existed, which was not the case.

Some experts might well wonder whether the Japanese planners were aware that there was a big discrepancy between what they hoped for and what was possible for them to achieve. It appears, however, that the single "big battle" idea had exerted such a hypnotic hold on the senior Japanese naval officers that they were unable to conceive any other way of viewing the situation. Even if what they planned was impossible to achieve, their blind spot was in reality a bog of quicksand, and it kept them from realizing that their plan was based on nothing more substantial than hopes and dreams. By blindly insisting on continuing along a path fraught with peril for the men who had to walk it to the bitter end, the Japanese planners clung to false hopes that constituted a betrayal of the truth and of millions of their own people.

On October 24, aircraft, which Kurita believed would protect him, left Clark Field on a hunt for American submarines. But as soon as they drew near the American carrier-based planes, these aircraft were torn to pieces. It was as though they were mere flies caught in the jaws of a hurricane.

When Kurita moved from the destroyer *Kishinami* to the battleship *Yamato* in the Palawan Passage, he breathed a sigh of relief. He had not been able to talk directly with his fleet on the *Kishinami* because its only communication devices consisted of light blinkers. Yet problems also existed on the *Yamato*. Half of the communications personnel had gone down with the *Atago*, and this loss would handicap Kurita's ability later on while directing his fleet in the coming battle.

As his force headed through the Sibuyan Sea that early morning of October 24, Kurita knew he would be encountering American forces in only a few hours; therefore, his ships would need an air umbrella for protection. Still unknown to Kurita, the Japanese plan called for their planes to attack the Americans, not to defend their Center Force. Thus, when Kurita asked Manila for fighters from its Fifth Base Air Force and newly arrived Second Air Fleet, his message was heard clearly, as battle communications between Kurita and Japanese headquarters around Manila were good. But the hoped for aircraft never showed up. The fact is, however, that Kurita had never really expected them to come, because there had never been good cooperation between the Japanese navy and army.

Furthermore, the severe aircraft shortage was now causing Vice Admiral Ohnishi to think of adopting desperate measures—launching kamikaze attacks instead of providing air cover for Kurita's fleet. Army planes would not be coming either. The relationships between the Japanese army and navy on the operational level were so fragmentary that no naval officer knew how many army planes—if any—might be sent out. In any event, the Japanese command organization, such as it was, stopped Kurita from directly asking the army for help, despite the fact that Japanese army units had been placed under naval operational control.

The first warning of what Kurita was about to face came early on the morning of October 24, when Manila reported the morning air strikes on and around the Luzon airfields. Kurita knew it would not be long before the Americans attacked his force, too. Soon after the Manila report, his radar picked up blips showing American planes were approximately 60 to 70 miles away.[12]

The Americans Strike Through the Air

Halsey's first wave of attack planes found the Japanese Center Force at 10:26 A.M. on October 24, and this act set in motion the Battle of the Sibuyan Sea.

Kurita had made certain that the Japanese fleet's formation was optimized for defense against air attacks. Their mighty ships were steaming in two concentric circles, with the huge battleship *Yamato* at the center. The battleships *Musashi* and *Nagato*, accompanied by three cruisers, sailed in a 2-kilometer diameter circle. The second circle was made up of seven destroyers; it steamed at a distance of 3½ kilometers from the *Yamato*.

Although the Center Force possessed an awesome antiaircraft defense system, it was not as modern as that of the American navy. The primary Japanese antiaircraft weapons were twin 12.7 centimeter (5-inch) guns. The *Musashi* had twelve of these and the *Yamato* had twice as many, twenty-four. These guns could fire up to fourteen rounds a minute and reach aircraft flying as high as 31,000 feet. Every ship in the force had numerous 25mm cannons. The *Yamato* had 152; the *Musashi* 130; the

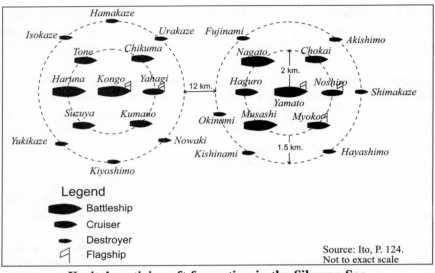

Kurita's antiaircraft formation in the Sibuyan Sea

cruisers had as many as 90; the destroyers carried up to 40 each. These cannons could only fire at a relatively slow rate, but each ship also had many 13mm machine guns.

The *Musashi* and *Yamato*'s 18.1-inch guns could also be used for anti-aircraft defense, because the two huge battleships carried *san shiki* shells, which also carried the nickname "Beehive." Each released hundreds of cylindrically shaped incendiary shrapnel shells when exploded by a time fuse. However, the 18.1-inch guns created special problems. When fired, the ultrahigh pressure created by the muzzle blast could knock unconscious a man within 50 feet of the big guns. Also, continuous use of the *san shiki* shells could severely damage the rifling of these guns, thus rendering them useless when needed in a surface battle. Therefore, the Japanese only used these shells as a last resort, after most of the other guns could no longer function. While the Japanese sailors manning all these antiaircraft guns were primed to put up a reasonable defense in facing the American Third Fleet, the American carrier aircraft forces, in the end, would prove to be too numerous and potent to be severely damaged by Japanese antiaircraft fire.

The loss of the *Princeton* had not been good news for the Americans, but the loss of one carrier was not a major setback, given the enormous power concentrated in the American navy and Halsey's naturally aggressive nature. The oncoming Center Force constituted a clear threat to the Leyte invasion. Therefore, Halsey sent orders by radio to Admiral Mitscher, commander of Task Force 38, on board his flagship, the fleet carrier *Lexington*. These orders read: "Assume Com Task Group 38.3 [under Adm. Forrest Sherman's command] is striking large enemy force Mindoros. Advise results of strike earliest possible."[13]

The Americans did not have all their carrier groups ready for an attack on the oncoming Japanese surface fleet, which had rounded Mindoro Island and headed into the Sibuyan Sea. As noted earlier, VAdm. John S. McCain's Task Group 38.1 had been sent to Ulithi Atoll for supplies and rest and relaxation. Admiral Sherman's Task Group 38.3 was too far north for its aircraft to reach the Sibuyan Sea and return at this time and was still recovering from the loss of the *Princeton*. Task Group 38.4, under RAdm. Ralph E. Davison's command, had steamed farther south than Bogan's Task Group 38.2 and could not respond until 1:13 P.M. to Halsey's orders to attack. Davison's aircraft found another Japanese naval force (Nishimura's Force C) in the Surigao Strait to the south and attacked it. Another one of Davison's search flights discovered two destroyers near Negros Island and attacked them. Therefore, Davison could not add support to Bogan's attacking force until he had recovered all his planes. If Davison moved his carriers prior to recovering his aircraft, the aircraft would not have been able to find their way back to their home ships before running out of fuel. Thus, Bogan's carrier group was the only one immediately available, so it had to make the first attack alone.

However, Bogan's group also was not up to full carrier strength. The carrier *Bunker Hill* was on its way back to Manus Island, and the *Independence* was being held in reserve for night action because she was the only carrier with planes, crews, and onboard equipment capable of conducting night searches. But Bogan did have at his disposal two remaining carriers, the *Intrepid* and the *Cabot*, and he used them to attack the oncoming Japanese force.

Excitement mounted in the Third Fleet's various Combat Information Centers (CICs). Bogan informed Halsey at 8:37 A.M. that he had forty-five planes ready to take off from the *Intrepid* and the *Cabot* to go after the newly discovered ships. Halsey's immediate reply—"Attack repeat Attack"—echoed an earlier command he had given to his beleaguered carriers during the dark days in the South Pacific after he became supreme commander: "Strike rpt [repeat] Strike!"

Halsey's crisp words stirred cheers in every ship in the fleet, especially among the men assigned to Mitscher's Flag Plot, inspiring them to listen intently on all radio frequencies for whatever reports the crews might send.

The *Intrepid* and the *Cabot* launched the first strike of forty-two planes (twenty-one fighters, twelve dive-bombers, and nine torpedo bombers) just after 9:00 A.M. The *Cabot*'s planes took off at 9:15 and rendezvoused with the *Intrepid*'s planes and the *Intrepid*'s strike coordinator, Lt. Cmdr. William Ellis. The torpedo bombers climbed to an elevation of 12,000 feet and flew in a loose V formation just beneath the dive-bombers. One division of the *Cabot*'s fighters flew at 14,000 feet, and the other flew at 16,000 feet.

Ellis radioed that he had assembled his force and was now heading west. Approaching the Center Force from the northwest, his attack formation was 25 miles northeast of the Japanese ships' position. As the American planes drew closer, they found the Japanese ships had moved into two circular formations—their standard antiaircraft defensive pattern.

At 10:26 A.M., the spectacle that lay below Ellis was one no American naval aviator had seen since Midway. The clear visibility over the Sibuyan Sea made the sighting all the easier. Although broken clouds were floating at 5,000 feet, Ellis saw the formation clearly, and what an awesome sight it was!

Below him lay a giant fleet of approximately twenty-five ships, on a course of 45 degrees at an estimated speed of 18 knots. A destroyer screen of about twelve ships encircled the group. Inside the destroyers' circle were two columns of four cruisers each. Three or four battleships steamed in a single column in the group's center. Two appeared to be Yamato-class battleships, while the other battleships seemed to be Kongo-class vessels.

This was the first time the Americans had seen the super battleships *Yamato* and *Musashi*. They were bigger than the America's largest battleships, the *Iowa* and the *New Jersey*. The Americans had heard that these giant ships carried 18.1-inch guns, larger than their own 16-inchers and able to shoot farther. Mammoth pagoda-shaped superstructures towered above the behemoths' armored decks. These great ships bristled with 110 guns, including 5-inch secondary batteries and machine guns that stuck out like pincushion pins from almost every corner of their superstructures. The antiaircraft gunfire these ships could send into the sky could form an impenetrable wall.[14]

• • •

Ellis received instructions for the attack by radio. Relaying these instructions, he ordered the planes to surround the fleet on all sides. The *Cabot*'s torpedo planes received orders to attack the leading battleship from its starboard side. The carrier's fighters not carrying bombs were directed to strafe the ships on the Japanese formation's starboard side.

The signal to attack crackled in the pilots' earphones. Lieutenant Alfred John Fecke, who commanded the *Cabot*'s fighters flying at 16,000 feet, ordered his pilots into a 70-degree dive. Moving from the southwest to northeast, they crossed the large Japanese formation's starboard side. Although vicious fire rose from the ships, the fighters kept coming, seemingly unstoppable. Firing from 3,000 feet, Fecke strafed a Japanese destroyer and pulled hard on the stick to climb upward. Another fighter, flown by Lt. John Thompson, followed immediately after, made a high-speed dive at 430 knots, and strafed what looked like a Tone-class heavy cruiser. The American plane moved from the cruiser's starboard quarter to its port bow, fired as the plane dove from 6,000 to 3,000 feet, and pulled up at 3,000 feet. Lieutenant (jg) Earl B. Sonner and Ens. Robert L. Buchanan followed their leader, strafed the Japanese destroyer, made a sharp turn, and escaped through a thick antiaircraft fusillade. After completing their strafing runs, these fighters headed toward a rendezvous point 20 miles away.

The *Cabot*'s planes were by no means through, however. Lieutenant Uncas Fretwell's division, flying at 14,000 feet, received an order to strafe the Japanese ships after the bombers attacked. The dive-bombers would zoom in first, followed by the torpedo bombers. The radio belonging to the intermediate cover fighters' leader stopped working for no apparent reason. Using hand signals, Fretwell ordered Ens. Melvin Cozzens to lead their strafing attack. The fighters approached from south to north and attacked without delay. Diving through the intense antiaircraft fire, Cozzens spotted a Kongo-class battleship and changed course to head straight for it. Firing as he dove from 8,000 to 1,500 feet, he raked the big warship from stern to bow. Fretwell also strafed the battleship, which steamed on a course of 30 degrees and pulled out at 2,000 feet. Lieutenant (jg) Bernard Dunn and Ens. W. H. Turner strafed a destroyer from bow to starboard quarter. As they made a sharp turn to leave the battle scene, the *Cabot*'s fighter pilots saw a bomb strike the battleship on its aft starboard side. They also saw a fighter, which had just completed a strafing run, burst into flames and crash into the water ahead of the ship. The pilot did not appear to escape.

While flying toward the rendezvous area, these two pilots saw Lt. John Wesley Williams from the *Cabot*'s Torpedo Squadron 29 land in the water about 10 miles south of Marinduque Island. The fighter's leader returned to the location of the downed American plane and joined the other pilots. The three fighters circled over the spot for twenty minutes, then saw Williams and his two crewmen, James Eugene Boland and Bronislaw Lawrence Raczynski, waving from their rubber boat. The planes were running out of fuel and had no choice but to return to their carrier base. The remainder of the *Cabot*'s fighters gathered together and escorted the bombers and torpedo planes back to the carrier.

Fanning out of the attack formation, the *Cabot*'s torpedo bomber pilots moved into a side-by-side formation to the right and began a gliding approach toward the Japanese ships, flying through a cloud cover to screen their path. Individually, the planes assaulted the ships, which were off the planes' starboard bow and still steaming straight ahead. However, the ships had slowed to about 23 knots and begun sending up a withering barrage of antiaircraft fire.

Lieutenant Randy McPherson led the formation that stormed the leading battleship. Lieutenant Raymond Anderson followed next. When Anderson emerged from the clouds, he could not get into alignment for an attack on the battleship, so he targeted what appeared to be a heavy cruiser. The ship was leading the battleships on the formation's port beam. He pointed his plane toward the ship's starboard beam, directing his aim one and one-half ship lengths ahead of its bow. As he approached the cruiser and passed across the leading battleship's bow, his turret gunner strafed the battleship. Anderson launched his torpedo, and as the torpedo bomber left the scene, its gunner spotted an explosion amidships on the cruiser's starboard side.

Lieutenant (jg) Howard H. Skidmore flew his plane at the leading battleship's starboard beam and released his torpedo, but he was not able to see the outcome. As his bomber attacked the battleship, his gunner saw two bombs from American dive-bombers hit the second Yamato-class battleship. The first bomb struck between the superstructure and the stack, and the second hit aft of the stack.

Skidmore's bomber took three antiaircraft hits while over the target area. A .50-caliber bullet hit one of his propeller's blades and tore out the propeller governor's gasket. A larger caliber bullet, probably a

40mm shell, entered the plane's starboard side and laterally pierced the fuselage just to the rear of the radioman's seat. The radioman, Daniel Joseph McCarthy, suffered shrapnel wounds to his left thigh and heel. A 5-inch shell's explosion bent the fairing at the port wing hinge.

Lieutenant John H. Ballantine attacked at about the same time as Skidmore. As he dove down around, rather than through the clouds, his plane was in almost perfect position to attack the second battleship. He approached the big ship from its starboard quarter and dropped his torpedo. It headed hot, straight, and normal toward the battleship. Ballantine did not see the outcome of the strike. As he approached the battleship, his radioman saw an explosion accompanied by plumes of black smoke rising from a cruiser on the formation's forward port side. The damage to the cruiser was probably caused by Anderson's torpedo striking the ship's side. None of the aircraft's crews saw what damage Lieutenant Williams's drop did. However, several crews saw his plane land in the water and burst into flames 15 miles northeast of the attack scene.

The Japanese ships did not turn or seriously try to evade the attacking Americans, although the leading battleship slowly turned to starboard. The ships appeared to have been caught off guard. However, the intense antiaircraft fire their crews sent into the air contradicted that line of reasoning. The American planes retired at 200 to 1,500 feet, made sharp turns in order to avoid the Japanese fire, rendezvoused 10 miles away, and uneventfully returned to their bases.

The American's first air strike was over. The losses in men and equipment were low. One man, McCarthy, was wounded. Williams had been shot down, along with his two crewmen. When last seen, these unlucky men were vigorously waving from their rubber boat.

But the Americans were by no means finished with the Japanese fleet in the Sibuyan Sea when the *Cabot*'s planes attacked again that afternoon. Their first wave had battered the fleet. When the second wave arrived, however, the ships responded by maneuvering themselves into two groups. Each group had two battleships surrounded by heavy and light cruisers, along with a screen of destroyers. The Americans saw heavy smoke arising from one of the battleships.

Two divisions' fighters from the *Cabot* resumed their attacks on the Japanese fleet. The pilots in the first division were Lt. Edward Van Vranken, Lt. (jg) Joseph Chandler, Ens. Francis Collins, and Ens. Robert Janda. The second division's pilots were Lt. Max Barnes, Ens. Robert

Murray, Ens. Henry W. Balsiger, and Ens. Emeral B. Cook. These fighters flew high cover until the dive-bombers and torpedo planes began their attacks. The fighters aimed for the battleships in the fleet's western group. In due course, smoke plumed up from one battleship. The vessels appeared to be heavily damaged.

Van Vranken led his division against the second battleship, evidently one of the Kongo-class. Intense antiaircraft fire rose from the Japanese ships to counter the oncoming fighters. The planes dove from 13,000 feet at a 70-degree angle toward the battleship, which was on a westerly course. The planes approached from a seven o'clock position. Van Vranken and his wingman, Ensign Collins, dove side by side, releasing their bombs at 3,000 feet. They pulled out at 1,500 feet, passed across the battleship's starboard bow, and executed a port 180-degree turn to avoid fire from the ships ahead. As the planes continued to turn, their pilots saw that Van Vranken's bomb landed 100 feet from the battleship, just to the rear of the port beam. Collins scored a near miss when his bomb hit the water 20 feet from the ship's port side, about 7 yards forward of the fantail.

Chandler flew behind Van Vranken, made a less steep dive, and, with Janda on his wing, they strafed the battleship from 10,000 feet. Both pilots continued firing as they dove to 4,000 feet. Chandler continued diving and dropped his bomb after descending another 1,000 feet.

Flying at 350 knots, Chandler pulled out at about 2,200 feet, and Janda followed behind. Janda released his bomb at 3,000 feet, retired in a northeast direction, and rendezvoused with Chandler over several Japanese cruisers and destroyers that fired at them from below. Van Vranken and Collins saw Chandler's bomb hit and explode about 30 feet off the battleship's starboard side and about 80 feet forward of the fantail. Janda's bomb hit the water about 500 feet from the port side, just slightly aft of the Japanese warship. All of the division's four pilots rendezvoused successfully about 10 miles northeast of the Japanese fleet and provided cover for the dive-bombers as all planes returned to the carrier.

As he dove while passing through 6,000 feet, Balsiger felt several hits as antiaircraft fire pierced his plane's skin. Turning to his right, he saw that more than half of his starboard aileron had been shot away. These collisions forced his fighter to roll around, but he could still control the aircraft, so he continued his dive. Balsiger aimed at the bow of the Kongo-class battleship, and released his bomb at 4,000 feet. No one saw whether the bomb hit anything. Balsiger pulled out of his dive at 2,500 feet but had some difficulty turning his plane. Still, he was able to rendezvous with his fellow pilots and return to the *Cabot*.

Lieutenant L. R. Swanson attacked what he thought was a Kongo-class battleship. Subsequent interviews with the pilots confirmed that he had made a direct hit almost amidships and slightly to the starboard side. Lieutenant J. L. Butts, Jr., also attacked the battleship, but his bomb failed to release. Therefore, he asked for permission from the air group commander to make a second attack, which was granted. He attacked a heavy cruiser, scoring a hit or a near miss.

Lieutenant P. R. Stradley and Lt. (jg) W. P. Wodell thought they had attacked a heavy cruiser. The results of Stradley's bomb drop are unknown. The belief is that Wodell's bomb probably hit the ship.

Lieutenant (jg) C. H. Bowen dove through the overcast, made a corkscrew turn around a cumulus cloud, and dropped down on what he perceived to be either a light cruiser or a destroyer. He pulled out after making a low dive. He and his crewman completely blacked out because of the dive's drastic pull. His crewman never saw the ship his plane attacked, so its identity remains unknown. However, A. F. Droske, who rode with Stradley and was taking pictures at the time, saw a destroyer explode, break into two pieces, and disappear almost immediately beneath the waves.

Back at the ship, reports by the flight commander to air intelligence confirmed and expanded on what had been said over the radio during the fighting. The reports of the *Cabot*'s planes did not exaggerate; the fliers on this second strike claimed only that they had attacked the Japanese ships.

Nevertheless, the excited pilots reported many things, and many pilots made reports. This was because 261 planes had attacked Kurita's force that day.

Meanwhile, the crews from Rear Admiral Sherman's Task Group 38.3 were busy fighting fires on the *Princeton*. But when Sherman recovered enough of the planes used in defending against the Japanese air attacks, he launched them at 11:00 A.M. Planes from the *Lexington* and the *Essex* arrived over the battle's area at about 1:30 P.M. and joined the fray. While Sherman's pilots achieved mixed results, their crews did not lack for enthusiasm or daring.

The *Essex*'s torpedo planes' formation divided into two eight-plane divisions. Lieutenant C. H. Sorenson led one and Lt. Cmdr. V. G. Lambert the other. Sorenson's group attacked first. Two pilots from Sorenson's division never returned, so what targets they attacked is a mystery.

Sorenson and Lt. (jg) L. G. Muskin led the division's attack. As they dove, two battleships were seen following behind a damaged Yamato-class battleship in an approximate columnar formation. Attacking first, Muskin dove his plane from 600 to 700 feet, flying at 250 knots. He was 1,300 yards away and made an approach to the rear battleship—a Kongo-class ship—30 degrees off its starboard bow on a southeast to northwest course. Muskin dropped his torpedo and reported later that he had an ideal shot, but the antiaircraft fire was so thick he could not see the result. Both crewmen on his plane said the torpedo ran "hot, straight and normal." Sorenson and another pilot claimed that the torpedo had hit the battleship amidships.

Sorenson attacked the smoking Yamato-class battleship with a bomb that made a direct hit on the rear of the ship's starboard side. After attacking a heavy cruiser and leaving the battle scene to the south, Lt. (jg) O. R. Bleech confirmed that the battleship had been hit when he reported he had seen a large explosion on a Yamato-class battleship.

Lambert and Ens. A. R. Hodges attacked two battleships in the column. One was identified later as the *Musashi*. The other was the *Kongo*. Lambert saw that the two battleships were so close together that one bow almost touched the other's stern. His plane was 1,500 yards away from the first battleship and 80 degrees on its port bow. At this range he couldn't miss. He dropped his torpedo at 650 feet while flying at 240 knots and was certain he had scored a hit. Hodges's crewmen confirmed that the torpedo had hit the ship. Both crews said they heard two explosions as they flew over the ships and pulled away.

Lieutenant (jg) R. L. Bantz came in next with Lt. (jg) S. M. Holladay and Lt. H. A. Goodwin right on his tail. Both Holladay and Goodwin reported that Bantz's bomb exploded on the battleship. The three planes' crewmen said all three pilots had hit the battleship, but they heard only two explosions. Later reports confirmed that the three attacking planes scored at least three hits; one was on the *Musashi*'s starboard side aft and the other two on its port side.

Lieutenant R. D. Cosgrove and Lt. (jg) R. D. Chaffe attacked the Kongo-class battleship. Cosgrove dropped his torpedo from only 450 feet from 2,000 yards away and claimed a hit on the battleship's bow.

Slightly ahead and south of the battleships was a Nachi-class light cruiser. Two pilots from Sorenson's torpedo bomber division attacked it. Lieutenant William S. Burns claimed he had scored a hit, and, as he watched her while pulling away, the cruiser appeared to slow. Lieutenant (jg) O. R. Bleech dropped from a 400-foot altitude from 1,200 yards away. He thought his torpedo ran directly at the target and watched as it zoomed toward the ship. However, his aircraft took several antiaircraft hits, and he did not know whether his torpedoes had hit the ship.

But Lambert and other pilots reported seeing two different explosions on two different cruisers. Another pilot said he saw at least one large explosion on the *Musashi*.

Two pilots, Lt. (jg) Paul Southard and Lt. (jg) W. F. Axtman, failed to rendezvous with their mates. Pilot reports suggest that Axtman and one of his crewmen were safe, but Southard and his crew apparently were lost.

During the determined American attacks on that day, other pilots from the *Lexington* ran into opposition from Japanese air forces. The account of Lt. (jg) W. J. Masoner, Jr., who led one of the most successful teams of fighters, reads as follows:

> We took off at 0610. My division escorting four SB2Cs [dive-bombers] on a 300-mile search from 275° to 285°. We entered a front spreading from about 50 miles from ship to about 20 miles inland. We flew instrument for 25 minutes and on emerging from the front the bombers were out of sight. We finally spotted them circling at 8000 feet over the eastern shore of Lingayen Gulf [Luzon]. As we came up to join them, they spotted a group of Bettys [bombers] and I saw them shoot down two. I saw four or five Bettys scattering in all directions; I picked one and went down on it with my division. I opened with a quartering shot and rode up on his tail. I observed his 20-mm gun firing from his turret. My incendiaries hit his fuselage and right wing root. He burst into flames and hit the water.
>
> I pulled up from this attack and saw eight Dinahs [dive-bombers] about 100 feet over me. They turned and spread slightly. I came up from below the right-hand plane and put a long burst into his starboard engine. It started to burn—the flames spread and it fell a mass of flames. During this time I saw four or five flamers and smokers crash on the shore.
>
> By this time no more planes were available so we rendezvoused and continued our search.

About 50 miles out one of the bombers tallyhoed two Nells [high-level bombers]. We dove down after them and chased them for five to six miles. I dropped my bomb and then caught up with them. I made a run from above and astern and his right wing burned, exploded, and fell off. He dove into the water and burned. I started to make a run on the other Nell but he was burning already and crashed. My wingman [Lt. (jg) W. E. Copeland] got him. These Nells had the new ball turret on their backs and one of these hit my section leader's engine. He was able to proceed, however.

We then joined the bombers—flew our cross leg and started home.

As we approached the shore of Luzon, we spotted five Nells at about 500 feet. My wingman and I went down on them and he burned one which crashed. His guns then stopped and he pulled up [Lt. E. E.] Bennett whose engine was damaged. I made a high quartering run on one Nell and observed hits. I did a wingover and came up under his tail to avoid his ball turret which was firing. I hit him in the fuselage at very close range. He exploded and pieces flew all over. He nosed straight down and hit the water—there was no fire.

I came up from behind and above on the next Nell and hit in the wing root and he exploded, throwing large pieces by me as I pulled up. He burned and crashed.

This left two Nells out of the five. I made two passes on one of them and on the second rode his tail until he burst into flames. This was very low and he hit immediately.

By this time my number four man [Lt. (jg) W. E. Davis III] had come down from escorting the bombers and we chased the last Nell over the land. We each had one gun firing and though we both got good hits, it wouldn't burn. My guns stopped entirely by this time so we withdrew.

These were definite kills. The film from his plane's gun cameras clearly showed all the Japanese airplanes he claimed to have shot down did indeed plunge into the sea in flames.

Other pilots had similar experiences. Lieutenant (jg) Copeland got on one Japanese plane's tail and fired a burst of gunfire. The unfortunate Japanese plane exploded into flames and crashed into Lingayen Gulf from 2,000 feet. Copeland was not finished, however. He caught another Japanese plane low over the water, fired a long burst, and the plane's two engines exploded in flames. His third kill that day was caught at 2,000 feet over Lingayen. Copeland stayed on its tail and tried to set the Japanese aircraft on fire, but it did not burn. Instead, its engines stopped working, and the plane crashed into a rice paddy.

Lieutenant Bennett got onto the tail of a Japanese bomber and later reported that he had shot "it down from 400, and then got an unidentified twin engine plane from 500, which also burned and crashed. I was hit by the turret gunner of a Nell and stayed up high from then on."

Lieutenant Davis got another Japanese bomber (a Betty): "I singled out one and fired several bursts into it. It started into a shallow dive and crashed and burned. Did not see any Bettys get away."

Obviously, the American pilots had achieved impressive results that day.[15]

Before the attacking aircraft from Task Groups 38.2 and 38.3 withdrew from the Sibuyan Sea at 2:15 P.M., another formation of American planes from RAdm. Ralph E. Davison's Task Group 38.4 appeared over the battle scene, making this the group's first strike against the Center Force. Davison's four carriers launched sixty-five planes at 1:13 P.M. near Samar Island. Like almost all of the other American attacks, no Japanese planes were anywhere nearby to stop them. The Japanese situation had become so desperate that they fired some of their battleship's big guns at the relentless Americans.

Commander Joseph Kibbe, the *Franklin*'s air group commander, enthusiastically reported that his planes had hit one of the Japanese super battleships with at least four bombs and between one and three torpedoes. Kibbe said he saw one bomb explode on the other super battleship's forward deck. He also reported that a member of the *Franklin*'s Torpedo Squadron 13, Lt. (jg) Robert Ransom, sank a light cruiser. The cruiser took a hit in the bow while it turned away in order to avoid the air attacks. When the torpedo exploded, the ship rolled over and sank. The *Enterprise*'s strike leader said bombs and torpedoes hit one of the super battleships and damaged a cruiser and two destroyers. Two of the bombs exploded on a heavy cruiser that seemed to be screening the more heavily damaged super battleship.[16]

By 1:13 P.M. on October 24, the carriers of the Third Fleet had launched five massive air attacks against Kurita's force in the Sibuyan Sea.

The Japanese land-based planes could not provide Kurita any effective air support. When some Japanese planes did indeed appear over the battle scene, the American pilots swiftly dispatched them to a watery grave. The American pilots made a point of concentrating on the super battleships, the *Yamato* and the *Musashi*. Most pilots claimed they had scored hits, inflicting heavy damage on both large ships, guessing they had been knocked out of action. In reality, the damage affected only one heavy cruiser and the *Musashi*. The cruiser in question limped back to its base and was out of action. The *Musashi* settled in the water and was still.[17]

At 3:18 P.M., after five massive air strikes had been carried out, Bogan radioed Halsey by TBS that the Japanese force had formed their ships into a circle when attacked, but nonetheless continued steaming on an eastward course. When the sixth and last of the American attacks launched by Bogan's Task Group 38.2 at 1:50 P.M. had finished by 3:35 P.M., its strike coordinator noted that the Japanese fleet had changed course and was heading back to the west. On receiving this news, the men in Halsey's flag plot exploded exclaimed, "We've stopped them!"

The planes from Bogan's Task Group thereupon returned to their carriers, where American optimism ran rampant. Bogan's Air Combat Intelligence (ACI) officers sent a message to Halsey reporting that one of the Japanese super battleships had been heavily damaged and appeared to be sinking. While this description turned out to be accurate, the rest of the message was too good to be true: "The enemy's course to the west may be retiring or may be protection of the cripples."

Just after Bogan's message arrived, Davison sent a message that seemed to confirm Bogan's report: "Enemy force on easterly course at first strike. When last seen, on westerly course."

Other reports of enemy damage also reached Halsey's flag plot. The Americans had pounded the Japanese all day long; the reports noted that two cruisers had been sunk and that a third had been forced to limp back to Brunei. By midday, another cruiser was seen dropping out of the Japanese formation. Officers in Halsey's flag plot first estimated that a total of 261 planes of the Third Fleet had hammered the Center Force's ships in a total of six successive strikes. Originally Halsey had planned to launch 1,000-plane strikes in the opening days of the Western Pacific campaign. However, because the Japanese could only muster a meager air defense, launching air strikes of that size was deemed unnecessary.

The people in Halsey's flag plot personally knew the ACI. The ACI's evaluations of the reports of returning air crews, which claimed many hits on the Center Force's ships, were regarded as accurate. However, wishes are one thing and reality another. These evaluations, in fact, reflected the aggressive and sometimes overly optimistic attitudes of the evaluators, and Halsey's staff, for its part, wanted to believe in the truth of these damage reports. But the fact is that two major questions remained unanswered: Did the Japanese really suffer a major defeat at the hands of Task Groups 38.2, 38.3, and 38.4? The related question then became whether the Japanese were indeed retreating.

At day's end, Halsey gave an affirmative answer to these questions when he sent a message to Nimitz and MacArthur, with a copy to King in Washington, in which he reported his assessment of the Third Fleet's battle against the big Japanese surface ships:

> Main Body reversed course to 270 about 1400 when 30 miles east of Tablas Island and while again being attacked. Score from incomplete reports: one Yamato-class bombed torpedoed left afire and down at bow. Kongo-class two bomb hits left smoking and apparently badly damaged. Bomb hits on one or both remaining battleships. Two torpedo hits on one of these bombed battleships. One light cruiser torpedoed and capsized. Torpedo hits on two heavy cruisers and bomb hits on another heavy cruiser. Night air attack probable.[18]

From the American perspective, they had forced the Japanese into retreating, sending them out of the Sibuyan Sea and back to their home bases. The Americans had lost only eighteen planes and believed they had won a great victory. Perhaps they were right. From the Japanese perspective, this view seemed justified. But this premature claim of victory overlooked the vigor of the Japanese naval defense, and the Japanese willingness to fight on.[19]

Chapter 8: The Japanese Fight Back

Kurita's lookouts had spotted the *Intrepid*'s search group, prompting him to issue immediate orders to increase speed to 24 knots and prepare for battle. Time passed tensely in Kurita's fleet as, at first, nothing happened. The American planes merely disappeared into the clouds. Minutes dragged by like a metronome, and still no action. Kurita guessed the American planes were a reconnaissance group, and that some time would elapse before the actual attack began. Accordingly, he reduced the fleet's speed to 20 knots and resumed zigzagging to frustrate any American submarines that might be in the area. Two hours passed as anxious Japanese sailors reported several aircraft sightings and a periscope. No attacks materialized, however. The powerful force rounded the north end of Tablas Island at about 10:00 A.M. while many radar antennae and lookout eyes scanned the still-empty skies.

Japanese radar detected the coming attack first. Their cathode-ray tubes showed that many air contacts were approaching from the east. Then, at 10:25, the lookouts saw a group of about thirty aircraft off the starboard beam.

Admiral Kurita had no air cover to protect his ships. But he did have at his disposal a powerful phalanx of antiaircraft guns with which to stop the oncoming American aircraft. At 10:26 he turned his glasses to the sky and saw a large formation of American planes approaching from the east. The planes began peeling off in the now familiar, disciplined formation that had become the hallmark of American naval aviation since

Midway. The first wave of American carrier-based planes included about twenty-five dive-bombers and torpedo-bombers.

Kurita immediately ordered his antiaircraft batteries to open fire. Even his battleship guns joined in the ever-increasing din. All the ships' guns sent up a withering wall of shells and concentrated their fire on the nearest attacking planes. Black smoke patches, chains of white phosphorous smoke, and tracer bullets trailing red light filled the sky. Any plane flying into that wall would surely be destroyed or seriously damaged. However, as Kurita watched the planes penetrate his presumably impenetrable protective screen, several hits blasted the *Yamato*'s sister ship, the *Musashi*. Thus, the pride Kurita had felt now turned to dread and apprehension.[1]

As long as the Japanese fleet kept within their circular formations, Kurita believed his ships' intense gunfire would be effective in inflicting serious casualties on the attacking Americans. However, if his ships scattered in an attempt to escape the American attacks, the gunfire's effectiveness would be severely diminished.

When the American planes attacked, the Japanese antiaircraft fire did not prove to be very accurate, so the American planes were able to press their attacks aggressively and relentlessly. Between 10:30 A.M. and sundown, more than 250 planes attacked the Japanese Center Force and only eighteen fell from the sky, prompting Admiral Ugaki to write laconically in his diary that night: "The small number of enemy planes shot down is regrettable."

The first battle lasted approximately one hour. While the Americans concentrated their efforts on the *Yamato* and the *Musashi*, their bombs literally bounced off the sturdy decks and plating, leaving the great ships relatively undamaged. One torpedo hit each ship but did not slow them at all. A second torpedo hit the *Musashi*, and several bombs exploded near her bridge section, knocking out the main battery synchronizers. Unfazed, this giant battleship continued on course at 27 knots.[2]

While the more heavily armored battleships seemed impervious to the American attacks, the same could not be said for the heavy cruiser *Myoko*. Like her sister ships that had been sunk in the Palawan Passage, she was a formidable vessel. However, she was not as large as some of the Center Force's heavy cruisers. The *Myoko* was more than 203 meters long and displaced just under 15,000 tons with a top speed of almost 34 knots. She was older than the other cruisers, since she had been built at the Yokosuka Naval Base in 1929 and was modernized later.

The aerial assault took its toll on her. When a torpedo hit her side, she began to slow, because, unlike her bigger compatriots, she did not have protective blisters.

The last attacking aircraft from the American first wave flew back to their bases on the carriers *Intrepid* and *Cabot.* Meanwhile, the staff of VAdm. Shintaro Hashimoto, the cruiser's division commander, moved to the heavy cruiser *Haguro.* The *Myoko* then limped back to Brunei. Another cruiser had already left the Center Force. And this was only the beginning of the agony.[3]

While the *Musashi* had survived the American's first attack relatively unscathed, later attacks by American torpedo-bombers critically damaged this super battleship. The big ship's armor, designed to protect her from torpedo damage, covered only 53½ percent of her hull. Her lead designers, Hiraga Yazura and Fukuda Keiji, had intended only to protect what they thought were the critical parts of the hull. They had taken special care in designing the bulges to explode when a torpedo struck the sides, thus absorbing the force of the explosion and protecting the ship's main hull from severe damage. But this did not prove to be enough.

Two major design flaws surfaced under battle conditions. The size of the bulges was too small and the 410mm-thick main armor belt riveted to the ship's bulkheads was not strong enough to withstand the torpedo warheads flung at them. The torpedo bulges on both of the big ships had been designed to absorb a blast of 500 pounds of TNT. But the American torpedoes now carried 600-pound warheads of Torpex, a substance twice as powerful as TNT. These deficiencies proved to be disastrous for both super battleships—for the *Musashi* at the Battle of Leyte Gulf and for the *Yamato* in the final days of the war.[4]

By noon, the fleet had just managed to re-create its original two circular formations when the second wave of American aircraft attacked. This time twenty-four heavy torpedo planes assaulted the oncoming Japanese ships. The Japanese crews had not eaten breakfast since the Americans had begun their attacks, and the second attack wave forced them to miss lunch as well. American torpedo planes split their attack by concentrating twelve planes on the *Yamato* and the *Musashi,* while another twelve focused on the other ships. Soon three torpedoes struck the *Musashi*'s sides. Smoke enveloped her as bombs crashed against her decks and superstructure. Seemingly unfazed, she maintained her position in the fleet's formation.[5]

Following a brief lull, another wave of American planes slipped out of the clouds. The *Musashi*'s chief gunnery officer, Shigure Noshino, begged the captain for permission to fire the type San Shiki Model 3 ammunition from the battleship's 18.1-inch guns. But his request was denied, because the captain wanted to save these big guns for a surface battle that might come at a later time.[6]

Utilizing prior attack patterns, the Americans assaulted the *Musashi* again. Smoke arose as bombs fell, and huge geysers of water from exploding torpedoes enveloped the ship. As the bombs hit the great battleship, machine-gun rounds from the American fighter planes made deadly clattering hits across the ship's topside decks and bulkheads. The big ship shook when yet another torpedo smashed against her sides and exploded.

The *Musashi*'s executive officer, Capt. Kenkichi Kato, had served for more than twenty-eight years in the Imperial Japanese Navy. Earlier in the war, he was executive officer on the heavy cruiser *Chokai*. His ship did not participate at the Battle of Midway or at Savo Island. However, he saw plenty of action that afternoon in the Sibuyan Sea.

One of Kato's responsibilities was supervising the *Musashi*'s damage-control parties. No serious concerns arose over the first torpedo hits. The outer hull's mammoth plates, which had once seriously depleted Japan's available steel supply, absorbed the early hits, minimizing the torpedo damage. However, even the strongest fortifications could not stand up to the incessant blows to the same places on the outer hull. An earlier torpedo had struck the outer hull at a spot near the number four engine room. A later one hit the same spot. At this point, the inner hull gave way, and water soon flooded the engine room. In vain, Kato tried to pump the rising water out of the large room, but hits from bombs also damaged some of the pumping equipment and the ship's internal communication system. Although the flooding was confined to the engine room, so much water rushed inside the hull that the big warship became unstable. The water's weight, and the loss of the number four engine's power slowed her, and she began to list to the port side.

Because the damage became so obvious, Noshino again asked the captain for permission to fire the huge antiaircraft rounds. As his lookouts saw yet another wave of attacking American aircraft emerging from the clouds, Capt. Toshihara Inoguchi reluctantly allowed Noshino to go ahead, for the guns could reach targets at 31,000 feet. While the crew fought desperately for their lives, their spirits lifted when the world's largest naval guns thundered defiantly at the Americans. This was the first time these great guns had been fired against an enemy. A colossal shock shook the decks below, which some of the crew thought was caused by another enemy hit.

The big shells scattered fire and shrapnel far into the eastern sky as the American planes attacked. Inoguchi and Noshino watched the approaching enemy planes, waiting for a large number of them to crash into the sea, trailing clouds of smoke. But not a single one fell. Inoguchi's fears about damage from firing the big guns came true, when some of the big shells damaged a turret.

Meanwhile, a third wave of sixty-five American aircraft delivered still another withering attack, pouring over the *Musashi* and striking her hard. Exploding torpedoes blew big holes into the already mangled port side as bombs continuously damaged her decks topside. One bomb exploded on the pagoda-like tower containing the command bridges, causing extensive damage throughout her command centers. For a short time, it seemed as though no one was in command of the ship. Inoguchi announced through a voice tube that all main bridge personnel had been killed and that he was shifting his command to the secondary bridge. A few moments later, more explosions poured heavy shrapnel on the *Musashi*'s command tower. This time, Inoguchi's luck ran out. In a weak voice, he announced through the brass speaking tube, "Captain is wounded. Executive officer, take command."[7]

Reflecting the situation facing his force, Kurita sent the following message to notify the Combined Fleet Headquarters in Tokyo and the Fifth Base Air Force in Manila of the fleet's activities and to request air assistance: "The First Striking Force [Center Force] is engaged in hard fight in Sibuyan Sea. Enemy air attacks are expected to increase. Request land-based air forces and Mobile Force to make prompt attacks on enemy carrier force estimated to be at Lamon Bay."[8]

The calmness of this message masked the anger and anguish of every man in Kurita's force. They had fought a five-hour, desperate battle, and no report from any friendly headquarters had been heard. There was no evidence that Japanese planes were making any effort to assault the American task forces. The Americans were moving around freely in Philippine waters and struck against Kurita's ships without air opposition. The thirty-two long-range scout planes transferred to land bases were nowhere to be seen. The navy had sent these planes ashore with the understanding that they would be used to search for American naval forces. The fleet was in a life-and-death struggle with the attacking Americans, but without air support from Japanese land-based planes, the situation was hopeless. To the men serving in the fleet, it seemed that their ships were being used for target practice.

However, Kurita did not know, nor did he have any way of knowing, that the Japanese land-based air force's size was down to fewer than 100 planes. Most of the Japanese carrier-based planes had been lost in the Air Battle of Formosa. The reality was that there was no help to send to Kurita's fleet from the air.

Meanwhile, on the *Yamato*, Ugaki watched helplessly as the *Musashi* slowly yielded to the relentless pounding of American aircraft. A huge wave piled up in front of one giant plate that had been torn loose from the *Musashi's* port side outer hull. Smoke poured from her gaping wounds. Her entire superstructure showed a noticeable port-side list. Her radios and signal searchlight stopped working as she lost all electric power. A flag signal issued from the bridge said, "*Musashi* capable of cruising at 15 knots. Listing to port about 15 degrees. One bomb hit first bridge; all members killed. Five direct bomb hits and twelve torpedo hits."

The Americans' savage attacks continued mercilessly. Additional aircraft from the *Intrepid, Cabot,* and *Essex* joined their comrades from the *Franklin* and the *Enterprise* and attacked Kurita's force. The Center Force had little or no hope of victory, or of survival without air cover. The endless supply of attacking aircraft from Halsey's great fleet left no doubt as to how this slaughter would end. Gradually, the Japanese antiaircraft fire was silenced.

Without question, both sides fought valiantly in this unequal contest. Brave men flew their aircraft and faced great danger while their opponents stayed at their posts and fired their guns, surrounded by an unspeakable slaughter. Only the pilots knew fully the risks they took that day as their aircraft maneuvered violently. Rear-facing gunners rode backward, while colored smoke bursts exploded all around them, and shrapnel struck their plexiglass canopies. On the other side, sailors tried desperately to rescue injured shipmates trapped inside compartments overrun by white-hot flames. Men who had little or no medical training tried to help the wounded and stop the continuous flow of blood.

The *Musashi* fell farther and farther behind the formation.

• • •

The *Musashi*'s crew tried to compensate for the inflicted damage by counterflooding on the bow's port side. The water's additional weight, however, made the bow sink still lower, and her speed decreased still more. She was now moving too slowly to remain with the fleet, and the Americans were not yet finished. A fourth wave of twenty-nine planes attacked at 1:25 P.M., followed by a fifth wave of approximately fifty American aircraft that appeared at 2:30 P.M., and the big ship's life span was now measured in hours.

More than thirty planes headed straight for the *Musashi* as she fell out of formation, slowing yet more. As water flowed over her bows, the crew bravely kept up withering fire from her antiaircraft batteries in a vain attempt to stop her attackers, and two American torpedo-bombers fell into the sea near the destroyer *Kiyoshimo*, with streaks of black smoke trailing from them as they crashed. More torpedo hits then reduced the *Musashi*'s speed even more.

Kato reported to Inoguchi—whose left arm was now lying useless in a sling—that the ship could not take any more damage. Inoguchi thereupon sent a message to Kurita on the *Yamato*: "Speed six knots, capable of operation. Damage great. What shall we do?"

Kurita's fleet had lost three heavy cruisers, including his flagship, the *Atago*, to American submarines in the Palawan Passage. He had been humiliatingly and unceremoniously plucked from the sea and placed on a new flagship with only half his original communications personnel still alive and able to carry out their duties. He had endured a succession of air attacks during the day, while the repeated pleas he sent for air cover went unanswered. Furthermore, he had watched as one of his two most valuable assets—the *Musashi*—disintegrated before his very eyes.

Kurita ordered the heavy cruiser *Tone* and the two destroyers *Kiyoshimo* and *Hamakaze* to remain with the hopelessly crippled *Musashi*. Once again he depleted his fleet by ordering three more vessels to stay with the maimed ship. A commander desirous of accomplishing his mission regardless of cost would not have made this kind of decision. A convoy commander would never risk his command's integrity by removing three protective ships to rescue a man who had fallen overboard in unfriendly waters. While this judgment of Kurita's decision may seem harsh, the sacrifice of crippled vessels must be weighed against a greater good, which in this case was the preservation of the fleet, whose mission was an all-out attack against a superior antagonist.

In warfare, decisions of this kind bring into play a variety of considerations. The utilitarian point of view preaches basing decisions on the greatest good for the greatest number. The "honor argument" reasons that one must never abandon one's comrades in peril. The end-justifies-the-means idea argues that an act must be judged on the value of the goal to be achieved, not on the means used to achieve it. Military commanders, being human beings, have all these arguments running through their minds when making decisions with life-or-death consequences. However, in military decision-making, the mission should always be given the greatest importance wherein the ultimate objective of victory is paramount. Historians always try to understand the mind set of a commander when trying to explain the reasons for that leader's decisions. Fortunately, historical perspective gives us the wherewithal to view the situation from hindsight, which is almost always superior to actually making the decision on the spot.

In an interview after the war, the rationale behind Kurita's thinking became clearer. During the interview, he noted that his ships did not have enough fuel to maintain a speed of 22 to 24 knots while moving toward Leyte Gulf. He said that if properly fueled, his ships were capable of traveling "for long distance voyages at high speed." He noted further that they had to "save their fuel for the trip back to Brunei." A commander on a suicide mission does not think in this way. Thus, he was unlike VAdm. Takujiro Ohnishi, who promoted the idea of the kamikaze attack when faced with enormous aircraft losses. Like any senior commander on a vital and complex mission, Kurita had to weigh a host of factors that might affect the mission's success. Clearly, the survival of his fleet was one of them.

As an apparently endless supply of American aircraft filled the skies above his fleet, Kurita pondered what lay ahead with no help forthcoming from any Japanese land-based aircraft. He had vigorously evaded the attacking aircraft, thus reducing damage to his fleet. His progress across the Sibuyan Sea was fast enough so that his fleet would be able to arrive at the narrow waters just ahead of the San Bernardino Strait's entrance during the daylight. If the Americans attacked again, however, his fleet's maneuvering room would be highly restricted, and his ships would be even more vulnerable than they were now.

The *Musashi* was now fatally wounded. As the other ships left her behind, the men of the fleet stood sadly at attention and bade farewell to the gallant but doomed ship. Adding to their apprehension were their thoughts of the fate awaiting them as they continued their mission. Was the loss of the *Musashi* a harbinger for the rest of the Japanese nation? We now know that the Japanese sailors who viewed the situation in this way were more correct than they realized at the time.

The sixth and final attack wave flew in at 3:10 P.M. More than 100 fighters and bombers screamed down from the skies to attack the battle-weary fleet yet again. The Americans daringly selected one damaged ship after another, and the *Musashi* was not spared. By this time, she could no longer fight back. Ten more torpedoes exploded against her now-buckled armor.

Realizing how desperate the situation was, the captain ordered every movable object shifted to the port side to bring the ship to a level keel. However, by 6:50 P.M., her bow sank below the water's surface. The last working engine died.

The day's sixth aerial attack also hit the *Yamato*, but she still had an ability to fight. Most of her antiaircraft guns were still operational, and her main 18.1-inch guns were not damaged at all. The battleship *Nagato* took two torpedo hits and slowed to 20 knots. The light cruiser *Yahagi* sustained heavy damage; her maximum speed was reduced to 22 knots. Other ships took such heavy damage that the fleet was forced to slow to 18 knots, which was the fastest speed of warships in 1894. Many men in the fleet had doubts as to whether they could navigate the hazardous San Bernardino Strait traveling at such a slow speed.

By 3:30 P.M., his operations officer informed Kurita that the Americans would be able to attack his beleaguered fleet at least three more times before dark. Undeterred, the fleet continued to move eastward toward the narrow entrance to the San Bernardino Strait.

The Japanese crews were exhausted, having fought off the American onslaught all day without rest. Nonetheless, they were as dedicated to their duties as ever and worked zealously to repair the damage in preparation for the next attack. The destroyer *Akishimo* rushed to the point of a reported periscope sighting and there dropped depth charges. Rumors of a submarine in the area set off a flood of torpedo sightings. It was highly likely that American submarines lurked around the many islands in these waters, and, if they did, they would have had a field day feasting on the many crippled ships in Kurita's Force.

The situation was not helped when the following message arrived from the Combined Fleet Headquarters: "Probability is great that enemy will employ submarines in the approaches to San Bernardino Strait. Be alert."[9]

The debris from the afternoon's engagements littering the water complicated the ability of the fleet's destroyers to search for American submarines. Fifteen destroyers had departed from Brunei. Now, only eleven remained available for antisubmarine operations. The *Asashimo* and the *Naganami* were towing the badly damaged cruiser *Takao* back to Brunei. The *Kiyoshimo* and the *Hamakaze* stayed behind to help the crippled *Musashi*. Because the fleet had to slow to 18 knots, every ship was a sitting duck for a torpedo attack. However, the fleet stayed on its course to the San Bernardino Strait.

Through it all, Kurita, in his customarily aloof manner, kept his composure. Just as the ships were about to steam into the narrowest passage of the San Bernardino Strait, and expecting the American's next aerial attack at any moment, he suddenly reversed the fleet's course to the west at 3:55 P.M. He explained his rationale for this unexpected, seemingly unwarranted maneuver in a 4:00 message to Combined Fleet Headquarters:

> Originally the main strength of [Center] force had intended to force its way through San Bernardino Strait about one hour after sundown, coordinating its moves with air action. However, the enemy made more than 250 sorties against us between 0830 [8:30 a.m.] and 1530 [3:30 p.m.], the number of planes involved and their fierceness mounting with every wave. Our air forces, on the other hand, were not able to obtain even expected results, causing our losses to mount steadily. Under these circumstances it was deemed that were we to force our way through, we would merely make ourselves meat for the enemy, with very little chance of success. It was therefore concluded that the best course open to us was temporarily to retire beyond the reach of enemy planes.

This message clearly shows Kurita's feelings of betrayal by the Combined Fleet Headquarters for its failure to send adequate air support. In the message, he refers to headquarters' promise to support him with friendly aircraft, and he cynically criticizes the commanders of the First and Second Air Fleets by sending them informational copies. In the first sentence he reminds Toyoda that the original SHO-1 plan stated that the air and surface forces would coordinate their actions. He also stated that their air forces "were not able to obtain even expected results."

Although Kurita's message states he hoped to move his fleet out of range of the attacking American aircraft by heading away from the San Bernardino Strait, any reasoned assessment of the situation shows that this hope was not realistic. Yet, for a reason unknown to Kurita, no American attacking aircraft appeared following his turn westward. With several hours before sunset, and with his ships still within range of the American aircraft, not a single American airplane was in sight. While he welcomed the puzzling respite, he felt uneasy nonetheless about what the Americans planned to do next.[10]

As Kurita's fleet headed westward, he again requested that land-based Japanese aircraft attack the Americans. But his pleas went unanswered. The Combined Fleet Headquarters had no planes to send.

In interrogations after the war, Japanese naval officers objected to Kurita's decision to turn back at this point. American admirals, however, saw it as a wise move. In addition to the basic logic governing Kurita's decision, another reason motivated his change of course. The Japanese SHO-1 plan called for Admirals Kurita and Nishimura to attack Leyte Gulf simultaneously, but the American air and submarine attacks had put Kurita behind schedule by six hours. He could move only at 22 knots because of the critical fuel shortage. If the fleet moved any faster, the tankers would not have been able to keep up. So, even if Kurita had been able to meet Nishimura at Leyte Gulf, he would not have had enough fuel to return to his base at Brunei.

The American attacks obviously had shredded the SHO-1 plan to tatters, and so it was critically important that Kurita's force approach the Leyte Gulf beachhead with all its remaining strength intact. Had Kurita continued on an eastward course, he would have exposed his ships to further air attacks and piecemeal destruction. By reversing course, he made it possible to avoid such devastating onslaughts and also provide some maneuvering room. Kurita's sudden retirement from the battle area caught the Americans by surprise and set in motion a chain of events that increased the Japanese chances of accomplishing their objectives. Looked at from this point of view, Kurita's maneuver was a tactical success.

There is another reason, too, for Kurita's reversal. At 10:00 A.M., a message had arrived from Nishimura stating the Southern Force had problems of its own as American planes from Davison's Task Group 38.4 had attacked his force. While Nishimura did not mention any specific damage, his message noted that the old battleship *Fuso* had taken some bomb hits, though this did not severely damage the vessel. Given the punishment Kurita's force had absorbed that day, he and his staff guessed that the ability of the Southern Force to meet its original objectives had diminished significantly. Also, they reasoned that Nishimura had understated the damage the *Fuso* had sustained, since it was common practice for the Japanese military to understate rather than overstate problems.

Oddly enough, for some inexplicable reason, Kurita failed to tell Nishimura about the American air attacks on his Center Force that day, and Nishimura blindly continued his drive northward toward the Surigao Strait.

Admiral Toyoda was not a happy man at 4:00 P.M., when he learned that Kurita had seemingly retreated from his assigned responsibility. He did not agree with Kurita's decision, and these sentiments circulated around the Combined Fleet Headquarters to the effect that Kurita was not doing his best.

Ugaki, on the other hand, assessed the situation differently. He expressed his views in a diary entry:

> It is true, if we are attacked by planes as often as this, it will appear that we have expended ourselves before getting to the battle area [Leyte Gulf], but our situation being what it is, we can't retire even if we chose to do so; there is a doctrine that in each and every instance the fastest means of settlement should be elected. My opinion at the time [of sailing] was that the only means available to us was to sortie determined to die. However, I am aware that to reverse course once until evening in order to deceive the enemy will be advantageous for tomorrow.

It is a common fact throughout military history that the commander knows much more about the situation at the battle site than any headquarters staff officer. Ugaki was on the spot and knew Kurita's retreat was but a temporary tactic. The admiral was attempting to remove his fleet from harm's way and also hoped for a miracle, which was that Ozawa's Northern Force would lure the Americans northward, away from the Leyte area. If the Americans believed Kurita was retreating, they would then send their aircraft to attack Ozawa's decoying force, thereby removing the threat they posed to Kurita.[11]

• • •

After the final American air attack ended at 3:35 P.M., one American plane continued to spy on the Center Force, keeping track of Kurita's ships. But around 4:20 that plane ceased tracking the Japanese force and turned eastward, leaving the scene. It never appeared again, which meant that American surveillance was now nil. This decision to withdraw surveillance then triggered a series of decisions that would end in disaster to the American ships guarding the Leyte beaches because the Americans assumed Kurita was going to continue his westward course, so they stopped the withering air assaults.[12]

Kurita Resumes His Mission

The SHO-1 plan's principal objective had always been to attack the American ships in Leyte Gulf. Therefore, Kurita was determined to forge on with his mission whatever the hazards. At 5:14 P.M., he reversed course, resuming the eastward direction, and headed for the San Bernardino Strait.

Imperial General Headquarters, for its part, dispatched Kurita a long-awaited message two hours after he had already altered his course eastward. This message became one of the most famous instances of extraordinarily bad timing: "Believing in divine help, resume the attack!"[13]

Many naval historians believe this message inspired Kurita's resumption of his advance through the San Bernardino Strait. However, this is logically impossible, because the message arrived two hours after he had already reversed his course. On reading this message, Kurita must have experienced a sense of overwhelming frustration at headquarters' abysmal ignorance of the tactical situation. This would explain the caustic reply he sent them: "Leave the fighting to us. Not even a god can direct naval battles from shore. Ignorant of enemy attacks, they can order anything. It would have been more realistic to say, 'Believing in annihilation, resume the attack!'"

A message to Kurita from Admiral Nishimura arrived shortly after the order sent by the Combined Fleet Headquarters. This message stated: "Our force will storm the center of the eastern shore of Leyte Gulf at 0400 on the 25th."

From this time forward, any hope of meeting Nishimura's Southern Force and executing a simultaneous attack on the Americans at Leyte

Gulf in a pincer's grip had vanished forever. Kurita's force was set to exit the San Bernardino Strait off Samar, and it was here that he would meet the American escort carriers of Taffy 3 shortly before dawn at approximately 6:00 A.M. on October 25.[14]

In a message to Admiral Toyoda, Kurita explained the reasoning that underlay his decision to resume his original course: "It is therefore considered advisable to retire temporarily from the zones of enemy air attacks and to resume the advance when the battle results of friendly units permit."[15]

Kurita showed his prudence by wanting to wait for help from the air forces, but he could not afford the luxury of waiting for it in these perilous circumstances. Realizing he was on his own, and dedicated to duty as he was, he decided to head to the other side of the San Bernardino Strait, and there he would meet his destiny.

A Valiant Lady Dies

After resuming its course to the east, Kurita's Center Force passed the dying *Musashi* at 7:00 P.M. The sun lay low on the western horizon, and the diminishing light that angled across the water increased the poignancy of this woeful sight. Ugaki stared yet again at this once grand, but now staggering colossus. The doomed *Musashi's* battle ensign slipped down as a sailor played the Japanese national anthem on a trumpet. Captain Kato, the doomed ship's executive officer, picked a strong swimmer from a group of volunteers, and then, in a solemn ceremony, with the ship's flag tied around his waist, the volunteer swam to another ship with his precious cargo, to be put away and saved for posterity. The *Musashi's* list increased. Empty shell casings rattled down the increasingly sloping deck.[16]

Inoguchi ordered a meeting of his senior officers on the battle bridge. Then he handed his final report to his executive officer and gave the order to abandon ship.

This was another in a now ever-growing list of sad times for the sailors in Kurita's force. As Ugaki contemplated the hapless ship that afternoon, he recorded his thoughts in his diary:

> It would appear that all of *Musashi's* officers and men are remaining at their posts without complaining. I thought that if things remained as they were, she might be able to hold out until the fol-

lowing morning. [The heavy cruiser] *Tone* is certainly a problem. She requested that she be allowed to join with the force in its penetration and at 1830 was ordered to rejoin its unit. Excluding some damage control personnel who remained aboard to help out, all other *Maya* personnel who had been accommodated on *Musashi* were transferred to a destroyer which pulled alongside of her.[17]

The *Musashi*'s sailors were now caught up in a hell of their own. Some of them were rescued from the *Maya*, after it had been destroyed in the waters of the Palawan Passage. Helplessly, they watched as the Americans mercilessly attacked and destroyed their place of sanctuary.

Ugaki continued his sad observations in his diary: "A little over an hour after sundown, a message was received from a destroyer, which had been ordered to stand by the damaged ship, that at 1937, *Musashi* had listed sharply."

Captain Inoguchi saw that his luck had run out. He obeyed Ugaki's advice and tried to beach his ship on the nearest shore. Only two of her four screws remained working. However, any attempt to change the great ship's direction caused the ship to vibrate. Furthermore, he realized that if he tried to change the ship's course, it might roll over. As her bow sank lower, she listed to starboard. Inoguchi ordered three of her four engine rooms flooded to keep the big ship level, but she was barely able to move using the engine she had left.

The fleet, meanwhile, continued toward San Bernardino Strait and soon disappeared over the eastern horizon. The cruiser *Tone* rejoined the main force, but the *Hamakaze* and the *Kiyoshimo* stayed behind to watch over the dying *Musashi*. Their lonely vigil lasted but a short while.

In her last death rattle, the great ship sank slowly by the bow. At about 7:30 P.M., the *Musashi* rolled slowly to port and gained momentum as she turtled. Sailors tried to stay on the ship's upward side as they ran along the rapidly turning hull. Anticipating they would have to swim, many took the precaution of discarding their shoes. The barnacles encrusted along the *Musashi*'s underwater hull cut into their feet as they tried to keep from falling into the sea. Some dove into the water but were sucked through gaping torpedo holes. After a few minutes, she stood upright with her stern trying vainly to remain afloat. Her gigantic propellers pierced high into the evening sky while her bow sank into the grim sea. Pausing for a moment, a convulsive explosion rumbled up from beneath the water's surface, releasing a great pillar of black smoke that covered the churning waters. It served as the frame for the great ship's descent into the depths.

In keeping with the traditions of the sea, her captain went down with the ship. He had been a battleship and big-gun advocate throughout the war, despite the amply documented power of aircraft against seemingly unsinkable, heavily armored ships. In his last report, he admitted he was wrong and expressed his profound apologies to his emperor and to the Japanese nation.

After the waters stopped churning above the doomed battleship, the two destroyers circled the gloomy site, picking up the survivors. Only half of the *Musashi*'s 2,200-man crew survived. The number of Japanese sailors lost when the *Musashi* sank equaled one-half the number of Americans who died at Pearl Harbor.

In a moment of moving melancholy, Ugaki wrote in his diary:

> This is like losing a part of myself. Nothing I can say will justify this loss. *Musashi*, however, was the substitute victim for *Yamato*. Today it was *Musashi's* day of misfortune, but tomorrow it will be *Yamato's* turn." Sooner or later both of these ships were destined to come under concentrated enemy attack. My sorrow over *Musashi's* loss knows no end, but when one conducts an unreasonable battle, such losses are inevitable. Should *Yamato* tomorrow meet with the same fate as *Musashi*, I will still have *Nagato* but there will no longer be a unit and my existence as division commander will be meaningless. As I had already made up my mind that *Yamato* should be my place of death, I firmly resolve to share the fate of the ship.[18]

These sentiments express clearly the *Bushido*[19] spirit of courage and resignation, a spirit difficult for a non-Japanese to understand. It would require both years of study of the Japanese way of life as well as true empathic gifts to comprehend the inner meanings of the deeply felt emotions Ugaki expressed. He and his other brave companions knew they were engaged in a deeply flawed operation. Nonetheless, their motivation was not success or personal survival but the preservation of the tenets of the *Bushido* honor code. It no longer mattered to them that their complex plan was a doomed one. Honor mattered most now. However, being the responsible naval officers that they were, they kept firmly in mind the practical realities that awaited them on the other side of the

San Bernardino Strait, for they were not only honor seekers, but also professional naval officers.

Ugaki had regained some of his former confidence and bravado when he set down his conception of his dedication to duty in his diary:

> We changed from circular formation to compound column and continued eastward. It would appear that the fleet headquarters has received a radio from Combined Fleet ordering our force to proceed ahead, trusting in divine faith. Today we underwent five or six air attacks, but neither our base air forces nor our own reconnaissance seaplane units were able to report any definite information on the enemy. The extent of the information was that a task force was present east of Manila, and that the enemy fleet in Leyte Gulf had moved out and there were no large ships in the gulf.
>
> At any event my firm belief has been that once we are able to transit the San Bernardino Strait we should conduct search attack in the area where we are able to approach and contact the enemy. . . .
>
> I have every faith in our ability to engage the enemy successfully. The only thing which worries me is that the enemy will successively reconnoiter our movements tonight and from after dawn will concentrate his air attacks on this force from a position over 100 miles from shore. Should this be the case, unless there is adequate cooperation from the base air forces, there will be nothing we can do, and our strength will be exhausted. We will have to expect decisive battle and annihilation with AA action alone.[20]

The crews of the American carrier-based planes that attacked Kurita's Center Force on October 24 showed the United States Navy's relentless spirit that had made them implacable adversaries. Ever since the Japanese navy had encountered the Americans at the Battle of the Coral Sea, its commanders were surprised at the persistence and bravery of American naval aviators. The Japanese propaganda machine had drilled into the minds of the Japanese people that the Americans were too soft and too accustomed to a comfortable lifestyle to equal the Japanese warriors. After their smashing, easy victory at Pearl Harbor, many Japanese senior naval officers had become convinced they were invincible. During the war, the Japanese Cabinet Information Bureau distributed highly inflammatory, derogatory propaganda about the United States. Any Japanese who praised the Americans in any way was branded a traitor. If any writers wrote something favorable about Americans, they were unable to publish it. After their defeats at Midway, Guadalcanal, the Philippine Sea, and in the islands of the Central Pacific, the men who fought the Americans came to realize that their nation's propaganda was mere rhetoric. Concrete experience taught Japanese sailors to deeply respect and admire the Americans, and they never hesitated to express the regard they held for the Americans' combat spirit and bravery.

By 1944, Japanese naval personnel had learned to hold in high esteem the ability of the American dive-bomber and torpedo-bomber crews who attacked with awe-inspiring mastery and fearlessness. The past Japanese defeats dealt out by American pilots at Midway, in the Solomons, and at the Marianas Turkey Shoot brought favorable comparisons with the Japanese fliers who sank the British Royal Navy's battleships the *Prince of Wales* and the *Repulse* off Malaya in 1941. Any Japanese who witnessed the American aerial attacks were always impressed by the relentlessness of the pilots who never retreated from their attacks. They kept coming with utter disregard for heavy antiaircraft fire until they had dropped all their bombs and torpedoes. They were willing to sacrifice everything they had, including their lives, to do their duty.

The Battle of the Sibuyan Sea had reached an end with severe Japanese losses. However, this battle proved not to be decisive. Kurita, his men, and his ships had showed an extraordinary, even inconceivable endurance in the face of merciless American aerial assaults. Therefore, the Center Force remained quite powerful. Kurita had the *Yamato* with its big 18.1-inch guns. He also had three other battleships, six heavy cruisers, two light cruisers, and about ten destroyers. The morale of the Center Force's crews was high, and they were spoiling for a fight. They had survived devastating but inconclusive American naval air attacks and were ready to face whatever awaited them.[21]

What was waiting for the Japanese would turn out not to be what they expected. Before their next test, a controversial decision would be made by Admiral Halsey that would result in the miracle that the Japanese had sought and perhaps bring about terrible consequences for the American naval forces guarding the Leyte beaches. One main objective of the SHO-1 plan would come to fruition.

Chapter 9: Making a Deadly Decision

Cape Engaño is the name of the northeastern tip of Luzon Island. Ironically, the Spanish word engañar means "to fool," and the literal translation of Cape Engaño might be "Cape of Fools." It was near this cape that the Japanese successfully executed their decoy plan, deceiving Halsey, Sherman, and other Task Force 38 commanders into taking the decoy bait that was part of the SHO-1 plan, which now had an excellent chance of success.[1]

Ozawa's battle plan was a wise albeit tragic one. American naval historians have called his part in the SHO-1 plan an all-out sacrifice. The Japanese intended it to be just that. Ozawa's mission was to lure Halsey's Third Fleet away from the San Bernardino Strait, even if this meant his fleet would be destroyed. Any attacks Ozawa might order were for the purpose of letting the Americans know the Northern Force was out there.

Ozawa was one of the few remaining talented naval commanders left in the Japanese navy and was as loyal to the emperor and to the Japanese nation as any other naval officer. If this meant he had to sacrifice his fleet to save the empire, he was prepared to do that unhesitatingly. He knew that if the American Third Fleet could be lured northward, he would buy enough time for Kurita to slip through the San Bernardino Strait, steam southward along Samar's east coast, and fall upon the relatively defenseless American forces in Leyte Gulf.

To keep the morale of his men high, he hid the idea of a suicide mission from them, so the order Ozawa sent to his fleet included enticing the enemy task forces northward and demolishing them. Nonetheless, the men serving in the Northern Force knew that their naval air forces had been severely weakened from prior battles with the Americans, but being dedicated sailors, these doomed men had no hesitation about sailing to their deaths, if that was what their superiors ordered. They had enough battle experience to know that their mission, as passed down to them via Ozawa's orders, was doomed to fail. The Americans had grown far too powerful for their meager Northern Force to inflict much damage. Still, every man in Ozawa's command had complete confidence in their commander and was willing to follow him anywhere into battle, including into the jaws of death.

Mishaps and misfortunes filled the Northern Force's voyage to the Philippines. Most befell the few remaining naval aircraft the Japanese had on their carriers. On October 21, Ozawa issued orders to launch twenty-one aircraft. One plane crashed at sea, another crash-landed aboard the carrier *Zuikaku*, and a third crashed on takeoff. The lack of experienced flight crews was now having a direct negative effect on actual Japanese operations.

The diminished Japanese resources for prosecuting the war at sea affected the surface fleet as well. Newer destroyers made up one-half of Ozawa's escort force, but clogged oil filters forced one new destroyer to fall out of formation. Realizing the danger the oil-filter problem posed if left unattended, Ozawa immediately ordered all oil filters cleaned. By 1944, most of the sailors in the crews of the newer, complex Japanese warships lacked both the knowledge and experience required to handle the intricacies of their ships. The destroyer that had dropped out had occupied an important escort position on the light carrier *Chiyoda*'s starboard quarter; its loss thus greatly increased the carrier's vulnerability. If any American submarines were hunting in the vicinity, the carrier's safety was an iffy proposition. Two submarine sightings were, in fact, reported, but they were never confirmed. The carrier was fortunate to escape danger, at least for the time being.

It was vital to the Japanese that the Northern Force lure Halsey's Third Fleet northward. By October 21, Ozawa realized he must act forcefully if he were to succeed, and so he embarked on a deception plan of his own to ensure that the Americans knew he was there. Making use of radios and call signs, he sent out a variety of signals concerning naval air operations with the aim of drawing the Americans' attention to his fleet.[2]

• • •

On October 24 at 11:15 A.M., the chance Ozawa and his fleet had sought so vigorously became a real possibility. A Japanese scout plane located an American force to the southeast, 160 miles from Ozawa's ships. Immediately, he ordered aircraft aloft to attack the American ships. In a remark added to the orders, Ozawa stated, "If the attacking planes deem it difficult to return to the carriers because of the weather, they are to proceed to land bases and notify the fleet at once upon their arrival."[3]

If the planes continued to bases on Luzon, his fleet would have no aircraft at all with which to attack the Americans. However, the sighting of the American Third Fleet raised Ozawa's hopes of successfully completing his mission.

A force of fifty-eight planes that included thirty fighter planes, nineteen fighter-bombers, four torpedo planes, and five attack planes left their flight decks at 11:45 A.M. After the last plane lifted into the sky, Ozawa looked away, then bowed his head. Given the many air struggles he had experienced at sea, he knew this force was not a fully integrated unit, but made up of thirty different aircraft types. It was a hastily gathered collection drawn from various units throughout Japan and was a pale imitation of the vaunted Japanese naval air force that had inflicted such a stunning defeat on the Americans at Pearl Harbor and had sunk the British warships *Prince of Wales* and *Repulse*. Ozawa wondered what results would issue from such a jumbled collection of planes.

The first group of planes left the carriers *Zuiho, Chiyoda,* and *Chitose,* engaged American fighters near the target area, then flew on to Clark Field. None of their crews saw any American ships. A second group, made up of six fighters, eleven fighter-bombers, and one attack-bomber, then took off from the *Zuikaku* and attacked several American ships. They reportedly set one fleet carrier and one light carrier afire. Following Ozawa's orders, they also flew to Clark Field. Three planes that had become separated from the second group returned to the fleet and, like their compatriots in the first group, saw no American vessels.

This last gasp of Japanese naval air power was in reality no more than a pathetic, futile gesture. Japanese naval airpower would never again duplicate the spectacular victories it achieved in the war's early months. The end of Japanese carrier-based air strength had arrived at last. In his own mind, Ozawa must have known this would eventually happen. While the morale of the untrained aircrews was high, their performance in no way matched their élan.

But something far more serious happened that caused Ozawa to change his tactical plan. The reports of Ozawa's aircraft attacks on the American task force never reached Kurita. As the Center Force fended off the continuous attacks by the American naval aircraft's second wave in the Sibuyan Sea, Kurita anxiously awaited the results of Ozawa's decoy tactic. But no message arrived because the *Zuikaku's* radio failed. Ozawa knew Kurita's fleet was under siege and that his mission of luring Halsey northward would not provide enough assistance. Therefore, he ordered RAdm. Chiaki Matsuda to move the converted battleship-carriers *Ise* and *Hyuga* ahead of his carriers and to engage the American fleet at night. At the same time, he moved his remaining ships in the direction of Luzon at maximum speed.

As October 25 dawned, Ozawa was convinced the Americans would attack his ships on this day. Trying to preserve the few planes he had left along with their inexperienced crews, at 6:10 A.M. he ordered all airplanes to Tuguegarao in the Philippines with the exception of the fighters. Five fighter-bombers, four attack planes, and one bomber lifted off and dipped their wings in a respectful farewell salute as they flew off to the west. Professional to the last, Ozawa always thought of his resources and mission first, which is why his name is still held in high esteem by friend and foe alike.[4]

The Japanese had done all they could to entice Halsey's fleet away from the San Bernardino Strait. Ozawa had more than fulfilled his mission. Now it would be up to Halsey to take the bait and give Kurita's still potent force an open door to Leyte Gulf.

A Time for Decision

Halsey earned the nickname "Bull" early in his career. Throughout his naval service, the nickname stuck, because he constantly acted like the proverbial "bull in a china shop." He always tended to be impatient even while achieving considerable success in his earlier assignments and command positions. His behavior approached the impulsive, because he attacked the Japanese without due regard for risks.

During September 1944, the Third Fleet had conducted a series of highly successful air raids on the Philippines. Flushed with these recent victories, Halsey recommended that the timetable for the Leyte invasion be moved up from December to October.

Admiral Raymond Spruance, Halsey's immediate predecessor and close friend, had been severely criticized when he failed to chase the

Japanese carriers aggressively after the Americans had thoroughly whipped the Japanese in the Battle of the Philippine Sea. Halsey was determined not to repeat what he thought was Spruance's major strategic blunder. After all, Nimitz's orders to Halsey included a provision that gave the impatient admiral the authority to attack and destroy the Japanese fleet should the opportunity arise. As Halsey placed the flag bridge aboard the *New Jersey*, he could hardly wait to find and destroy the Japanese carriers he knew were out there somewhere. It almost seemed as though it was his destiny to fight a great carrier battle and achieve a great victory, one he knew he deserved. Halsey was deeply grateful to his superior for having been given those orders, because his restless, forceful personality matched them very well.

As darkness loomed in the eastern skies off the Philippine east coast on October 21, Halsey's impatience increased as his great fleet steamed back and forth. In a radio message he sent to MacArthur, he showed that he was aching to do something dramatic:

> My present operations [are] in strategic position to meet threat of enemy fleet forces [but] are somewhat restricted by necessity to cover your transports. . . . [Need] early advice regarding withdrawal [of transports and other] such units to safe positions . . . will permit me execute orderly rearming program for my groups and at same time give me more freedom for further offensive action.

The message surprised Nimitz. Halsey was up to something. Immediately Nimitz asked Halsey what he meant by "further offensive action." The Third Fleet commander answered Nimitz's question, but apparently that answer was totally unsatisfactory to Nimitz. CINCPAC sent a strong message stating clearly that Halsey did not have the freedom of movement he thought he had: "General plan and tasks assigned . . . continue in effect and restrictions imposed by necessity to cover forces of the Southwest Pacific are accepted. Movement of major units of the 3d fleet through Surigao or San Bernardino Straits will not be initiated without orders from me. Acknowledge."

MacArthur minced no words either in his response to Halsey's message: "Basic plan for this operation in which for the first time I have moved beyond my own land-based air cover was predicated upon full support by Third Fleet. . . . Our mass of shipping is subject during this critical period to raiding enemy elements both air and surface. . . . I consider that your mission to cover this operation is essential and paramount."

Halsey's orders could not have been clearer. Both MacArthur and Nimitz told him to stay where his orders said the Third Fleet should be and to support the landings. Any movement to go after any Japanese fleet that would take him out of his allotted position was not sanctioned. Halsey rapidly, almost apologetically, replied to Nimitz that his message was meant as an exploration of an option and not as a definite plan. Since the Third Fleet was not going to pursue any of the Japanese fleets, Halsey ordered his task groups to proceed to Ulithi on a rotating basis to refuel, rearm, and restock and then return to Philippine waters. Admiral McCain's Task Group 38.1 was the first task group ordered in that rotation.[5]

A full twenty-four hours before the *Darter* reported seeing Kurita's Center Force in the Palawan Passage, several strong hints had begun to flow into the *New Jersey*'s flag plot indicating the Japanese navy was going to oppose MacArthur's October 20 invasion. At 7:47 A.M. on October 22, a message arrived from Admiral Nimitz containing an analysis of the latest Japanese radio intercepts that came from ULTRA and the code breakers at Station HYPO in Oahu. According to this analysis, the Japanese Mobile Fleet or carrier force probably had left the Inland Sea on the 20th. At least nine American submarines were patrolling the area west of Luzon Strait, because at that location they would have the best chance of attacking merchant-convoy targets. However, these submarines kept seeing Japanese warships. The *Seadragon* had attacked seven warships at night, claiming two torpedo hits on one, which it identified as a carrier. Later that evening, the submarine *Shark* sent a message stating it had made contact with a force of seven warships earlier that day. They were on a course heading 190 degrees south of the Pescadores at 22 knots. Halsey was in his flag plot on October 22 when he carefully examined the intelligence charts, correctly deducing that these seven warships were the same ones the *Seadragon* had attacked earlier in the night.

By this time, the *Darter*'s reports had begun to arrive one after the other, providing the first solid information that the Japanese navy had reacted at last to the Leyte landings. These reports made Halsey more convinced than ever that the Japanese carriers were on their way and should be attacked.

Halsey's operations officer, Capt. Ralph E. (Rollo) Wilson, handed the *Darter*'s latest dispatches to the admiral as he sat in his wardroom at a big table. As Halsey looked the dispatches over carefully, the admiral's chief of staff, RAdm. Robert B. (Mick) Carney, observed that submarine skippers often misidentified the ships they saw in their periscopes. However, they were seldom wrong about a ship's course and speed. Wilson observed that, "He's trackin' 'em, and every one of his reports says they're headed straight up the channel and at 16 knots." Halsey's air officer, Capt. Horace Douglass (Doug) Moulton, chimed in, "At that rate they could get to Coron Bay by sundown."

Halsey's assistant operations officer, Cmdr. William McMillan, brought another message from the flag plot. It stated that on October 21 at 9:30 A.M., the submarine *Icefish* had spied two heavy cruisers and three destroyers heading south in the same place that the submarines *Seadragon* and *Shark* had made their sightings. Rollo Wilson ordered the flag plot to track the course of these ships and report on whether they turned in the direction of Coron Bay. An officer in the flag plot called back a minute later with a report that these ships could easily arrive at Coron Bay by sundown. But at this point their mission was unclear; one fact was clear, however: the Japanese navy was going to make some major movements soon.

What were the Japanese going to do next? Halsey recalled thinking prior to the Leyte invasion that the Japanese might disperse their warships in small, scattered groups close enough to the Leyte beaches so they could make short, fast Tokyo Express runs.

Marine Major General William E. Riley, Halsey's plans officer, reminded the others in the room that MacArthur's Leyte invasion plan had made mention of a second possibility: the Japanese navy might attack his exposed transports while they were unloading supplies and men on the Leyte beaches, an idea that brought back memories to those who had been at Guadalcanal the night after the landing. On the evening of November 7, 1942, Adm. Kelly Turner, the amphibious commander, had removed his transports from the beaches, and then a Japanese cruiser force completely surprised the Americans off Savo Island and sank four Allied cruisers. Carney made the point that the Japanese force now included at least four battleships, whereas Halsey had only four battleships currently deployed in the two task groups assigned to defend the approaches to Leyte. The rest were with Davison's Task Group 38.4 on station to the south but too far from the northern exit to the Surigao Strait to help with any Japanese battleships that might break through to the Leyte beaches.

Doug Moulton interjected that MacArthur's plan also included a scenario of a Japanese air attack during the Leyte landings. Four weeks of spectacular air victories leading up to the Leyte invasion had given the Americans air supremacy over the Philippines. So, if the Japanese attacked with a potent fleet, they would need to fly in air reinforcements from China, or maybe from Japan itself to achieve victory by air. In that event, the 388 planes in Sherman's Task Group 38.3 and Bogan's Task Group 38.2 might not be sufficient to maintain American air supremacy around and over Leyte.

The debate among Halsey's staff continued on board the *New Jersey*. Meanwhile, on October 22, 600 miles to the southeast, Admiral Kinkaid, aboard the *Wasatch*, asked the same question: What will the Japanese navy do? He and his staff had tracked the courses of Kurita's fleet and the two other Japanese fleets, Nishimura's and Shima's, moving along the western side of the Philippines. Kinkaid believed the Japanese ships' destination was Coron Bay. His staff's analysis of radio intercepts showed that tankers might be assembling there. If the Japanese ships did manage to reach Coron Bay, the danger to the American invasion force would increase dramatically. If the Japanese had their tankers in Coron Bay, these vessels had sufficient refueling and resupply facilities to top off the Japanese ships' fuel tanks, thereby keeping their fleets operational for some time. Furthermore, Coron Bay was only one day's sailing time from the Leyte invasion beaches. Kinkaid felt reassured by the thought that he had ordered his resupply group to station itself nearer the beaches in Leyte Gulf rather than remain at sea to the east. This meant that the old battleships and cruisers deployed to protect the American troop and supply transports, and to bombard the invasion beaches, could remain in the vicinity of Leyte Gulf and not leave the area to refuel.

Both Kinkaid's and MacArthur's plans did *not* include contingencies for attempts by the Japanese navy to oppose the Leyte landings. Admiral Mitscher's plan for the Third Fleet's fast carriers also had no provisions for the appearance of large Japanese naval forces. Nimitz did not expect these forces to show up either. Nimitz had a plan for the Third Fleet to attack the Japanese home islands on November 11, 1944, one he never mentioned to MacArthur. It is a fact that no prudent senior commander would ever plan such a major operation without having every ship and plane at his disposal. If Nimitz knew the Japanese were going to oppose the Philippine invasion, why would he plan to pull out the Third Fleet and send it north for another major operation while the invasion was still in doubt? The answer is that he did not anticipate any major Japanese naval operation near the Philippine Islands.

The reports from the *Darter* continued to stream into Kinkaid's command. It was clear that a large, powerful surface fleet was approaching Leyte Gulf through the Palawan Passage. However, several disparate and confusing sightings also reported Japanese ships nearing the Philippine Islands from the northwest. Scattered submarine reports of southbound Japanese warships forced Kinkaid to conclude that a force, probably including cruisers and destroyers, was indeed approaching Coron Bay.

But there were two additional sightings that also drew his attention. Both of them—one by the submarine *Seadragon* and the other by a China-based plane of Gen. Claire Chennault's Fourteenth Air Force—sighted aircraft carriers in the South China Sea. Although these sightings were uncertain, Kinkaid concluded that at least some carriers had arrived in Philippine waters. On October 23 at 10:42 A.M., he changed his estimate of Japanese intentions and radioed them to Halsey: "I regard the approach of enemy combatant ships and tankers toward Coron Bay as the first phase of the buildup of magnified Tokyo Express runs against Leyte. . . . It is also possible that enemy carriers will support surface forces and strike from west of Palawan."

Kinkaid felt the Japanese fleet movements were a prelude to landing reinforcements on Leyte—either at Ormoc on Leyte's Japanese-held west side or via the Surigao Strait to some area of Japanese-held territory on eastern Leyte. He also warned that the Japanese seemed to be concentrating a large number of Japanese aircraft in the Luzon area in support of Tokyo Express–like runs.

With new information still pouring into Halsey's command every minute, he, like his Seventh Fleet counterpart, reexamined the rapidly changing situation. Halsey knew perfectly well the plan to attack Japan was his next big scheduled operation, requiring every ship and plane in the Third Fleet. Halsey believed that his fleet's raids leading up to the Leyte Gulf operations had most likely destroyed Japan's Philippine land-based air strength. But he knew as well that his superior had firmly reminded him on October 19 that he had to continue to give MacArthur's forces close support as long as the situation around Leyte Gulf was in doubt.

Trying to organize the choices that confronted Halsey, Mick Carney, his chief of staff, summed up the situation, a habit he had developed since joining Halsey's command. And Halsey appreciated his subordinate's bright mind and swift, organized way of thinking. One of Halsey's strengths was that he knew some of his own weaknesses and surrounded himself with people who filled in the gaps. On a later occasion, Halsey noted about Carney, "I had sense enough to know that I had a man who could talk so well, and I used him as I am not in his class in that respect." Carney had negotiated with MacArthur and his staff when Halsey's South Pacific operations moved closer to MacArthur's Southwest Pacific domain. He had the authority to speak for Halsey on many other occasions as well. Carney now succinctly summarized the current situation: "No operation plan can ever include the enemy's reactions. We must always be ready to make instant decisions on changes in the situation resulting from unpredictable enemy reactions."

With the entire Japanese navy now converging on the Philippines, Carney saw three possible battle alternatives available to the Japanese. First, they could attempt to reinforce their ground troops on Leyte with fast Tokyo Express runs. This was what everyone in Halsey's command initially expected that the Japanese would do. Second, there were too many heavy ships on their way to merely make fast runs and to reinforce troops as the Japanese had done at Guadalcanal. This being the case, they might have something else in mind. The Japanese could attack MacArthur's forces on the beach by air and sea. Halsey interjected that the Japanese had done that at Guadalcanal. Then, months after the initial Guadacanal landings, Halsey reminded everyone that the Japanese had sent battleships close inshore to bombard men and planes on the beach. Third, the Japanese could attack the Leyte forces using their battleships and heavy cruisers. Halsey noted that they had never done that before. However, the Japanese had always surprised everyone by doing the unexpected, and there was no reason to believe they had abandoned this practice now.

Carney summarized the situation: the Third Fleet must be reinforced.

Meanwhile, Bogan's task group, which included Halsey's flagship, the *New Jersey*, began filling its tanks. The tanker *Neosho* moved alongside the *New Jersey* at 10 knots to pump fuel into the flagship's tanks. The cruiser *Miami* also took on fuel from the *Neosho* on the tanker's other side. On the *New Jersey*'s starboard, the *Hancock* received oil from the tanker *Ashtabula*. Two destroyers pulled alongside the *Monongahela* and filled their tanks. Bogan reported that fueling for his task group was on schedule and would be completed by noon.

Carney next spread a chart on the conference table, which showed the placement of Halsey's forces around the Philippine islands. After examining the chart, Halsey decided he would send Bogan's Task Group 38.2 to join Sherman's Task Group 38.3, now located near the shore east of the Philippines. Both task groups, therefore, would arrive at their next fueling rendezvous 500 miles east of Leyte on October 26.

Meanwhile, Carney continued with his presentation. The Japanese forces now converging on the Philippines's western side would have at least eighteen ships, maybe more. Radio intercepts had indicated that the Japanese had kept six battleships in the Singapore-Brunei area. There were at least four battleships among the heavy ships moving into the Philippines. The two fast carrier groups currently supporting MacArthur had but four battleships, not enough to ensure a victory if these opposing heavy forces should engage in a slugging match.

The possibility of Japanese air attacks also had to be considered. Carney said he expected the Japanese to fly more planes rapidly into the Philippines to support their big ships. Undoubtedly, these aircraft would operate from Philippine bases. However, Vice Admiral Kinkaid noted that several carriers had been seen in the South China Sea, which meant that Japanese carrier planes could attack from that direction. Although some of the Japanese carrier planes were 300 miles away, they still could touch down on land bases, refuel, and attack the Third Fleet. The Third Fleet's air forces needed strengthening, but this was not as important a matter as adding more big guns.

Listening to Carney's arguments, Halsey decided his previous plans for his fast carrier forces would no longer work. Nimitz had reemphasized his orders to support MacArthur the previous day, so he was well aware that he had to be ready for Japanese fleet movements. Even if Kinkaid's assessment that the Japanese would make "magnified Tokyo Express" runs was correct, Japanese battleships were now one day's steaming time from the Leyte beachhead. If the Japanese tried to land troops on Leyte, or attempted to ambush Kinkaid's transports off Leyte, Halsey would have to change his forces' locations by moving two of his fast carrier task groups nearer to the Philippines's eastern shores. So, Halsey decided Sherman's Task Group 38.3, which included the battleship *Massachusetts*, would stay where it was—90 miles east of Luzon. Bogan's Task Group 38.2, which had the Third Fleet's two most powerful battleships, the *New Jersey* and the *Iowa*, along with the *South Dakota* would move just east of the San Bernardino Strait approach to the Leyte beachhead, instead of joining Sherman off Luzon. Admiral Davison's Task Group 38.4, which had the battleships *Alabama* and *Washington*, would move off Leyte southward to be nearer the Surigao Strait's northern exit. Halsey did not recall his fourth carrier group, McCain's Task Group 38.1, from its retirement toward Ulithi because he did not expect a major fleet battle. However, when Halsey learned that major Japanese naval units were converging on the Philippines, he changed his mind and ordered McCain to reverse course and rejoin the Third Fleet at maximum speed.

Davison's group had two battleships, while McCain's Task Group 38.1 had none. The *Washington* was the flagship of Adm. Willis A. (Ching) Lee, commander of the Third Fleet's battleships. Task Group 38.4 had only 207 planes while Task Group 38.1 had 326 planes. However, the two battleships in Davison's task group tipped the decision in favor of sending them to fend off the Japanese battleship threat.

Also on October 23, Halsey's staff took control of the flagship's communications and installed a teletype machine and pneumatic tube for a fast, reliable link between the flag plot and Radio One, the ship's communication center located three decks below. Rollo Wilson wrote the dispatches carrying out Halsey's decisions and gave them to the communications liaison officer, Lt. Cmdr. Kenneth Gifford, in the flag plot. Gifford sent a message to the assistant communications officer, Charles Fox, who commanded Radio One, which said, "Important messages coming." He then rolled the papers into a container and put them into the pneumatic tube. In the *New Jersey*'s radio room, Fox and his assistant, Lt. Burt Goldstein, waited for the incoming messages with sixteen coding officers and the same number of radiomen.

The container shot out of the pneumatic tube and slammed into a basket in Radio One. Realizing the importance of the dispatches, the men encoded them in four minutes. At 8:59 A.M., the first message went out, ordering Davison to head westward to a point close inshore off Leyte, to launch teams of bombers and fighters westward across the southern and central Philippines at dawn on the 24th, and search for the approaching Japanese ships. A second set of orders directed Bogan's Task Group 38.2 to finish refueling, head for a point just east of the San Bernardino Strait, and launch search aircraft westward at 6:00 A.M. on October 24 across the central Philippines. There were no new orders for Task Group 38.3 because they were unnecessary. A dispatch sent at 2:52 A.M. had ordered Sherman to position his task group east of Luzon and to launch search planes and fighters westward over Manila and the northern Philippines at first light on the 24th.

When dawn broke on October 24, three of the four fast carrier groups were close to the shore along the eastern edge of the Philippines. One was east of Luzon, a second near the eastern approaches to the San Bernardino Strait, and the third near the northern approaches to the Surigao Strait. Search aircraft soon would be launched to cover the entire 1,000-mile span of the Philippine archipelago, to clarify Japan's naval picture, and to find targets for the Third Fleet. MacArthur and Kinkaid, who had been uneasy about the safety of their men and ships at Leyte, were pleased when they learned how Halsey had positioned his forces.[6]

By midday on October 24, Carney had sized up the situation as one in which major forces from the Japanese fleet were moving toward a predetermined rendezvous. Furthermore, he reckoned they would gather on October 25 at the earliest. However, in Carney's view, their exact physical objective was not yet clear.

Halsey's intelligence officers, on the other hand, had a clearer picture of the situation. They believed that two Japanese surface forces were advancing through the Surigao and San Bernardino Straits for the purpose of simultaneously attacking the Leyte beachhead. Carney brought forth yet another possibility—the Center Force, now thought to be moving toward the San Bernardino Strait, might shorten its passage toward Leyte Gulf by not passing through the San Bernardino Strait and instead traverse the narrow passage between Samar and Leyte.

While Carney mused about what the Japanese were going to do, Kurita's Center Force was being pummeled by American carrier aircraft. Meanwhile, Kinkaid had sent orders over the radio, which were heard by Halsey's communications personnel, that instructed the heavy ships of the Seventh Fleet to ready themselves for a Japanese thrust through the Surigao Strait.

However, there was still some confusion concerning the whereabouts of Ozawa's carriers. Mitscher's carriers were defending themselves from attacking Japanese aircraft. When a Japanese aircraft, which could have come from a carrier, dropped a bomb that seriously damaged the carrier *Princeton*, Halsey's staff started to think about the possibility that the Japanese carriers might be in Philippine waters, perhaps west of Luzon. From there they could shuttle-bomb the American carriers by using land bases, then return to carriers outside American aircraft range.

Halsey guessed that a major coordinated Japanese naval movement was under way, but still did not know the location of the Japanese carriers. They might have been lurking west of the Philippines, as Mitscher and others suspected, or they might be coming from the northeast of the Philippines, where Halsey's planes had searched earlier that morning.

However, the reality was that a fleet containing several large Japanese capital ships was on its way, moving closer and closer on a course that led to the Leyte beachhead. Naturally, if this threat should manifest itself, Halsey did not want to be unprepared. Therefore, at 3:12 P.M. on October 24, his operations officer, Rollo Wilson, sent out a message entitled "Battle Plan," which would become a source of controversy for years to come. It alerted all Third Fleet ships that a new task force would be formed consisting of the battleships *New Jersey, Iowa, Washington,* and *Alabama,* two heavy cruisers, three light cruisers, and two destroyer divisions. These ships would come from Task Groups 38.2 and 38.4 and be called Task Force 34. It would be under the command of Adm. Willis A. Lee aboard the *Washington.*

The dispatch stated that Task Force 34 would decisively engage the oncoming Japanese heavy ships at long range. It also ordered Davison's Task Group 38.4 and Bogan's Task Group 38.2 off the San Bernardino Strait to move out of the way of any major surface action. Halsey himself would be the officer in tactical command on the *New Jersey.* Halsey intended that this order be contingent on future orders according to the evolving situation. However, at 5:10 P.M., when Davison's carriers came within voice-radio range, Halsey sent the following message to his subordinate: "Operate in this vicinity until further orders. Keep [carrier] groups concentrated. If enemy sorties [appeared through the San Bernardino Strait], Task Force 34 will be formed when directed by me."[7]

Bogan also heard this message, but no one else did. Everyone assumed Task Force 34 was about to become real. The most important people who believed the "formation" of Task Force 34 was a reality included MacArthur, Nimitz, and Kinkaid.

Kinkaid's staff heard Halsey's 3:12 P.M. message and reported to their superior that the Third Fleet's battleships would be guarding the San Bernardino Strait. Kinkaid breathed a sigh of relief at the welcome news. It fit perfectly with his own plans for his battleships and heavy cruisers. While Jesse Oldendorf stopped the Japanese Southern Force, Task Force 34 would presumably protect his northern flank. Halsey's powerful battle line had the most modern and fastest battleships afloat. These ships and the aircraft of the Third Fleet's powerful carriers would have more than enough power to stop the approaching Center Force. Nonetheless, the two admirals were not able to agree, in the end, on a common strategy with which to face the approaching threat because of the divided command structure. Kinkaid assumed that Task Force 34 would be there, though he was never able to confirm that Halsey's Task Force 34 formation order would be put into effect.

After the war, Halsey wrote about the reasons he gave this order in his postwar autobiography:

> This dispatch, which played a critical part in the next day's battle, I intended merely as a warning to the ships concerned that if a surface engagement offered, I would detach them from Task Force 38, form them into Task Force 34, and send them ahead as a battle line. It was definitely not an executive dispatch, but a battle plan, and was so marked. To make certain that none of my subordinate commanders misconstrued it, I told them later by TBS, "If the enemy sorties [through San Bernardino Strait], Task Force 34 will be formed when directed by me."[8]

On board the fleet carrier *Lexington*, VAdm. Marc Mitscher watched the planes returning from their mission over the Sibuyan Sea. He had heard many radio reports throughout Task Force 38 of the pilots' resounding successes. Landing airplanes on the carriers was much like a well-coordinated ballet requiring the utmost in skill and teamwork among the men on the flight deck. Any mistake could be fatal. Every plane, however, landed without incident. Mitscher eagerly anticipated the results of the debriefings.

The reports he received were full of positive information. As is the case with pilots of all nationalities, the American pilots returning that day were naturally optimistic, combining a natural aggressiveness with a positive outlook. If their narratives were to be believed, the Japanese Center Force was finished as an effective fighting force. The pilots reported that they had inflicted punishing damage on the Japanese, leaving many ships behind as burning, useless hulks. They reported also that the Japanese fleet was retiring to the west, apparently heading back to their base in Brunei. If these accounts were true, then the Japanese fleet posed no further threat to the Leyte landings, and so there was no need to continue attacking them. Also, American losses were light; they had lost only eighteen planes.

The overwhelmingly positive messages continued to pour into Mitscher's Combat Information Center, and so he sent the following joyful message to Halsey at about noon:

> Morning search reports 2 Natori-class cruisers, 1 dead in water just offshore northwest tip Mindoro. The other under[water] off west shore Lugang Island, 1 damaged Nachi cruiser in Manila Bay. Enemy has been flying several large groups twin engine planes from Formosa to Luzon. About 100 enemy planes shot down. Now striking enemy fleet east of Mindoro no reports yet of results. We have another large blip [probably Ozawa's Northern Force] heading from the northeast. Launching search 350 [degrees] to 040 [degrees] at 1305 [1:05 p.m.]. The *Princeton* still afloat.

On the *New Jersey*, Halsey's staff received Mitscher's battle reports. Halsey, in turn, reported to Nimitz in Pearl Harbor as the attacks progressed. According to the messages he sent Nimitz, American planes had stopped a destroyer, scored hits on a cruiser and a destroyer, scored bomb hits on two battleships, rocket hits on a cruiser and two destroyers, and torpedo hits on battleships and cruisers. So many similar reports poured in that it appeared that the Japanese were taking an enormous beating in the Sibuyan Sea. As sundown approached, Mitscher reported that the Japanese ships were "milling around aimlessly in several groups." Based on this report, it seemed reasonable to conclude that the Japanese ships posed no further threat to the landings at the Leyte beaches. Later reports caused Mitscher to revise his damage estimate to the effect that 150 Japanese planes had been destroyed on that day. However, the news was not all good in that latest message. The loss of the *Princeton*'s fighter aircraft had considerably hurt Task Force 38's ability to protect the American fleet against further Japanese air attacks. Unfortunately, there was no way to *verify* whether the American strike reports of sinking ships were true or not.[9]

A plane from the *Intrepid* observed the apparent Center Force's retreat as it unfolded and immediately informed his task group, which in turn quickly forwarded the information to Halsey, who received it at 4:20 P.M.

Not every senior American naval officer was as sanguine as his superiors about this apparent good news. Rear Admiral Bogan cautiously assessed the Japanese course change in a message over the TBS:

> Flash report 3rd strike enemy force reported at 1600 at 12-42 N 122-39 E. Course 270 speed 17. This force has been 14 miles to the east of this position but reversed course during time attack was over target. 2 battleship[s] reported to be of Kongo-class were damaged and circling. Apparently not controlled, at 12-39 N 122-48 E. The first was listing and afire [probably the *Musashi*]. The second less damaged. Course to west may be retiring or may be protection for cripples.[10]

The Americans had been fortunate to find Kurita's fleet as it entered the Sibuyan Sea. They were not as lucky in locating the Japanese carriers.

The American submarine *Besugo* led a wolfpack with the mission of watching the Bungo Channel, which was the exit from Japan's Inland Sea and the likely place from which the Japanese carriers would sortie. The submarine stayed at its assigned post for several days and saw nothing. The *Besugo* then asked for and received permission to hunt a convoy. Thus, when the Japanese carriers sailed southward, no American ship saw them depart. Long-range reconnaissance aircraft based on Saipan searched the seas around the Japanese home islands, but missed the carrier force moving to the south at the airplanes' extreme range. American naval intelligence in Hawaii intercepted Japanese radio messages that ordered tankers to a southern rendezvous. After analyzing the Japanese interceptions, they reasoned that the Japanese carriers were at sea and relayed that estimate of Japanese intentions to Nimitz.

But where were the Japanese carriers? During the evening of October 20, the submarine *Hammerhead* saw a formation of enemy warships northwest of Manila. The submarine's captain identified an aircraft carrier in the force. He attacked the ships and claimed a hit. Based on this report, American senior commanders ordered searches for the Japanese carrier force west rather than east of the Philippines.

Halsey's Third Fleet was east of the Philippines. In that position, he became increasingly concerned about his northern flank. When Nimitz's intelligence report estimated that the Japanese carriers had left the home islands on October 20, Halsey sent a message on October 24 at 8:55 A.M. to Mitscher, who was aboard the *Lexington* with Sherman's northernmost carrier group: "Enemy carrier strength not located. Keep area to north under observation."

The message arrived in Mitscher's hands at 11:25 A.M. That morning Sherman's Task Group 38.3 had defended themselves against three land-based air attacks from Luzon. A bomb had struck and disabled the *Princeton*. Almost all of his fighters had been launched trying to keep the Japanese planes from inflicting further damage. By 11:00 A.M., the action had died down enough so that Task Group 38.3 could launch its first strike against Kurita's Center Force in the Sibuyan Sea. At 11:55, which was three hours after Halsey had sent out his search orders, enough fighters had returned to escort search aircraft to the north in search of the approaching Japanese carriers.

However, the search had to be cancelled because, when the aircraft lined up to leave at 12:45 P.M., they had to share the flight decks with the second strike about to depart to attack the Center Force again. Task Group 38.3 had been defending themselves from air attack from the west. American radar screens showed a large group of Japanese aircraft 105 miles away and approaching from the northeast. The appearance of this greater, more immediate threat forced Sherman to cancel the search. He promptly launched the planes already loaded for the second strike and scrambled twenty-three fighters from the *Lexington* and the *Langley*, which had been originally assigned to the search, in order to intercept the new danger.

The Hellcats met the oncoming Japanese planes about 45 miles from Task Group 38.3. After the encounter, the American pilots claimed they shot down eleven planes, while the rest of the Japanese aircraft retreated. Meanwhile, the *Lexington*'s radar picked up another large group of Japanese planes about 60 miles away and again approaching from the northeast. Sherman scrambled more fighters from the *Essex* and intercepted the newest threat about 25 miles away. These Japanese fliers fought better than their immediate predecessors; some managed to get past the American fighter protection and to draw dangerously close to the task group. A pilot from these American fighters, Lt. Dan Morris, observed: "The enemy pilots were the most aggressive encountered since the fleet action of 19 June [Marianas Turkey Shoot]. They flew excellent formation, kept good sections and traded head-on shots. They evidently were part of the No. 1 team."

At 2:58 P.M., the *Essex*'s lookouts sighted a plane on fire through the clouds about 10 miles away. Almost immediately thereafter, five Japanese carrier-type planes—identified as Judys—dove out of the clouds and attacked the big carrier. All five planes successfully released their bombs, but they exploded harmlessly in the water between 100 and 300 yards away. One plane, hit by the carrier's antiaircraft fire, swerved sharply and crashed into the sea just beyond the destroyer screen. At 3:44, another Judy attacked the *Lexington*, dropped a bomb that missed astern, then escaped through the clouds toward Luzon.

The Japanese air attack caused no damage, but these planes were of the type that could be launched from carriers, and so it seemed probable that they came from Japanese carriers nearby. Rear Admiral Sherman later said that the presence of these aircraft made him, "strongly suspicious of the presence of Japanese carriers to the northeast." Even prior to the attack on his task group, Sherman realized that the quest for the Japanese Northern Force could no longer be delayed. Search planes had to be launched immediately even if they had no fighter escort, so he asked for and got Mitscher's permission to do just that. At 1:05 P.M., five Helldivers left the *Lexington*'s flight deck and headed on a northeasterly course to search for the elusive Japanese carriers about 350 miles away.

While Sherman withstood the Japanese air attacks, losing the *Princeton* earlier in the morning notwithstanding, Mitscher and Task Group 38.3 were too far north of the *New Jersey* and the rest of the Third Fleet to hear the aircrafts' radio communications. The only information they could glean came via longer-range message radio. However, Mitscher radioed a flash message at 12:07 P.M. to Halsey, describing the morning searches, the shooting down of 100 attacking planes, and the heavy damage inflicted on the *Princeton*. The flag bridge on Halsey's flagship received Mitscher's message at 1:31, a message in which Mitscher added another cryptic, albeit extremely important, piece of information: "Large bogey from northeast approaching to attack. Searchers to north launched at 1300."

That tidbit gave Halsey a clue that the Japanese carriers might have finally arrived in the Philippine Islands area. However, that was all the information he received. Many messages were sent between Mitscher, Sherman, and Sherman's force over the course of the next hours, but Halsey and his staff could not hear them. At 3:40 P.M., a message to

Mitscher from two of Sherman's search planes reported the first American sighting of Ozawa's Northern Force—a force of surface ships at 18°10'N, 125° 30'E. One hour later, another pilot relayed another sighting report, radioing that he had "got a good look" at the carrier force slightly northward of the first sighting: "Four carriers, two light cruisers, five destroyers."

Mitscher assembled the two reports and evaluated their implications, and at 5:17 P.M. radioed a message to Halsey: "New contact: Afternoon search reports 3 CV 4 to 6 CA and 6 DD at 18°10'N, 125°30'E which is 180 miles east of Aparri [at Luzon's northern tip]. One of CVs is of Ise-class. On course 110 speed 15 knots."

Thirteen minutes later, the report was in Halsey's hands. The elusive Japanese carriers had at last been found and conclusively identified. By that time Mitscher and Sherman had already agreed that it was too close to sunset to attack the approaching carriers. Any action would have to wait until the next morning. The highly impetuous admiral finally had enough firm information to make a decision, and he would have to make this decision quickly.[11]

But the Americans were having problems in starting the pursuit of Ozawa's Northern Force. The Japanese shore-based air attacks on Sherman's Task Group 38.3 that morning had been so intense that its carriers could not launch an early strike on the Northern Force's heavy ships until after noon. Another delay then took place when Sherman's aircraft had to defend their task group against two more waves of attacking planes. These planes had been launched from Japanese carriers that moved toward the Philippines from the northeast and on the offensive.

Confusion now reigned. Mitscher was having a difficult time sorting out what was happening to his Task Force 38 carriers. Sherman had sent unescorted Helldivers northward in search of the Japanese carriers. One aircraft had spotted a surface force at 3:10 P.M., but no carriers. One hour later, a Task Group 38.3 plane found the Northern Force carriers steaming about 60 to 100 miles farther north. However, Mitscher did not get the complete picture until the pilots returned to their ships and reported that the enemy ships were sailing in two formations. The second group reportedly had two Zuikaku-class carriers and one light carrier along with other ships. By this time, the information was now firm that the Japanese carriers had arrived undetected, had attacked twice, and were still untouched. Lieutenant Commander John Lawrence, who was in Halsey's Air Combat Intelligence unit, expressed uncertainty when he wrote up the Third Fleet's action report about its activities for that day.

By 8:00 P.M. on October 24, many things had happened since the Japanese navy had entered Philippine waters. The Battle of the Sibuyan Sea had escalated to the point that Halsey felt it necessary to report the day's events to his contemporaries and superiors. He and his staff crafted a note that they sent to Admiral Nimitz, General MacArthur, Admiral Kinkaid, and the task group commanders of the Third Fleet. In that message, Halsey relayed what he thought he knew:

> On 24th launched strong dawn search teams from 3 groups across Luzon and Visayas. At 0745 search planes contacted enemy force 4 BB [battleships] 8 CA [heavy cruisers] 2 CL [light cruisers] 13 DD [destroyers] 15 miles south of Mindoro. [Task Group] 38.2 [Bogan] launched strike immediately and repeated during day. 38.3 and 38.4 [Sherman and Davison] struck same force after initial strikes on other targets. 38.3 reported 1 CA 1 CL 1 DD Manila Bay, all damaged. After first strike 38.3 under heavy air attack and shot down about 150 planes. [This was the series of attacks that resulted in the sinking of the *Princeton*.] *Princeton* heavily damaged and *Birmingham* had personnel casualties resulting from explosions on *Princeton* while alongside her. 38.4 first strike enemy force southeast of Negros [Nishimura's Southern Force] consisting of 2 Fuso-class BB 1 CA 4 DD making two bomb hits on each BB, rocket hits on CA and 2 DD, strafed 2 remaining DD. None of these seen to sink. Main body [Center Force] reversed course to 270 about 1400 when 30 miles east of Tablas Island and while again being attacked. Main body: score from incomplete reports; 1 Yamato class [*Musashi*] bombed torpedoed left afire and down at bow. Kongo class 2 bomb hits left smoking and apparently badly damaged. Bomb hits on one or both remaining BB. 2 torpedo hits on one of these bombed BB. 1 CL torpedoed and capsized. Torpedo hits on 2 CA and bomb hits on another CA.[12]

The last two sentences in this part of the message turned out to be overly optimistic as to the extent of the damage inflicted on Kurita's fleet. The next part of the message was just what Halsey was waiting to tell the message's recipients. According to Halsey, the next part of his note was new information and solved the mystery about the location of the Japanese carriers.

> At 1540 [which was just after he learned that the Japanese fleet in the Sibuyan Sea had turned to the west] plane from 38.3 sighted enemy force near 18E10NN 125E30N report evaluated as two Ise class [battleships converted to aircraft carriers] 2 CA 1 CL, 6 DD course 210 speed 15. At 1640 another group [Ozawa's Northern Force] sighted 18-25 N 125-28 E, 2 Zuikaku [fleet carriers], 1 CVL [light carrier], 3 CL, 3 DD, course 270 speed 15. 2 DD 100 miles northeast this group course 240 [heading for northern Luzon.] Planes from this force may have been attacking 38.3 prior to contact, CTG 38.3 has scuttled *Princeton* and is closing 38.2 and 38.4, which are now concentrated off entrance to San Bernardino Strait. Night air attack by enemy probable. More later.[13]

Halsey's planes had at last found Ozawa's force. For a change, the Japanese SHO-1 plan was working according to schedule. The Northern Force was just where Kurita had hoped it would be. If Ozawa succeeded in his mission, the pressure would be taken off Kurita and give his Center Force a free hand as he exited the San Bernardino Strait. If the Americans took the bait, nothing would stand in Kurita's way when his force arrived off the Leyte beaches.[14]

The dispatch, which was sent to Nimitz and MacArthur and initialed by Carney, summarized the day's action, which led to the Halsey's decision to launch the dawn search. It reported:

> 1. Air strikes had found two powerful surface forces exercising a pincer movement toward Leyte.
> 2. The Luzon-based Japanese air raids on Task Group 38.3.
> 3. The all day attacks by American carrier planes and the apparent victory over the Japanese Center Force (Main Body): "Main Body score from incomplete reports: 1 *Yamato* bombed torpedoed afire down by bow, one battleship left smoking apparently badly damaged, one light cruiser torpedoed capsized."
> 4. The sighting of the Japanese carriers.
> 5. A tentative assessment about the source of the attacking aircraft: "Planes from this force may have been attacking TASK GROUP 38.3 prior to contact."

• • •

It did not matter whether the sighting of the Japanese carriers was late or not. Halsey now knew the answer to his primary question—where are the Japanese carriers? At long last, he had located the target he had sought ever since returning to sea and taking command of the Third Fleet. The American attack on the Philippines had forced the Japanese to send out their carriers. Now they were within the Third Fleet's range.[15]

Halsey faced a difficult decision that evening. He knew the possibility existed that Kurita could turn around again and head eastward toward the San Bernardino Strait. Based on the information he had, he identified three alternative actions he could take:

1. Guard the San Bernardino Strait with all three available task groups. This alternative would place the Third Fleet between Japanese airfields and carriers, a situation all World War II naval commanders avoided under almost all circumstances. The Third Fleet would then become a target for two converging air forces, because the Japanese could shuttle their aircraft between the airfields and carriers for refueling and rearming, thus having greater range than the American carrier-based planes.

2. Guard the San Bernardino Strait with Task Force 34 while attacking the Northern Force with part of Task Force 38. Halsey would have to leave at least one carrier group to protect Task Force 34's battleships and cruisers from Japanese land-based planes. McCain's Task Group 38.1, which had more planes and carriers than the other groups, was still too far away to engage the Japanese. Thus, a weakened and divided American carrier force would have to destroy an unknown number of enemy carriers.

3. Leave the San Bernardino Strait unguarded and attack the Northern Force with all three Task Groups. Halsey thought this choice was the best one. His orders from Nimitz obliged him to attack an enemy fleet if the opportunity presented itself. The enemy carrier fleet was out there somewhere. From his perspective, the Japanese carriers were the greater threat with the greatest ability to inflict the greatest amount of damage on the American landings because of their operating range and other capabilities.

Furthermore, Halsey's task group commanders had reportedly inflicted extensive damage on Kurita's Center Force. Bogan's Task Group

38.2 had damaged the battleship *Yamato* with four torpedo hits and two bomb hits; the battleship *Nagato* with one torpedo and one bomb; the battleship *Kongo* with two torpedoes and six bombs; the heavy cruiser *Mogami*, which was possibly sunk by torpedo; the heavy cruiser *Nachi* with one torpedo; and the heavy cruiser *Tone* with one torpedo. Admiral Sherman's Task Group 38.3 had damaged three battleships, one badly, four heavy cruisers, and two light cruisers. Davison's Task Group 38.4 damaged the battleship *Musashi* with a torpedo and, seeing it down by the bow, was probably sunk; damaged the battleship *Yamato* with one to three torpedoes and two bombs and one heavy cruiser and another destroyer; and sank one light cruiser and one destroyer and probably sank another destroyer.

If (and that was a big "if") these reports were to be believed, Kurita's Center Force had been decimated and essentially eliminated as an effective fighting force. Kinkaid's old battleships and jeep carriers should make short work of them, so Halsey thought.[16]

In Halsey's mind, the Northern Force presented the greatest threat, and his primary task was to destroy the Japanese carriers. The destruction of these carriers would, in Halsey's judgment, make the greatest contribution to an American victory.

Halsey was not worried about Kurita's Center Force. If it should come through the San Bernardino Strait, it would be attacked by American land-based planes from the just-captured airfield at Tacloban and by jeep carrier planes from Thomas Sprague's Taffy 1, Taffy 2, and Taffy 3. It also would have to run Rear Admiral Oldendorf's gauntlet of battleships and heavy cruisers. Doug Moulton felt strongly that the Center Force would never reach Leyte Gulf. Its ships' guns and fire control had been too heavily damaged by the Third Fleet air attacks in the Sibuyan Sea for it to remain an effective fighting force.

Halsey reasoned: (1) If the Center Force reached Leyte Gulf, what damage could it do? Assuming the rosiest possible scenario, Halsey believed Kinkaid could have scout planes tracking every move the Center Force made; (2) if the big Japanese ships entered Leyte Gulf, Kinkaid would have sufficient warning to get ready to defend himself and to move his amphibious ships out of harm's way; and (3) if the Japanese should break through, there would be no ships to attack, and their Southern Force would have been destroyed by Kinkaid's fleet. Thus, the Japanese plan to squeeze the Americans in a pincer movement would be in ruins. Although Oldendorf's battleships were older and slower than those of the Japanese, he could set up a static defense using his 14- and 16-inch guns and pound the already heavily damaged ships into submission. So, the only alternative left to them would be to retire westward at high speed in order to escape Halsey's carriers. After all, they had no assault troops to land on the beaches for the purpose of annihilating the Americans ashore.[17]

Emotions now ran high in Halsey's immediate circle. Carriers had decided every major battle of the Pacific war. To be victorious, hitting first was vital. The Japanese carriers' aircraft had attacked first, and Ozawa's ships were untouched. For Halsey, annihilating these ships with his overwhelmingly superior force could bring an early end to the war. If the Americans could get near the Japanese carriers at night, they would be able to surprise them and crush them at dawn's early light. The victory he had sought for as long as he could remember was so close; Halsey could almost smell it. The Japanese force had no way of escape. Task Force 34's battle wagons, under the command of Admiral Lee, was already alerted. It would move in quickly and finish them. Once these carriers were destroyed, the Third Fleet could operate freely off Tokyo. The temptation to seal the fate of the Japanese Empire was far too strong for Halsey to resist.

Halsey's staff held a hastily called meeting in the flag plot on the evening of October 24. Moulton, who had advocated the morning search, now argued that the day's delay was an ideal situation that had to be exploited. Task Group 38.1 was returning at maximum speed to a mid-ocean fueling rendezvous at dawn. When they got within range, all twelve of the Third Fleet's fast carriers could launch an overwhelming attack and slaughter the Japanese. If the Japanese carriers were destroyed now, MacArthur would have maximum freedom in his next scheduled moves to retake the Philippines in December and January.

The impulse to attack came naturally to Halsey. His aircrews had repeatedly attacked the big Japanese surface ships all that day. Halsey wanted to accept the interpretation of the fact that claimed the initial reports of heavy damage to the Japanese Center Force were accurate. The pilots' final report had asserted that the Japanese ships were retreating westward as the American aircraft left the target area. Halsey's assistant air officer, Herbert L. (Jack) Hoerner, stated that the six air strikes had exploded so many bombs on the topsides of Japanese warships that their guns could not put up any precise air defense. Rollo Wilson observed that the Third Fleet could not wait around at the San

Bernardino Strait to see whether the battered enemy would venture through it. There were ships out there to attack that had *not* been hit—the Japanese carriers!

No one in the meeting that night offered any alternative courses of action. Carney certainly did not, although he would say years later, "I might have had other ideas." Halsey's chief of staff was a brilliant advocate of his ideas, a person with an agile mind who saw quickly what had to be done. Carriers had been the deciding force in every naval engagement of the war thus far, and they were out there, untouched, with their capacity to shuttle bomb the Americans. Carney had seen them do this at Saipan, Tinian, and Guam.

However, several officers on Halsey's staff, men who had cooler heads, did not attend that meeting. One of these was Maj. Gen. William E. Riley, just the sort of man to bring up alternatives. Another was Capt. Marion O. Cheek, Halsey's intelligence officer. Still another was Cmdr. Gilvin M. Slonim, radio intelligence officer, who had heard radio intercepts all day and did not find out about the meeting until it was over.

Halsey could have left Task Force 34 to guard the San Bernardino Strait with one of the task groups providing air cover. Several of Halsey's commanders, including Willis Lee, thought Halsey would do this. However, one of Carney's cardinal rules was that the fleet should never be divided in battle. Some felt the Third Fleet was so powerful it was really several fleets, although Halsey did not seem to think of it in this way. The almost Lorelei-like prospect that beckoned Halsey was an opportunity for which he had planned ever since leaving Manus, an opportunity he felt he must not miss.

Probably no argument could have persuaded Halsey of any other course of action. On sweeping his arm over the big flag plot chart that lay before them, he said to Carney, "Here's where we're going, Mick." It was clear that he was going to send every ship he had.

In rapid-fire succession, orders went out to the fleet. At 8:06 P.M. the following order was sent to Task Group 38.1: "Proceed at best speed toward Point Mick (rendezvous)."

Three minutes later the following was sent to Task Groups 38.2 and 38.4: "Head north." And at 8:22 another order went out to Mitscher, with copies to all group commanders: "At 2300 [11:00 P.M.] Groups 38.2 and 38.4 pass through 14°28'N 125°50'E course 000 [due north] speed 25 knots. Upon joining Commander Task Force 38 [Mitscher] take charge all three groups attack enemy carrier force. Keep CTG

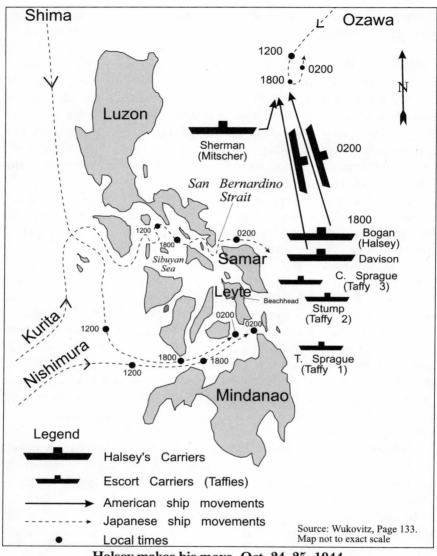

Halsey makes his move, Oct. 24–25, 1944

38.1 [McCain] advised your movements. He is herewith directed join you earliest."

After sending these orders to the Third Fleet, Halsey sent an urgent message at 8:24 P.M. to Kinkaid. For some reason, the message did not contain the information that the Japanese ships that his forces had attacked all day were turning back: "Enemy force Sibuyan Sea 1925 position 12°45'N 122°40'E course 120 speed 12 knots. Strike reports indicate enemy heavily damaged. Am proceeding north with three groups to attack enemy carrier force at dawn."

Although he now had moved decisively in the direction of Ozawa's carriers, Halsey delayed the decision to attack because it was getting too dark to launch air strikes. If the pilots left now, they would have to return in total darkness. With the exception of the pilots on the *Independence*, none of the other pilots in the Third Fleet had been trained in night operations. Also, the Japanese aircraft had a longer operating range than the American aircraft. Therefore, he decided on closing the range with the Japanese carriers and attack at first light.

The tension of the last few days had totally exhausted him. With a euphoric air of finality, Halsey made his decision and then went to bed.[18]

Misunderstanding and Discontent

Most of Halsey's senior officers gave wholehearted support to his decision once it became clear the Third Fleet was heading north. Among these supporters was Rear Admiral Sherman, who said, "They were close enough so that they could not get away. The situation was entirely to my liking, and I felt that we had a chance to completely wipe out a major group of the enemy fleet, including precious carriers, which he could ill afford to lose."

Captain James Thach, Mitscher's assistant chief of staff, echoed similar sentiments several years after the war's end, when he said: "If I were Halsey and had the whole thing to do over again, even knowing what's written in all the books, I'd still go after those carriers. I think he did exactly right. . . . There's a little calculated risk in everything, but in my opinion he certainly should have gone after those carriers."

Thach's superior and Mitscher's chief of staff, Commodore Arleigh A. Burke, was not among those who agreed with Halsey's decision. He did not think Halsey had assessed the situation carefully enough. Japanese aircraft had attacked Sherman's Task Group 38.3 earlier that day. Burke surmised that these planes must have come from carriers located north of Luzon. Another apparent fact was that the Japanese air attacks were not coordinated with land-based aircraft on Luzon. If Burke's observations and deductions were correct, what was afoot here?

The only possible conclusion was that the carriers had not coordinated their attacks because they were not able to do so. And they were not able to do so because they did not have enough air strength.

Burke had witnessed the terrible losses of Japanese aircraft during the Marianas Turkey Shoot and the great Formosa Air Battle. These losses had depleted the Japanese fleet of enough trained aircrews to make anything approaching an effective attack impossible. Without their aircraft, the Japanese carriers were as helpless as an effective fighting force as they had been during the American invasion of the Gilbert Islands. So, why would the Japanese send their once-prime carrier fleet off to the north? There was only one possible answer to that question. They were there to lure the Third Fleet away from the Leyte landings.

Burke voiced his conclusions to Mitscher, asking the admiral to forward them to Halsey. Mitscher told Burke, "Well, I think you're right, but I don't know you're right. I don't think we ought to bother Admiral Halsey. He's busy enough. He's got a lot of things on his mind." In Mitscher's mind, a subordinate never questioned a battle order once it was under way.

Admiral Lee, who came to the same conclusion as Burke, was not as bashful in expressing his opinion to Halsey, so he flashed him a light signal. But an indifferent reply came back, for Halsey and his staff thought it was absurd that the Japanese would risk the rest of their precious carriers just to protect a small number of less lethal battleships.

Halsey's message caused a number of key people to misunderstand his intentions. Nimitz and King assumed the message meant that only the three carrier groups would be heading north, and Task Force 34 would remain behind guarding the San Bernardino Strait. This assumption never fit in with Halsey's way of conducting a major naval battle.[19]

Halsey's decision to go after Ozawa's carriers did not add any significant worries to Kinkaid's burdens, because his communications center had read Halsey's October 24, 3:12 P.M., message to the effect that Task Force 34 was guarding the San Bernardino Strait. Kinkaid and his staff, like Nimitz and King, also assumed that while Halsey was heading northward with his three carrier groups, Lee's Task Force 34 was still on the job. As the Third Fleet moved northward, Kinkaid informed Halsey of the upcoming battle with Nishimura's Southern Force. Kinkaid's chief of staff, Commodore Leland G. Shaffer, remembered what happened that evening:

We notified Halsey of our expected night engagement with the enemy Southern Force and that we would be able to take care of them without any assistance from him if he could handle the Jap Center Force. . . . At this point we were not at all concerned as to the outcome of an encounter with the oncoming forces of the Jap fleet. As a matter of fact we rather relished the idea of taking part in a major naval battle which this was promising to be.[20]

Kinkaid would write later: "It was inconceivable that Halsey would have scrapped a perfect battle plan."[21]

If Halsey did what Kinkaid, Nimitz, and King assumed he was going to do, this assumption would not fit with Halsey's view of naval tactics. He was not a commander who would send his carriers into battle against an enemy of unknown size without taking his battleships, cruisers, and destroyers along to protect them. It would have been poor naval strategy to leave a powerful battleship force behind waiting for an enemy force that had been heavily damaged, given the fact that it is unlikely that a force in this condition would be able to come through the San Bernardino Strait.

However, Kinkaid and the others failed to grasp one vitally important piece of information. If Halsey was going northward with his carriers, his flagship *New Jersey* would go, too, for it was part of Task Force 34, as well as being a part of Task Group 38.2, and would not remain behind. If the *New Jersey* went northward, the rest of the fast battleships would follow. And when that happened, there would be no Third Fleet ships to guard the San Bernardino Strait. We now know that this is what happened. With the benefit of historical hindsight, it seems inconceivable that these gifted senior officers did not understand the psychological and strategic structure of the situation. And this misunderstanding came to the light of day in an appalling way, when Clifton Sprague's jeep carriers came under attack.[22]

Some junior officers also saw an inherent danger in leaving the San Bernardino Strait unguarded. One of these unhappy officers was Lt. Harris Cox, who was present at the Air Combat Intelligence station in the flag plot when Halsey made his decision to head north. Halsey's decision stunned him, and on returning to his room, he discussed the situation with his roommate, Lt. Carl Solberg. Upset, Cox came right out with his view that Halsey was doing what the Japanese hoped he would.

Solberg, in his book *Decision and Dissent*, reveals an interesting insight about this infamous episode in American naval history. Cox had spent many days in his quarters studying a rare captured Japanese document that he had obtained when the Third Fleet had stopped at Ulithi on October 6. Solberg had seen his roommate poring over this twenty-eight-page translation, trying to unravel its mystery. This document was not the usual piece of captured intelligence that naval intelligence officers routinely analyzed. Instead, it was the Japanese overall plan for repelling the expected American Pacific invasions, called the Japanese navy's Z-Plan.

Junior officers rarely saw intelligence data of this type, but an improbable series of events placed the invaluable document in American hands at this critical juncture.

When Admiral Yamamoto was in command of the Japanese Combined Fleet, the Japanese High Command had no need to set up large-scale plans with which to defend the empire. Every foe standing in their way had fallen. The Imperial Japanese Navy seemed to be as invulnerable as Hitler had seemed in the early years of World War II. However, an ULTRA radio-intercept message led to the charismatic Japanese admiral's death on April 18, 1943, and an American battle plan was evolving with which to push back the Japanese. In the end, the Americans executed a series of leapfrogging invasions along New Guinea's northern coast that brought the Americans ever closer to the Japanese homeland. The war's momentum and initiative had clearly shifted to the Americans, and so the task of developing a comprehensive, detailed defensive plan was assigned to Yamamoto's successor, Adm. Mineichi Koga.

This vital document fell into American hands some months prior to the Battle of Leyte Gulf. On March 31, 1944, Admiral Koga and his staff tried setting up a shore command on the southern Philippine island of Davao. Two big flying boats departed from Palau but ran into heavy weather. Mechanical problems delayed a third plane. Admiral Koga's plane was one of the planes that ran into heavy weather, and it disappeared into the sea. The second plane tried to make a midnight landing in shallow water near Cebu and crashed. All eleven men reached shore, where they were captured by Filipino guerrillas. Among the prisoners was the badly injured Admiral Koga's chief of staff. In the plane's wreckage, the Filipinos found several important papers, including a red-bound document. Soon, the papers reached Col. James Cushing, chief of guerrilla forces on Cebu. Immediately recognizing the papers' importance, he arranged for a submarine, the *Crevalle*, to transport them to MacArthur's headquarters in Australia. Allied intelligence in Brisbane quickly translated the document, which bore the title "Operation Orders: Secret Fleet Orders Operation No. 73, 8 March 1944, aboard flagship *Musashi* at Palau by Mineichi Koga, Commander in Chief of the Combined Fleet."

They sent one copy of this document to Admiral Nimitz's headquarters in Pearl Harbor. Its arrival drew the interest of naval intelligence officers Edwin Layton and Jasper Holmes. Immediately they asked for and received MacArthur's permission to make additional copies. The Third Fleet's intelligence officers received one copy while they were in Ulithi for supplies and mail.

The Z-Plan had been developed prior to the American invasion of the Marianas in June 1944 and was the master framework for subsequent Japanese defense plans. It included the A-Plan and the SHO-Plan, which included the plan used in defending the Philippines. The Z-Plan laid out Japanese naval intentions as regards the defense of the North Pacific, the Marianas, and the Indian Ocean. The plan gave considerable detail on the importance of land-based air in Japan's war strategy and laid out four broad options. According to the plan, the Combined Fleet had (1) use of the whole fleet for operations; (2) use of the carrier force as a prelude to an offensive by the main body of surface ships; (3) use of the carrier planes to strike first from a distance offshore, followed by air strikes from bases on shore; and (4) use of surface forces alone in operations.

The Japanese high command had chosen the third option in unsuccessfully defending the Marianas in June. In that battle, they had tried to extend the range of their carrier planes while attempting to shuttle bomb the American carriers from bases on Saipan, Tinian, and Guam.

The document came into the Americans' possession too late for use by Admiral Spruance's Fifth Fleet forces in invading the Marianas. When it arrived on the *New Jersey*, Halsey and Carney examined it with intense interest because of its heavy emphasis, on page after page, on shore-based air counterattacks. The Third Fleet had experienced these very tactics when raiding Okinawa and Formosa near the Japanese homeland. Halsey feared the Japanese would put repeat the same tactics in the Philippines.

However, Lt. Harris Cox conducted an analysis of the captured document and arrived at a conclusion different from Halsey and Carney. Cox was not one of the Third Fleet senior staffers who had been with Spruance in the Marianas and witnessed the Japanese shuttle-bombing tactics used there. But Carney and Moulton had been with Spruance. Also, Cox had not been assigned officially to Halsey's command as an air combat intelligence officer, as Solberg had. Cox's training was as an Office of Naval Intelligence reservist assigned to American surface ships and, as such, paid close attention to the big Japanese surface ships and the role they might play in the Battle of Leyte Gulf.

Cox kept the document in his quarters, where he examined it exhaustively and discussed its contents with Solberg and with Captain Cheek, who was Cox's section chief.

There was no doubt in Cox's mind that the Japanese would attack with every land-based aircraft they had, an idea that was an integral part of the Z-Plan. Of course, they did not have many planes left after the devastating losses they had suffered in the Formosa Air Battle. However, the Japanese still had some carrier-based aircraft that could be used against the Americans. No one in Halsey's command knew exactly how many carrier-based planes the Japanese actually had. But Halsey's people did believe that the Japanese still had too many aircraft to ignore. Everyone in the admiral's inner circle also foresaw that the Japanese would try to implement a coordinated advance, which would make use of their heavy surface ships, sending them toward the Surigao Strait and the San Bernardino Strait.

After spending many long hours pouring over the Z-Plan, Cox observed that the vitally important document stated one clear aim:

> Bear in mind that the main objectives which must be destroyed are [the enemy's] transport convoys. Surface forces will make the transport convoys their primary objective, and will deliver a sudden attack. . . . The carrier nucleus will try as far as possible to operate outside the limits of the area [and] attack the enemy striking force on the flank.

Cox concluded that this was exactly what the Japanese were doing. Their carriers had operated beyond the range of American search aircraft and had attacked the American northernmost task group. The document noted that the highest priority for the Japanese was to have their large surface ships fight their way into Leyte Gulf and wreak havoc on the American beachhead crowded with transports and troops.

The sightings that reported the approach of Japanese surface ships from the north and south convinced Solberg that his roommate's conclusions were correct. The Japanese appeared to be ready to sacrifice their carriers to lure Halsey northward so that their main body (Center Force) could get through the San Bernardino Strait and attack MacArthur's invasion forces. But the orders to go after Ozawa's carriers had already been given. From Cox and Solberg's point of view, Halsey's decision was clearly wrong. Allowing this potentially tragic mistake to proceed would leave the thinly armored transports open to annihilation. Something had to be done, and Cox took the first step when he presented his conclusions to Cheek.

Cheek had already argued with Moulton earlier that evening. Search aircraft from the night-operations carrier *Independence* had found Kurita's Center Force moving toward the San Bernardino Strait under the cover of darkness. When Cheek approached Moulton again to confer about this latest discovery, the discussion between the two men became, to put it mildly, animated. The normally cool, calm Cheek declared, "They're coming through, I know. I've played poker with them in Tokyo." But Moulton brushed aside all of Cheek's arguments. Halsey's orders had already been issued, and there was, in Moulton's mind, no turning back.

Moulton's word was not final, however. As 10:00 P.M. approached, Cheek tried to convince Carney that Halsey was doing just what the Japanese hoped he would. Cheek was now certain that the Japanese had a coordinated plan when he learned that Ozawa's carriers had been sighted. However, he had not yet concluded that the Japanese were using their carriers as decoys, as Cox and Solberg had.

Unfortunately, Cheek did not have the kind of influence with Halsey and his close advisers as his predecessor, Col. Julian Brown. Brown had shared his quarters and developed a close personal relationship with Halsey while serving under the admiral's command in the South Pacific. Cheek, who had assumed the colonel's duties when Brown returned to the United States for medical reasons, never achieved the same level of familiarity with the admiral.

An Annapolis graduate before World War I, the navy recalled Cheek from reserve status when the Pacific war began, and he had a reputation for being passive. Solberg comments in his book that, "It took our being caught in a great typhoon to draw from him the remark that he'd served on a destroyer that rolled 89 degrees and recovered in the North Atlantic in World War I." His modesty about his past was so great that it prevented other men with whom he served from knowing that he had won the Navy Cross for intelligence service before escaping with his life from the Philippines in 1942.

While serving as his intelligence officer on the *New Jersey*, Cheek's way of communicating with Halsey was to send brief notes to the chief of staff, which Carney would sometimes forward to Halsey. Cheek could not argue his position assertively and could not compete with the other strong-willed members of Halsey's staff. It was just not the way his personality was constructed. Not surprisingly, when he returned from his meeting with Carney, he related that Carney had told him that Halsey was asleep and could not be disturbed.

Meanwhile, Bogan had an uneasy suspicion that Kurita's Center Force had changed course again and was not retreating at all. In an effort to allay or confirm his fears, he ordered his night-search aircraft to continue following Kurita's force, since the latest American air surveillance had been aloft at around 4:20 P.M. The *Independence*'s aircraft did indeed sight the large force of surface ships on a course of 120 degrees at 12 knots, so Bogan was correct in his assessment. Like a tiger on the hunt, Kurita was heading back toward the San Bernardino Strait.

Halsey was wrong.

At 7:35 P.M., the *Independence* confirmed the sighting. Then, one hour later, the *Independence* added another report to the effect that the Japanese fleet was now off the middle of Burias Island's west coast, which was just slightly west of southern Luzon. The force then reached Burias Island's southern tip and turned northeastward between Burias and Ticao Islands. Later sighting reports affirmed that Kurita's fleet was nearing the western entrance to the San Bernardino Strait.

Bogan ordered his staff to draft a message to Halsey. It was ready to be sent a short time later. As he consulted with his staff, he remembered that the Japanese kept the San Bernardino Strait dark. However, on this night, Bogan learned that the Japanese had turned on the navigational lights in the strait, and there could be only one reason the Japanese would do this. The waters in the San Bernardino Strait were too narrow to safely navigate in the dark, so they needed the lights in order to proceed safely. On gathering this information, Bogan ordered the American search planes return to the *Independence*. Bogan sent a message over the TBS that the Japanese were still moving toward the San Bernardino Strait, but before he could complete the transmission of the message, the Third Fleet Communications Center cut the transmission short. A short, cryptic response, presumably from Moulton, reflecting the finality of Halsey's decision, stated, "Yes, yes, we have that information."

Bogan readied another message, stating that if the Third Fleet headed north, the San Bernardino Strait would be left unguarded. But he never transmitted this message.

Meanwhile, Lee was on his flagship, the *Washington*. He also was tracking the Japanese ships' progress. Before darkness descended, he sent a blinker message to the effect that the Northern Force was nothing but a decoy and that the Center Force was coming through the San Bernardino Strait. The *New Jersey* received the message but made no reply.

Years later, the pilot of the aircraft from the *Independence* that had followed the big ships, Lt. William Phelps, said he saw the Japanese warships shine their searchlights at the steep shores as they steered in a column through the narrow waters toward the San Bernardino Strait. When the plane landed on the *Independence* at 11:44 P.M. on October 24, the big carrier was already rushing north with the rest of the Third Fleet. Thus, just as Bogan had predicted, the San Bernardino Strait's eastern exit was indeed wide open.[23]

Chapter 10: Crossing the "T"

The Battle of Surigao Strait was the last time a naval fleet used the classic "crossing the T" maneuver. For centuries of naval warfare, warships had tried to bring the maximum firepower to bear on their opposition. The top of the "T" would sail across an approaching enemy's bows and fire broadsides at them while their opposition could only fire ahead with their forward-facing guns. The T-crossing force had the advantage, because they could outgun their approaching enemy by firing more guns. Because the Americans successfully executed this classic naval tactic against the Japanese, the Battle of Surigao Strait has received the most attention when people discuss the Battle of Leyte Gulf.

When the Japanese ships steamed up the Surigao Strait's narrow waters between Dinagat and Leyte Islands, they encountered an overwhelming American force of battleships, cruisers, and destroyers. In the larger scheme of things, what happened in the Surigao Strait was an overwhelming American tactical victory, but it did not ultimately determine the outcome of this momentous struggle. However, the Battle of Surigao Strait did indeed leave some vivid, indelible memories in the minds of many navy veterans and influenced many naval historians, because it is an exciting example of outstanding planning and execution by the United States Navy.

None of the battles that were part of the Battle of Leyte Gulf actually took place in Leyte Gulf itself. The Battle of Surigao Strait took place in Leyte Gulf's backyard.[1]

Destiny Lost

Shoji Nishimura was a war-worn veteran of the Pacific naval war. As the escort commander of the Japanese naval force that had decisively beaten the Dutch and Americans in the 1942 battles around the Netherlands East Indies, he had carried out a series of unremarkable assignments before receiving command of the Southern Force.[2]

His Force C was one part of the Southern Force, while the other part was the responsibility of Admiral Shima's Second Striking Force, composed of cruisers and destroyers. Force C was far less powerful than Kurita's Center Force; nonetheless, it had a critical mission. Nishimura's fleet consisted of two old battleships, the *Yamashiro* and the *Fuso;* one heavy cruiser, the *Mogami;* and four old destroyers, the *Mitsushio, Asagumo, Yamagumo,* and *Shigure.* The *Fuso* and *Yamashiro* were more than thirty years old, and the first two dreadnoughts built for the Japanese navy. While they had powerful 14-inch guns, they lacked the speed, range and armament of their newer, modern counterparts such as the *Yamato.* Until now, they had been used as training ships operating exclusively in the Inland Sea. The use of aged warships such as these in combat indicated serious weaknesses in the SHO-1 plan, revealing how desperate the Japanese were to stop the American capture of the Philippine Islands. Both these ships had undergone modernization but were so old they could never be brought up to the level of the newer battleships in the Japanese navy.

The *Yamashiro* and *Fuso* were not very nimble either, and this may explain why they were selected to approach Leyte through the narrow Surigao Strait, where maneuverability was not needed. Their slowness and lack of maneuverability would have hindered Kurita's force, which was the principal battering ram of the SHO-1 plan. The mission of these battleships was to appear off the Leyte beaches as the southern half of planned pincer movements and use their 14-inch guns to sink as many transports as possible before being sunk by the American Seventh Fleet.

Like all Japanese admirals, Nishimura accepted his orders in a fatalistic fashion with a dedication to carrying them out at whatever cost. Undoubtedly, he realized his mission was to sacrifice his force if necessary, and so he acquiesced to Kurita's plan, unquestioningly resigning himself to what might well be a suicidal journey toward Leyte Gulf.

Force C entered the Mindanao Sea about 9:00 A.M. on October 24. The sea was calm, but the weather forecast predicted rain squalls for

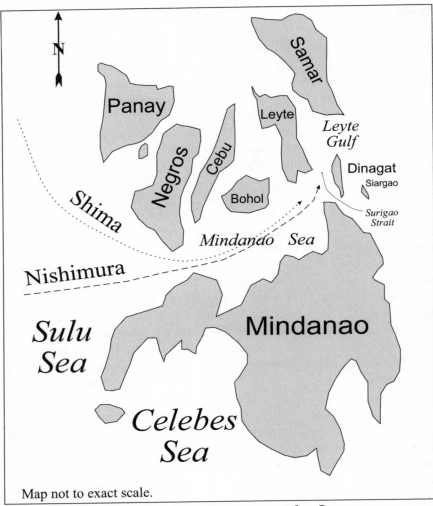

Japanese Southern Force approaches Leyte

the rest of that day. As Nishimura mulled over what lay ahead, his lookouts spotted American aircraft. In no time at all, about forty American Grumman fighters dove out of the sky and destroyed the *Fuso*'s scout plane and catapult. The aircraft attack knocked out the destroyer *Shigure*'s number one turret and rendered it useless. Compared to the damage inflicted on Kurita's Center force in the Sibuyan Sea, however, this damage was light and did not slow Nishimura's advance toward the Surigao Strait.

After the Grummans called it a day, Nishimura continued his eastward course almost without incident until later that afternoon. At 2:00 P.M., a few American torpedo boats showed up and attacked them. Despite this seemingly annoying interruption, Force C arrived three hours ahead of schedule to a spot that was just four hours of cruising time from Leyte Gulf. Meanwhile, the incessant American aircraft attacks delayed Kurita's Center Force by more than six hours from reaching its planned position off the beaches of Leyte Gulf. Trying to arrive at Leyte Gulf so as to coordinate with the now-delayed Kurita, Nishimura reduced his force's speed to 13 knots, which increased its vulnerability to American torpedo attacks.

No one knows whether Nishimura received Kurita's three messages which were sent on October 24. One asked for help from Japanese land-based air forces; the second notified Combined Fleet headquarters of his temporary retirement westward; and the third reported he was resuming his original, planned course toward the San Bernardino Strait. In any event, if Nishimura had received these messages, he did not change his plans.

After the war, the Japanese naval historian Masonori Ito interviewed several former Japanese admirals who knew Nishimura. All agreed that Nishimura's determination to continue toward Leyte Gulf never wavered. Like many of his counterparts in the Japanese navy, he felt that his mission must be completed at all costs. One possible reason for his determination was to relieve some of the pressure the Americans could inflict on Kurita. This view contradicts the conclusion reached by some American naval historians who have argued that Nishimura's action was strategically flawed and arbitrary.

Attempting to rendezvous with a friendly force at sea when the opposing force is very strong is always a complicated operation. Since Kurita's Center Force had been relentlessly attacked all day, while Nishimura's Force C had steamed freely toward the Surigao Strait, the possibility of the two Japanese forces meeting in Leyte Gulf was almost nil. Kurita still had to traverse the narrow, treacherous waters of the San Bernardino Strait. Nearly an insurmountable task in daylight, in darkness it was probably impossible. What Nishimura had not been told was that the Japanese planned to illuminate the San Bernardino Strait to make Kurita's task easier. Despite those considerations, Nishimura rightly reasoned that he would never be able to rendezvous with Kurita at the planned time.

Nishimura must have had a sense of foreboding as he pressed on to Leyte Gulf. He was in no hurry because of the need to coordinate with Kurita. Slowly, cautiously, therefore, he approached the Surigao Strait.

When Nishimura entered the Mindanao Sea in the early morning of October 24, he launched the lone plane he had from the cruiser *Mogami* to find out what was awaiting him. At 6:50 A.M., the aircraft arrived over Leyte Gulf and sent back the following report: "Sighted four battleships and two cruisers to the south of the bay. There are also about eighty transports off the landing area. There are four destroyers and several torpedo boats near Surigao Strait. In addition there are twelve carriers and ten destroyers in position 40 miles southeast of Leyte."

This message was the first and only intelligence report the Japanese naval commanders received about the disposition of the American forces during the entire Battle of Leyte Gulf. Kurita received this message in turn at about 2:10 P.M. The paucity of intelligence was due to a variety of reasons. First, no Japanese land-based aircraft left their bases to gather any intelligence information about the Americans. Second, no Japanese submarines were either near enough to the Philippines or in positions that would permit them to gather useful information. The third reason was a total lack of coordination among the senior Japanese commanders—Kurita, Nishimura, and Ozawa. These commanders relied instead on the flawless execution of the complex SHO-1 plan, hoping everything would turn out alright.

The *Mogami's* scout plane report was partially accurate as to the array of Americans ships in Leyte Gulf. The grouping actually consisted of six battleships, six cruisers, and thirty-odd destroyers. Although Nishimura's search plane had observed the Americans from a high altitude, its pilot confirmed the presence of a powerful American fleet in Leyte Gulf, with Halsey's fleet carriers only two hours away. Nishimura now knew that the American naval forces waiting for him in Leyte Gulf were three times larger than his own. What his feelings were on realizing that he faced certain extinction is something we will never know. There is, however, one fact we do know: he never retreated. He confirmed his intentions to Kurita when he sent a message at 10:30 P.M. on the 24th: "It is my plan to charge into Leyte Gulf at 0400 hours on the 25th."

Kurita replied: "Kurita main body plans to dash into Leyte Gulf at 1100 on the 25th. You are to proceed according to plan, rendezvous with my force ten miles northeast of Suluan Island at 0900."[3]

The Japanese destroyer *Asagumo*'s captain, Cmdr. Kazuo Shibayama, remembered the mood on that fateful day as Force C entered the Surigao Strait. The weather was worsening, which added to the feeling of impending doom. An ominous darkness was descending rapidly. Danger appeared like a specter and surrounded the small force as a light fog fell on the waters like a funeral pall. As Force C changed course and headed northward around Panoan Island's southern tip, American PT (motor torpedo) boats appeared on the horizon. Nishimura was about to experience one of the most devastating defeats in the Pacific War.[4]

Finding a Prime Target

At 9:05 a.m. on October 24, a flight of planes from the *Enterprise* and the *Franklin* cruised above the Sulu Sea. As their pilots scanned the sea below, they saw the ships of Vice Admiral Nishimura's Force C looming up to meet their gaze. Three large vessels were sailing about 50 miles west-southwest of Saiton Point, Negros Island, and 75 miles southeast of the Cayagan Islands. A screening force of four ships followed behind.

Between 9:10 and 9:50, an American patrol aircraft sighted Force C again. Although Shima's force was not sighted by the patrol aircraft, both Shima's force and Nishimura's Force C were still converging and heading for the Surigao Strait, which exactly matched American naval intelligence predictions.

The Americans did not sight any more Japanese ships near the Surigao Strait during the daylight hours of October 24. The entire Southern Force sustained no more air attacks during the afternoon and evening of that day. The major reason Nishimura's Force C was able to steam freely toward the Surigao Strait was that Rear Admiral Davison's fast carrier force had moved out of range in order to assault Kurita's Center Force in the Sibuyan Sea.[5]

The American pilots, in fact, reported a much smaller force than was actually present. The crews said they saw two old-style destroyers and a larger ship, possibly a Katori-class light cruiser. The American aircraft strafed, fired rockets, and bombed the Japanese force. The larger vessel was reported as sunk. Later, eight fighters and eleven bombers attacked, inflicting further damage on the remaining ships. However, the Americans could not confirm any more sinkings.

As had happened in the past, the damage reports of the American pilots were more optimistic than the facts warranted. The actual damage on Force C included one minor hit on the battleship *Yamashiro*'s fantail, one gun crew member on the destroyer *Shigure* killed, and the *Fuso*'s float plane shot down, which wiped out the battleship's ability to see what lay ahead of it. Meanwhile, an American Fifth Army Air Force bomber that had found Shima's force again reported: "Confidential. Urgent 7615. From: Fifth Bomber Command. To: All interested CurOps. This is my second report this force. Two Fuso class BB [battleships]. One unidentified heavy cruiser, four unidentified (garbled) latitude 121-35. Course 60 true. Speed 15 knots. I am returning to base."

There were two errors in this message. The message had garbled the identity of the last group of ships, which were most probably destroyers. Second, the ships had been misidentified. Shima's force actually had two heavy cruisers, one light cruiser, and four destroyers. Nonetheless, the incorrect bulletin did not change any decisions American naval commanders would make on that day. Halsey still would send every plane he had to attack Kurita's more powerful Center Force and would never attack either Nishimura's or Shima's force again.[6]

Vice Admiral Thomas Kinkaid sat at his desk on his flagship, *Wasatch*, after finishing a staff meeting with his officers. He had received encouraging dispatches about the Sibuyan Sea battle. The Japanese Center Force had absorbed seemingly crippling losses. Reports of sinkings of several Japanese capital ships poured in. Halsey's fliers, like all pilots, were optimists, and Kinkaid knew from experience that just because a pilot reported a ship's sinking did not necessarily make it a fact. Despite the optimistic reports, an uneasy feeling nagged at him that all was not as well as Halsey's reports made it appear.

Kinkaid had his own worries as well. Japanese land-based aircraft had attacked a fuel dump on Leyte and set it afire. He knew the Southern Force would soon be within range of RAdm. Jesse B. Oldendorf's force. Despite his misgivings, he took comfort in knowing that Halsey was still in a position to cover the Seventh Fleet's northern flank and to protect his transports against an attack by the Center Force. If Oldendorf could intercept and cripple, or perhaps even destroy, the Southern Force, and if the Center Force remained under Halsey's control, his worries could be confined to the immediate areas facing him on Leyte Island. The crews on his escort carriers could handle most contingencies on the ground.

Kinkaid sent two Black Cats (radar-equipped, night-search PBY patrol planes) to look for Nishimura, but they found nothing. He still had the feeling Nishimura would attempt a breakout into Leyte Gulf through the Surigao Strait. These feelings would be confirmed later by American naval intelligence. Kinkaid's confidence rose when he realized Oldendorf's force was ready for the Japanese.[7]

Setting the Trap

Kinkaid issued an alert for a nighttime naval engagement. It arrived on Oldendorf's flagship *Louisville* on October 24 at 2:43 P.M.:

> Jap force estimated at two battleships, four heavy cruisers, four light cruisers, and ten destroyers reported under attack in eastern Sulu Sea by our carrier planes. Japs able to arrive Leyte Gulf tonight. Make all ready for night battle. Your force to be reinforced by Admiral Berkey's Task Group. Motor torpedo boats in maximum number to be stationed in lower Surigao Strait and to stay south of 10°10' north latitude during darkness.

Oldendorf conferred with his chief of staff, Capt. Richard W. Bates, and both men agreed Kinkaid's intentions were clear. However, Oldendorf had some concerns as to the makeup of the ships he would be commanding. Rear Admiral Russell S. Berkey and the two Australian ships—the heavy cruiser *Shropshire* and the destroyer *Arunta*—had never before operated under his command. Oldendorf was never one to leave things to chance, and so he ordered his chief of staff to make clear the threat that was coming their way: "Our force will attack by torpedo and destroy by gunfire Jap forces trying to enter Leyte Gulf through Surigao Strait or south."

American carrier-based aircraft had attacked the Japanese ships as they entered and steamed through the Mindanao Sea and inflicted some damage. Oldendorf did not, in fact, know the extent of the damage, but these ships still were within striking distance of Leyte Gulf.

Another gnawing problem kept buzzing through Oldendorf's head. Kurita's Center Force had been attacked and was reported retreating westward away from the San Bernardino Strait. But what if this powerful force should reverse direction again, pass through the San Bernardino Strait, and pounce upon the vulnerable transports unloading supplies and troops in Leyte Gulf? Although Halsey's Third Fleet

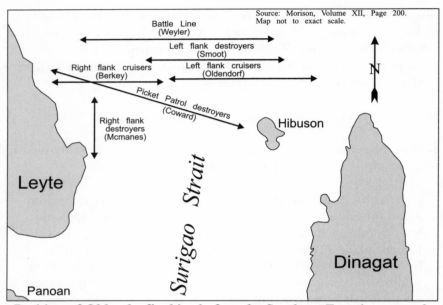

Position of Oldendorf's ships before the Southern Force's approach

guarded his northern flank, Oldendorf realized he had to use his own resources to stop the threat from the south. He could not leave either Leyte Gulf or the Surigao Strait unguarded.[8]

His fleet had been sailing across the mouth and into the waters of the Surigao Strait for the last two days, waiting for information that would clarify the situation. Based on the information from Kinkaid and his own intelligence officers, Oldendorf modified his battle plan to prepare for Nishimura's force.

Oldendorf's force was a formidable one and organized into three battle groups. While Oldendorf had overall command of this force, residing on his flagship, the heavy cruiser *Louisville,* he also had tactical command of the left flank group. RAdm. George L. Weyler commanded the battle line, which had the battleships plus some destroyers. Admiral Berkey commanded the right flank of cruisers and destroyers. The following table shows the ships in Oldendorf's force and their respective commanders.

It was clear the Americans enjoyed overwhelming superiority in ships and firepower vis-à-vis Nishimura's force, which Kinkaid and Oldendorf planned to destroy completely. This was the time to exact revenge for

Ships in Oldendorf's Force

Left Flank (Oldendorf)	Battle Line (Weyler)	Right Flank (Berkey)
Heavy Cruisers	**Battleships**	**Heavy Cruiser**
Louisville, Portland	*Mississippi, Maryland,*	HMAS *Shropshire*
Minneapolis	*West Virginia, Tennessee,*	(Australian)
	California, Pennsylvania	
Light Cruisers	**Light Cruisers**	**Light Cruisers**
Denver, Columbia	None	*Phoenix, Boise*
Destroyers	**Destroyers**	**Destroyers**
Captain Smoot	Commander Hubbard	Captain McManes
Newcomb, Richard P. Leary,	*Claxton, Cony, Thorn,*	*Hutchins, Daly, Bache,*
Albert W. Grant	*Aulick, Sigourney, Welles*	*Killen, Beale*
Captain Conely		Captain Coward
Robinson, Halford, Bryant		*Remey, McGowan, Melvin*
		Mertz
Commander Boulware		
Heywood L. Edwards, Bennion,		Commander Phillips
Leutze		*McDermut, Monssen,*
		McNair

the humiliating defeat the Americans had suffered at Savo Island. Many Pacific naval veterans would give everything they had to erase the memory of that horrible battle. They felt confident their plan would wreak havoc and destruction on the approaching Japanese. Oldendorf positioned his ships to block Nishimura's passage into Leyte Gulf.

The battle line would steam east and west across the strait's mouth. The left flank cruisers would sail 2½ miles south on a course parallel to the battleships. Oldendorf positioned the right flank cruisers about the same distance south of the battle line and west of the left flank cruisers. Berkey's westernmost position brought his ships very close to Leyte Island. The Surigao Strait is only 12 miles wide where his ships were to steam. The ships came quite close to the beach, but Leyte's land mass supplied firm, visible radar echoes that clearly showed where the land was, thus reducing the chances that his ships would run aground.

One destroyer force (the Picket Patrol) ranged across the strait on a diagonal course between Hibuson and Leyte Islands. Another destroyer force (the left flank) steamed on a parallel course with the battle line just north of the left flank cruisers. A third destroyer force (the right flank) sailed a north-south course just east of Leyte Island.

Oldendorf summoned Berkey and Weyler aboard the *Louisville* to review his plan and to discuss a severe supply problem. Oldendorf's initial mission before being called to support the Leyte landings was the bombardment of Yap. Most of the shells aboard his battleships, therefore, were the high capacity explosive (HC) type, designed to destroy beach defenses. Because each ship had limited storage space, the number of 14- and 16-inch armor-piercing (AP) shells that would be used against heavy capital ships were cut to make room for the high explosive shells, which produced a shortage of AP shells aboard the battleships. After their staffs analyzed the ammunition situation, the admirals realized they had enough AP ammunition for just five salvos, which they hoped would be sufficient to destroy or cripple the enemy battleships so the high explosive shells could be used against the smaller ships. Because of the shortage of AP ammunition, they decided they would open fire at ranges between 17,000 and 20,000 yards to improve their accuracy. The number of main armament shells on each American battleship is shown in the table.

Main Armament Shell Inventory for Oldendorf's Battleships

Battleship	AP	HC	Caliber
Mississippi	201	543	14-inch
Maryland	240	445	16-inch
West Virginia	200	175	16-inch
Tennessee	396	268	14-inch
California	240	78	14-inch
Pennsylvania	360	93	14-inch

The destroyers also had no replacements for their torpedoes. In addition, these ships had only 20 percent of their normal 5-inch ammunition supply, because they had used most of it during their bombardment of the Leyte beaches. Therefore, the PTs would have to make up for this shortage. Also, more mines would have to be laid in the Japanese fleet's path.

The order of battle followed the traditional battle plans taught at the United States Naval Academy for the past fifty years. The PTs would be placed at the southern entrance of the Surigao Strait, where they would provide an early warning of the Japanese force's approach. When the Japanese ships came within the boats' range, the PTs would attack to reduce their numbers. Next, the left and right flank destroyers would follow up with a classic torpedo attack from each side of the Japanese ships. Commander M. H. Hubbard's destroyers would screen the battle line.

Destroyer Squadron 54, with Capt. Jesse G. Coward in command, would augment Oldendorf's destroyer attack on his own initiative because he was under VAdm. Theodore S. Wilkinson's command. Although not officially part of Oldendorf's force, he nonetheless would contribute to the attack. At 7:50 P.M. on October 24 Coward sent a message to Oldendorf that showed his intentions: "In case of surface contact to the southward I plan to make an immediate torpedo attack and then retire to clear you. With your approval I will submit plan shortly."

There was no doubt as to what Coward would do. He did not merely volunteer; he was going to be an integral part of this night's battle. This was another example of the American naval officers' courage, initiative, and innovation that had already been seen in the Palawan Passage and would be seen again and again that day in the Surigao Strait and in the days to follow. Any Japanese ships that escaped the PT and destroyer attacks would approach the American battleships and cruisers in a line and be summarily destroyed by the Americans' overwhelming superiority in firepower.

After Oldendorf explained his plans, he looked around the table at Berkey and Weyler. Everyone felt the tension of the moment. Although they did not realize it that night, capital ships would execute the classic crossing the T maneuver for the last time in naval history. Oldendorf would direct maximum fire onto the oncoming Japanese, while they, in return, would direct only minimum fire from their forward guns. The last time this had been done on such a large scale was at the Battle of Jutland in 1916.

Every sailor in San Pedro Bay in north Leyte Gulf would be depending on Oldendorf's success. The rest of the Seventh Fleet could not provide any direct support, though they had plenty of hope and prayers for him and his command. The Americans on Leyte needed the victory that was to come.

The "Peter-Tares" Attack

Thirty-nine PT boats lay in the smooth-as-glass water. The partial overcast that had been lingering earlier in the afternoon on the 24th had now dispersed. The sky was clear and a quarter moon shone brightly on the water. A light, 5-knot wind ruffled small ripples in spots across the strait, and since the weather pattern typical of this time of year included sudden rain squalls, the crews of the PTs were not surprised when small squalls appeared just after midnight to the east-southeast in the Mindanao Sea. Veteran sailors had cause to reminisce about nights like this when the Pacific Fleet had battled the Japanese navy in Iron Bottom Sound, up the Slot, and in Empress Augusta Bay in the Solomon Islands in 1942 and 1943.

The views by American naval strategists of motor torpedo boats had significantly changed since the bombing of Pearl Harbor. At the beginning of the war, naval strategic thinkers saw these small vessels as the fleet's messengers and eyes, and during the Japanese invasion of the Philippines, they were used for this purpose. But after the PTs had some success in sinking Japanese warships, the strategists saw their potential, and they were now seen as offensive weapons.

These boats had certain advantages over other warships. They were much faster, and their shallow draft allowed them to safely navigate the shallow, shoal-infested waters of the Pacific Islands. The PTs had been used to intercept Japanese barges attempting to reinforce the Japanese ground troops in the Solomons. The PT crews who were now waiting for Nishimura's Force C to come up the Surigao Strait had not had any torpedo attack experience since the action in Blackett Strait in the Solomon Islands on August 2, 1943.

In one of their most heralded missions, PT crews had safely transported General MacArthur, his family, and staff part of the way to Australia. These boats were now going to be used in the Battle of Leyte Gulf in an offensive role—the way their designers had intended them to be used. Taking advantage of their exceptional speed and high-powered torpedoes, they would attack a superior Japanese naval force as part of a larger fleet action and establish for themselves a permanent place in naval history.

Tonight the PT crews and their comrades in the Seventh Fleet were as well trained and prepared for the battle to come as any had ever been. PT boats, destroyers, cruisers, and battleships were ready to intercept, harass, and ultimately destroy the approaching Japanese ships. The fast boats had been dispersed over an area 60 miles east-southeast from Surigao Strait's southern entrance in the Mindanao Sea to 25 miles inside the strait. Because of a critical shortage of night-flying patrol planes, the

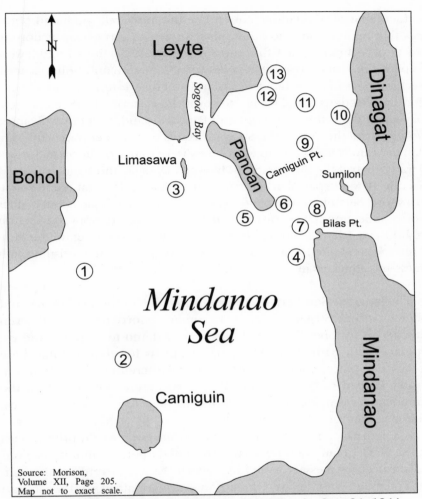

American PT boats' positions in Surigao Strait, Oct. 24, 1944

PTs were acting as the eyes of the fleet, with orders to report any enemy fleet movements, either by radar or sight, and to attack independently. The northernmost boats had instructions to stay clear of Admiral Old-endorf's battleships, cruisers, and destroyers, while the other boats could attack if and when the opportunity arose. Before dark on October 24, all boats were on station, anxiously awaiting orders.

Lieutenant Commander Robert Leeson, in overall command of the PTs that night in Surigao Strait, placed thirteen three-boat sections in the approaches to and within the Surigao Strait. Sections 1 and 2 were to patrol the southernmost area between Camiguin and Bohol Islands. Section 3 was to cover Limasawa Island and the western entrance to Sogod Bay. Sections 5 and 6 were to cover the eastern entrance to Sogod Bay and around the southern tip of Panoan Island. Sections 4, 7, and 8 would patrol the area at the Surigao Strait's southern entrance off Mindanao Island's northern tip where they were to patrol the area. Section 9 was to patrol the Surigao Strait between Dinagat and Panoan Islands. Section 10 was to patrol in a north-south course off Dinagat Island's western shore. Section 11 was to motor across the Surigao Strait about 3 miles north of Section 9. Sections 12 and 13 were to patrol opposite Section 10 off Leyte Island's southeastern shore. Any ships coming up the Mindanao Sea and into the Surigao Strait had to run a gauntlet bristling with harassing attackers in order to enter Leyte Gulf.

The Japanese Southern Force, comprised of Nishimura's Force C and Shima's Second Striking Force, was a combined force in name only, even though on October 21, Shima had been ordered to "support and cooperate" with Nishimura. The Japanese plans for coordinating these forces in its pincer concept gave Shima total discretion, resulting in confusion instead of coordination. When Nishimura tried to attack the American landings in Leyte Gulf and to help Kurita's Center Force, Shima maneuvered independently.

While the Japanese naval planners had sincere hopes for the success of the SHO-1 plan, their hopes were dimmed when Nishimura received a disheartening message from Kurita at 4:00 P.M., reporting that the Center Force had been delayed due to American air attacks in the Sibuyan Sea. Despite this report, Nishimura maintained his force's course and speed. His confidence mounted on receiving a heartening message from Admiral Toyoda at 7:00 P.M.: "All forces will dash to the attack." Determined to fulfill his mission, Nishimura steamed on.

A gloomy darkness descended on the waters of the Surigao Strait despite light from the moon. However, it was not bright enough to make a serious dent in the darkness. Current weather conditions would give Nishimura a reasonable chance to penetrate Leyte Gulf, for the gloom would hide his movements. He knew no air cover or combat air patrol would be forthcoming, nor would he receive help from Kurita. He ordered the heavy cruiser *Mogami* and three destroyers to move in front of his battleships to see what lay ahead. The big cruiser and accompa-nying destroyers maintained a northeast course, while Nishimura's main body remained behind near Bohol Island.

Kurita's Center Force had been delayed, but Nishimura could not risk being caught in the Surigao Strait's narrow waters in daylight, because American aircraft could easily find and destroy his small force. The com-mander of the *Shigure* related later that Nishimura was "the sort of fel-low who would prefer to fight a night battle."

The Japanese navy had been quite successful in night battles earlier in the war, but then it had adequate air support. Now Nishimura was be-ing forced to rely entirely on his own resources, and this placed him in a difficult position.

Ensign Peter Gadd's *PT-131* of Section 1 was in the smooth water off Bohol Island when his radar operator picked up Nishimura's battleships at 10:36 P.M. When the report was repeated to the section's other two boats, all three increased their speed to 24 knots, their boats' bow waves making V-shaped wakes through the still water. The engines' roar grew louder as each boat's captain pushed throttles to the maximum. Water swished past the boats' hulls as they quickly reduced their range to the Japanese ships. Every crew member, officers and enlisted men alike, knew this was the moment for which they had trained. The ensuing twenty minutes seemed like an eternity, but at 11 P.M., several large ships loomed 3 miles ahead.

Nishimura's peaceful passage toward Leyte Gulf ended. The historic Battle of Surigao Strait was about to begin.

At 10:54 P.M., lookouts aboard Nishimura's flagship, the *Yamashiro*, screamed out that they saw American PT boats coming toward them. Nishimura ordered an emergency starboard turn to escape the rapidly onrushing boats. Two minutes later, Japanese searchlights pierced the darkness, pinpointing the American PTs. Night turned to day as the Japanese destroyer *Shigure* fired its 4.7-inch guns. Plumes of water strad-dled the Americans as shells exploded around the fast-moving boats. The Japanese naval gunfire was as accurate as it had always been, and the PTs zigzagged violently to avoid the incoming shellfire, making smoke to hide their movements.

The American boats tried getting closer but failed. A shaft of lumi-nescence from the *Shigure's* searchlight fell on *PT-152*, and a shell from the destroyer struck her, knocking out her 37-mm gun and killing one man and wounding three of her fifteen-man crew. Another shell passed through *PT-130* while she made smoke to protect *PT-152*. Luckily, the shell did not explode, but all of *PT-130*'s radio equipment went dead. The skirmish ended as quickly as it had begun, and *PT-130* sped away to report the location of the Japanese force. Since *PT-130*'s radio no longer worked, her captain used his signal lamp to report the Japanese contact to the nearest boat, *PT-127*. At 12:10 A.M., *PT-127* relayed her report to the American support ship *Wacapreague*.

Sixteen minutes later, at 12:26, Oldendorf received the message. At last, he had the first definitive enemy contact report since 10:00 A.M. on the previous day. Japanese intentions were clear, and Oldendorf knew he had put his ships in the right place.[9]

Oldendorf guessed that Kurita's Center Force was about the same size as his own Fire Support Task Group. The Center Force had entered the Sibuyan Sea where it was attacked by Halsey's carrier aircraft, sustained considerable damage, and then appeared to retire toward the west. However, contrary to Halsey's expectations, Kurita turned around again and headed back toward the San Bernardino Strait. Based on the intelligence Oldendorf had received up to this time, he conjectured about the comparative size and makeup of each force (see table).

Comparison of Oldendorf's Task Group and Kurita's Center Force[10]

Ship Type	Oldendorf's Task Group	Japanese Center Force
Battleships	6	5
Heavy Cruisers	4	10
Light Cruisers	4	1–2
Destroyers	26	About 15
Motor Torpedo (PT) Boats	39	Probably none

It was not clear which force was superior. Oldendorf saw that if he went after the Center Force, the Southern Force would be able to enter Leyte Gulf unopposed and destroy the landing forces now placing troops and supplies on the Leyte beaches. If the Southern Force entered Leyte Gulf successfully, the Japanese could bring in reinforcements, making MacArthur's situation on Leyte extremely tenuous. His forces could be annihilated on the beaches, because MacArthur would be totally cut off from any help, just as he had been on Corregidor. However, Oldendorf was certain that Halsey's Third Fleet was guarding the San Bernardino Strait, keeping Kurita's Center Force at bay. He had received a message from Kinkaid stating that Halsey was forming Task Force 34, which included all of Adm. Willis Lee's fast battleships. These newer ships would be more than a match for the older, slower Japanese battleships; furthermore, Oldendorf's battleships were even older and slower than Kurita's. However, they could still deliver a withering fire on Nishimura's force as it steamed in line up the Surigao Strait.

Oldendorf's decision was, therefore, an easy one. Given his assumption that Halsey's fleet would be in place to stop Kurita, the only thing for Oldendorf to do was to attack the Southern Force now attempting to enter Leyte Gulf through the Surigao Strait. Of course, what Oldendorf did not know was that Halsey had already sent the Third Fleet northward, in pursuit of the Japanese Northern Force, taking Lee's battleships with him and leaving the northern approach to Leyte Gulf unguarded.[11]

Aboard his flagship, the heavy cruiser *Louisville*, on the night of October 24, Oldendorf was unable to sleep. The air seemed clear, but still he could see no more than 2 or 3 miles down the Surigao Strait. Furthermore, the overpowering darkness blotted out the land. The stars stood like aloof signals in the sky. But this was not one of those spectacularly beautiful nights to which he had grown accustomed while serving in the tropics. The moon shone only up to a few minutes after midnight; then, when it had set, the Big Dipper hung upside-down all evening in the northern sky. The Southern Cross stood upright in the south, then disappeared behind gathering clouds until it was as faint as the North Star in the northern sky. There was no wind at all. The sea was flat. Only the faintest reflection of the stars on the water appeared as the ships moved along, leaving phosphorescent foam in their wakes. Oldendorf's battleships to the north had disappeared into the darkness, and the ships on both flanks vanished into the gloom as they pulled away from the *Louisville*.

Oldendorf was able to see only two ships—those immediately in front and behind him. The screening destroyers did become visible for a few brief moments, however, as they maneuvered nearby. The *Louisville* meanwhile stayed on station on the formation's left flank, steaming west, gliding on into the darkness. The moon disappeared behind the western clouds, and the ships changed course at 12:10 A.M., heading east again.

Reports burst in from the PT boats farther south in the strait. These boats had encountered Nishimura's Force C after 11 P.M. *PT-127* reported that three Japanese destroyers and two large, unidentified ships were passing near Bohol Island just before midnight, 10 miles offshore and heading north.

Oldendorf and others on the *Louisville*'s bridge eagerly received each report. Lieutenant Van Derwerker wore a headset trailing a long wire behind him as he followed the admiral around the bridge. He relayed every word from the crowded flag plot, where four officers and six enlisted men helped the commander in the densely packed room. Surrounding them were large quantities of communications, electronic, and plotting equipment used for the transfer of messages and information throughout the fleet.

The admiral's favorite spot was the open bridge, a space on the superstructure's sides and back, below the command bridge. As the Japanese approached, Oldendorf stood on the bridge's starboard side and remained there throughout the battle. Oldendorf's signal officer, whose normal duties during daylight hours were supervising signals to ships in the admiral's command, was on the bridge with him. In the darkness of that fateful night, Oldendorf's subordinate had little to do, so he watched and listened. Every so often someone would come outside from the flag plot for a breath of fresh air or to get away from the crowded room's constant noise. Nerves in that room were being rubbed raw from the metallic, almost constant comments erupting from the "squawk box."

Oldendorf was surprised at the small size of Nishimura's force steaming through such a narrow channel in almost total darkness. Time and time again, however, the Japanese had proved they were capable of doing the unexpected. American radar screens began revealing that the leading Japanese ships were indeed heading up the strait. More PT boats produced reports of additional sightings of two large ships in the Japanese formation. These had to be the battleships predicted by naval intelligence. Captain Coward, commander of the Picket Patrol destroyer formation, which included the ships under Commander Richard H. Phillips, reported that he was starting his run in preparation for attacking the oncoming enemy. Further reports incorrectly indicated that the Japanese admiral had his battleships in the lead position without any destroyer screen in front of them. Oldendorf could not believe a senior naval commander would be so foolish.[12]

• • •

Meanwhile, the *Mogami* and the other destroyers passed near Camiguin Island and escaped detection by PT boat Section 2. The Japanese battleships and the other group steamed forward at 18 knots. The American torpedo attacks had not stopped them. At 11:30 P.M., Nishimura radioed Kurita and Shima: "Advancing as scheduled while destroying enemy torpedo boats."

Twenty minutes later, Lt. (jg) Dwight Owen's Section 3 sighted the *Mogami* and her escorts. *PT-151* and *PT-146*, accelerated to top speed, came within range at 12:15 P.M., and fired one torpedo each at the Japanese ships. As the PTs attacked, the *Mogami*'s searchlight beamed down on the speedily approaching boats. Both torpedoes missed. The boats reversed course and retired at high speed while zigzagging and making smoke. The Japanese destroyer *Yamagumo* fired her guns at the retreating PTs but hit nothing, even though *PT-151*'s port engine stalled for three minutes. Although the PTs were not damaged, their captains did not send any sighting reports, perhaps due to enemy jamming or mechanical failures.

There were reruns of this scenario, as Nishimura's force advanced farther up the Surigao Strait. Several PT groups would sight the enemy, attack, receive ineffective Japanese fire, hit nothing, and retire at high speed under smoke cover. Although the PTs did not slow the oncoming Japanese ships, they reported their course, speed, and position to Oldendorf's command. The Americans now knew precisely what was coming toward them.

The *Mogami* group rejoined the battleships at 12:40 A.M. on October 25. In recombined form, this force moved into an approach formation at 1:00 A.M. The destroyers *Asagumo* and *Michishio* led the way, and the battleship *Yamashiro* followed 4 kilometers back and flanked by two other destroyers, the *Shigure* and the *Yamagumo*. The battleship *Fuso* and the heavy cruiser *Mogami* followed in line at 1-kilometer intervals.

Nishimura's progress satisfied him thus far. The "nuisance" motor torpedo boat attacks had not succeeded. At 1:00 A.M. on October 25, he advised Kurita, already out of the San Bernardino Strait, and Shima, 35 to 40 miles astern, that his ships would "penetrate into Leyte Gulf a little after 0130. Several torpedoes sighted but enemy situation otherwise unknown."

Obviously, the lack of Japanese land-based air reconnaissance kept any

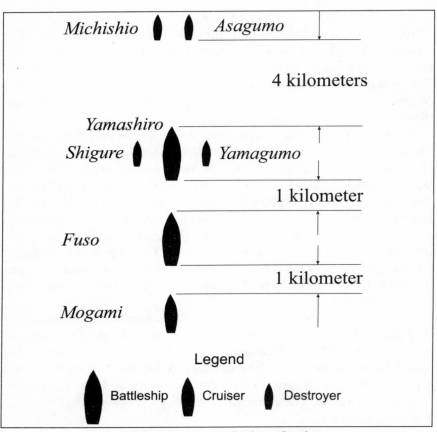

Nishimura enters Surigao Strait

knowledge from reaching Nishimura about what and how many American ships awaited him.

Stationed in the narrows between Panoan Island and Sumilon Island, Leeson, in direct command of PT Section 6, had received the earlier sighting reports of the oncoming Japanese ships. As the Japanese ships drew near Leeson's boats, he commanded his section to attack the approaching Japanese force at 2:05 A.M. The Japanese returned fire and drove off the American PTs. At 2:07, Lt. John M. McElfresh's PT Section 9 was moving south of its assigned patrol area when it attacked the

Japanese ships and fired four torpedoes that missed their targets. More American PTs pressed the attack. Seeking clear targets for their guns, the Japanese turned on their searchlights and fired star shells, causing eerie spots of light to mark the night sky. Gunfire crisscrossed between the American and Japanese ships.

The American PTs continued to press their so far ineffective attacks. *PT-490* launched two torpedoes, but a shell smashed into her, so she reversed course and left the battle scene. *PT-493*, its torpedo hung in the rack, covered *PT-490's* retirement in smoke while three 4.7-inch shells smashed her chart house and blew a large hole in her bottom, killing two men and wounding five others. Its skipper, Lt. (jg) R. W. Brown, probably because his boat was under fire in a desperate battle and had sustained heavy casualties, reported tersely over the radio: "All hands in the cockpit were blown aft, but resumed station."

Petty Officer A. W. Brunelle saved *PT-493* by stuffing his life jacket in the hole and stopping the water's inflow. The boat's engines still ran, but the damage was so great that eventually Brown ordered the boat beached on Panoan Island. He and his crew waded ashore and established a defensive perimeter until *PT-490* rescued them shortly after sunrise. When the tide reached its highest point, *PT-493* slid off the rocks and slipped beneath the deep water's surface.

PT Section 8, commanded by Lt. Cmdr. F. D. Tappaan, shed light on the Japanese by firing star shells, then attacked from the southeast, firing six torpedoes. The Japanese searchlights illuminated the PTs, and the Japanese fired back at the American boats, forcing the undamaged PTs to retire while leaving the Japanese also damage-free.

As far as Nishimura was concerned, the American PTs completed their operations, ending the battle's first phase at 2:13 A.M. Every American attack had been repelled. Thirty of the thirty-nine PTs had engaged the Japanese and fired thirty-four torpedoes. All but two ran "hot, straight, and normal." Still, only one torpedo had hit its target—a destroyer. The Japanese had not been stopped. Instead, they continued steaming up the strait.

At 2:25, *PT-327* from Lt. C. T. Gleason's Section 11 saw Nishimura's force at a distance of 10 miles. The torpedo boat reported the Japanese ships' course, position, and speed to Captain Coward, who ordered the boats to leave the scene as his destroyers approached from the north.

Although the PTs did no serious damage to the Japanese ships, they rendered an invaluable service to the rest of the American fleet by providing accurate reports that alerted Oldendorf as to position, course, and speed. The PTs had shown determination in coolly pressing their attacks in the face of powerful Japanese return fire. Thirty PTs received enemy fire, ten were hit, but only one had been sunk. The total casualties were three killed and twenty wounded.

Relentlessly, Nishimura steamed ahead to an uncertain future.

Here Come the Greyhounds

When Nishimura peered through his binoculars up the Surigao Strait at 2:13 A.M., he must have been pleased. He believed that gunfire from his ships had severely damaged and even sunk several of the American attackers. Quiet descended again on the Surigao Strait. Nishimura continued on his way, a course that would lead him to face a division of American destroyers under the command of Capt. Jesse G. Coward.

Captain Coward had positioned his squadron on the Surigao Strait's eastern side. His Picket Patrol destroyer group included the seven destroyers *McGowan, Melvin, Mertz, McDermut, Monssen, McNair,* and his flagship *Remey.* Commander Phillips was part of this group. Coward's destroyers patrolled along a diagonal course between Leyte Island and Hibuson Island. At 2:13 A.M., his destroyers were on Surigao Strait's eastern side, which meant they would be on the Japanese ships' starboard quarter when they steamed forward.

It was hot that night, at least 80 degrees, with almost no breeze. The destroyers' decks and bulkheads dripped with moisture from the stifling heat and humidity. The technology of the time did not allow for air conditioning on naval vessels, so sailors welcomed every opportunity to go on deck. The ships' fuel supply was down to 45 percent capacity, so the captains had slowed their ships' speed, meaning hardly any breezes would pass through the vents to the lower decks. Occasional lightning flashes illuminated the canyon-like walls of the islands on both sides, giving Coward a view about 3 miles down the strait.

The initial contact reports that began coming in at 12:26 A.M. on Oldendorf's ship had identified Nishimura's Force C ships. Twelve minutes later, another contact report showed that Admiral Shima's Second Striking Force had been spotted as well. The Americans realized they were facing two widely dispersed forces and changed plans accordingly. At 1:07 A.M., *PT-523* reported star shell bursts 10 miles west of Panoan Island in the Mindanao Sea. At 2:00 A.M., *PT-134* reported a ship steaming north on Panoan Island's beam. This message was relayed to all American forces. Coward thus realized the Japanese were only 30 miles south of his destroyers and put his ships on battle alert by issuing the command "general quarters."

Coward planned an "anvil attack" using ships from two destroyer groups. Leaving the *McNair* and *Mertz* behind on picket duty at the Surigao Strait's northern exit in case the other Japanese force appeared, the western group with the destroyers *McDermut* and *Monssen* and the eastern group with the *Remey*, *McGowan*, and *Melvin* would steam south toward the approaching Japanese ships and launch a torpedo attack on their flanks. The destroyers would approach the Japanese at 30 knots and slow only to fire their torpedoes accurately. Following the attack, Coward would withdraw close to the land areas alongside the strait to make way for the American cruisers and battleships. A sailor's natural inclination is to fire everything he has. However, Coward knew that gunfire would reveal his position to the Japanese and was well aware that his destroyers' 5-inch shells could not stop a battleship.

The destroyers were to be used in a classic way. They would launch an offensive torpedo attack before the Japanese ships came within range of the heavier ships. This technique was taught at the United States Naval Academy and been part of American surface battle doctrine for years. But it had been seldom used during World War II, and, when it was, it never quite worked. This time, however, things would be different.

The anticipation of a deliberate night attack rubbed the destroyers' crews' nerves raw. Surprise attacks were actually easier. To calm everyone's nerves, each destroyer's captain ordered coffee and sandwiches served after midnight.[13]

Cecil M. Kent was a destroyer veteran who had served on the old four-stack destroyer *Bainbridge* after he joined the navy on January 3, 1941. He fought in the Battle of the North Atlantic for two and a half years before being assigned to the *McGowan*, where he rose to the rank of Machinist Mate First Class. On October 11, 1944, as a "seasoned" nineteen-year-old veteran, he and his ship left Manus Island for the Philippines. Kent was aboard the *McGowan* in the Surigao Strait on October 25.

All that night the TBS never stopped squawking about the approaching Japanese fleet. At 1:30 A.M., the *McGowan*'s captain, Cmdr. W. L. Cox, ordered the crew to bring the steam pressure to its maximum level and stand by. Over the intercom, he told the crew the ship was going into battle against a force of Japanese ships and would try something that had never before been successful—attack a battleship with torpedoes. The *Remey*, with Captain Coward on board, would attack the first large ship in line, a battleship, and their ship, the *McGowan*, would attack the second ship in line, another battleship. The *Melvin* would attack a third target—a cruiser.[14]

General quarters sounded at 2:06 A.M. on the *McGowan*. Two columns of destroyers formed, attacking on the starboard (eastern) and port (western) flanks of the Japanese warships. Leading the eastern group, Coward issued a "follow me" order at 2:30 to the *McGowan* and the *Melvin*, and the group steamed south at 20 knots. The western destroyer group under Commander Phillips headed south on a 170-degree course. Commander C. K. Bergin, *Monssen*'s skipper, gave a characteristic before-the-battle speech: "To all hands. This is the captain. We are going into battle. I know each of you will do his duty. I promise you that I will do my duty to you and for our country. Good luck to you, and may God be with us."

At 2:40, a blip that was 18 miles away on a 184-degree heading appeared on the *McGowan*'s radar screen. Five minutes later, the blip became a column of ships steaming due north 15 miles away at a speed of about 20 knots. The two opposing groups of ships now headed for one other at a combined speed of 40 knots. They would meet each other in about twenty to twenty-five minutes.

In the meantime, Nishimura's ships were changing position from approach to battle formation and had almost completed the reformation. Four destroyers would head his column, followed by the flagship *Yamashiro* and, at 1-kilometer intervals, followed by the *Fuso* and the *Mogami*.

A lookout stood in the Japanese destroyer *Shigure*'s crow's nest, scanning the seas. Any Japanese sailor would be proud of having such an honorable assignment, as it meant he had sharp eyesight. At 2:56 A.M. three ships suddenly appeared in his glasses about 8 kilometers away. Picking up the intercom telephone, he immediately reported his sighting to the bridge below.

The *Yamashiro*'s biggest searchlight flashed on, sweeping the seas ahead, but its beam, piercing the darkness, revealed nothing. The Americans were too far away to be seen by searchlight, but this would not be true for long.[15]

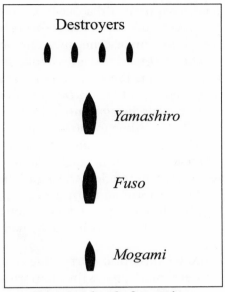

Japanese battle formation

The *McDermut* remained at its assigned patrol station across the Surigao Strait. The men on midwatch aboard this destroyer were nervous but silent. Some time after 2:00 A.M., they felt the ship turn and increase speed. Their monotonous routine—waiting—had come to an end. One of the torpedo men glanced quickly at the gyro-repeater, which showed they were heading in a southward direction. Someone muttered, "This is it." Butterflies fluttered somewhere deep in their stomachs.

Torpedoman's Mate 3d Class Richard Parker was at his battle station on the port bridge wing along with the torpedo officer, Lt. (jg) Daniel Lewis. Lewis ran the port torpedo director. Both men had a unique vantage point where they could hear incoming radio accounts. Parker spoke into the sound-powered phone system to relay the reports to the torpedo stations. Torpedoman's Mate 3d Class Roy West sat at his battle station, the gyro-setter for torpedo mount number two. He looked at his mount captain, Torpedoman's Mate 2d Class Harold Ivey, as each man listened over their sound-power telephone headphones. American PT boats were on the attack. Each time the word "battleship" was uttered, West and Ivey looked into each other's eyes. No words were needed.

Everyone who has served on board a warship knows quiet times can be a curse or a luxury. As a curse, they are an overwhelming boredom that can sink one's soul. As a luxury, they mean no one is firing at you. For the men aboard the *McDermut*, thoughts about quiet time vanished rapidly. A few minutes following the attack reports, activities aboard the destroyer escalated, which meant the *McDermut* was going into battle. The men calculated a torpedo firing solution as the ship decreased its distance to the Japanese. According to the information that came down from the port torpedo director, the men on both torpedo mounts quickly matched pointers, set the firing angles on the gyros, and turned the torpedo mounts to match the angles. The night's heat and hard work made heavy beads of sweat form and drip from their foreheads. Roy West's heart beat heavily as he concentrated on the job at hand. His mind and fingers worked instinctively, based on what he had learned in countless training exercises.

The *McDermut*'s rudder turned to port as the destroyer's speed increased. She heeled over to starboard as the quartermaster in the wheelhouse pulled the wheel for a 40-degree turn. The destroyer steadied as her course paralleled the target's approach course. The two ships were heading straight toward each other. If they continued on course, no correction of the gyro angle would be needed. The *McDermut*'s firing solution was nearly perfect. West had never been as close to a Japanese ship as he was now. The two ships closed the distance at a relative speed of nearly 50 knots.

Meanwhile, deep within the *Remey*'s hull, it was dark in the Combat Information Center. Captain Coward listened intently as the reports from the PT boats came in. When the reports made clear that the Japanese had passed the last of the PT sections, Coward sent a message to Oldendorf to the effect that he was taking his destroyers down the strait. The *Remey* led the way, followed by the *McGowan* and the *Melvin*, along the strait's eastern side, while the *McDermut* and *Monssen* continued southward on the western side.

Not many minutes passed before the *Remey*'s radar picked up the Japanese ships coming up the strait. Although the approaching Japanese ships were still unseen to the human eye, small green blips on the radar screens, blips that flared, faded, and reappeared, told an unmistakable truth. A number of Japanese ships were 38,000 yards away on a compass bearing of 184 degrees, heading straight for the American destroyers.

Convinced he could direct the action from the bridge, Coward left the CIC, climbed the ladder to the main deck, opened the hatch door, and walked outside. The night's blackness and humid air surrounded him like a warm, woolen blanket. After climbing another set of stairs, he reached the *Remey*'s bridge.

A few moments passed, and at 2:40 A.M., the bridge's speaker crackled to life. The CIC reported they could clearly see the blips of seven Japanese ships on the radar screen. As the range closed, the radar operator was able to make out the relative sizes of the approaching warships. There were four destroyers, two battleships, and a cruiser. Coward's destroyers continued at full speed, and five minutes later, the volume of words increased over the bridge speaker as voices excitedly reported the rapidly diminishing radar ranges in a language totally unrecognizable to anyone who has never served on an American naval vessel, a language as colorful as the people who invented it and used it: "Skunks [Japanese ships] bearing one-eight-four, distance fifteen miles, over." "Standby to execute speed four. Jack Tar and Greyhound One acknowledge." "This is Jack Tar [*McGowan*], WILCO." "This is Greyhound One [*Melvin*], WILCO." "This is Blue Guardian [*McDermut*], I am coming left to zero-niner-zero to fire fish."[16] And so on.

Two sections of five American destroyers now raced toward the Japanese column. This small force, with a total displacement of about 12,500 tons, was about to engage a force nearly eight times its size. The Americans did not stop to consider the odds and moved toward their targets.[17]

Coward ordered the *Remey* to attack the first battleship, the *McGowan* the second battleship, and the *Melvin* the cruiser.

Signalman 2d Class Jessie D. Dye occupied a ringside seat on the *Melvin*'s bridge, excited and tense with anticipation. Questions raced through his mind as he kept his station: Would we be successful? Would they find us? Not much time would pass before his questions found answers.[18]

Captain Coward's destroyer flotilla was busy as well on the strait's eastern side. The destroyers *Remey*, *McGowan*, and *Melvin* closed on Nishimura's ships at 45 knots. At 2:50 A.M., Coward ordered his flotilla to change course to 150 degrees in order to secure a better firing angle. Coward's plan was to make three successive turns to 120 degrees before firing his torpedoes. At 2:54, his radar detected the Japanese to the south, so he decided to maneuver his column toward the Japanese to get a 50-degree torpedo firing angle on his bow 7,500 yards away. Coward closed the enemy almost head-on.

This was the moment for which every naval officer had trained and waited. The Japanese were well within torpedo firing range, and the firing solution could not have been any better. Calmly setting the tone for his command, Coward sent a message to the *McGowan* and *Melvin* at 2:57: "I [*Remey*] will take first target, you [*McGowan*] and Melvin take second; Comdesdiv 108 [*McDermut, Monssen*] take small one and also number 3."

As the range closed, the oncoming targets became somewhat more visible. *Melvin*'s lookouts saw Nishimura's ships at 2:58, about 12,800 yards away. Coward ordered funnel smoke, turned left, closed at 30 knots, and ordered, "Fire when ready."

Just after 3:00 A.M., the *Remey*, *McGowan*, and *Melvin* launched torpedoes. When a large Japanese searchlight bathed the *Remey* in bright light, it made her crew feel as exposed and vulnerable as "animals in a cage." About seventy-five seconds later, twenty-seven Mark-15 torpedoes whooshed out of three destroyers' tubes and sped through the water at 33½ knots. The torpedoes' range was set to 10,000 yards, although the Japanese ships lay at a distance of between 8,200 and 9,300 yards. Knowing it would take approximately eight minutes for the missiles to find their targets, Coward ordered a hard turn to port and fled the battle scene on a 21-degree course. Each American destroyer made smoke and zigzagged violently. As the destroyers turned, the *Yamashiro* and Japanese destroyers opened fire, ringing Coward's ships with salvos of shells and geysers of water. The men aboard the *Melvin* thought the exploding shells were depth charges and noted that the star shells gave off such a brilliant light that a book could actually be read on deck. Despite this sound and fury, they signified nothing, for the American destroyers escaped without damage. Not a single Japanese shell made a direct hit.[19]

In his diary, Cecil Kent described what happened on the *McGowan* during this early morning encounter.

> October 25 - 0301 hours: Three of us began attack. The other two of our squadron will head in from left side of [the Surigao] Strait.
>
> When the *Remey*'s torpedoes hit the destroyer, the whole area lit

up like the 4th of July. It blew up. At this time we had broadsided
the battleship *Fuso* and fired our ten torpedoes.

The *Fuso* put their searchlights on us and started laying out a 14-
inch broadside that straddled us. The bridge used to lay out smoke
from our boilers. Then they said to get more speed. We were already flanked out wide open (30–32 knots). The battleship *Fuso's*
attack on us lasted until the first torpedoes hit her then another.
Then the search lights went out.[20]

The *McDermut* and her companion destroyer, the *Monssen*, moved on
toward their targets. The men in the *McDermut's* CIC had been listening
to Coward's orders, and the first word that torpedoes had been fired by
the eastern destroyer contingent came over the TBS. Richard Parker repeated the message over the sound-powered phone to the men in the
McDermut.

Roy West stared into the pitch blackness on the ship's port side, trying to make out what was happening on the strait's eastern side, but it
was too dark to see anything. Just when he thought he would never find
out what was going on, orders came over his earphones to get the torpedoes ready for firing. A sudden burst of light in the sky loomed above
the *McDermut* as a Japanese star shell lit up the night sky. The burning
flare floated slowly toward the water as it hung from its parachute's
shrouds and cast an eerie gray-white light on the water's surface. West
looked toward the *McDermut's* stern and saw the *Monssen* illuminated in
an ashen-gray pallor. He hoped the Japanese did not spot either destroyer. Up ahead, a green searchlight started sweeping the sea. Its beam
made broad half circles on the water's surface, trying to see the approaching American destroyers in its brightness.

At 3:09 A.M., West heard the familiar explosive whooshing sound beneath him as electrical commands from the bridge fired five torpedoes.
All five missiles leaped from the ship and splashed into a sea now boiling in the destroyer's wake as she accelerated to attack speed. Both of
the *McDermut's* quintuple torpedo mounts fired everything they had. Ten
lethal harbingers of death left wakes in their paths as they sought their
Japanese targets. The *Monssen* unleashed a full salvo of ten more torpedoes. The Surigao Strait was now not a safe place for any ship.

Knowing there would not be enough time to reload the torpedo tubes
and fire again, the bridge sent orders to secure the torpedo mounts. West
and his fellow torpedo men quickly obeyed the order and gathered

around CPO Virgil Rollins, who, using a flashlight with a red-filtered lens, stared at a stopwatch. All knew it would take some time for the torpedoes to reach their targets, but that did nothing to lessen the anxiety. As they counted the seconds, the *McDermut* heeled over sharply as she made a hard, tight 180-degree starboard turn and headed back up the strait. She moved fast and the wind swept across her decks. The heaving deck made everything seem out of control.

Suddenly, the ghastly pall of a green searchlight poured over the destroyer's deck. The Japanese had found them. West then felt a shock that radiated from a nearby explosion as a large geyser of water rose from the sea off the *McDermut*'s port side. Warm saltwater drenched the *McDermut*'s weather decks as several more rounds exploded nearby.

Before he lost his reason, West heard Chief Rollins—who was still studying his stopwatch—calmly say, "It's about time for something to happen."

Rollins' words were prophetic. The dark gloom to the southeast exploded into a brilliant glow as a monstrous fireball took form. Two more

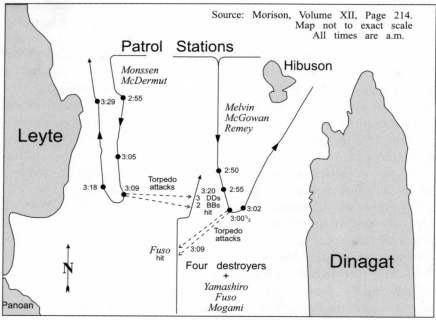

Coward's destroyers attack Force C

blasts then lit up the southeastern sky. A strange mixture of fear, awe, and exhilaration filled Roy West as he gazed at this ironic mixture of beauty and death. He transfixed his eyes for a moment, but then explosions closer at hand diverted his attention, because the *McDermut* now frantically dashed northward, weaving like a football halfback trying to avoid tacklers.[21]

Standing on the *Remey*'s bridge, Coward turned his glasses on the Japanese ships. Enough time had elapsed for the torpedoes to reach their targets, but, amazingly, the Japanese ships had not changed course in response to the American torpedo attack. Glancing at his watch, Coward saw it was between 3:08 and 3:09 A.M. Flashes of light filled the distant darkness as the thunder of deadly explosions reached Coward's ears. Gunfire was not their cause however; the battleship *Fuso* took one hit from the *Melvin*'s torpedoes. Slowing, she turned 180 degrees, caught fire, and fell behind the others in the Japanese column. The light from her fires could be seen for miles. Thinking this light was from a burning American ship and remaining blissfully ignorant of what had happened to his command, Nishimura did not know that he had lost half of his battleship strength. Without altering his course, he continued northward up the Surigao Strait.[22]

At least six explosions erupted as some of the torpedoes from Coward's destroyers struck their targets. The men aboard the destroyers speeding up the strait's western side could not see the fireballs produced by the destroyers' torpedoes on the Surigao Strait's eastern side. As both destroyer groups fled up the strait, the blips on American radar showed that the Japanese column had greatly reduced speed with its ships seemingly circling.

Japanese shells no longer fell near the rapidly retiring *McDermut* and *Monssen*. Staying close to the Leyte Island's shoreline, they tried to avoid radar detection by hiding in the island's radar shadow, leaving the strait clear for the American ships lying in wait for the oncoming Japanese. A section of American PT boats failed to realize that the *Monssen* and the *McDermut* were American ships, however, and started their engines and sped toward the unsuspecting destroyers under full throttle.

Commander Phillips, leading the Picket Patrol's western contingent, had been listening continuously to the PT boats' radio traffic as well as his own from the *McDermut*'s bridge. When he heard that the PT boats

were attacking, he quickly guessed that the range and bearing information they passed over the radio pointed directly at his ships. Swiftly,
Phillips contacted the wayward PTs and prevented a terrible tragedy.
Thus, the *McDermut,* the *Monssen,* and the other destroyers on the strait's
eastern side continued retiring northward without mishap.[23]

More Greyhounds Coming

Captain Coward's destroyers had inflicted crippling losses on Nishimura's command. Half of his battleship power lay wallowing up to its
gunnels. Two other ships lay at the water's bottom. But the American destroyers were not through yet.

Ten minutes after the *Monssen's* and the *McDermut's* torpedoes
smashed into the Japanese ships, the destroyers under Capt. K. M. Mc-
Manes' command attacked on the Japanese left flank. At 2:54 A.M., Rear
Admiral Berkey sent a radio message to McManes: "When released, attack in two groups. Until then, stay close to land."

Another message arrived at 3:02: "Proceed to attack, follow other
groups in and return northward, make smoke."

Five of McManes' destroyers were of the newer 2,100-ton class. His
flagship, the *Hutchins,* was the first of her class to have the new CIC. It
would prove a valuable tool in directing the attack by providing important information to the squadron and group commanders. More important, it also supplied complete gunnery and torpedo information to
the ship itself. McManes broke naval tradition by directing the attack
from the CIC rather than from the ship's bridge. This technique would
be used many times by future naval commanders during World War II
and for naval engagements fought in later years. However, it was an ironic
twist of naval history that destroyers would never be used in this way
again.[24]

McManes' squadron cruised south in two sections. The first section
contained the *Hutchins, Daly,* and *Bache;* the second section, under
Cmdr. A. E. Buchanan of the Royal Australian Navy, had HMAS *Arunta,*
followed by the *Killen* and *Beale.* At 3:17 A.M., McManes ordered his ships:
"Boil up! Make smoke! Let me know when you have fired."

As they approached the oncoming Japanese ships, one of the Japanese
destroyers, the *Yamagumo,* hit by one of the *McDermut's* torpedoes, exploded, setting the horizon brilliantly ablaze and providing more than
enough light for Buchanan's attack.

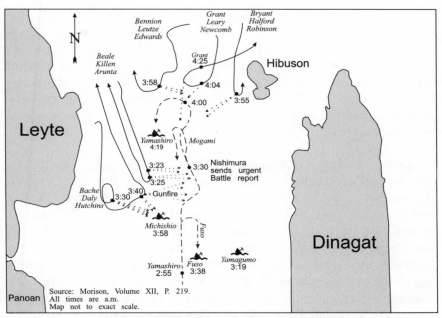

McManes's and Smoot's destroyers attack

The *Arunta* closed the range to 6,500 yards with the leading Japanese destroyer, the *Shigure*, and, at 3:23 fired four torpedoes, all of which missed. Two minutes later, the *Killen* launched five torpedoes at the *Yamashiro* from a distance of 8,700 yards. One hit its target. The Japanese battleship slowed temporarily to 5 knots but kept moving. Fifteen seconds later, the *Beale* launched five torpedoes from 6,800 yards; none hit their targets. All torpedoes spent, Buchanan's group turned 180 degrees and headed up the strait at high speed.

It was now McManes's section's turn to attack. Moving due south at 25 knots, at 3:30 they fired fifteen torpedoes at Nishimura's fleet at ranges of between 8,200 and 10,700 yards, then reversed course. Immediately after launching, two torpedo wakes of unknown origin crossed the *Daly*'s bow. The *Bache* opened fire with her guns, and the Japanese returned several salvoes. However, these proved to be inaccurate.

Charles Fast, on duty in the *Daly* that night in the forward fire room during what was called "the burner watch," clearly remembers bringing the boilers on line and increasing steam pressure as the *Daly*'s speed accelerated during their torpedo run. After their torpedoes were launched, the boiler room crew turned on the smoke burners and laid down its smoke screen. Deep in the ship's bowels, the only way the men below could find out what was going on topside was via the ship's telephone. Moments before the *Daly* launched several torpedoes, two enemy torpedoes sped by the *Daly*, scaring the men in the forward fire room and everyone else besides.[25]

After steaming in a complete loop, McManes executed a wide turn to the east and north, then closed the range with the Japanese. The *Yamashiro* had recovered from its earlier torpedo assault by the *McDermut* and increased speed to 15 knots on a 340-degree course. The *Mogami* steered due north at 20 knots, and the *Shigure* made 26 knots. At 3:40 A.M., the *Hutchins*, *Daly*, and *Bache* fired their 5-inch guns. When the American torpedoes hit the Japanese ships, three gigantic explosions rocked the humid night air. Huge, round, orange fireballs filled the horizon. Although no one has ever learned the cause of these fires, some historians have speculated that either the *Fuso* blew up or the *Yamashiro* fired her main guns.

It was now clear that the American destroyers had inflicted serious damage on Nishimura's fleet. The blips on the radar scope in the *Hutchins*'s CIC showed the effects of the relentless attacks. The once orderly Japanese column had taken on a ragged look. Still seemingly unperturbed by the tumultuous action raging around her, the *Yamashiro* pressed ahead, though the *Mogami* and *Shigure* sheered off starboard. The other crippled ships were either aimlessly drifting or had retired southward. Just as McManes was about to resume his attack, Admiral Berkey ordered him to cease his attack and leave the scene, fearing the American destroyers would run afoul of battleships and cruisers waiting farther north to engage the Japanese. The *Hutchins* nonetheless launched five more torpedoes a minute later at the *Asagumo*. Another crippled Japanese destroyer, the *Michishio*, drifted into the torpedoes' path and took all five torpedoes. She blew up and sank immediately at 3:58 A.M.

As the *Hutchins*, *Daly*, and *Bache* retired, they caught up with the *Yamashiro*. The Japanese battleship opened fire but overshot its targets, and the American destroyers escaped undamaged.

But the American destroyers were not done with Nishimura's doomed force. Destroyer Squadron 56, under Capt. Roland N. Smoot's command, was responsible for protecting the left flank cruisers. But at 3:35 A.M., his assignment changed when Smoot received an order from Oldendorf: "Launch attack. Get the big boys!"

Smoot's Destroyer Squadron 56 was deployed into three sections:

Destroyer Squadron 56 Deployment

Section	Section Commander	Destroyers
1	Capt. R. N. Smoot	*Albert W. Grant, Richard P. Leary, Newcomb*
2	Capt. T. F. Conley	*Bryant, Halford, Robinson*
3	Cmdr. J. W. Boulware	*Bennion, Leutze, Heywood L. Edwards*

Assigned to predetermined areas, all the destroyers in Sections 1, 2, and 3 sped southward at 25 knots, approaching the Japanese bow to bow. At 3:45, as Conley's section reached its assigned firing area, a bright glow appeared on the southern horizon, the result, so Conley thought, of Japanese gun flashes. He ordered his yeoman to transmit a flasher message to his section: "This has to be quick. Stand by your fish."[26]

At 3:51 the Japanese sighted Conley's section and opened fire. Uncharacteristically, their aim was inaccurate, so their shots fell short and wide. Conley, afraid gun flashes would betray his position, did not fire back. Between 3:54 and 3:59, all three destroyers in his section fired five torpedoes each from a distance of 8,380 to 9,000 yards. His section then turned and rapidly retired northward; not a single one of the torpedoes found its target.

The *Edwards, Bennion,* and *Leutze* of Section 3 sped toward the *Shigure* and *Yamashiro.* The Japanese returned gunfire when the destroyers fired their torpedoes at around 3:58 from a distance of 7,800 to 8,000 yards. Shell flashes and geysers of water mobbed the Americans, who, in response, made smoke and raced toward Leyte Island. The *Shigure* reversed course from 010 degrees to 180 degrees. In this encounter between Nishimura and Sections 2 and 3, neither side inflicted any damage on the other.

Smoot's section planned to make a head-on attack in the exact center of the Surigao Strait. Carefully, Smoot evaluated the radar blips to avoid hitting Conley's squadron.

A deadly pyrotechnic display ensued, filling the sky with light. The Japanese fired continuously for fifteen minutes using main battery gunfire. Shells fell around the American destroyers as they made their escape. Meanwhile, shells from the American battleships and cruisers roared overhead, converging on the *Yamashiro.*

Lieutenant (jg) Jack Conley remembers that his fellow officer, Lt. (jg) Harris Warren, said the shells sounded like freight trains roaring overhead. From Conley's position in the *Newcomb's* CIC, he knew his destroyer was now moving at 40 knots and saw, too, that the distance to the *Yamashiro* was 1,500 yards. The American destroyers were so close to the battleship that its big guns could not be depressed to a level low enough to fire at the nearby American destroyers.

Just before the *Leary, Albert W. Grant* and *Newcomb* turned to port, the *Yamashiro* slowed and turned to port from a northerly course to a westward one. The American destroyers changed their planned port turn by turning to starboard and paralleling the battleship's course. Now the American destroyers' torpedo-firing solution became much simpler. At 4:04 A.M., the *Leary* fired three torpedoes, while the *Newcomb* and *Albert W. Grant* each fired five fish from 6,200 yards away. Seven and a half minutes later, two torpedoes crashed into the *Yamashiro's* beam, raising two huge water columns against her side as they exploded.

As soon as the destroyers launched their torpedoes, they turned 180 degrees and headed back up the strait at flank speed. Later, Conley noted he did not recall hearing a single explosion. Fear had consumed him, shutting out all sounds. Nonetheless, his earlier intensive training carried him through his fear and enabled him to concentrate on his job. A destroyer that makes a torpedo run against a battleship is on a suicide mission, making the likelihood of surviving such an operation very small. All on board a warship in the heat of battle know this. Nonetheless, the men concentrated on their duties, and any evidence of fear never surfaced.

The *Leary* and *Newcomb* led the retiring column and escaped damage. The *Albert W. Grant* was not so lucky. As the *Leary* and *Newcomb* headed up the strait, a message arrived in the *Newcomb's* CIC that the *Albert W. Grant* had apparently taken friendly fire and was badly damaged. The *Newcomb's* captain, realizing the two destroyers may be hitting the *Albert W. Grant,* got on the TBS and screamed to the *Newcomb* and the *Leary:* "Cease fire! Cease fire! You are hitting our ships!"[27]

The *Newcomb* immediately stopped firing. Just as the *Albert W. Grant* began a turn, however, a large caliber shell rocked her, so she launched all her torpedoes at the Japanese ships and tried to escape as fast as she could go. Eighteen more shells shook the now hapless destroyer, and she was dead in the water. Her skipper, Cmdr. Thomas A. Nisewander, was wounded as he tried to rescue the men trapped below decks. Smoot ordered the *Newcomb* to come alongside. The rescuing ship's crew was petrified because there were many unexploded 6- and 8-inch shells on the *Albert W. Grant*. Conley remembered that the *Newcomb* stayed alongside her heavily damaged companion for an hour or so. Using a towline, they pulled the *Albert W. Grant* to safety, thus saving her to fight another day. However, thirty-four officers and enlisted men lost their lives in her misadventure, and, to this day, no one was sure whether the gunfire that pummeled the *Albert W. Grant* came from the Japanese or was friendly fire.[28]

Coward was sure they had scored at least three hits on the Japanese out of the forty-seven torpedoes launched from his two columns. In actual fact, they had scored five hits and sunk three ships, including the battleship *Fuso*, which sank beneath the waves at 3:38 A.M. After the war, Admiral Oldendorf called the attack "brilliantly conceived and well executed."

The American destroyer actions in the Surigao Strait were among the finest in the Battle of Leyte Gulf action. Although Coward and McManes received a certain amount of criticism for launching their torpedoes from a longer range than was customary, their decisions were based on the need to avoid running aground in the strait's narrow waters. The brave attacks of the American destroyers inflicted severe damage on Nishimura's command, sinking 75 percent of his force's firepower. This battle yielded the best demonstration to date of how America's high-speed destroyers could be used to disable an enemy. Yet the heroism of the American destroyer crews in the Surigao Strait would be repeated in spades in just a few hours in the waters off Samar.[29]

Exacting Revenge

While the Seventh Fleet's primary mission was to directly support MacArthur's amphibious landings on Leyte, its bombardment forces of escort carriers and old battleships along with smaller warships (cruisers, destroyers, and motor torpedo boats) made it a formidable naval force in its own right. When Nishimura's pair of old battleships and supporting ships had been spotted from the air on October 24, Kinkaid planned a warm welcome. He assigned the task of defending the Leyte landings from this threat from the south to Admiral Oldendorf's bombardment and support group. Its battle line would be led by six old battleships, five of which had survived the Pearl Harbor attack. Two of these had once lain on Pearl Harbor's bottom but had been raised to sail again.

At the center of the battle line were three 35,000-ton battleships—the *West Virginia*, the *Tennessee* and the *California*—which had undergone thorough modernization. The *West Virginia* had eight 16-inch guns; the *Tennessee* and *California* had twelve 14-inch guns. The only ship not a Pearl Harbor veteran was the *Mississippi*, which had been modernized prior to the war. She had twelve 14-inch guns and led the battleship line. The 16-inch gun *Maryland*, although modified extensively since Pearl Harbor, was not as modern as her former sister ship, the *West Virginia*. The *Pennsylvania*, the sister ship of the *Arizona*, was last in line with her twelve 14-inch guns.

Admiral Weyler commanded the battleships as they patrolled the Surigao Strait's northern entrance. Two lines of cruisers steamed south of the battleships on each side of the strait. Admiral Oldendorf was in the heavy cruiser, the *Louisville*, on the eastern or left flank with the heavy cruisers *Portland* and *Minneapolis*, which were sister ships built between the world wars. Commanded by RAdm. Robert W. Hayler, the modern light cruisers *Denver* and *Columbia* followed. The prewar Brooklyn-class light cruisers *Phoenix* and *Boise* and the Australian heavy cruiser *Shropshire*, commanded by Rear Admiral Berkey, were on the strait's right or western side.

The *Shropshire, Phoenix,* and *Boise* are interesting because the *Shropshire*, which flew the white battle ensign of the British Royal Navy, was the largest ship, representing what once had been the most powerful navy in the world. It was abundantly clear, at this stage of the war, that the Americans had built the world's most powerful navy. (After the war, the two cruisers were given to the Argentine navy. One of them, the *Phoenix*, was renamed the *General Belgrano* and was the first—and so far the only—warship to be sunk by a nuclear-powered submarine, in the 1982 Falklands War. This cruiser had participated in what has been acknowledged to be the end of an era in naval warfare—the last battle between super dreadnoughts in naval history. Thus a new era began in the Falklands when a new kind of capital ship sank one from a past era.[30]

Oldendorf paid close attention to the destroyers' reports and watched the light flashes to the south. While he knew it was possible some of the flashes were gunfire, the destroyer reports and radar suggested something else. Too many flashes resembled torpedoes exploding against the sides of Japanese ships. The destroyers evidently had been busy whittling Nishimura's fleet down to size.

Captain Coward sent a message to the effect that two large ships and one small one were heading in Oldendorf's direction. The *Fuso* lay in two smoldering hulks farther south, and Japanese battleship strength had been cut in half. Only one battleship and two smaller ships were moving up the Surigao Strait. Oldendorf's confidence in the ultimate outcome rose, because he knew he had both superior battleship strength as well as supremacy in cruisers and destroyers.

Oldendorf sounded general quarters at 2:30 A.M. At 3:12 a searchlight beam flashed far to the south. Oldendorf recalled later that it looked like a "walking stick of a blind man being waved through the night, though what it touched we could not see."

The light went out as suddenly as it had appeared, and at this moment Coward reported that his destroyers had fired all their torpedoes and seen five hits, though two was a more likely number.

At 3:30 all three American task groups steamed eastward near the western side of the Surigao Strait. The crew on the *Louisville* saw a flare of light, followed by the sound of an explosion. One destroyer division in Captain Coward's command reported that one of their torpedoes had struck a Japanese ship, thus causing the explosion.

Oldendorf reviewed the situation. The Japanese ships had been steaming northward in a single column consisting of one battleship, one heavy cruiser, and one destroyer, all moving directly into the jaws of an American trap. Their column was set to form the vertical portion of a classic T, while the Americans were in a line that formed the broad horizontal part of the T. However, the Japanese began to change direction when the American destroyers attacked. Also, their formation became less organized, even though its general direction was north. Oldendorf was set to cap the T just as Togo had done to the Russians in the Battle of Tsushima Strait. Now it was the Americans' turn.[31]

• • •

Oldendorf's anticipation mounted as he asked for the range to the Japanese ships every few minutes. From the *Louisville's* flag bridge, one deck below the command bridge, he looked up to the next deck and saw the skipper, Capt. Samuel H. Hurt, leaning on the rail. Hurt looked down at him, and while no words passed between them, it was clear that both were anxious to get into the upcoming battle.

Oldendorf broke the silence: "What range do *you* get, Sam?"

"Seventeen thousand yards, sir," Hurt replied.

"Have you got a good set-up?" the admiral asked.

"Yes, we have."

Seventeen thousand yards was about 8½ miles away, a moderate range for the guns of Oldendorf's battleships and cruisers. However, he wanted to make certain every shot counted, because he did not have as many armor-piercing shells as he would have wished. So, he waited a little longer. When the range had closed to 15,600 yards at 3:51 A.M., he turned to Van Derwerker and commanded, "All right, give the order to open fire."

Derwerker picked up the phone and issued the order, one rapidly echoed on every American ships' squawk box. The ominous darkness of that fateful night broke into bright flashes of deadly light.

The radar screens in the American ships' CICs revealed the location of the Japanese ships. At 3:33 A.M., from a range of about 33,000 yards, Admiral Weyler ordered the battle line to open fire when the Japanese ships came within 26,000 yards. Like his superior, Admiral Oldendorf, he had no wish to waste the few AP shells he had and wanted to get closer to improve his guns' accuracy. With the oncoming Japanese ships 22,600 yards away at 3:53, the resurrected battleships from the Pearl Harbor disaster would wreak their revenge. The great guns of the old battleships filled the early morning darkness of October 25 with thunder and light.[32]

The *Louisville's* six forward guns' muzzles exploded with a deafening noise and a blinding light. Oldendorf sat but a few yards away from them. As they fired it seemed as though a powerful lightning storm had brewed, covering the black waters. Smaller light flashes in the distance from Admiral Berkey's cruisers' guns punctuated the night sky. The light flashes bounced off the hillsides of Leyte's eastern shore. Flashes from the battleships' guns to the north penetrated the darkness with still more light as their big shells passed overhead, making the roaring sound of a fast express train crossing over a bridge. Scores of arching light streaks curved over the *Louisville* and converged on their distant targets.

However, Oldendorf missed a great deal of this brilliant display. He was so close to the *Louisville*'s guns that the flash temporarily blinded him when they fired. Spots danced before his eyes for several minutes, preventing him from seeing the entire show. Still, he saw enough to appreciate what was happening.

In order to see more of the effect of his ships' fire, he went impatiently to the flag plot to see what was happening on the radar screen. Here the effect of the glare disappeared, and he was able to locate sixteen blips on the radar screen. Reflecting there might be sixteen Japanese ships, Oldendorf thought to himself, "Well, there won't be that many very long."

His curiosity satisfied, the admiral returned to the flag bridge, sat down, lit a cigarette, and took in the sights and sounds of the battle. Heavy shells roared overhead. Giant flashes erupted miles to the north as the battleships fired broadsides. The rumble from the gunfire rolled down the strait's waters like thunder from a distant storm. The tracers seemed to draw closer together as the shells' accuracy improved with each salvo. Every man on the *Louisville*'s bridge could see plainly the effects of the shells. Flares bloomed as they hit, exploded, started fires, and sometimes caused still more explosions.

Captain Smoot recorded his recollections of what happened that night:

> It was a privilege of the Destroyer Squadron Commander to watch the gunfire . . . from a position considerably removed from the line of fire. The devastating accuracy of this gunfire was the most beautiful sight I ever have witnessed. The arched line of tracers in the darkness looked like a continual stream of lighted railroad cars going over a hill. No target could be observed at first. Then shortly there would be fires and explosions, and another enemy ship would be accounted for. I witnessed, personally, three ships destroyed one after another in this fashion.[33]

Using the newest Mark-8 fire control radar, the *West Virginia, Tennessee,* and *California* had a firing solution for its main batteries and were ready

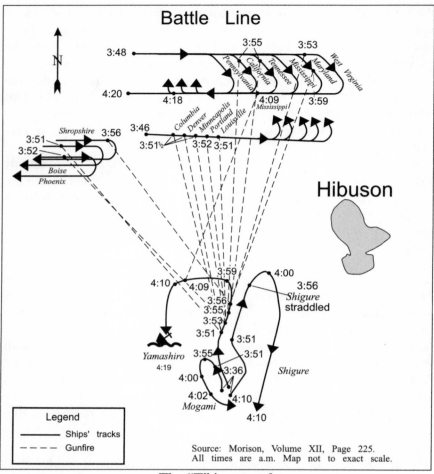

The "T" is crossed

to fire well before the Japanese came within range. These three ships would make the greatest contribution to the battle action. The *West Virginia* opened fire at 3:53 A.M. and sent ninety-three 16-inch armor-piercing shells at the Japanese before ceasing its fire. The *Tennessee* and *California* commenced firing at 3:55 and shot sixty-nine and sixty-three 14-inch armor-piercing shells, respectively. Equipped with the older Mark-3 fire control radar, the remaining three battleships could not find a target. The *Maryland* found its targets by getting the range from the

West Virginia's splashes and fired forty-eight rounds of 16-inch shells in six salvos. The *Mississippi* fired one salvo at 3:59, while the *Pennsylvania* never found a target and did not fire its guns that night.

The battle line's speed increased to 15 knots and had traveled too far east to get a good firing angle for its main guns. Oldendorf therefore ordered two turns in order to reverse the ship's easterly course so as to steam westerly. Now the *Mississippi* had a better firing angle and opened fire on the *Yamashiro*, which was 20,990 yards away on a 192-degree bearing. The Japanese heavy cruiser *Mogami* was 3,000 yards farther away and appeared to be reversing course. Although Oldendorf ordered all ships to cease fire, the *Mississippi* fired its full salvo at 4:09 and thus had the honor of firing the last large gun salvo of this battle, thus ending an era that had begun in the seventeenth century.[34]

Nishimura's Troubles Continue

The *Yamashiro* slowed to 12 knots at 3:52 A.M. and continued its 20-degree course. It continued firing only at visible targets, because it had no fire control radar. Seemingly oblivious of what was happening around him, Nishimura steamed boldly into a terrible gunfire inferno, bringing with him only the heavy cruiser *Mogami* and the destroyer *Shigure* for support. To the sinking *Fuso*, he sent a futile message ordering it to make top speed, and then "all hell broke loose."

Admiral Shima, in the meanwhile, had not received any messages from Nishimura and thus had no idea of what he was about to face.

Many naval historians have criticized Nishimura as having been too reckless with his command in the Surigao Strait. This line of criticism should not be accepted in a light or casual manner, given what happened to this beleaguered commander and the unique circumstances of his assignment. Other naval historians reasonably argue that the criticisms leveled at him have been far too harsh. To better understand his experiences and the perceptions they engendered during the last desperate hours of his life, it is necessary to consider what happened to him and his command during the final fight for their lives.

American torpedo boats had attacked him with ferocity and frequency ever since his force had steamed into the Surigao Strait's southern entrance. Then the American destroyers assaulted his force. By 2:20 A.M., the old destroyers *Yamagumo* and *Mitsushio* had been attacked and sunk. The destroyer *Asagumo* sustained heavy damage and had to retreat southward. The *Fuso* lost her ability to steer and dropped back. Nonetheless, despite these heavy losses, Nishimura held fast to his mission, steaming northward with the four ships he had left in his command, arranged in a single column. At 3:20, acting on his orders, they proceeded on to Leyte Gulf.

As Nishimura scrutinized the darkening eastern sky from the *Yamashiro's* flagship bridge, his radar showed approaching American ships. At 3:23, he radioed the information to Kurita and Shima: "We have sighted what appear to be enemy ships."[35]

Seven minutes later he radioed again: "Enemy torpedo boats and destroyers present on both sides of northern entrance of Surigao Strait. Two of our destroyers torpedoed and drifting. *Yamashiro* sustained one torpedo hit but no impediment to battle cruising."[36, 37]

This is the last message Nishimura sent to Kurita. A second torpedo then hit the *Yamashiro*, heavily damaging the old battleship, so Nishimura signaled his ships: "We have been torpedoed. Proceed independently to the attack."

These words capture perfectly the fighting spirit of this valiant man. Moments after he sent them, a third torpedo hit the *Yamashiro*.[38]

Life aboard the *Yamashiro* and *Mogami* now became unbearably chaotic, as crews struggled mightily to repair the awful damage, but American and Australian 6-inch, 8-inch, 14-inch, and 16-inch shells slammed onto the doomed ships' decks and sides. A torrent of destruction fell like a deadly rain from the sky as the American heavy and light cruisers, including the *Denver*, *Minneapolis*, *Columbia*, and *Portland* continued the devastating barrage after the battle line ceased firing. Since 3:51 A.M., the cruisers had fired an incredible 3,100 shells. Although totally overwhelmed, the Japanese ships nonetheless boldly returned fire, the *Mogami* for a short time and the *Yamashiro* for a little while longer. The crippled *Yamashiro* directed her main batteries' fire at the American cruisers and her secondary guns at the torpedo attackers.

The only splashes from Japanese large caliber fire that the American battle line could see landed near the destroyer *Claxton*, which was screening the larger battleships. The destroyer's captain remarked: "If we had been the leading battleship, it would have resulted in an extremely well-placed hit."

The Japanese fire proved to be so ineffective that even their star shells fell far short of their intended targets. And the battleships were never visible to the beleaguered Japanese vessels. Soon their crews would join their fellow shipmates aboard the *Fuso* by sinking into the Surigao Strait's shark-infested waters.

The Slaughter Continues

Before Oldendorf's cease-fire order, Admiral Berkey's right flank cruisers, the *Phoenix* and *Boise*, fired countless shells into the hapless *Yamashiro*. The *Phoenix* fired fifteen 8-inch gun salvoes every fifteen seconds. Berkey noticed that a strong easterly breeze blew away the gunfire smoke, making it easier to see the Japanese ships. The Australian heavy cruiser *Shropshire* was having trouble with her fire control radar and had to fall back on optical sighting. Belatedly, she fired her 8-inch guns. As returning Japanese shells splashed on both sides of her, she increased her firing pace. The American cruisers *Denver* and *Phoenix* stopped firing when they turned right to a westerly course, but the *Shropshire* continued firing as she turned with the Americans. The *Denver* and *Phoenix* then resumed fire as they completed their turn at 4:00 A.M.

The eventful midwatch ended at midnight, but this had no effect on the rush of events. The *Yamashiro* had been zigzagging in a northerly direction, firing purposefully, absorbing many heavy caliber hits, and straightening her course in a west by south direction. Bright flames stretched the entire length of her decks, illuminating her 5-inch turrets. The *Mogami*, meanwhile, retired to the south, while Nishimura's sole remaining destroyer, the *Shigure*, moved sharply eastward. One 8-inch shell hit the destroyer, penetrating her decks, but did not explode. Several near misses knocked out her gyro compass and radio. Since she had no radar, she could not find the American attackers to fight back with her torpedoes.

Nishimura and the officers and crew of the *Yamashiro* regarded Oldendorf's cease-fire as a gift from the gods. Although severely damaged, the battleship turned south in a desperate attempt to escape. In reality, she had only ten more minutes to live. At 4:19 A.M., a violent explosion from her magazines tore huge holes in her hull. She rolled over and sank, taking Nishimura and all but a few crew members with her. When the Americans rescued the battleship's few survivors later, they were too dazed and exhausted to report accurately on what had happened.

When the shelling began, the *Mogami* absorbed even more damage than the *Yamashiro*. She turned left at 3:53 A.M., increased speed to 15 knots, and began retreating southward. At 4:01, she launched torpedoes while taking gunfire from Captain McManes' destroyers. She caught fire, turned south, and made smoke. American shells continued pummeling her as she tried to escape. At 4:02, a salvo, probably from the *Portland*, exploded on her bridge, killing all officers on board, including her captain and executive officer. Other shells crashed into the engine and fire rooms, and she slowed to a near stop. While she had taken a severe beating, she could still move and managed to escape to the south.

The American destroyer *Richard P. Leary* reported that torpedoes had passed nearby, fired by the *Mogami* before she retired. This torpedo sighting report rekindled respect for Japanese torpedo attacks, prompting Weyler to order the *Mississippi*, *Maryland*, and *West Virginia* to turn north and leave the battle scene. Admiral Thomas E. Chandler ordered the remaining battleships on a westerly course. Weyler's order took half the battleships out of the conflict. When Admiral Oldendorf ordered all ships to resume firing at 4:19, no Japanese ships appeared on the radar screens. The *Mogami* had moved out of range, and the *Yamashiro* had disappeared beneath the waves.

By 4:20 A.M., Nishimura's force, previously scheduled to arrive in Leyte Gulf, was utterly finished. Of its two battleships, only the *Fuso*'s burning stern was still afloat. Three destroyers had been sunk or disabled by torpedoes in the middle of the Surigao Strait, and a badly damaged heavy cruiser and a damaged destroyer were retiring southward. The Japanese could extract not a drop of consolation from this defeat, for the only American ship to suffer any appreciable damage was the destroyer *Albert W. Grant*, which had been damaged most likely by friendly fire.

Yet the Japanese had more to face in the Surigao Strait. Admiral Shima's Second Striking Force was about to encounter the wrathful presence of American sea power.[39]

Who Should Be Blamed?

As an effective fighting force, Nishimura's command no longer existed. Its only remaining large warship, the *Mogami*, had been damaged so badly she could barely inch down the strait toward her eventual demise. The destroyer *Shigure* was relatively undamaged, so she was able to retreat and arrive in Brunei on October 27. Who was responsible for this debacle? The perished commander, Nishimura, could not answer, since he was beyond the reach of such worldly concerns.

In fact, no single senior Japanese officer survived to tell of the gallantry of such men as the rear admirals Katsukiyo Shinoda in the *Yamashiro,* Masami Ban in the *Fuso,* and all the others. Commander Shigeru Nishino of the *Shigure* was the only surviving commanding officer after this battle.

After the war, the U.S. Strategic Bombing Survey questioned him, and in these interviews, he revealed that Nishimura prepared his men for battle by underscoring that spiritual readiness was as important as combat readiness. Nishimura placed the coming battle in the broadest possible context. Knowing how slim the odds for success were, he reinforced in his men the tenets of the *Bushido* code that preached it was an honor to sacrifice oneself for emperor and nation. His attitude set the tone, and his men willingly followed him into a situation in which they faced almost certain extinction. While no memorial exists today for this heroic fighting man and his command, no one should fault this brave admiral and the men of his command for their gallant stand against overwhelming odds.

A Strange Paradox Indeed

A constant array of strange and inexplicable Japanese tactical naval decisions characterized the Japanese modus operandi in the Battle of Leyte Gulf. After Nishimura's Force C ceased to exist, another Japanese force came on the scene. The Japanese destroyer *Shigure* desperately signaled this force and learned it was the Second Striking Force, part of the Southern Force, and under VAdm. Kiyohide Shima's command. Shima's flag flew in the heavy cruiser *Nachi.* The time of the encounter was 4:30 A.M. on October 25.

Why did Nishimura's and Shima's fleets approach Leyte Gulf separately? What plans existed to coordinate the two admirals' actions? Allied historians have criticized what transpired as a glaring example of command disunity, but Japanese naval historians have a different point of view.

Admiral Shima's force originally consisted of ten ships, the heavy cruisers *Nachi* and *Ashigara,* the light cruiser *Abukuma,* and the destroyers *Akebono, Kasumi, Ushio, Shiranuhi, Wakaba, Hatsushimo,* and *Hatsuharu.* This force's makeup was no match for its mission. It had too few ships and, more importantly, not enough firepower to engage the American battleships of the Seventh Fleet. So why was Shima's force thrown into the maw of the Seventh Fleet? An explanation exists for this deadly puzzle, one that spotlights the disarray existing at Combined Fleet Headquarters in Tokyo.

Shima's ships were not under Kurita's command, nor were they part of Ozawa's Northern Force. Shima reported directly to the Combined Fleet Headquarters and was tactically independent in the Leyte operation. Five days before Kurita's ships left Brunei, Shima's force had been placed in VAdm. Gunichi Mikawa's Southwest Area Fleet but was still answerable only to Tokyo—an odd situation indeed.

Shima's force had been shifted about from command to command and from area to area so many times that Admiral Shima might well have felt like the proverbial stepchild. His fleet's original mission had been to defend the northeastern part of the Japanese homeland. When the entire Japanese fleet was reorganized in August 1944, following its defeat in the Marianas, Shima was assigned to Admiral Ozawa's First Mobile Fleet. Shima's ships trained with that fleet in the Inland Sea until mid-October, 1944.

The situation for the Japanese became more complex in mid-October, when Halsey's fast carrier forces attacked Formosa. According to the inaccurate, misleading reports filed by surviving Japanese pilots, the Formosa Air Battle constituted a great Japanese victory, and these overwhelmingly optimistic reports led the Japanese Naval High Command to falsely believe that twelve American capital ships had been sunk and another twenty-four heavily damaged. The Combined Fleet Headquarters thus assumed that the Americans would not be returning any time soon. The actual damage to American ships was an entirely different matter, however. Only two American cruisers had been damaged, while the Japanese had lost hundreds of planes. The Formosa Air Battle was a clear American victory. Of course, the Japanese had a great desire to believe in the tempting illusion that their pilots had unwittingly portrayed.

Because of these groundless reports, the Combined Fleet Headquarters ordered Shima's fleet to hunt down what was assumed to be a crippled American fleet fleeing south of Formosa and, at the same time, to rescue downed Japanese pilots. The Combined Fleet Headquarters picked Shima's ships because they were fast and mobile. Shima's men confidently looked forward to their forthcoming mission, expecting an easy time attacking crippled American ships. As Shima's ships approached the approximate location of the supposedly sinking American ships, an astonished Shima was met instead by two enormously powerful naval forces completely intact and spoiling for a fight. Knowing that his small force would last less than five minutes in a battle with such a powerful array of ships, Shima wisely turned his cruisers and destroyers around and headed at a flank speed of 34½ knots for Amami O Shima (a small island approximately 400 kilometers south-southwest of the Japanese home island of Kyushu) and comparative safety.

New orders arrived on October 18, assigning Shima's ships to the main body of a mobile surface counterattack force, which could mean but one thing: his force was going to become a counterlanding force. After the war, staff officers assigned to the Combined Fleet Headquarters admitted that these new orders were more than an attempt to cover up the mistake they had made of sending these unfortunate ships on the illusionary "mop-up" operation near Formosa five days earlier. With Shima's ships now part of the Southwest Area Fleet under Vice Admiral Mikawa's command, they were sent to Mako in the Pescadores to await further orders.

Mikawa's Southwest Area Fleet included Vice Admiral Ohnishi's Fifth Land-based Air Force (First Air Fleet) in the Philippines, and Vice Admiral Fukudome's Formosan Sixth Land-based Air Force (Second Air Fleet). Despite the devastating losses in the three-day Formosa Air Battle of October 12–14, these air forces still had some power. However, the surface naval component of the Southwest Area Fleet was far weaker than its air strength, since the only surface ships were the ten in Shima's command. At noon on October 21, an order arrived from the Combined Fleet that was relayed by Mikawa's headquarters to Shima. This order stated: "It is deemed advisable for Second Striking Force (Shima) to storm into Leyte Gulf from the south through Surigao Strait, and cooperate with the First Striking Force."

This was the third change in orders Shima had received in one week. First, he had been sent on a fruitless chase after the Americans near Formosa. Then he had been told to wait for new orders. Now he had been ordered to engage an American force of unknown size and strength at Leyte Gulf. It should come as no surprise, therefore, that Shima's officers believed the Naval High Command viewed their pitifully undersized force of ten ships as no more than a plaything.

Shima's and his staff's patience had been stretched almost to the limit, yet the critical importance of the Leyte operation to the empire forced Shima and his command to put personal feelings aside and obey the orders given. On the morning of October 21, the Combined Fleet ordered three of Shima's destroyers, the *Wakaba*, *Hatsushimo*, and *Hatsuharu*, to

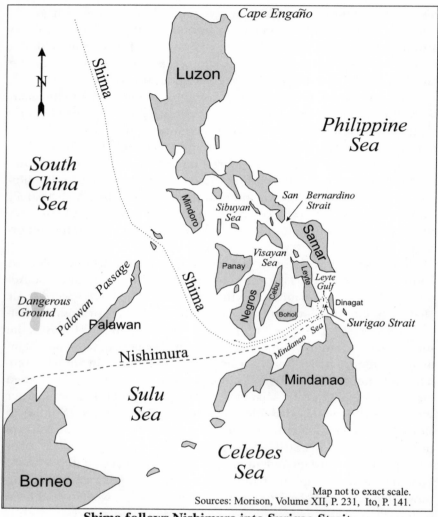

Shima follows Nishimura into Surigao Strait

act as transports between Tokyo and Manila, and so Shima's already small force of ten became three destroyers smaller. At 4:00 P.M., the rest of Shima's force hastily departed from Mako for Coron Bay, on the other side of Mindoro Island. But Shima then received some information about what would happen next. Messages arrived notifying him of Nishimura and Kurita's operational plans.

Adding to the confusion, the Combined Fleet Headquarters also sent Nishimura's orders to Shima that let him know that he would not meet with Nishimura in a prebattle conference or receive any specific orders from either Nishimura or Kurita. Headquarters hid the fact from him that the operation would turn out to be a suicidal one or, at the least, one with very low odds for success. The only fact he did know was that he was to act as a rear guard for Nishimura's Force C. Despite these changes in orders, Shima displayed the characteristic Japanese obedience even to the vaguest of orders and led his seven ships into the Mindanao Sea on the morning of October 24.

It is important to keep in mind that, in visualizing this situation, Shima was not in Nishimura's chain of command but was, rather, the senior admiral on the scene. Therefore, there was no reason for Shima to take orders from Nishimura. On the other hand, since Nishimura was in command of the main force entering the Surigao Strait and did not know that Shima was steaming into the Surigao Strait as well, he had no reason to seek out or to obey any orders from Shima. Lacking detailed, definitive plans for the advance up the Surigao Strait and lacking clear directives from Combined Fleet Headquarters, these totally uncoordinated, independent commands were, in effect, hurled haphazardly into the same battle area with no senior commander on the scene in charge of them both. As a consequence, Nishimura and Shima steamed forward on courses independent of one another, with Nishimura going first and Shima deciding to follow one hour later.

Shima overheard Kurita's radio message to Nishimura soon after 10:00 P.M., ordering their two forces to meet 10 miles southeast of Samar Island at 10:00 A.M. on the 25th. On his initiative, Shima decided to join these forces at their rendezvous, and so he increased speed to arrive at Leyte Gulf at 4:00 A.M. on the 25th as well. Consequently, he arrived deep in Surigao Strait at the battle's scene just after Nishimura's Force C had been annihilated.[40]

Shima's Second Striking Force had enough power to make it a force of some consequence. Shima had two heavy cruisers, the *Nachi* and the *Ashigara*, each mounting ten 8-inch guns and eight torpedo tubes and each having a 36-knot cruising speed. An old four-stack light cruiser, the *Abukuma*, also sailed with the Second Striking Force. She was built in 1925 and was a veteran of the Pearl Harbor attack. Because of this fact, the Americans had a special incentive to sink her. The four destroyers *Akebono*, *Ushio*, *Kasumi*, and *Shiranuhi* made up the rest of the force.

Shima believed that if he could link up with Nishimura's Force C, their combined fleet could wreak havoc on the American landing force. The only contact he had with Nishimura let him know that Nishimura's Force C was under attack by motor torpedo boats. At that time, Shima's Second Striking Force was approximately 40 miles astern of Nishimura. At 1:00 A.M., gunfire flashes appeared in the distance, and Shima's officers overheard radio messages sent by Nishimura, ordering his ships to evade American torpedo attacks.

The next two hours passed uneventfully. At 3:15 A.M., the ships passed into a rain squall that made the ships' hulls ring with a peppering sound. Lookouts sighted torpedoes fired by the *PT-134*. All missed their targets. At 3:20, Shima ordered a simultaneous starboard turn and increased speed to 26 knots.

Five minutes later, however, Lt. (jg) I. M. Kovar's *PT-137* fired a torpedo at the *Abukuma*. It exploded against its port side, killed thirty men, and forced the cruiser to slow to 10 knots. She fell out of formation as the rest of the ships continued on a 20-degree course. Kovar aimed the torpedo at a destroyer heading south to assume a position to Shima's rear, but it hit the cruiser instead.

Admiral Shima's column minus one cruiser changed course to due north and increased speed to 28 knots. As the column turned, lookouts saw what appeared to be two large ships on the surface. Deducing these might be the *Fuso* and the *Yamashiro*, Shima's heart sank. Two hulks burned furiously as his formation passed. Actually, these smoking derelicts were the two pieces of the *Fuso*, which were formed when the old battleship disintegrated in a violent explosion earlier that night. Shima realized it was now more important than ever to give whatever support he could to Nishimura. A disturbing fact that he could not know at this time was that Nishimura had perished with the *Yamashiro*.

The heavy cruiser *Ashigara* trailed the *Nachi* on a northwesterly course of 330 degrees. Orders went out to search for targets and to get the ships' torpedoes ready for firing. Shima looked at his radar monitor, where he saw two blips, believed to be American ships bearing north at a distance of 9,000 yards. At 4:24 A.M., Shima ordered both cruisers to launch torpedo attacks at them. The two cruisers turned right to course 90 degrees, and each ship fired eight torpedoes. All sixteen missiles missed their targets and bubbled harmlessly to the north. Two were found later on a Hibuson Island beach. Shima's Second Striking Force would make no further contributions to the battle.

As Shima quickly took stock of his situation, he had no idea what had happened to Nishimura and assumed the worst, for the American destroyers' heavy smoke blinded his vision to the north. He recalled his forces, retired southward, and showed unusual discretion for a Japanese admiral when he sent a message to all Japanese naval forces in the Philippines: "This force has concluded its attack and is retiring from the battle area to plan subsequent action."

Captain E. Kanooka, the *Nachi*'s skipper, noticed the burning *Mogami*, which appeared to be lying dead in the water. Actually, however, she was moving very, very slowly. Kanooka, thinking the *Mogami* was not moving, ordered the *Nachi* to change course to 110 degrees so as to avoid the burning cruiser. He made a serious error of judgment in changing course, and thus the two cruisers collided, badly damaging the *Nachi*'s stern. The *Mogami*'s distressed crew wondered why the fully functional *Nachi* had not been able to avoid their flaming ship. From their perspective, the *Nachi*'s crew was clearly in the wrong.

The damaged *Nachi* slowed to 18 knots as water flooded some of the decks below. The *Mogami*, on the other hand, made an extraordinary effort to increase its speed in order to join Shima's column and managed to stay even with the *Nachi*. Shima ordered the *Shigure* to join his formation, but the destroyer's steering malfunctioned because of her inoperable steering engine. While she lagged behind, she could still attack Lieutenant Gleason's PT section and inflicted slight damage on *PT-321*.

By 5:00 A.M., and with sunrise only an hour and a half away, Nishimura's Force C was broken and defeated and what was left of it was retreating. The battleships *Fuso* and *Yamashiro* had been lost in the middle of the Surigao Strait, joined by the destroyers *Yamagumo* and *Michishio*. The lucky *Mogami*, although severely damaged, and the swift *Shigure*, had thus far escaped. Shima's force, minus one light cruiser, retired safely southward.[41]

The total action by Shima's force in the Surigao Strait lasted only five minutes. The Americans declared this minibattle a rout. From the Japanese perspective, it was an ineffective hit-and-run action. Nonetheless, the orders that had directed Shima's force to take part in this operation were flawed from the beginning.

In interviews with American investigators after the war, a staff officer who had participated in the planning observed that the Shima force had added nothing at all to the battle and had been a mere useless addition. Japanese newspaper reporters have noted that Shima's mission had no chance of success. The problem, they said, was that the planners at Combined Fleet Headquarters had been too optimistic and incompetent. To blame Shima for Japan's failures in the Surigao Strait was, in the opinion of these Japanese reporters, a great miscarriage of justice. In their view, the unfortunate admiral had simply carried out his duties to the best of his ability given the information he had, which was very little.[42]

Mopping Up the Leftovers

Rear Admiral Robert W. Hayler scanned his radar screen. On it three Japanese ships appeared—the *Nachi*, the *Ashigara*, and the *Mogami*—heading southward, 14 miles away. The radar images were large enough to be cruiser-size at the least. Hayler reported his sighting to Oldendorf.

"Oley" was then steaming south in the *Louisville* with the other cruisers in a column with Captain Smoot's destroyers providing screen support. Oldendorf ordered the right flank cruisers to move south along the Leyte shore and sent a message to Admiral Kinkaid at 4:40 A.M.: "Enemy cruisers and destroyers are retiring. Strongly recommend an air attack."[43]

Oldendorf had added screen strength to the battle line. Although no Japanese submarines had been sighted, he dared not risk the old battleships, because they were needed to protect the Leyte landings. Despite his caution, the admiral ordered some of his destroyers, under Commander Hubbard, to steam south and join the cruisers as their screening force. The destroyers continued south at 25 knots but never got close enough to the escaping Japanese ships to mount an attack. By 5:35 A.M., they overtook the pursuing left flank cruisers.

The *Claxton*, Hubbard's flagship, sighted approximately 150 Japanese survivors in the water about twenty minutes later. Oldendorf ordered the recovery of a few of them, but because they were still in a battle zone, the destroyer could not stay very long to rescue many survivors. Accordingly, the *Claxton*'s crew lowered a whaleboat into the water and it moved toward the men. True to tradition, the Japanese sailors refused rescue, preferring death to the dishonor of capture. Of course, this only made it more difficult to pull them out of the sea. A Japanese officer ordered the whaleboat to stay clear, but the boat's crew persisted and, in the end, pulled three sailors from a watery grave. One of these, a warrant officer, spoke English. He confirmed that his ship, the *Yamashiro*, had indeed sunk—welcome news to the Americans.

The American left flank cruisers maintained a 15-knot southerly course down the strait in pursuit of the retreating Japanese. This cautious, slow speed unfortunately allowed the fleeing Japanese to escape temporarily further American surface attacks. Although the American radar screens did detect Shima's force, Shima, realizing the Americans outnumbered and outgunned his small force, continued his retreat.

Dawn pierced the darkness hanging over the Surigao Strait. As the American sailors on duty on the various ships' bridges scanned the looming land masses of Leyte and Dinagat on both beams, Philippine patriots gazed back at them. These land-bound people had seen the flashes in, over, and around the Surigao Strait all night and wondered what had happened, hoping the hated Japanese ships had been sunk. Their hopes were rewarded when they saw Japanese sailors swimming toward shore. Memories of the brutal Japanese occupation of their homeland boiled up, and as the Japanese sailors swam to the seeming safety of the shores, angry Filipinos bent on revenge met them, but not with safety on the natives' minds. Knives and bolos greeted the luckless warriors who reached the beaches.

The American sailors, for their part, sought relief from the oppressive heat below decks by coming topside to breathe in the cool morning air and to discuss the previous night's battle. Many wondered how many Japanese ships were still afloat. How good it felt to be alive that morning, with a dry, safe deck beneath their feet.

Thousands of sailors in San Pedro Bay stayed awake all night and saw a multitude of flashes in the distance. The sailors were, however, too far away to hear the gunfire. Later on, radio transmissions brought news of a vaguely encouraging nature that made them feel the Japanese Southern Force was no longer a threat. Unfortunately, this feeling of security was temporary.

By 5:20 A.M., Oldendorf's left flank cruisers reached the site at which the *Mogami* and *Nachi* had collided an hour earlier. American lookouts saw two Japanese ships burning and a third one with no apparent damage. The admiral ordered the column to turn right to 250 degrees. The lookouts verified that the ships were Japanese, and the *Louisville, Portland,* and *Denver* fired their guns at the *Mogami*. The crippled Japanese cruiser took several direct hits. Lookouts on the *Louisville* reported the hapless cruiser was "burning like a city block," but she was not yet finished. As the Japanese ship burned, Oldendorf ordered the American left flank cruisers away from the action to concentrate on the possibility of another battle to the north.

At about 6:00 A.M., the lookouts on *PT-491,* commanded by Lt. (jg) H. A. Thronson, and part of Lieutenant McElfresh's cross-strait patrol, spotted a large Japanese ship with several smaller ships, 4 miles off Panoan Island and steaming south at 6 knots. The larger ship was the *Mogami,* and *PT-491* was following her. The PT boat's crew attempted to report these ships' positions, courses, and speeds, but the Japanese jammed the radio circuit. The Japanese cruiser opened fire with 8-inch shells. Shells exploded around the beleaguered boat for about twenty minutes. Some came as close as 25 yards, lifting the small boat out of the water and drenching its deck with sea water. As the PT rapidly retired under heavy fire, it fired two torpedoes at the cruiser, but both missed.

Shima's force headed for the Mindanao Sea at high speed to shake off the pursuing Americans. The American right flank cruisers pulled out of the chase so they could join the battle line. But the Japanese met with more trouble from other PTs. Lieutenant R. G. Mislicky's PT Section 5 picked up the Japanese cruisers at about 6:20 P.M. *PT-150* fired one torpedo at the *Nachi.* The cruiser dodged, returned fire, and hit *PT-194,* seriously wounding the section commander and two other men. *PT-190* encountered a column of "six large ships."[44] Two Japanese destroyers left their positions and opened fire on the PT. The boat made smoke and retired toward Sogod Bay. The Japanese column moved toward the Mindanao shore at 16 knots to avoid the PT attacks, a maneuver that was successful.

But, the battle was not over. American aircraft and ships entered the picture. The Americans tried to attack the swiftly retreating Japanese ships with land-based bombers, but found these planes lacked the range to locate the ships. However, American naval aviators did have sufficient range to relentlessly and effectively pursue the retreating Japanese ships. Admiral Sprague's escort carriers launched an attack with torpedo bombers and fighters at 5:45 A.M.

Meanwhile, daylight came for Oldendorf at about 6:17 A.M., when he again turned southward. At 6:43, Oldendorf ordered Admiral Hayler to send his two light cruisers and three destroyers southward a second time "to polish off enemy cripples." At 7:07, all five American ships fired at the destroyer *Asagumo,* which had lost its bow in earlier action with Captain Coward's destroyers. As the crippled Japanese ship swapped fire with two American destroyers, the *Denver* and *Columbia* appeared and opened fire. Several American shells struck the Japanese ship, dealing out mortal blows. Her bow was under water as she gallantly returned fire from her rear turret. She fired her last salvo as her stern sank at 7:21 A.M.

At around 8:17, seventeen Avengers sighted Shima's retreating fleet, followed by the injured *Mogami*. They peeled out of formation and attacked the damaged cruiser just after 9:10 A.M. Several torpedoes found their mark and the *Mogami* lay dead in the water. The Japanese destroyer *Akebono* removed the mortally damaged cruiser's crew and administered the coup de grâce by firing one torpedo and sinking her. The gallant cruiser had run out of lives. Although she had given a good account of herself, in the end she followed her fellow ships of Force C by vanishing beneath the sea. American B-24 Liberators and B-26 Marauders sank the *Abukuma* on October 26. The *Nachi*, heavily damaged when she collided with the *Mogami*, headed for Manila, where she eventually sank when attacked by American carrier-based aircraft in early November.

Of the ships in Nishimura's force that had departed Brunei in October, the destroyer *Shigure* was the sole survivor. The Southern Force, which included Nishimura's Force C and Shima's Second Striking Force—sent to navigate the Surigao Strait and to attack American landing forces, had only six survivors at the battle's end—one heavy cruiser, the *Ashigara*, and five destroyers.

Admiral Oldendorf recalled Hayler's forces. Then, at 7:32 A.M., an astonishing report reached him. A new battle had begun off Samar. It pitted Kurita's Center Force against Cliff Sprague's escort carriers. Oldendorf hadn't slept the night of October 25, but that didn't matter now, because he had plans to make to meet the new threat. At 10:18 A.M., the *Shigure*'s captain, Commander Nishino, sent a dispatch to Admiral Toyoda in Formosa, his commander in chief, and to Admiral Kurita: "All ships [Force C] except *Shigure* went down under gunfire and torpedo attack."[45]

Kurita received this message as he was being attacked by the Seventh Fleet's escort carrier planes off Samar. This is one of the factors that influenced the outcome of the Battle of Leyte Gulf.[46]

In no other naval battle in World War II did the United States achieve such a sweeping victory. They did it with overwhelming strength on the surface and in the air, a strength that would become more evident in the battle off Cape Engaño. Other factors contributed as well to the crushing Japanese defeat. Admiral Oldendorf's tactical deployment and maneuvering of the battle line, his effective use of all forces at his disposal, and the telling destroyer torpedo attacks all made significant contributions. Japanese casualties, though officially not counted, numbered in the thousands, while American losses were few. Thirty-nine Americans lost their lives, and only one American ship, the destroyer *Albert W. Grant,* suffered heavy damage.

Nishimura lost all but one ship from his Force C. His torpedo tactics and attack execution fell far short of earlier Japanese naval successes in 1943. Probably the most intelligent act executed by a Japanese admiral in the Surigao Strait was Shima's decision to retreat against overwhelming American power.

End of an Era

Before the Battle of Surigao Strait, twentieth-century naval history had witnessed only two other episodes in which the crossing the T maneuver was used. The first took place four decades before the Battle of Leyte Gulf, when Japanese Adm. Heihachiro Togo capped the Russian "T" at Tsushima in 1905. At Jutland in 1916, British Adm. John R. Jellicoe used it vis-à-vis the German High Seas Fleet, though he never realized he had done it.[47]

The Battle of Surigao Strait was the last naval battle in which airpower played no significant role, except in pursuing the retreating Japanese. Instead, in this conflict, a battle line was the dominant factor. Little wonder old sailors wax lyrical when discussing what happened in these narrow Philippine waters.

The battle line dates back to the days of King James I of England, when Sir Walter Raleigh ordered the Royal Navy to abandon boarding enemy vessels and to batter enemy naval fleets with withering, accurate broadsides. This "new" naval tactic had been successfully used first in 1655 by James, the Duke of York, against the Dutch in the Battle of Lowestoft. It then became the standard order of battle in all great sea battles for nearly 300 years, including Beachy Head, Ushant, the Capes of the Chesapeake, Battle of the Saints, Cape St. Vincent, and Trafalgar. As shipboard guns improved in accuracy and range, powerful ships formed a "battle line" with which they tried to pummel their adversaries into submission.

History is replete with examples of how technology increased the deadly effects of naval warfare. In the nineteenth century, ships donned steel armor, became steam powered, and mounted increasingly accurate, larger-caliber guns. The battle line then became a truly formidable force. Large groups of what would eventually be called battleships would line up to deliver punishing fire at an enemy, to pound them into submission, to defeat them piecemeal, or to force them to retreat.

Air power sounded the battle line's death knell. During World War II, only four naval battles were fought without air power: (1) the nighttime naval battles off Guadalcanal in 1942 and 1943, (2) in Empress Augusta Bay on November 2, 1943; (3) the Battle for the Komandorskiye Islands on March 26, 1943; and (4) in the Surigao Strait on October 25, 1944. This latter battle in the Aleutians involved neither aircraft nor submarines.

When the *Mississippi* fired its last 14-inch broadside at 4:09 A.M. on October 25, 1944, this battleship not only delivered a coup-de-grâce but also a funeral salute to the end of a naval era. One can imagine the ghosts of great admirals such as Raleigh, Hood, Nelson, Dewey, Sampson, Togo, and Jellicoe standing at attention as this classic maneuver disappeared into oblivion along with the cavalry charge, the Roman legions' phalanx, and the English longbow at Agincourt.[48]

Chapter 11: Band of Brothers

Of all the battles comprising the vast naval engagement that became known as the Battle of Leyte Gulf, the one people remember as the "make-it-or-break-it" event for the Americans was the naval Battle off Samar Island. In the epochal struggle that took place there, luck, courage, perseverance, misunderstanding, confusion, and good and bad judgment all played key roles, and it is this mosaic that, in the opinion of this author, makes the Battle off Samar a history-making, crowning achievement for the United States Navy in World War II. Although the Battle of Leyte Gulf was the largest naval battle ever fought, the Battle off Samar is the one in which Americans have justifiably taken enormous pride as a primal manifestation of American ingenuity, guts, and self-sacrifice. Samar was the culmination of miscalculations on the part of both American and Japanese admirals who previously had shown effective command ability. But Samar is a battle that makes clear that even naval commanders as fine as these could, and did, make tragic errors of judgment.

It is a piece of historical irony that the Battle off Samar took place on October 25, Saint Crispin's Day, as did two other historical battles. The first was the Battle of Agincourt in 1415, when the vastly outnumbered English under the command of Henry V defeated a formidable French army. The second was the battle at Balaclava, a seaport on the Black Sea, during the Crimean War in 1854, when the British Light Brigade made its famous charge against heavily entrenched Russian guns. These two conflicts and the Battle off Samar had one outstanding quality about them. They were examples of extraordinary military heroism.

The Setup

The Japanese SHO-1 battle plan to defend the Philippines from American invasion included the powerful Center Force of battleships, cruisers, and destroyers. This fleet, under the command of Admiral Kurita, attempted entry into Leyte Gulf through the San Bernardino Strait but was pushed back by American naval air forces during the morning and afternoon of October 24 in the Battle of the Sibuyan Sea. The Americans thought the Japanese Center force had retreated, but, while it did reverse course to the west, it did not actually retreat. Instead, Kurita regrouped and reassembled his ships, reversed course again eastward, and traveled through the San Bernardino Strait to appear in the waters off Samar Island.

The key circumstances that made the Battle off Samar possible were the movements of the Japanese Northern Force commanded by Ozawa and the subsequent actions taken by Admiral Halsey, who drew his powerful Third Fleet of carriers and battleships away to the north in pursuit of Ozawa. When Halsey took the bait of Ozawa's force, a gap had been opened, and Kurita's Center Force leaped into it.[1]

Some Disturbing Thoughts and a Big Surprise

As Kurita's force steamed toward the east coast of Samar during the night of October 24–25, miseries filled the admiral's mind. Information arrived stating Nishimura's Force C had been attacked by American bombers as he steamed toward the Surigao Strait. Kurita's concerns increased when he realized that, without Nishimura's force to close the southern half of the planned Japanese pincer attack, Japanese forces could no longer meet simultaneously in Leyte Gulf.

As October 24 wore on, Kurita saw how much damage American aircraft had inflicted on his own force. If the Americans had attacked Nishimura's ships with the same ferocity, Kurita deduced that the damage to Nishimura's less powerful force would be proportionally greater. Kurita could easily imagine a specter of burning, sinking ships as he made his way through the San Bernardino Strait. This mental picture would prove to play a major factor in his decision-making on October 25.

A basic problem with the complicated SHO-1 plan was that it choked off nearly all communication among the Japanese commanders. Kurita should have received up-to-date communication on the disposition of all Japanese *and* American forces in the Philippines. But, the totally disconnected Japanese command structure prevented the relay of hour-by-hour information as to what was happening to the other Japanese forces. The lack of a coordinated Japanese air search strategy also prevented Kurita from knowing what the American navy was doing. Of course, it could be argued that the Japanese did not have enough planes and trained air crews to execute any sizable air searches. But the essential point remains that, with the deaths of senior naval officers like Yamamoto and Koga, the Japanese lacked the necessary top-level planning skills and discipline to establish and implement an effective, well-coordinated search plan.

The Center Force entered the San Bernardino Strait with its navigational lights turned on to assist Kurita and the ships' captains in steering through the strait's treacherous waters. A bright moon's light shimmering on the calm water's surface also added luminescence to the night's darkness, thus making the navigation of the narrow strait even easier. As Kurita thanked his superiors for the lights, his mind nonetheless conjured up disturbing mental images. The latest Japanese intelligence estimates were that the American fleet carriers and fast battleships were located between 80 and 100 miles off the Samar coast. The danger of again facing American naval bombers raised the specter of complete annihilation via incessant bombing and shelling by American aircraft and ships.

Furthermore, the submarine attacks that his force had sustained in the Palawan Passage, coupled with the air attacks that had pummeled his command in the Sibuyan Sea, had severely damaged some of his ships that were still afloat. The battleship *Nagato*'s communications system was severely damaged, inhibiting communications with the other vessels. Timely and accurate communication among ships could make the difference between destruction and survival in battle.

Whatever doubts he had about the tasks facing him, a strongly worded note arrived from his superior, Admiral Toyoda, and quelled them just as he turned westward in the Sibuyan Sea. Kurita's Center Force was ordered to move on to Leyte Gulf, disregarding all perils. The life of the Japanese Empire hung in the balance.

By 10:00 P.M. on October 24, Kurita still hoped for help from the Japanese land-based air forces stationed throughout the Philippines. Be-

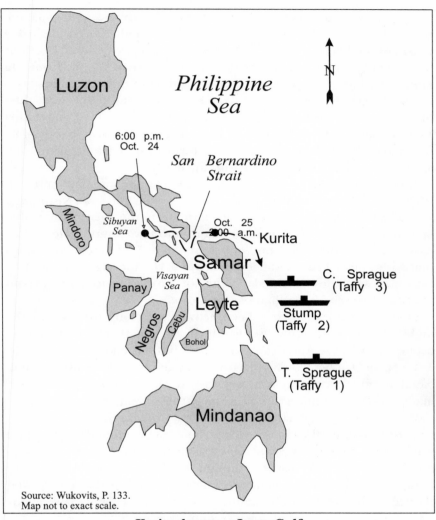

Kurita threatens Leyte Gulf

ing a practical man, however, he was aware that realization of this hope was not likely. But he still had twenty-three of the thirty-two ships that had left port at Brunei Bay, and it was still a formidable force. Kurita ordered his ships' captains to form into a single column and to begin moving through the narrow San Bernardino Strait.

A little over two and one-half hours later, on October 25, the Japanese Center Force exited the other end of the strait and entered the broad waters of the Pacific Ocean. Preparing for battle, he ordered his ships to change positions from a single column to a broad 13-mile front. He knew the Americans' powerful carriers and battleships could easily do severe damage to his ships. He steamed eastward until 3:00 A.M., then ordered a southward course change toward the Leyte Gulf target area south of Samar. When the Center Force neared the Leyte beaches, he planned to place his ships in a circular formation to defend against the air attacks he knew would come with the dawn.

Kurita had almost no information about what was happening to Nishimura's force. Only one message had reached him from Nishimura. At 3:35 A.M., Nishimura reported to Kurita from the Surigao Strait that he had seen three American ships. When almost two hours of silence had passed, a radio message from Shima arrived at 5:32, informing Kurita that Nishimura's force had been destroyed. The message also said that two Japanese battleships now lay at the bottom of the Surigao Strait, and the heavy cruiser *Mogami* had been set afire.

Japanese flying boats had been actively searching throughout the night and relayed highly useful information to their land-based air headquarters. Four American ship concentrations had been located by 4:00 A.M. on October 25. This piece of information would be used in land-based air attacks over the next few days. Kurita saw none of this information, however, until hours after the Battle off Samar was over.

When the Center Force left the narrow confines of the San Bernardino Strait, the sky was clear. The ocean undulated with a light swell. This time of year was the rainy season along the Philippines's eastern coast, and if the weather followed its customary patterns, the sky would darken as low, overhanging clouds and rain squalls pockmarked the ocean's horizon. Ships steaming in these regions could expect many drenching, though brief, deluges of rain.

Just before Kurita sent the orders at 6:44 A.M. for his ships to move into a circular, anti-aircraft formation, Japanese lookouts spotted four masts, presumably belonging to destroyers, on a port bearing of 60 degrees about 37 kilometers from the *Yamato*. Lookouts from the light cruisers *Noshiro* and *Yahagi* saw masts just five minutes after the *Yamato*'s reports. Immediately following these sightings, the *Yahagi*'s lookouts saw three carriers. The *Kongo*'s lookouts reported seeing four carriers and ten more warships. The final sighting report, at 6:50 A.M., came from the

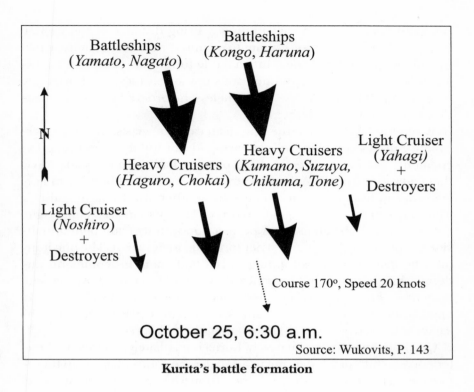

Kurita's battle formation

battleship *Haruna* when her lookouts announced they had sighted American ships.

At that time, the sea had a slight chop, and scattered, broken clouds and rain squalls dotted the sky. The 14-mile visibility might interfere with the accuracy of the Center Force's gunnery; however, other than in the areas beneath the rain squalls, the calmness of the sea would assist aiming accuracy.

Japanese lookouts had never seen American escort carriers. The profiles they sighted on the distant horizon therefore confused them, since what they were seeing were actually converted tanker hulls. Since no Japanese sailor dared report uncertainty as to what they were actually seeing, they reported what they *thought* the distant ships were. Thus, when Kurita read his lookouts' messages, he concluded that the American fleet consisted of heavy cruisers and fleet carriers. The commander of the Center Force's battleships, Vice Admiral Ugaki, thought that Halsey's

powerful fleet carriers were within easy flying distance of the Center
Force. As Kurita's ships were about to go into the circular, defensive formation, Kurita ordered them into a battle formation, causing total disarray. Not expecting to see American ships at this location, Kurita was
taken completely by surprise. Nonetheless, he ordered the fleet to battle speed and turned southeast.

When the Japanese saw the American carriers' masts, the chaos per-
vading Kurita's command nonetheless did not nullify a mounting excitement. The forces directly ahead of them had to be the same force
that had supported the American attacks on the Gilbert Islands, and every other invasion since that time—the southernmost half of Halsey's
Third Fleet. If these sightings were correct, Halsey's Third Fleet was right
there, waiting to be attacked. A perfect opportunity had opened to divide the powerful American carrier force and to destroy it. The one hundred hours of strenuous training Kurita had made his command un-
dergo while stationed in Lingga Roads was about to pay off. Kurita sent
an optimistic message to Combined Fleet Headquarters: "By Heaven-sent
opportunity, we are dashing to attack the enemy carriers. Our first objective is to destroy the flight decks, then the task force."[2]

Quick action was now a necessity. Kurita immediately ordered his Center Force to full speed, steering to a 110-degree course. Each ship therefore had to move toward the Americans from whatever position they were
in and, consequently, steamed independently, with no direct coordination from Kurita's flagship.

Every Japanese commander in the Center Force certainly knew what
Kurita meant by "destroy the flight decks." Unfortunately, Kurita's order
had not faced and answered one vital question: Should the ships fire incendiary shells or the big armor-piercing ones available on the battleships? Meanwhile, the Japanese lookouts had not definitively identified
the types of American ships they were facing. Were they relatively lightly
armored carriers or more heavily armored battleships? The choice of ammunition was crucial. An incorrect decision could make the difference
between victory and defeat.

If the Americans launched an all-out air attack, Kurita's force had no
chance of survival. Their only chance of success lay in firing everything
they had before the Americans could launch their aircraft. Kurita knew
the American carriers were lightly armored and could not withstand hits
from the Japanese battleships and cruisers' shells.

When the Japanese fired their big guns, this would be the last time the Imperial Japanese Navy would engage in a ship-to-ship naval battle, and this would be the first and last time the *Yamato*'s huge 18.1-inch guns would be fired at an enemy's surface vessels.

The battleship's big guns boomed away, belching flame and smoke from their first salvo at 6:59 A.M., thus signaling the beginning of the Battle off Samar.[3]

Chapter 12: A Morning to Remember

R ear Admiral Clifton A. F. Sprague stood on the escort carrier *Fan-shaw Bay's* bridge, surveying the scene in the early dawn hours just off Samar's east coast. Since Sprague had led his crew aboard the seaplane tender *Tangier* on that disastrous day, December 7, 1941, much had happened in the life of this talented, modest man. He had risen to flag rank in less than three years, a significant achievement for any officer, even in wartime. Behind him was the completion of a multitude of complex tasks.

For his outstanding leadership aboard the *Tangier* at Pearl Harbor, he attained the rank of captain and was ordered to the Gulf Sea Frontier on the Atlantic coast. Nazi submarines were inflicting serious losses to American shipping along the United States's eastern coast. Sprague brought organization and discipline to the situation by establishing a convoy system and supervising the construction of escort vessels, and losses dropped precipitously.

His performance at the Gulf Sea Frontier earned Sprague the command of the new Essex-class carrier *Wasp*. After directing the finish of her construction and taking her out for sea trials and her shakedown cruise, he took her into harm's way along with the carriers *Essex* and *San Jacinto* for the bombardment of Wake and Marcus Islands.

The *Wasp's* next assignment was to be part of the massive Fifth Fleet under the command of Admiral Spruance to support the invasion of the Marianas Islands. There the crew of the *Wasp* distinguished themselves by being an integral part of the American victory at the Battle of the Philippine Sea.

On July 9, 1944, Sprague's command of the *Wasp* ended. President Roosevelt appointed him to the flag rank of rear admiral along with three of Sprague's famous classmates: Forrest Sherman, James L. (Jocko) Clark, and Thomas Sprague. (Thomas Sprague would become Cliff Sprague's superior officer in the upcoming Battle of Leyte Gulf.)

Sprague stayed aboard the *Wasp* until relieved on July 21. The next day, he was given command of Carrier Division 25, which encompassed the escort carriers *Fanshaw Bay* and *Midway* (renamed *St. Lô* on September 15), and four destroyer escorts. As had been the case when he had arrived to take command of the *Wasp*, he had little need of fanfare. When he left his ship, he left in the same way.

In developing exemplary leadership skills while commanding the *Wasp*, Sprague had proven his qualifications for leading large groups of men into battle. He had molded an unfinished carrier and an unpolished, inexperienced crew into a corps of formidable fighters. Many predicted a bright future for Sprague. Lieutenant John A. Roosevelt wrote: "We were all happy that his fine quality of leadership had been recognized but, at the same time, we felt a personal loss when he left the ship." When the *Wasp*'s newspaper, *Waspspirit*, reported its captain's promotion to flag rank, it said:

> There was no evidence that anyone was surprised at the announcement. Nor need there have been. The career of the USS *Wasp*, during the months since she first hoisted her commissioning pendant, was ample proof that Sprague's promotion was justly deserved. As a matter of fact, before shuttling off from Pearl Harbor, the Supply Department wisely laid in a set of bars, shoulder boards, and gold braid in anticipation of the coming event.[1]

Now here he was on October 25, 1944, the commander of Taffy 3. At the time of the American invasion of the Philippines, Sprague's command was placed in Admiral Kinkaid's Seventh Fleet, which had the mission of directly supporting MacArthur's return. A force of sixteen escort carriers, separated into three units called Taffy 1, Taffy 2, and Taffy 3, had the task of providing direct air support for the landing troops and of protecting against Japanese submarine attacks. The carrier units were under the command of Thomas Sprague, with Clifton Sprague in command of Taffy 3.

On October 25, 1944, Taffy 3's position in the larger force of escort carriers is shown in the table.

American Escort Carriers off Samar, October 24, 1944

Taffy 1	Taffy 2	Taffy 3
RAdm. T. L. Sprague	RAdm. F. B. Stump	RAdm. C. A. F. Sprague
Escort Carriers*	**Escort Carriers**	**Escort Carriers**
Sangamon, Suwannee,	*Natoma Bay, Manila Bay,*	*Fanshaw Bay, St. Lô,*
Santee, Petrof Bay	*Marcus Island, Kadashan Bay,*	*White Plains, Kalinin Bay,*
	Savo Island, Ommaney Bay	*Gambier Bay, Kitkuh Bay*
Destroyers*	**Destroyers**	**Destroyers**
McCord, Trathen,	*Haggard, Franks, Hailey*	*Hoel, Heermann, Johnston*
Hazelwood		
Destroyer Escorts	**Destroyer Escorts**	**Destroyer Escorts**
Richard S. Bull,	*Richard W. Suesens,*	*Dennis, John C. Butler,*
Richard M. Rowell,	*Abercrombie, Le Ray Wilson,*	*Raymond,*
Eversole, Coolbaugh	*Walter C. Wann*	*Samuel B. Roberts*

*The escort carriers *Saginaw Bay* and *Chenango,* along with the destroyer *Edmonds* and destroyer escort *Oberrender* left for Morotal on Oct. 24, 1944 for resupply.

Veteran American sailors considered the escort carriers—also known as "baby flattops" or "jeep carriers," nicknames given to them by navy personnel—as outsiders. Designated by the navy as CVEs, they were initially used in the Atlantic in 1942, they brought Allied airpower to the landings on the Moroccan coast. These little ships proved their flexibility when they gave air cover to amphibious landings and protected the North Atlantic Allied convoys by effectively defending them against the Nazi submarine threat. Inexpensive to build, American shipyards produced these versatile vessels in record numbers. By the war's end, they had paid for themselves many times over.

While the big fleet carriers earned well-deserved fame and most of the glory during the Pacific War, the escort carriers operated in the background in ever-increasing numbers and performed highly critical, albeit monotonously routine tasks by providing air cover for convoys and amphibious landings. The men who served in these little ships faced much tougher living conditions than their big carrier compatriots. An escort carrier could become oppressively hot even in moderate outdoor temperatures. For example, in the *San Marcus* pilot ready room—a place where pilots would meet prior to flying their missions and for the purpose of receiving their briefings—temperatures exceeded 100 degrees during the Battle off Samar.

Three of the first escort carriers, the *Sangamon*, *Suwannee*, and *Santee*, which would face the onslaught from the war's first kamikaze attack, came from a converted tanker class of ships that underwent tough battle exposure off Casablanca in 1942. The remaining CVEs were built by Kaiser Shipbuilding on the American West Coast during 1943–1944.

While operating in Leyte Gulf, they more than exceeded their primary objectives when they successively executed air support missions, such as bombing enemy airfields and protecting the landing zones from attacks by Japanese planes. They also flew combat air patrol over the landing operations and looked out for Japanese submarines around the entire Leyte area. Since there were no army air forces in the Philippines during October 1944, the escort carriers' aircraft admirably filled in by attacking Japanese truck convoys, bombing fueling facilities, and dropping supplies to the troops ashore. However, conspicuously absent from this mission list was the bombing, strafing, and torpedoing of enemy warships. It would not be long before they would have to perform this difficult task, too, and learn how to do it against great odds.[2]

An Overwhelming Presence

When Kurita concluded that the American ships on the distant horizon were an immediate threat to his powerful Center Force, the reality was that Kurita had nothing to fear from them, because his force could fire more large and small shells at an enemy than any fleet afloat. He had the 68,000-ton *Yamato*; the battleship *Nagato* with eight 16-inch guns and twenty-six 5.5- and 5-inch guns; the battleships *Kongo* and *Haruna* with eight 14-inch guns and twenty-two 6- and 5-inch guns; twelve heavy and light cruisers and fifteen destroyers that escorted the battleships and added a combined eighty 8-inch guns, more than 150 5-inch guns, and more than 200 torpedo tubes that fired the deadly long lance torpedoes. Kurita's five battleships alone possessed 112 guns larger than anything Sprague had.

A poem written by an American sailor contrasts what the puny American escort carriers had against such an overpowering force:[3]

They build a flight deck on a tanker hull,
Jam almost thirteen hundred men on board;
They load it up with aviation gas,
With bombs, torpedoes, ammunition, fuel,
And then, in case the poor guys have to fight,
What have they got? One stinkin' five-inch gun.

On October 18, Taffy 3's location was east-southeast of Samar's southern edge. There Taffy 3 could prepare for the day's strikes, which would initiate the Philippine campaign. Taffy 1, Taffy 2, and Taffy 3 were 30 to 50 miles apart and spread along the Philippine eastern coast. South of Taffy 3, the escort carrier group commander, and Cliff Sprague's immediate superior, RAdm. Thomas Sprague, placed Taffy 1 off northern Mindanao. Fifty miles to his north, RAdm. Felix B. Stump's Taffy 2 had been placed closest to Leyte Gulf, while Taffy 3 protected the northern approaches off Samar.

The three Taffies conducted extensive air strikes against the Japanese airfields on Negros, Cebu, Mindanao, and Luzon, flying 471 sorties for two days before MacArthur's troops landed on Leyte. They dropped 82 tons of bombs and destroyed over sixty enemy aircraft on the ground. On the 19th of October, the escort carriers *Gambier Bay* and *Kitkun Bay* joined Cliff Sprague's group, which now brought Taffy 3 up to its full strength of six escort carriers, three destroyers, and four destroyer escorts.

Every night Sprague moved his force 50 miles out to sea so it could more effectively defend itself against Japanese submarines. Taffy 3 zigzagged all night until dawn, when Sprague moved his force closer to the shore to lessen the distance for his aircraft to carry out their softening up and ground support missions. The Japanese did not offer much in the way of opposition, so Sprague concentrated his duties on the more humdrum, but indispensable, support operations and antisubmarine patrols.

Some men in Taffy 3, impatient to take the war to the Japanese, wanted more action, but realized service in jeep carriers or destroyer escorts hardly ever involved combat. Like many of his shipmates, Sonarman 3d Class H. Whitney Felt of the *Samuel B. Roberts* had never seen his ship's guns fire at an enemy ship or aircraft: "Most of us hoped that we'd at least see an enemy airplane. We never expected anything big, though."

MacArthur's triumphant return to the Philippines took place on Oc-

tober 20. By midnight of the 20th, more than 100,000 men and 200,000 tons of equipment had landed on Leyte, and hundreds of supply transports had disgorged a steady stream of supplies ashore. Within a day, there were only twenty-eight Liberty ships and twenty-five landing craft left in Leyte Gulf, an impressive contrast to the traffic jam of the hundreds of ships that had dotted the waters off Leyte just two days before.

During the campaign's first week, Taffy 3's contribution brought great satisfaction to Sprague. By itself, the *Fanshaw Bay*'s VC-68 squadron had flown 245 sorties that included bombing and strafing land targets as well as conducting combat air and antisubmarine patrols. All of Sprague's aviators' confidence grew with each day's successes.

Because many in his command had never experienced action in a war zone, Sprague tried to keep his men's morale high by informally talking with his officers and men. Standing watch near his gun and never having been in combat before, a pleasantly surprised Duane Iossi remembered a conversation in which Sprague came over to him and spoke some encouraging words. Iossi muttered a startled reply. After talking with the young sailor for a few minutes, Sprague ended the conversation with, "Keep up the good work."

By such informal, compassionate acts as this, Sprague was able to restore his escort carrier sailors' self-respect under highly tense conditions. So, when Kurita's overwhelmingly powerful force appeared at dawn on October 25, these measures proved to be important, because every sailor in his command went into battle in a spirit of confidence rather than of doubt and fear. An officer serving under Sprague wrote: "With Admiral Sprague these constant plaguing doubts of the jeep-sailor gave way to the confidence we had in him as a leader and as a personality who was working for our best interests."[4]

The Storm Cometh

Cliff Sprague awoke at 4:00 A.M. on the 25th, and strode to the *Fanshaw Bay*'s bridge to begin what he thought would be a very busy day. Taffy 3 was 35 miles east of Samar, and Sprague wanted to get an early start planning and organizing a schedule of strikes and patrols that "would keep my deck crews on the jump until sundown." There were routine combat air patrols and antisubmarine patrols to be flown, photo and search missions to be launched, and any emergency strikes executed that MacArthur's forces might need in order to aid the fighting ashore.

Sprague's previous few days had passed peacefully. No Japanese aircraft had endangered his thinly armored escort carriers, and the ground war on Leyte was progressing satisfactorily. The two Japanese naval forces that had threatened Leyte the previous day had been seemingly repulsed. Oldendorf's battle line had thoroughly destroyed Nishimura's Force C only hours earlier in the Surigao Strait. The airpower of Mitscher's carriers in the Sibuyan Sea and the submarines *Darter* and *Dace* in the Palawan Passage had presumably severely crippled Kurita's Center Force.

Because he felt no Japanese naval forces threatened his command, Sprague thought with confidence that this day would be a long one and believed that the only demand on his force would be frequent air support missions to help the troops ashore. His ships had more than adequate protection from both the north and south. Kinkaid's powerful Seventh Fleet blocked the Surigao Strait in the south, while Halsey's Third Fleet protected Sprague's northern flank as they guarded the San Bernardino Strait. The *Gambier Bay*'s Lt. Henry Burt Bassett had flown his torpedo plane on October 24 and seen some of Halsey's carriers just north of the San Bernardino Strait. He noted that Taffy 3 was "well-protected because this huge group was nearby."

The *Gambier Bay*'s commander, Capt. Walter Vieweg, echoed some of these "feeling safe" sentiments when he characterized the early days off the Philippines as "uneventful in that we received no air attacks, and life was quite peaceful aboard ship." While most men welcomed this quiet time, others could hardly wait for the action to begin. Some officers and seamen on Taffy 3's destroyers and destroyer escorts expressed disappointment that their ships were screening the "puny" jeep carriers instead of escorting a fast carrier.

Aboard the destroyer *Johnston*, its gunnery officer, Lt. Robert C. Hagen, and its skipper, Cmdr. Ernest E. Evans, discussed their feelings of the night before. "Well, Hagen, we're within three days of being one year old. It's been an uneventful year." Hagen replied, "Yes, sir. I wouldn't mind a little action."

It seemed the war had passed them by on this new and apparently uneventful day. Of course, neither Hagen nor Evans could know that Hagen would get his wish and then some. Perhaps, he should have remembered the old adage, "Be careful what you wish for. You may get it."

Early that morning at 1:55 A.M., Kinkaid ordered Thomas Sprague to launch three daylight air searches, one of which was to cover the north-ernmost waters of Leyte Gulf. The Taffies' commander chose Taffy 2 to carry out this mission through a message sent at 3:30 A.M. Receiving Thomas Sprague's order one hour later, Admiral Stump examined his carriers' positions and at 5:09 A.M. ordered the *Ommaney Bay*, which was in the best spot, to launch its search aircraft. Because of the little car-rier's cramped deck space, it took a long time to get the aircraft aloft. Therefore, the first plane took off two minutes before seven, almost two hours after the launch order had been issued. By then, it was too late.

No one realized that a potential disaster was on the way. All three Taffy groups moved closer to shore to conduct their normal daytime opera-tions, and as dawn broke, they turned northeast into the wind so they could launch planes from their flight decks or catapults. The southern-most group, Taffy 1, launched a strike at 5:45 A.M. to attack the retreat-ing Japanese ships in the Surigao Strait. The next northernmost groups, Taffy 2 and Taffy 3, launched their planes from 60 miles off Samar.

At 6:14, the sun rose, shedding its light on another beautiful day. Soft winds of 6 to 8 knots, varying in direction from east-northeast to north-northeast, blew lightly over the calm sea, and scattered cumulus clouds obeyed the mild zephyrs' commands as they moved slowly across the sky. It would be a fair day for sure, but any smoke that was certain to come from the impending battle would hang low on the water, hiding the smaller American ships from the approaching, much larger Japanese ves-sels.

At this time of year, in these waters, rain squalls were common, and a few had appeared on the horizon. However, none threatened any op-erations or affected the fine visibility that stretched 8 to 12 miles in ev-ery direction.

Following his usual disciplined routine, Cliff Sprague put all his ships on morning alert. Eight search and patrol planes took off just before sun-rise. At 6:15, being a prudent commander, he ordered six more fighters aloft to fly combat air patrol. Also, obeying his superior's orders, Sprague readied two additional planes armed with torpedoes and two more armed with 500-pound bombs on deck in case Oldendorf needed more help to the south. Now confident that he had done all that was needed at this time, Sprague ordered Taffy 3 to stand down from morning alert and took time out to enjoy another cup of coffee.[5]

This day's peaceful beginning was deceptive, however, for Sprague's mood was soon to change to one of desperation.

• • •

Ensign Hans L. Jensen's Avenger torpedo bomber left the *Kadashan Bay*'s flight deck at 5:51 A.M. for an antisubmarine patrol. For about forty minutes, he and his crew saw nothing but empty ocean as his plane ducked into and out of heavy, damp clouds. Abruptly, Jensen's radioman, D. G. Lehman, staring at his radar scope, stirred nervously when a large number of blips suddenly appeared. They could not be American ships, that much he knew, since his position was north of Taffy 3. All at once, bursts of antiaircraft fire surrounded the aircraft as the Japanese gunners spotted it. While Jensen knew the radar sighting was outside his assigned patrol area, he banked his plane and headed toward the gunfire's source.

Gradually losing altitude and closing range to the radar blips, his plane broke out of the clouds at 1,800 feet. About 20 miles north of Taffy 3, a frightening sight loomed on the surface of the water. It was Kurita's Center Force, shimmering, powerful, and deadly. Based on their training in recognizing the types of Japanese warships, the plane's crew identified at least four battleships plus twelve cruisers and destroyers heading straight for the unsuspecting American carriers. Jensen quickly picked up his radio microphone and sent a message reporting the position, course, and speed of the huge force.

The Japanese force was steaming on a 170-degree course in four columns at 20 knots. They swept the horizon from 60 degrees to 240 degrees relative to the plane's cockpit. The column of ships farthest to the east had the light cruiser *Yahagi* along with the destroyers *Urakaze*, *Isokaze*, *Yukikaze*, and *Nowaki*. The heavy cruisers *Kumano*, *Suzuya*, *Tone*, and *Chikuma* were in the next westward column, and about 3 miles to their stern, the battleships *Kongo* and *Haruna* followed. The next column to the west had the two heavy cruisers *Haguro* and *Chokai*. Following them approximately 3 miles back were the battleships *Yamato* and *Nagato*. The last and farthest west column consisted of the light cruiser *Noshiro* and seven destroyers—*Kishinami*, *Okinami*, *Hayashimo*, *Akishimo*, *Hamanami*, *Fujinami*, and *Shimakaze*.

The sailor in the *Yamato*'s crow's nest was scanning the horizon southward, while the intraship intercom crackled with talk about American warships to the south. He strained his eyes for some moments and, then, sure enough, he saw warships where they should not be. Picking up the ship's intercom microphone, he reported, "Enemy warships to the south. Appear to be aircraft carriers."

Kurita saw Jensen's plane himself as the American aircraft dropped what appeared to be depth charges. The ships in the distance were aircraft carriers with airplanes parked on their decks, and Kurita thought these might be part of Halsey's fleet. Some of his lookouts, however, reported the ships were Ozawa's. From about 25,000 meters away, Kurita could not identify them precisely, but carriers they were, and they might not be friendly. Also, light and heavy cruisers might be among them. Kurita's people urged him to withhold fire, given the uncertainty of identification. His chief of staff tried to convince him they might be one or two battleships, four or five fleet carriers, and at least ten heavy cruisers.

Many Japanese officers below flag rank were elated at the fact that their journey since traversing the San Bernardino Strait had been uneventful. They expected easy pickings in pounding the American invasion fleet to smithereens with no opposition. However, Kurita did not share in these feelings. His recent experience of being attacked by American aircraft on the previous day had inspired little confidence in his antiaircraft defenses, and so he did not have any desire to meet any more American carrier airplanes, since they had already inflicted serious damage on his command.

It was inconceivable to him that these American carriers were only small escort carriers, not the heavily equipped fleet carriers whose aircraft had attacked him earlier. It was also inconceivable to him that these small ships mounted only one 5-inch gun and carried significantly fewer planes than their larger, more powerful cousins. Kurita was well aware that he had only a few float planes at his disposal, and that these would be no match for the experienced American pilots he had encountered during the last two days.

Japanese gunners saw the American Avenger and opened fire with an intense, albeit inaccurate, barrage of antiaircraft shells. As Jensen watched, he saw the Japanese ships open fire at Taffy 3. Putting his plane into a glide, he descended to the dangerous altitude of 1,200 feet and dropped three 350-pound depth charges on a heavy cruiser. Although the bombs he dropped could not materially affect the big cruiser because they were intended for submarines, they splashed and exploded close enough to wet the cruiser's decks. Having no more bombs left, Jensen turned his plane around and headed back to his home ship. As the plane zoomed away, Jensen's gunner, M. M. Soter, fired his machine guns at the cruiser. The Japanese flak's accuracy did not improve until Jensen was almost back in the shelter of the clouds. Suddenly, two shells exploded near enough to the Avenger to rock it violently.

Jensen maneuvered so as to stay unseen at the clouds' edge, and here he saw one of the battleships launch a float plane. The Japanese plane lurched from the ship's catapult, gained altitude, and headed in the direction of the American aircraft. Waiting till the Japanese float plane was almost directly beneath him, Jensen pounced on the unsuspecting pilot as he dove out of the clouds. Jensen fired his two .50-caliber wing guns and watched as their bullets made large holes in the float plane's wings, but the plane did not go down. Jensen pulled out and rolled over until he was upside down above the Japanese plane. Using the machine guns in his rotating turret, Soter opened fire, hitting the Japanese plane again. Realizing he was overmatched, the float plane's pilot turned around and headed back to his ship. However, the battleship was now too busy firing on Taffy 3's carriers to stop and pick it up, so the float planes took no further part in the action that day.

Jensen's attack may have affected the tactics the Japanese adopted later in the battle. Jensen saw the Japanese just before they saw the Americans, and, as a result, the Japanese were prevented from sending a spotter plane aloft to help them gauge the best ways of assuring their shooting would be on target (called the "fall of shot") as they aimed their fire at the American jeep carriers.

Jensen was not able to land on his home ship, the *Kadashan Bay*, because it was now attempting to dodge Japanese gunfire. Therefore, he landed at Tacloban, refueled, and rearmed his plane in order to attack the Japanese ships with bombs and machine guns later that day.

Although Jensen was the first American pilot to sight the Japanese, his report, in fact, never reached Sprague. When he radioed his report on the Center Force, the only clear receipt was at the *Natoma Bay*, Taffy 2's flagship. As it happened, only a garbled version of his sighting report reached the *Fanshaw Bay*'s radio room. The credit for the first sighting report that reached Sprague belonged to another flyer, Ens. William C. Brooks.[6]

Brooks flew over Taffy 3 on the lookout for submarines. He had not seen anything since he took off from the *St. Lô* earlier that morning and tried to keep himself awake. As had been the case over the last few days, the Japanese sent no submarines into Philippine waters and seemed to be posing no significant threat to the American invasion. As he gazed at the water below, however, a remarkable sight met his eyes. Spread across the broad expanse of ocean beneath his plane was a large group of warships, white foam wakes trailing behind them. Steaming southward at what looked like high speed, they headed directly for Taffy 3. Ensign Brooks quickly picked up his radio microphone and sent the alarming news to Sprague's flagship, the *Fanshaw Bay*: "Enemy surface force of four battleships, eight cruisers, and eleven destroyers sighted 20 miles northwest of your task group and closing in on you at 30 knots."

The message abruptly shook Sprague out of his reverie and startled everyone else on the bridge and in the flag plot. Springing out of his chair, Sprague yelled into the squawk box, "Air Plot, tell him to check his identification."

Sprague was angry at the report, because everyone knew the only naval forces of any size near Samar were his own Taffy 3 and Halsey's Third Fleet. Disturbed, and ignorant of the fact that Halsey had turned north to go after Ozawa, Sprague thought, "Now, there's some screwy young aviator reporting part of our own forces. Undoubtedly, he's just spotted some of Admiral Halsey's fast battleships."

At 6:48 A.M., Brooks banked his plane and reduced altitude to get a closer look in accordance with the *Fanshaw Bay*'s request for confirmation that these ships were indeed Japanese. As Brooks drew closer, the unmistakable pagoda-shaped masts of the Japanese battleships took shape before his eyes, so he pressed the send button on his microphone, transmitting, "Ships have pagoda masts."

These crisp words sent shock waves throughout the *Fanshaw Bay*'s bridge. As the impact of Brooks's message sank in, Lt. Verlin Pierson, standing directly above the *Fanshaw Bay*'s bridge and scanning the horizon with his binoculars, screamed at the command bridge, "Those ships look to us like Japanese battleships from here."

The escort carrier's Combat Information Center confirmed the sighting when their radar picked up the ships' images on the radar screen. The rapidly closing ships were only 16½ miles away, and the CIC intercepted the Japanese radio traffic.

Horrified, Sprague shouted, "It's impossible! It can't be, it can't be!"

But all doubts vanished the moment Sprague saw smoke puffs of antiaircraft fire peppering the skies to the northwest, near the spot where

Brooks's plane was flying. Rapidly surmising the true nature of the situation facing him, he could not contain his anger. Sprague's visual fighter-director officer, Lt. Vernon D. Hipchings, Jr., standing watch above the bridge where the furious Sprague now paced, overheard the admiral growl, "That son-of-a-bitch Halsey has left us bare-assed!"

The *Fanshaw Bay* was not the only American ship to be horrified at the sighting of the Japanese ships. When the Japanese ships appeared to the north, sonarman Felt of the destroyer escort *Samuel B. Roberts* called his executive officer, Lt. Everett E. Roberts, to the bridge, where Roberts confirmed the ships were indeed Japanese. But Roberts never imagined they could be the Center Force. Instead, he surmised they were remnants of the force Oldendorf's battle line had destroyed earlier that morning in the Surigao Strait—Nishimura's Force C. Speaking into the ship's loudspeaker microphone, Roberts announced: "Now hear this. After you finish breakfast and before you relieve the watch, you might want to go astern and look back of us to see a remnant of the Japanese navy."

The ship's crew not on duty rushed topside and over to the destroyer escort's stern to have a look for themselves. As one man hurried past his quarters, the skipper, Lt. Cmdr. R. W. Copeland, yelled at the bridge: "Lay to the topside hell! If there are any Japs out there, sound the battle stations alarm and pass the word to man your battle stations!"

One of the *Kalinin Bay*'s pilots, Ens. Richard G. Altman, awoke from a sound sleep and learned from the ship's supply officer that Japanese ships were approaching from the north and that he should get ready to take off in his torpedo plane. Altman remembered later, "I didn't believe him at first and stayed in my bed, but when he came back a second time and sounded extremely serious, I put on my clothes and rushed to the ready room."

After Japanese antiaircraft fire had chased Brooks about the sky, 14- and 16-inch shells from the battleships that one seaman remembered as being like "long tree logs pointed at us with smoke puffing out" now screamed toward the escort carriers from 15 miles away. Within seconds, geysers in a variety of colors straddled the *White Plains* and the other carriers. The multicolored water columns appeared to the American sailors as some kind of ghastly carnival with a deadly purpose. The Japanese in fact used various colors to help them spot their fall of shot, and Sprague remembered later that, "in various shades of pink, green, yellow, and purple, the splashes had a kind of horrid beauty."

This surreal scene would have made a "a beautiful camera shot," as

Lieutenant Pierson recalled later, but he also noted that, "We didn't have a ghost of a chance and that it would only be a matter of a few minutes until we would all be blown sky high."

Sprague realistically estimated that his force would last about fifteen minutes, given such an overwhelming display of firepower. In view of the long odds, Sprague reflected, "What chance could we have—six slow, thin-skinned escort carriers, each armed with only one 5-inch peashooter, against the 16-, 14-, 8-, and 5-inch broadsides of the 22 [sic] warships bearing down on us at twice our speed?"

Sprague later stated that the battle's opening minutes did not seem at all nightmarish. He said, "For my mind had never experienced anything from which such a nightmare could have been spun. . . . The thought that six of us would be fighting 22 Jap warships at gun range had never entered anyone's mind."

Sprague believed his opponent would simply send a few cruisers to handle Taffy 3's ineffective challenge while continuing on its way toward Leyte Gulf with the rest of his force.

Sighting the American carriers, however, caught Koyanagi completely by surprise. He thought their images on the horizon were "a miracle. Think of a surface fleet coming upon an enemy carrier group. Nothing is more vulnerable than an aircraft carrier in a surface engagement."

The old Japanese naval adage "A sighted enemy is the equivalent of a dead enemy" seemed to be coming true. After the war, Sprague expressed a similar thought when he wrote in the margin of the naval historian C. Vann Woodward's *The Battle for Leyte Gulf,* alongside Woodward's recital of the events, a laconic, "Thought so too."[7]

Splashes from the Japanese salvos crept closer and closer to Sprague's escort carriers as tall, broad geysers of water drenched the carriers' decks. By this time, Sprague realized his command was in a desperate situation and that he had to act quickly. Only bold, audacious, swift action could answer the challenge he faced, and he rose to the occasion in one of the finest demonstrations of determination, courage, and perseverance exhibited by any naval commander in history.

Borrowing an idea that could have come right out of a Japanese military manual, Sprague decided that the only way the Japanese Center Force could be stopped was by sacrificing his command in the hope that Kurita could be diverted away from the Leyte beaches. His reasoning:

"If we can get this [entire] task force to attack us, we can delay its descent on Leyte until help comes, though obviously the end will come sooner for us." Throughout the Pacific War, the Japanese had used suicide tactics in order to achieve victory. Now the tables would be turned. An American commander would implement suicidal tactics off Samar, for it was Sprague's intention to sacrifice his entire command to protect MacArthur and Kinkaid's forces inside Leyte Gulf.

His determination to "give them all we've got before we go down" opened with a rapid fire communication over the TBS that drowned out all other talk in the *Fanshaw Bay*'s command center. While many officers used the network that morning in a frantic effort to avoid the apparent fate awaiting them, Sprague's voice over the radio interjected an aura of calm and reason. He knew his classmate Tommy Sprague's Taffy 1 carriers were steaming about 130 miles south by east, and that Rear Admiral Stump's Taffy 2 lay between his command and Taffy 1. At 6:50 A.M., Sprague changed course from due north, heading directly for the approaching Japanese, to east, so that Taffy 3 headed away from Kurita's ships and Leyte Gulf. He formed his escort carriers into a circle about 2,500 yards in diameter and placed an outer screen of destroyers and destroyer escorts to protect them. By moving eastward, Taffy 3 headed into the wind so its aircraft could get into the air as fast as possible.

Trying to dodge the Japanese salvos, the escort carriers made many frequent course changes. Sprague ordered all ships to maximum speed in an effort to reach a rain squall that could provide shelter before the falling Japanese shells found their intended targets. The only offensive weapons Sprague had were his aircraft, and these he sent into action.

He asked the Leyte air controller to order any Taffy 3 planes that were executing missions over the beachhead to return, and ordered all of Taffy 3's escort carriers to launch every available aircraft to attack the oncoming Japanese ships. Some of the escort carriers' captains complained that their fighters and torpedo planes lacked the proper ammunition to attack the heavily armored battleships and cruisers. Briefly losing his temper, Sprague demanded, "Get the damn things up!"[8]

Time was the only ally he had, and he needed it to reach the rain squall's protective cover to shield Taffy 3 from prying Japanese eyes, to think, and to wait for help to reach him. It did not matter whether the planes had the right bombs or ammunition, or whether they had any armaments at all. What did matter was to get the planes aloft in order to torment Kurita in any way they could. Another danger existed, too, another reason for the planes to take off. Aircraft loaded with gasoline sat on the carriers' decks. If any of the Japanese shells hit the flight decks, they could set off the very same kind of conflagration that had destroyed the Japanese carriers at Midway. When American bombs hit those Japanese flight decks, they were littered with fully fueled aircraft and armed bombs that exploded, sinking four large carriers. In this instance, too, all six American escort carriers faced the same risk.

Sprague knew it would take approximately fifteen minutes to reach the nearby rain squall. Until then, he needed to secure added protection for Taffy 3. At 6:57 A.M., he therefore ordered all ships' commanders to make smoke. Taffy 3 now steamed into the wind so the smoke would drift between the Japanese and Taffy 3. Within minutes, two types of smoke belched from the destroyers and destroyer escorts. A white chemical smoke poured from large canisters and generators placed on the ships' fantails, and, drifting atop the white smoke, a thicker black smoke billowed from their funnels creating a double-layered, smoky curtain that hid Taffy 3 from Japanese eyes.

Kurita's operations staff officer, Cmdr. Tonosuke Otani, during interviews by American intelligence agents after the war, credited Sprague's skillful use of smoke with thwarting the accuracy of the Japanese salvos. The Japanese had never upgraded their warships with accurate fire control radar such as the Americans possessed. Therefore, their guns were not able to follow Sprague's maneuvers, which the American admiral executed with increasing frequency in an effort to avoid the Japanese shellfire. Lieutenant Commander Copeland, captain of the *Samuel B. Roberts*, watched from his bridge and later expressed admiration for what he saw when he said Taffy 3's use of this camouflaging tactic was "one of the most effective smoke screens that anyone on the *Roberts* had previously observed."

Taffy 3 headed for the rain squall at the fastest speed its 18-knot escort carriers could move. Knowing the reality of the situation, Sprague sent a message in plain English asking for help from any American forces in the area. Only Taffy 1's and Taffy 2's airpower were close enough to give immediate support. The other Taffy commanders, Tom Sprague and Felix Stump, could send only some of their aircraft, those that could be recalled from their current mission or that were waiting to take off from their carriers' flight decks. Furthermore, their screening ships were too far away to reach Taffy 3's position in time to be of any help. An indication of the tension of those moments is apparent in a small, telling incident in which Admiral Stump's voice rose to an uncharacteristically high pitch as he tried to assure his beleaguered colleague that he was doing all he could: "Don't be alarmed, Ziggy! Remember, we're back of you—don't get excited—don't do anything rash!"

Momentary smiles broke out on the *Fanshaw Bay*'s bridge as Stump's voice came over the TBS. As the battle unfolded during the next action-filled hours, Stump's Taffy 2 would be of enormous help to Cliff Sprague as he desperately fought off the powerful advances of Japanese warships.

Taffy 1's position was closer to Leyte Gulf. Thus, its aircraft were con-ducting an air support mission over the beachhead. Thomas Sprague could not believe much less imagine what was happening, but he sent all the resources he possibly could. Turning to his chief of staff, he yelled about his namesake to the north: "That damn fool can stir up more trou-ble than a small boy sticking his fish pole into a hornet's nests. Tell the boys to get out their flit guns and go help him."[9]

Kinkaid's ships had used so much ammunition during the action in the Surigao Strait that their supply was low, and Kinkaid still had to keep watch over Shima's retreating force. All he could do was send Olden-dorf's battle line northward to try to lend a hand. However, the old bat-tleships were so slow they couldn't possibly reach Taffy 3's position in time.

Sprague was well aware that his frenzied message for help would reach Halsey. However, since the Third Fleet commander was under Nimitz's command, Sprague's message had to go through MacArthur's decoding station on Manus. Therefore, another hour would pass before Sprague's appeal would reach Halsey.

As Kurita's ships drew closer and closer, Sprague realized he had to depend largely on his own resources to fight off the faster, more pow-erful Japanese force, and so he needed to make use of every cunning maneuver he could think of. He would have to send inadequately armed aircraft into the fray and deploy his thinly armored screening destroy-ers and destroyer escorts so that they would be more than toothless tigers. Somehow he would have to put the brakes on Kurita, at least for a while.

Taffy 3's path to the protective cover of the rain squall's clouds seemed to take a lifetime, though in reality it was now only ten minutes away. At the rate the Japanese were closing the range, Sprague wondered how he was going to escape immediate, total annihilation. The near misses of Japanese shells had begun to rock the *Fanshaw Bay* as Sprague glanced toward the *White Plains*, steaming on his exposed left rear flank and closest to the Japanese guns. The Japanese salvos bracketed the *White Plains*, sending up such a deluge of water that the *White Plains* almost disappeared from Sprague's view.

A signalman aboard the endangered carrier, seeing the blinking signal lamps on the oncoming Japanese ships, yelled, "I can't read their signals but [they] certainly send a lot of dashes." Responding in the characteristically American style of stoic cynicism, one that masks a large reservoir of courage, another signalman sneered, "Yeah, and they are likely to be periods when they get here."[10] Three 14-inch shells straddled the carrier and sent up gigantic splashes that doused the little carrier in floods of water that spread over her upper decks and superstructure. The last shell exploded so near to her that she twisted savagely in the water, throwing men on deck off their feet, tossing gear all over her decks, and temporarily cutting power to her steering engine.

Sprague later recalled in an April 1945 *American Magazine* article: "Wicked salvos straddled *White Plains*, and their colored geysers began to sprout among the other carriers from projectiles loaded with dye . . . yellow and purple, the splashes had a kind of horrid beauty." A *White Plains* sailor, shocked by all the shells falling around his ship, screamed, "Hey, they are shooting at us in Technicolor." But the carrier survived the relentless attacks and launched her aircraft two minutes later.

Sprague's action report, written in the cryptic prose characteristic of these types of documents, does not adequately convey the grim reality of what really happened: "At this point, it did not appear that any of our ships could survive another five minutes of the heavy caliber fire being received, and some counteraction was urgently and immediately required. The Task Unit was surrounded by the ultimate of desperate circumstances."

Despite all the chaos, turmoil, and confusion swirling everywhere around him in this inferno of terror, Sprague kept his composure. Although the appearance of the Japanese ships had come as a total surprise to him, he made at least eight major command decisions in the fourteen minutes that Kurita's force loomed onto the northern horizon. It was not by chance that he was able to make so many effective decisions in such a short period of time. His capacity to perform well under stress came from years of training as a naval aviator. The repetitive exercises a pilot undergoes in making fast decisions under potentially life-threatening circumstances permanently ingrained in Sprague an outstanding ability to command under the most trying battle conditions.

During his long career in naval aviation, Sprague developed quick reflexes and self confidence in his ability and learned to trust his instincts. He had received his wings in the early days of naval aviation, when many of his friends and colleagues had died due to the hazards that come as a consequence of experimenting with any new technology. Despite all the adversity he experienced, Sprague survived unharmed. One of the keys to his survival is that quick reactions in a crippled airplane often give a pilot an edge in the form of a few precious moments in which to make correct life-or-death decisions. Whereas relying solely on first instincts is not an infallible guarantee of longevity, a tested ability in making the right decisions at the right time, under almost unspeakably difficult circumstances, greatly improves the odds for success.

As Sprague gazed at Kurita's rapidly approaching ships, seeing the shells falling all around him that early morning on Saint Crispin's Day, he faced the crisis with self-assurance, knowing he would do the right things at the right time. No prudent commander relies on an ambiguous intuition alone when the lives of the men under his command are at stake. Sprague's ability to act quickly, the fruit of years of experience in assessing situations and options, gave him a fund of wisdom on which to draw. He created an initial, though not too detailed, strategy and used it to make tactical decisions based on the assumption that his force would be attacked. This gave him a steady framework from which to calmly issue orders.

A pilot from the *Gambier Bay*, Lt. (jg) Henry A. Pyzdrowski, recalled that "Sprague was a cool customer. I got the impression he role played ahead of time and played this out, like he lay on his bunk and thought things through from every vantage. He must have done a lot of mental chess." Another testimonial to Sprague's demeanor and coolness under fire was voiced by a personal acquaintance, historian Thomas Vaughan, who said, "Sprague looked like he belonged in a library. He had a reflective nature and was always thinking."

When Kurita's more powerful force appeared off Samar, Sprague could not call on the naval tactics taught at the naval academy, for none had anticipated such conditions. Thus, he had to improvise, to create his own tactics as the situation evolved. As the *Johnston*'s Lieutenant Hagen noted, "Sprague was an innovator and he learned quickly. At Samar, he improvised and sort of grew into the battle."

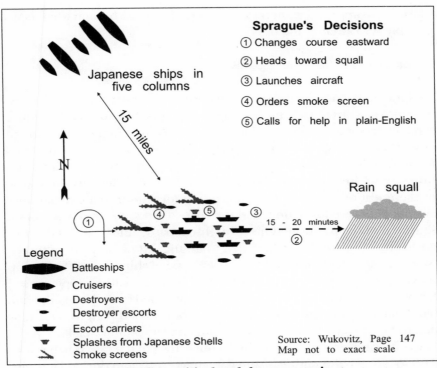

Japanese ships in five columns

15 miles

N

Sprague's Decisions

① Changes course eastward

② Heads toward squall

③ Launches aircraft

④ Orders smoke screen

⑤ Calls for help in plain-English

Rain squall

15 - 20 minutes

Legend

Battleships

Cruisers

Destroyers

Destroyer escorts

Escort carriers

Splashes from Japanese Shells

Smoke screens

Source: Wukovitz, Page 147
Map not to exact scale

Taffy 3's first critical and desperate minutes

Sprague's philosophy was, "Pull up your socks and just do it," and he never yielded to the temptation to procrastinate. The only decision for him at this moment was not *if* he would fight the Japanese, but *how*. And Taffy 3 was all that stood between Kurita's guns and MacArthur's defenseless Leyte Gulf beachhead.

Sprague's demeanor of calm decisiveness and aggressive decision-making inspired the other officers in his command to follow suit, and this was a factor that proved to be decisive in determining the battle's outcome. Because of his attitude, which set the tone of command, his men were willing to sacrifice everything they had, including their lives.

An officer writing about the Pacific War commented that there were few heroes who "can compare with the courage, coolness, and tactical genius of 'Ziggy' Sprague. His aggressiveness bewildered the Japanese and infected all his forces, surface and air." A rephrasing of Arthur C.

Clark seems appropriate here, that the only way to go beyond what seems possible is to attempt the impossible.

Kurita Reacts to Sprague's Moves

As Sprague headed for the rain squall with his screening escorts spewing smoke, Kurita made two decisions. The first was to send his entire force after Sprague, because his Center Force had more than enough power to destroy Sprague's command and to pulverize the Leyte beaches. Kurita's next order, however, was one that threw his command into confusion, because at the time he ordered a general attack, his ships were in the midst of changing from a cruising formation to a circular anti-aircraft defensive formation, and this turned out to be an unwise move. Kurita should have formed his ships into a battle line, with his destroyers leading the way. Since he failed to do this, all his ships were forced to attack independently, and since every type of ship has a different top speed, each ship in his force headed hell bent for leather in piecemeal formation. The Center Force was thus transformed into a jumbled, bumbling mass of disorganization, lacking a coordinated plan for attack or defense in the event the Americans launched a counterattack.

Kurita's move to follow Sprague's course toward the rain squall rather than to move to the southeast and cut Sprague off from the land was not, however, a totally foolish decision. He did indeed want to get in front of Sprague to deny him the wind advantage. However, if had he moved toward the Leyte beaches instead of chasing after Sprague, Kurita would have cut Sprague's path to Leyte Gulf and could have easily destroyed Taffy 3 before turning toward his main objective—the Leyte beachhead.

Why did Sprague's decisions turn out to be the right ones while Kurita's decisions proved to be wrong? One possible explanation lies in the Japanese naval training Kurita received at the Etijima Naval Academy. A fundamental principle in Japanese culture is to make decisions by consulting with all parties concerned. While this may be an excellent form of decision-making when there is ample time to examine all aspects of the alternatives, to discuss them fully with subordinates, and then reach a conclusion, the dynamics of a naval battle often give a commander little time to respond. At such moments, brilliant, split-second decisions are required.

If the Americans had done what Kurita had expected them to do, the Japanese could have achieved their objectives. However, unlike Sprague,

Kurita fixed his mind on his mission. Thus, when confronted with choosing between staying with his mission or attacking Sprague, uncertainty paralyzed him. He had never been convinced that the SHO-1 plan could succeed. Nonetheless, a historic opportunity to bring glory to himself and to the Japanese navy stared out at him across 15 miles of ocean. The vaunted American carriers were out there just waiting to be crushed, and if he could have called upon the same initiative his opponent was displaying, he might have destroyed Sprague and stopped the Leyte invasion. But the indecisiveness implicit in his second decision had a dramatic effect on the ultimate outcome of the Battle off Samar.[11]

Another possible explanation for Kurita's hesitancy can be found in his service record. Kurita had a reputation for coolness under fire. Aggressive, he nonetheless had compassion for the sailors in his command and respected his subordinates and staff. As a person, he was competitive and enjoyed sports, playing tennis and baseball and developing skills in archery. Kurita's World War II record was broad and extensive. His first assignments were in Japan's early campaigns in the Netherlands East Indies, where he commanded invasion groups and naval escorting forces. He commanded a cruiser squadron that attacked Allied bases in the Indian Ocean. He saw action at Midway, Guadalcanal, the Solomons campaign, and the Philippine Sea. His battleships had mercilessly bombarded the marines on Guadalcanal and had the American aircraft carrier *Hornet* under their guns. The Japanese lost no carriers at the Battle of the Philippine Sea when Kurita's ships escorted them. Clearly Kurita could both command and lead men into battle.

Despite this exemplary war record, there were also calamitous losses. While chasing the cruisers *Houston* and *Perth* off Java during the war's first days, some of his ships were sunk by torpedoes. His cruiser, the *Mikuma*, collided with the *Mogami* at Midway and sank under a torrent of American torpedoes and bombs. Some of the *Enterprise*'s planes bombed and heavily damaged his flagship at Santa Cruz. In November 1943, incessant American air raids ruthlessly attacked his cruiser force at Rabaul. His own Center Force, on entering Philippine waters in October 1944, had undergone an ordeal of destruction.[12]

The Battle Escalates

Many men on the *Fanshaw Bay*'s bridge held little hope for Taffy 3's survival. Increasingly accurate Japanese shells howled overhead, exploding

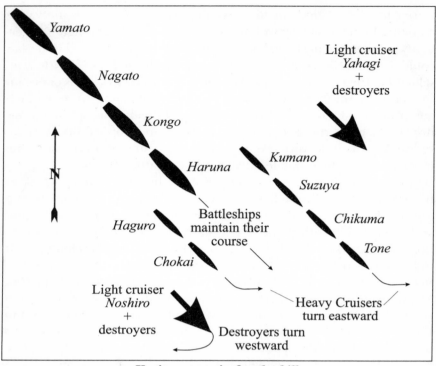

Kurita moves in for the kill

in the waters around Taffy 3 as the six slow-moving escort carriers and screening force of destroyers and destroyer escorts moved as fast as they could toward the rain squall. Water geysers from falling shells drenched the destroyer escort *Samuel B. Roberts's* captain and anyone near him on the small ship's deck. To Sprague and the others, it must have seemed like a nightmare in slow motion with a ferocious predator trying to catch up with them before they could reach the temporary safety of the squall's rain and mist.

Kurita's force charged ahead in roughly five separate formations, rapidly closing the range to its apparently hapless victims. Two columns of cruisers and one column of battleships, protected by destroyers on both flanks, were now a scant 11 miles away. The Japanese formation then began to separate so that its ships could trap Taffy 3 between two forces. The Japanese cruisers steamed at high speed eastward in order to keep Sprague from moving into the wind and farther out to sea and to keep him from launching more aircraft.

Meanwhile, the destroyers moved westward so that they could attack from that direction. The battleships stayed on a steady course to be able to continue bombarding the sterns of the Taffy 3 ships. Even though this meant that the battleships were chasing the American escort carriers from their rear quarter, they had such an overwhelming speed advantage over the slower-moving escort carriers that they could easily catch them. There was no doubt that the carriers would soon be within range of the battleships' guns. To some of Sprague's officers, the battle scene developing before their very eyes might have seemed like watching a Hollywood western in which attacking Indians circle a slow, cumbersome pioneer wagon train.

Taffy 3 reached the shelter of the rain squall at 7:21 A.M., just as splashes from Japanese shells engulfed the American ships. Invisible now to the Japanese spotters, Sprague had time to evaluate the situation and plan his next move. He still clung to the vain hope that Halsey's Third Fleet was nearby, reasoning that if he could lure Kurita farther away from the Leyte beaches, the Japanese force would be in a place "where somebody could smack him, for if we were going to expend ourselves I wanted to make it count." However, moving eastward so he could launch aircraft, and reaching the rain squall's shelter, conflicted with the objective of luring Kurita away from Leyte. Taffy 3, in fact, had to head south so that it could become a barrier between the Japanese and the Leyte beaches, and Sprague had to bring his command closer to any help that might come from that direction.

Sprague made a swift and difficult decision. He ordered a course change to 170 degrees. Putting Taffy 3 on a course toward Leyte Gulf was a maneuver that could easily prove to be disastrous, because if Kurita moved southeast, Taffy 3 would be placed directly under the guns of the Japanese battleships and cruisers. In this spot, the outgunned American ships would be annihilated. But just as Kurita's lookouts could not see what Sprague was up to while Taffy 3 was in the rain squall, Sprague also suffered from the same disadvantage. He could not know what Kurita was doing. Sprague decided to move southward, leaving the rain squall's sheltering cloud cover, and hoping against hope that Kurita would then make a wrong move.

Sprague later told reporters, "I figured we'd be blown out of the water the instant we came out of the rain squall." He was flabbergasted, however, when he saw that Kurita did not move to the southeast and cut off Taffy 3 but, instead, "stupidly followed us around the circle."

Sprague's gamble therefore is one that paid off handsomely because it bought fifteen precious minutes for Taffy 3. The escort carriers, shielded from view by the rain clouds, escaped to the south, while Kurita stayed on an eastward course. However, that advantage proved to be a brief one, for when Kurita realized what Sprague had done, he turned his ships in pursuit. But the fifteen minutes thus gained Sprague and his commanders a chance to assess the situation facing them.

Serving on the *Fanshaw Bay*'s bridge and close enough to Sprague to be within earshot, Lieutenant Pierson said later that Sprague's decision to turn southward was "the order that saved us." Pierson reasoned that while most officers would have continued moving eastward in hopes of a miracle, Sprague exercised boldness and made the unconventional, hard decision. "A miracle happened all right but the admiral sure helped the situation," Pierson said.

When the Japanese shells started falling, Pierson thought Taffy 3's chances for survival were dwindling fast. As Taffy 3 moved southward out from under the rain squall's shelter, and Pierson saw that the Japanese had not immediately moved to pursue them, he expressed a bit of optimism by observing that they "might be able to get away with this after all." Another officer who overheard Pierson's optimistic exclamation tried to burst Pierson's bubble by retorting, "Don't be silly."

After looking at the Japanese to the north through his glasses, Sprague knew it would not be long before their faster warships would make up for their mistake. Soon they would have Taffy 3 within point-blank range of their guns.[13]

Chapter 13: Swarming Bees

Sprague had more things to worry about than "merely" dodging the Japanese. He had to prevent Kurita's force from reaching the Leyte beaches by using effectively the two weapons at his disposal: the aircraft on his escort carriers and the destroyers and destroyer escorts that were screening Taffy 3. Attacks by Taffy 3's planes on the Japanese ships had to be properly directed. Due to Sprague's earlier order to launch all aircraft, a bizarre hodgepodge of torpedo bombers and fighters made uncoordinated attacks on Kurita from mixed altitudes, angles, and directions.

By the time Sprague changed course southward and moved out from under the rain squall's protection at 7:30 A.M., about 100 fighters and torpedo planes began attacking Kurita with torpedoes, bombs, and bullets. Only a few planes attacked at one time, but the cumulative effect must have seemed like an assault from a swarm of bees. Each attacking plane forced Kurita to turn his attention away from the ships of Taffy 3 and to defend his force against their incessant assaults.

Although each pilot might have felt they did not do much in the way of damage to the powerful Japanese warships, the cumulative effect of the attacks most assuredly affected Kurita with a far deeper impact than the American pilots could know or even imagine at the time. These gnat-like assaults were a decisive part of Sprague's tactics aimed at forcing the oncoming Japanese warships to turn back. Sprague wanted to pressure every Japanese ship's captain into believing that every attacking plane carried bombs or torpedoes, therefore forcing them to maneuver their ships with extraordinary care to avoid being damaged. In so doing, Kurita's columns became confused and jumbled as they tried to evade the ever-present, ever-attacking American aircraft.[1]

By 7:30 A.M., ninety-five aircraft had left the decks of Taffy 3's carriers. Each carrier launched a different number of aircraft types. The table shows how many aircraft each Taffy 3 carrier launched and the armaments they carried when they took off.

Taffy 3's Aircraft and Their Armament

Carriers	Aircraft Launched	Bomber Armament
Gambier Bay	10 fighters, 8 torpedo-bombers	2 bombers, no bombs; 3 had two 500-pound general purpose bombs; 2 had two 350-pound depth bombs; 1 bomber, one torpedo, but only 35 gallons of gas
Fanshaw Bay	1 fighter, 11 torpedo-bombers	10 bombers, one 500-pound high explosive bomb; 1 bomber, two 350-pound depth bombs
St. Lô	15 fighters, 4 torpedo-bombers	2 bombers, eight 100-pound general purpose bombs; 1 bomber, no bomb; 1 bomber's load unknown
White Plains	5 fighters, 4 torpedo-bombers	4 bombers, one 350-pound depth bomb each with contact fuses
Kalinin Bay	10 fighters, 10 torpedo-bombers	3 bombers, one 500-pound bomb each and eight 5-inch rockets; 6 bombers, ten 100-pound general purpose bombs and eight 5-inch rockets
Kitkun Bay	11 fighters, 6 torpedo-bombers	6 bombers, four 500-pound high explosive bombs each

None of the planes had the proper armament for use against heavily armored warships. Instead, the fighters just had their .50-caliber machine guns to attack the oncoming Japanese warships. The aircrafts' crews had been trained to attack lightly armored merchant vessels and submarines, as well as to support ground troops. As more planes returned from ground support missions after 7:30 A.M., they immediately rearmed, refueled, and took off again. Any aircraft on combat air patrol and on antisubmarine patrol attacked as soon as they received orders from Sprague. All of the aircrews realized that a dire situation faced their command and were more than willing to attack with what they had.

Because of the chaos inherent in the situation, the American planes' attacks could never be coordinated. Therefore, they struck the Japanese in small groups of one, two, or three aircraft at a time. There was no way to establish points of rendezvous; the Japanese ships had appeared too suddenly to allow for any planning. As far as doing any heavy damage to the powerful Japanese battleships and cruisers, their attacks would have as much effect as bee stings on the hide of an armadillo. But they relentlessly and repeatedly attacked and would not give up until the Japanese quit.

Lieutenant Commander Edward J. (Hux) Huxtable waited for his breakfast in the *Gambier Bay*'s wardroom when the general alarm's clanging sound jolted him. Thinking this was just another warning about another mission into the Sulu Sea, Huxtable was too hungry to pay much attention. He was determined to have at least some juice and toast before he went anywhere. But when his personnel officer rushed into the wardroom exclaiming, "Captain, you better get up to the ready room in a hurry! They are already manning the planes!"[2] he leaped to his feet and ran at a full gallop, as much in the dark as before the alarm rang.

Huxtable grabbed his plotting board and ran to his plane. Climbing onto the wing of his Avenger and preparing to enter the cockpit, he asked his plane captain what bomb load his aircraft had. Startled when he found out there was none, he asked the man to tell Cmdr. Fred E. (Buzz) Borries, the ship's air officer, that he needed a bomb load; there was no point in taking off without any bombs. Huxtable looked up at the carrier's superstructure island, where he saw Borries move forward to talk to Captain Vieweg. He got his answer when Vieweg made a large sweeping gesture with his arm as if to say, "Get 'em off!"

From just behind his left ear, an extremely loud noise sounding like a shot from a high caliber gun drew Huxtable's attention. Large splashes doused the *White Plains*'s flight deck. He knew now why the alarm had been sounded. Later he said, "I was more than ready to get on the catapult." Three Avengers catapulted into the air ahead of him; soon after, he pushed his plane's throttle forward to full power, making the engine vibrate. When the catapult officer suggested his engine had enough thrust by dropping the flag, Huxtable released his brakes, and the single-engine bomber accelerated across the fight deck and shot up into the air. As soon as his plane's wheels left the deck, he called the *Fanshaw Bay* for his orders and got a short, simple answer: "Attack immediately!"

Three more Avengers rose from the hangar deck on the ship's elevators after the first four took off, ready for launching. The first plane waddled onto the catapult, and Lt. (jg) William Gallagher and his crew climbed in. The plane captain screamed, "Wait! Wait! It's got no gas!" Unfortunately, Gallagher's plane had only 35 gallons in its tanks, far less than its 300–500 gallon capacity. However, time was too short to take on more fuel. As Vieweg gave the signal to launch, Gallagher nodded his head, waved his hand, gunned the engine and took off. He banked, turned the Avenger left, and headed for the Japanese ships.

Unlike Gallagher's plane, the next Avenger about to be launched had full fuel tanks and carried a torpedo slung under its belly. Lieutenant (jg) Robert E. Weatherholt and his crew climbed aboard and waited for the catapult to yank the plane aloft. Weatherholt sat in the cockpit and calmly smoked a cigarette. Just as the catapult officer was about to give the launch signal, he took a last drag from his cigarette, then flicked it away. As the plane accelerated down the deck, he looked at the deck crew as a broad grin crossed his face.

The last Avenger was being hooked to the catapult when the ship changed course, trying to dodge the Japanese shells falling all around the carrier. Hank Pyzdrowski and his crew were already aboard and impatient to go. Pyzdrowski yelled, "She's charged! Let 'er go!" Looking up at the bridge, he saw Borries pointing at the ship's ensign. The carrier's course change meant there was not enough wind for his plane to take off.

Pyzdrowski jumped from his plane, ran to the bridge, and pleaded with Borries to let him launch. The only answer was "wait." Determined to take off and attack the oncoming Japanese under any conditions, Pyzdrowski disgustedly ran back to his plane and ordered his crewmen to get out. If necessary, he would take off by himself. However, the shell splashes now surrounded the carrier; he would have to wait until the carrier turned into the wind.

Once again, Pyzdrowski climbed down from the cockpit, unable to understand why his planes could not be launched, wind or no wind. It had been done before. He ran up to Borries as the air officer pointed at the catapult. The pilotless Avenger shot off into the air, crewless. The launch was picture-perfect as the big plane rose into the sky, flew for a few seconds, rolled off on its wing, and splashed into the sea. The *Gambier Bay* would launch no more planes.

Meanwhile, Huxtable led his group of bombers against the Center Force. Flying in some broken clouds, his formation broke into clear air. Below them were four cruisers making foam-flecked V-shaped waves through the water. Farther to their rear on the gloomy horizon, four battleships followed. Huxtable pulled his stick back and ordered his formation into the shelter of the clouds. He wanted to draw near enough to be able to dive on the ships from the cloud cover and to reduce the time the Japanese gunners had to shoot at them. His dead-reckoning navigation led his planes over the cruisers. Breaking out of the clouds, they dove on the Japanese cruisers' starboard side.

Red lines from tracers filled the sky as the Japanese gunners tried to find the American planes. Suddenly, bursts of flak engulfed the planes with puffs of black, red, and assorted other colored smoke. Dodging the bursting antiaircraft shells, Huxtable violently banked his plane to the left and dove for the last cruiser at 190 knots. Pressing the attack, he moved in until he was 2,000 yards away. Although his plane had no bombs, he was unwilling to commit suicide like a kamikaze pilot, so he pulled out of the dive 4,000 yards on the cruiser's other side. He thought that if he did not directly attack the cruiser, the Japanese would not fire at him, an assumption that soon proved to be wrong. Five flak shells exploded in several colors 150 yards in front. Flying through the smoke of the middle burst, Huxtable saw one near miss on the second cruiser.

Huxtable radioed the *Gambier Bay*, asking where to rearm and was told "Tacloban." Not knowing what kinds of supplies he could get there, Huxtable resumed attacking the Japanese without any bombs. He opened his bomb bay doors to make the Japanese believe he was attacking with torpedoes. Continuing the fake attacks until about 9:00 A.M., he finally headed for Tacloban. These ersatz attacks by Huxtable and many of the other "jeep" pilots disturbed and confused the Japanese and was a major factor preventing them from boring in on Taffy 3 and sinking it.

Bill Gallagher joined Huxtable in attacking the Japanese ships while "Hux" prepared to make another run. Gallagher's Avenger had several holes in its skin; heavy, black smoke belched from his engine, and his fuel tanks were nearly empty, but he flew directly at the Japanese cruisers, took aim at one of them, dropped his torpedo, then headed for

Tacloban. The last time anyone saw his plane, it had landed in the water. Gallagher's plane and crew were never seen again.

Lieutenant Bassett was on Huxtable's wing when his squadron commander dove on the trailing cruiser. Bassett instead decided to attack the leading Mogami-class cruiser. The ship wiggled like a polliwog in shallow water when Bassett dove his plane at it. Red fingers of flak reached up from all over her superstructure, pointing at his aircraft. When he dropped his first 500-pound bomb, his plane trembled from gunfire ripping through it. Bassett wasted no time in dropping his second bomb and then just as quickly escaped into the clouds. Neither bomb hit its intended target. When Bassett emerged from the cloud cover, he looked to his right. A huge hole had been torn in his starboard horizontal stabilizer. The plane still flew, but not wanting to tempt fate, Bassett headed for land, touching down at Dulag just after 11:00 A.M.

Taking off before Huxtable, Ens. Robert L. Crocker and Ens. William C. Shroyer joined with their skipper to do as much damage as they could on the Center Force. Crocker carried no bombs, so he could do little damage. However, he followed his commanding officer in making dummy attack runs and effectively diverted gunfire to himself. Some of the heavier Japanese guns tried to take their revenge on his airplane and achieved some success. When Crocker eventually landed his plane at Dulag, his instruments no longer worked and there was a gaping big hole in his left wing. Adding insult to injury, a fighter ran into his Avenger on the ground and damaged its propeller.

Unlike his wing man, Shroyer had two 500-pound bombs and put them to good use. The low clouds forced him to strafe the cruisers first, but heavy antiaircraft fire surrounded his plane and made him retreat. Banking his plane toward the Japanese warships, he looked down. His plane was flying over a Tone-class cruiser, and he saw more than twelve Wildcat fighters spraying the vessel with machine-gun fire. Shroyer pushed the stick forward into a shallow glide and dropped his bombs, which hit and exploded on the cruiser's stern. Another pilot from a different squadron confirmed the hits. Heading for Dulag later, Shroyer again flew over the cruiser; it lay dead in the water.

Other fliers from the *Gambier Bay*'s fighter squadron also let the Japanese know they were there. Lieutenant (jg) Charles J. Dugan's Wildcat was one of the first to take off, albeit over a 40mm mount instead of straight off the deck. Wondering why everyone was in such a rush, his questions were answered when he saw the Japanese ships. The next thought that occurred to him was to puzzle over where were the "rich kids" (the fast carrier pilots): "This is their kind of work. We haven't been hired to fight the whole Jap fleet by ourselves."

In his younger days as a hunter, Dugan had always pursued the biggest game. Today, the largest quarry in his sight was the giant *Yamato*. To Dugan, launching an attack at a battleship with a puny fighter was on-the-job training because, "The books and manuals that [he] had read on how to be a fighter pilot did not anywhere tell you where you should shoot a battleship with .50-caliber machine guns to mortally wound it."

Dugan decided the only way to inflict any damage on this behemoth was to shoot at its most vulnerable spot—the area around its bridge. He put his plane into a steep dive and started firing his machine guns. He saw the .50-caliber bullets bounce off the *Yamato*'s bridge and make miniature, twinkling-like colored explosions when they hit. Violently pulling back on his stick at 900 feet, his Wildcat climbed steeply into the air, and he blacked out. Dugan reasoned that while he did not hit many people on the bridge, his machine-gun fire inevitably took "a lot of paint off their front door."

He made several more strafing runs and lost consciousness each time he pulled out of his dives. The Japanese antiaircraft fire relentlessly followed him as he pulled into the clouds but all missed his plane. Disdaining the Japanese gunners' abilities, Dugan said later, "It made a lot better war of it knowing the bastards couldn't shoot." Finally exhausting his ammunition, he made several dummy runs and eventually headed for Tacloban.

Like Dugan, many pilots also ran out of ammunition. However, they returned again and again to make fake attacks on the Japanese ships, thus forcing them to change course to avoid the American aircrafts' assaults and keeping them from getting nearer the escort carriers. But this fighter squadron was not the only one to be so effective. Almost all of Taffy 3's squadrons accomplished as much.

One Japanese officer later described the harassing tactics used by the American flyers in attacking the Center Force: "The attack was almost incessant, but the number of planes at any one instant was few. The bombers and torpedo planes were very aggressive and skillful, and the coordination was impressive; even in comparison with the great experience of American attack that we already had, this was the most skillful work of your planes."

• • •

The *Fanshaw Bay* launched twelve planes as four more already on combat air patrol joined them. Using their advantage of a higher altitude, the four CAP fighters sprinted ahead and immediately started strafing the leading battleships and cruisers. Diving at a 60-degree angle, most of their attacks began at 4,000 feet; they continued firing until pulling out at 1,000 feet. Heavy antiaircraft fire climbed to meet the attacking Wildcat fighters. However, the Japanese gunners failed to accurately follow the American planes' paths and most of their fire exploded well behind the planes.

Like his comrades, Lt. Ray Anderson machine-gunned the bridge of a battleship. Although no one saw any damage from the attacks, the American fighters returned again and again to continuously strafe the heavily armored ships. Not seeing any visible damage from the assaults disturbed the fighter pilots, Anderson lamented later, "I would have felt much less insignificant had I had four 5-inch H.E. [high explosive] rockets on zero length launchers or one or two 250-pound bombs. As it was, I jettisoned about 450 pounds of gasoline, which I would gladly have traded for the above."[3]

The rest of the *Fanshaw Bay*'s fighter planes appeared over the frantic struggle a few minutes later. Their commanding officer, Lt. Cmdr. Richard S. Rogers, first led his group northwest, then turned northward at 8,000 feet while flying through moist, dark gray broken clouds. After turning his planes north, Rogers reduced their altitude to 1,000 feet to get a sighting of the Japanese ships. Flying through the broken clouds' mist and haze, a group of six cruisers and battleships emerged as the American planes broke out of the cloud cover at about 7:35 A.M. Rogers quickly radioed the rest of the planes that had been above him to come down.

Despite Japanese perceptions, and like most of the earlier attacks, little coordination existed among the American planes for they attacked from every direction. Strafing fighters led the way as eight Avengers attacked two heavy cruisers, probably the *Haguro* and the *Chokai*. While black, purple, yellow, and green flak bursts dotted the sky, the bombers unerringly headed for the Japanese cruisers. Although he only had two depth bombs, Ens. George F. Smith pointed his plane's nose at the second cruiser and dove at her. As the wind screamed by his canopy and exploding flak shook his Avenger, Smith stayed on target. He released his bombs at 2,000 feet and kept diving until he was just above the water. Smith turned around and saw his bombs explode near the cruiser's port bow. Few American flyers could tell whether they hit anything, because their planes violently jerked, banked, dived, and turned as they tried to avoid being hit by Japanese antiaircraft fire.

Having no more bombs, Smith saw a battleship in his sights and fired his wing guns. As he sped past the big battlewagon, his two crewmen sprayed its deck with turret and belly guns. Wanting to keep attacking with something more than ineffective machine-gun fire, Smith headed back to his ship to rearm with more bombs. However, the *Fanshaw Bay* was too busy evading heavy Japanese shellfire to land any aircraft. Forced to land on Taffy 2's *Marcus Island,* he found six other wandering Avengers that had to land there also. Feeling the desperation of the battle's situation, the little carrier's arming crewmen quickly and furiously rearmed the torpedo bombers with torpedoes. Soon, all seven Avengers were in the air again to resume their attacks.

While Smith attacked one cruiser, Lt. William J. Slone went after another. Slone saw two battleships just disappearing under a rain squall's clouds and mist. Following them were the light cruiser *Yahagi* and four accompanying destroyers. Before losing sight of them, he dove from 8,000 feet and began his attack run. Flak shells exploded all around as his plane dove toward the water. As he passed 4,000 feet, one shell struck his Avenger and almost cut its main wing spar. Nevertheless, Slone pressed the attack by trying to drop three 500-pound bombs at 3,000 feet, but only two bombs actually left the bomb racks in his plane's belly. The third one stuck in the rack and failed to drop. Always optimistic, like all flight crews, his gunners reported that all three bombs hit the *Yahagi,* while another pilot stated the ship later sank. However, the ship the bombs hit was not, in fact, the *Yahagi.* She would survive until April 1945, when she sank with the *Yamato.* Whatever ship the bombs hit, its identity remains unknown to this day.

False reports of damaged or sinking ships were common in the heat of battle. As air crews dove through murderous flak, firing machine guns, and dropping bombs and torpedoes, the increased adrenaline flow led the crews to make exaggerated claims. (This book tells what happened from the perspective of those who were there, and while every attempt has been made to render events accurately, in some instances it has not been possible to confirm the reports made since they are the only records available.)

Rogers's other pilots attacked every Japanese ship in sight. Lieutenant (jg) Jerry J. Jacoby claimed his 500-pound bomb hit a cruiser. According to Lt. (jg) Harvey L. Lively, three of his bombs hit the same ship a few minutes later. The damaged cruiser most likely was the heavy cruiser *Suzuya*. The American attacks forced her to steer away from the American escort carriers and to lose speed. Another pilot's bomb hit and exploded on one of the battleships but did little harm.

By 8:05 A.M., the Avengers had used every bomb they had so they flew back to their carrier to rearm. Meanwhile, every one of the twenty-odd fighters still flying over the Japanese fleet strafed the ships continuously, paying particular attention to the ships closest to the American carriers. They kept up their attacks for about forty-five minutes, relentlessly tormenting the oncoming warships, forcing the Japanese captains to execute violently evasive maneuvers that delayed their pursuit of Taffy 3.

Rogers and his pilots had made several dummy strafing attacks at the Japanese ships. Shooting machine-gun bullets at heavily armored warships was as effective as shooting spitballs at them. These pilots had no way to defend themselves, and Rogers's own words put the episode in a true perspective: "You know you can't shoot back and rattle the guy who is shooting at you. Psychologically, it's like getting into the ring with a good boxer and having your arms tied behind you."

Rogers's aircraft had carried out three attacks, in the process using up his supply of ammunition. Since Taffy 3's carriers were now steaming downwind, trying to dodge the Japanese salvos, Rogers could not land his plane and rearm on his home carrier. Knowing he could not stay aloft forever, he radioed Sprague, asking what to do next. Sprague replied, "Well, look, you just make dummy runs on the ships because every time you do, you draw fire away from my ships."

For Rogers that order meant that the pilots under his command were being asked to sacrifice their lives so Sprague's carriers could buy time. Rogers would say later, "Sprague had to give the order to make dummy runs. It shows you the type of leader he was—he had his priorities in order and he did what he had to do. There's a time you've got to do things for the greater good, like falling on a grenade. This was one of those times."[4]

Throughout the battle, these strafing, often feigned attacks greatly affected the Japanese more than the American pilots imagined possible. While damage to the Japanese ships was considerable, the psychological damage done was still greater. Eventually it took its toll. Nonetheless, despite the persistent American air attacks, the Japanese cruisers kept coming after the vulnerable little carriers, getting closer with each passing minute.

At 5:30 A.M., the *St. Lô* launched six planes for an antisubmarine patrol, but two aircraft never entered the battle. The remaining four, responding to Sprague's call for help, joined in when the battle began about one hour later. These four pilots, after making a quick sweep of their sectors, came on the scene and dropped their depth bombs near several ships shortly after Bill Brooks had seen the Center Force and after Hans Jensen had dropped his depth bombs near either the *Tone* or *Chikuma*. After they finished, two pilots landed on *Marcus Island* to rearm; the third landed on *Ommaney Bay*; and the last went to Tacloban.

Hidden beneath the protective cover of the squall, the *St. Lô* began launching four Avenger torpedo bombers and fifteen fighters at 7:18 A.M. The fighters followed their comrades' lead by strafing the ships with .50-caliber machine guns until they exhausted their ammunition supply and had to head for land to rearm. While the fighters did their best, the Avengers' leader, Lt. Cmdr. R. M. Jones, claimed three hits on a battleship; Lieutenant (jg) J. R. Gore hit a cruiser's deck with a string of five 100-pounders and strafed it and as many other ships as he could, until his ammunition ran out. Lieutenant (jg) Leonard E. Waldrop made eight attacks with bombs, machine-gun fire, and rockets on four cruisers and a destroyer. Having neither bombs nor rockets, another pilot strafed the Japanese ships several times until he also exhausted his ammunition. Waldrop headed back toward the carriers; the rest turned toward Dulag or Tacloban.

The *White Plains* could launch only five fighters and four bombers because of the gigantic geysers of water from Japanese shells that engulfed her. Just as the planes were about to take off, a salvo bracketed the carrier that caused two fighters to collide so they could not be launched.

Just as the other fighters did that morning, the *White Plains'* fighter pilots strafed the onrushing Japanese. Lieutenant (jg) Solen N. Hales said later, "I couldn't find anything else to do so I made some strafing runs on a battleship." However, his squadron commanding officer also made the point, "There are no confirmed reports of enemy battleships sinking as a result of these strafing attacks."

Lieutenant (jg) Walter P. Owens led the four *White Plains'* Avengers when they probably attacked a heavy cruiser (probably the *Haguro*) as she and the other cruisers closed their range to the escort carriers. All four bombers peeled off in echelon formation from 8,000 feet and glided down to 6,000 feet. From that altitude, their pilots pushed their sticks forward to put their planes into 50-degree dives and headed straight toward the cruiser. One after the other, they descended, dropped their bombs, and pulled up so steeply their guts felt like a hundred-pound rock lay on them. Leaving the cruiser behind with their throttles pushed fully forward, two planes headed back and landed on the *St. Lô.* The rest headed toward American bases on Leyte. Miraculously, all the planes' crews survived.

By 7:25 A.M., the *Kalinin Bay* strengthened the initial air attacks by launching seven fighters and ten Avengers; three more fighters left the carrier's deck twenty-five minutes later. However, the poor visibility caused by the rain and the smoke screen delayed their rendezvous as they headed toward the Japanese ships. Lieutenant Commander William Keighley's radio failed, and so he could not coordinate his group's attacks. He delegated the leadership of his bombers, therefore, to Lt. Patrick "Patsy" Capano.

After flying for fifteen minutes, Capano spotted four cruisers, two battleships, and several destroyers making white-foamed wakes as they steamed south at high speed and immediately ordered the bombers to attack. The planes dove out of the broken clouds and pounced on the Japanese ships. Keighley dropped his 100-pound bombs on a Tone-class cruiser. Three bombs apparently hit the cruiser, but the comparatively small bombs caused little damage. Capano dropped his bombs on the formation's leading cruiser with unknown results. He then joined with Keighley to strafe the cruisers. Keighley's planes continued strafing any ship they could see until he left for Dulag about 11:30 A.M.

Ensign Richard G. Altman picked the *Haruna* as his target. He flew straight for the big battleship until he was directly above it. Altman pushed the stick forward and put his plane into a steep dive using the now-common American dive-bombing tactic. He fired four 5-inch rockets and hit the big ship amidships. Not finished, he dropped two 500-pound general purpose bombs. One just nicked the *Haruna*'s bow, and the other exploded near it. Altman pulled the stick to his belly and looked for another target. On the periphery of his vision, Altman saw a cruiser slicing through the water. He leveled off, dove his plane, and fired his remaining rockets from 1,000 feet. With all his armaments spent, he headed for Leyte to rearm. Later, Altman claimed two hits on the cruiser's superstructure.

Four more of the *Kalinin Bay*'s Avengers followed Keighley's group into the conflict. At about 7:50 A.M., they attacked the same group of ships at almost the same time. Lieutenant Walter D. Crockett approached the *Haruna* from astern and dropped his bombs from 2,500 feet. He pulled up into the clouds and could not tell whether his bombs had hit the battleship. Unhappily, he did see another squadron's Avenger suddenly burst into a brilliant ball of flame and head, comet-like, into the sea. He also saw another Avenger follow that doomed aircraft as it, too, plunged into the water.

Crockett's fellow pilots were just as busy. Lieutenant (jg) Earl L. Archer, Jr., strafed a destroyer and then attacked the two leading cruisers. He dropped his bombs one after the other on the second cruiser while diving between 4,500 and 3,000 feet. Continuing his dive toward the leading cruiser, Archer fired his eight rockets and saw them explode in sequence across the cruiser's deck. Pieces of the ship flew into the air as each rocket exploded on the deck and disappeared in billowing balls of fire and smoke.

Ensigns G. Neilan Smith and James R. Zeitvogel fired their rockets at several ships. Smith also dropped two 500-pound bombs near a cruiser's side. Before they headed away from the battle, they dove and wove while firing their machine guns, trying to match the ships' wildly twisting maneuvers. However, they could not keep this up as they used all their ammunition and had to land to rearm. Crockett and Smith landed on the *White Plains* at 10:15 A.M. as Archer and Zeitvogel flew to Tacloban. Archer received a new assignment the next day when he transferred to Dulag to become the landing field's landing signal officer. The landing conditions there were so bad that carrier landing procedures needed to be established.

The *Kalinin Bay*'s fighter pilots also kept busy. Making repeated runs at the Japanese ships, many of them dove at steep 65-degree dives and pulled up dangerously close to the water's surface. Any resemblance to coordinated attacks went out the window as many aircraft approached, attacked, and then left to and from many directions. Most of the planes attacked by themselves or haphazardly joined with other planes that happened to be nearby.

While most of the confrontations were of the plane-against-ship variety, some of the carrier's fighters also engaged in aerial combat with Japanese aircraft. Ensigns George A. Heinmiller and Geoffrey B. King each shot down a Japanese dive-bomber that bumbled into their gun sights during this savage action. Unable to land on the *Kalinin Bay*'s flight deck because she was dodging Japanese shellfire, most of the fighter pilots flew to Tacloban.

Archer's new assignment became more challenging on the now crowded, busy airstrip. However, all his skills could not overcome the effects of heavy rains that turned the field into a muddy quagmire and made it increasingly unsafe to land aircraft. Three fighters crashed trying to land and were total wrecks; one Wildcat ditched in Leyte Gulf and sank; four other aircraft sustained so much damage they could not fly without being repaired.

At 6:55 A.M., the *Kitkun Bay*'s pilots heard the "on the double" flight alert. Commander Richard L. Fowler and his men ran so fast out of the ready room and into their planes that the first fighter took off only about a minute later. As the last Avenger leaped off the carrier's deck, the technicolor geysers sprouted like fast-growing weeds and surrounded the little carrier. The American pilots easily found the Japanese ships. All they had to do was make a 180-degree turn, fly for about two minutes, and the massive fleet appeared below.

The fighters led the bombers as they vertically dove on the ships, pulled out just above the wave-tops, regained altitude, and attacked again. Angry red lights spouted from each ship's guns, suggesting that many Japanese gunners had survived the earlier, repetitious American strafing runs. Most of the planes attacked the heavy cruisers closest to the *Gambier Bay*'s port quarter. Lieutenant Paul B. Garrison attacked the cruisers twenty times, firing his guns on twelve passes and feigned attacks eight times with no ammunition. As he made his last pass, a large-caliber shell ripped through his left wing and turned him over on his back. Out of ammunition and with only about 20 gallons of gas left in his tanks, Garrison sensed he might be running out of luck, too. He turned his damaged craft toward Tacloban and landed there at about 10:00 A.M.

The *Kitkun Bay*'s Avengers began their attacks over one hour after the first fighter left its flight deck. Fowler needed that much time to gather his planes and to coordinate their attacks. There was a heavy cloud cover, and Japanese gunners aimed their flak barrages at holes in the clouds.

One of these fusillades shot down one American bomber and set another on fire. He had watched the other planes attacking from above as they went after the *Kongo* and the *Haruna*. What made Fowler unhappy was that some Avenger pilots chose to attack by horizontally bombing the Japanese from 6,000 feet. These assaults failed because the Japanese ships twisted and turned, causing the bombs to fall far from the ships and to explode in the water. These tactics might have worked on stationary targets using a group of six Avengers and twenty fighters that had been aloft on ground support missions when the Center Force attacked earlier that morning; they definitely would not work against moving ships trying to avoid being hit.

Fowler became frustrated at seeing the lack of coordination among the *Kitkun Bay*'s planes attacking the Japanese cruisers in groups of two or three aircraft. From his long experience with naval aviation, he knew that to damage or to sink these heavily armored ships, the American attacks had to be made in large, coordinated groups. Therefore, he stayed aloft to coordinate not only his carrier's air attacks, but others as well. By 8:30 A.M., the American aircraft attacks became more effective and inflicted much heavier damage than they had done earlier that morning.

Finally, Fowler ordered his own planes to dive and attack. Never designed to be used as dive-bombers, only three Avengers were able stay with Fowler as they dove from 8,000 feet. The planes directed their attacks at the heavy cruiser *Chokai*, which had closed the range to the escort carriers such that 5-inch shells from the *White Plains*'s lone stern-mounted gun hit her.

Paying exclusive attention to the American carriers, the big cruiser's crew did not see the plunging planes until it was too late. Twelve 500-pound, semi-armor piercing bombs left the Avengers' bomb bays, and nine hit the ship. One exploded on the cruiser's stern and sent her into a sharp right turn. Heavy black smoke billowed from the stricken cruiser and her forward progress slowed. Soon the destroyer *Fujinami* came alongside, removed her crew, increased the distance from the *Chokai*, and put a torpedo into her. The cruiser immediately sank. Fowler landed on the *Manila Bay* at about 10:00 A.M., rearmed, and planned another major strike against the Center Force.

While Fowler's four planes destroyed the *Chokai*, Lt. Charles Lee had more to worry about than attacking the Japanese. An antiaircraft shell exploded and destroyed his wingman's plane. Unfortunately, that was not the only damage done. The shell's explosion also set fire to Lee's Avenger, put a hole in an oil line, and tore a big piece from one of his propeller blades. His Avenger became harder to fly, but Lee doggedly pressed his attack. The fire went out, then flared up again; however, Lee went into a gliding dive at a battleship and dropped his bombs. He might have hit the battleship and missed a destroyer. With his plane now crippled, he tottered back to Tacloban and landed safely.[5]

Taffy 2 Joins In

Taffy 3 was not the only escort carrier group to attack Kurita's Center Force in this desperate conflict. Taffy 2, under RAdm. Felix Stump's command, steamed westward to its assigned daytime operating area, about 20 miles south-southeast of Taffy 3 and about 15 miles from Kurita's Center Force.

Even though Taffy 2 had not been alerted to the already raging battle, Admiral Kinkaid ordered this carrier group to be ready to load torpedoes at a moment's notice so they could immediately attack the Japanese ships coming up the Surigao Strait. The carriers' ground crews had been awake all night placing torpedoes into the bellies of the Avenger torpedo-bombers, which was a highly fortuitous decision. When Stump ordered all planes aloft at 6:57 A.M., all of Taffy 2's available Avengers were already properly armed and ready for action.

It took some time to assemble the rest of Taffy 2's planes, because they were on other missions when Stump's attack order went out to assault the menacing Japanese fleet. Those planes were not armed to attack capital ships, but that did not matter. They attacked with what they had, even though some of the bombs these planes carried inflicted minimal damage. The *Marcus Island* had only two properly armed Avengers, since the rest of that carrier's planes were delivering water and K-rations to the American troops ashore.

Despite these complications, Taffy 2 sent three strikes with thirty-six fighters and forty-three torpedo-bombers to attack the Japanese within one and one-half hours after Cliff Sprague asked for help. That carrier group's planes launched forty-nine torpedoes, the only truly effective weapon against capital ships, at the Japanese that day and claimed between five and eleven hits, all but one on battleships and heavy cruisers. The fighter planes attacking the Japanese dropped 133 500-pound bombs and hundreds of 100-pounders and fired 276 rockets. These weapons probably did the greatest amount of damage to the Center Force's ships because of the planes' relentless and courageous attacks and being properly armed to effectively attack battleships and cruisers.

Sending his screening destroyers, the *Haggard, Hailey,* and *Franks,* to his rear to guard against a Japanese destroyer attack, Stump turned his carriers into the wind and sent his planes aloft at 8:05 A.M. for combat air patrol. Thirty minutes later, he launched eight fighters and sixteen torpedo-bombers and recovered six Avengers from Taffy 3 that had lost their way. The Japanese were about 17 miles astern. Several Japanese heavy shells straddled the three screening destroyers at 8:41 A.M. The pagoda masts of the approaching Japanese battleships appeared on the horizon as their shell splashes came closer and closer. After a half hour of shelling, Stump recalled the destroyers to remove them from the approaching menace.

As Taffy 3 finished another air attack, Stump sent its third and fourth air strikes to attack the approaching Japanese battleship and cruisers. The Avengers, with Wildcat support, persistently and repeatedly attacked the enemy ships. They scored several torpedo hits on the *Chikuma,* which had been observed by the *Tone*'s crew to lose way (that is, to slow down so much that steering becomes difficult) due to the damage. The fatally damaged cruiser soon disappeared from view, another Japanese casualty in this conflict.[6]

Chapter 14: Deadly Delays and Unanswered Pleas for Help

D espite the boldness and bravery of the officers and enlisted men in Taffy 3, confusion reigned unchecked as Sprague tried to get help. Adding fuel to the fire, extraordinary delays took place in the sending and receiving of messages among the three commanders—Sprague, Kinkaid, and Halsey. The time lag for messages almost nullified the good achieved by Sprague's brilliant tactics. At 4:12 A.M., Kinkaid sent a message asking whether Task Force 34 was guarding the San Bernardino Strait, but this message did not reach Halsey until shortly before 7:00 A.M., just as Kurita's first shells were in the air and on their way toward Taffy 3, an unsatisfactory delay of almost three hours.

A delay of this magnitude most certainly should not have occurred in that day of rapid radio transmissions. Until Halsey received Kinkaid's message, he had assumed that Kinkaid and other Seventh Fleet commanders realized that he had taken Task Force 34 with him when he went north to go after Ozawa. Halsey also had assumed that Kinkaid would keep an air reconnaissance presence over the San Bernardino Strait in order to detect any Japanese movement through the strait. However, he now knew that Kinkaid had intercepted his October 24, 3:12 P.M., message about forming Lee's battleship force. Immediately trying to clear up this misunderstanding, Halsey replied with a highly disturbing message that Task Force 34 was heading north with his carriers and was not guarding the eastern approaches to the San Bernardino Strait.

While Halsey tried to figure out how to respond to this first dispatch, Kinkaid and Sprague desperately flooded the radio waves with five new appeals for help from Halsey, all in just over a thirty-minute period. Kinkaid sent a dispatch at 7:07 A.M. in plain language, stating that Japanese battleships and cruisers were firing at Sprague's ships.

Eighteen minutes later, Kinkaid sent a second message, stating that Oldendorf's battleships had run low on high-caliber ammunition and therefore could not help Sprague's ever-worsening situation. Trying to reduce the transmission delays, he sent another radio message in plain language at 7:27 A.M.: "Enemy forces attacking our [escort carriers] composed of four battleships, eight cruisers and x other ships. Request Lee proceed top speed cover Leyte. Request immediate strike by fast carriers."[1]

Another plea went out from Kinkaid at 7:39 A.M.: "Fast battleships are urgently needed immediately at Leyte Gulf."

That message left Kinkaid's communications center only four minutes after Sprague sent his own message notifying Halsey of the Japanese attack. Sprague's message was sent just as his ships left the rain squall's shelter.

Showing the desperation of Taffy 3's situation, Kinkaid sent the following message at 8:29, again in plain English: "My situation is critical. Fast battleships and support by air strike may be able prevent enemy from destroying [escort carriers] and entering Leyte."[2]

Sprague's and Kinkaid's tension and frustration grew when Halsey did not respond immediately to their urgent appeals. Kinkaid's 7:07 A.M. dispatch took seventy-five minutes to reach Halsey; his 7:25 A.M. message took almost two hours; the 7:27 A.M. message arrived on Halsey's flagship ninety-three minutes later; and Sprague's 7:35 A.M. plea took forty-seven minutes. It is not known how much time elapsed before Kinkaid's 8:29 message arrived in Halsey's hands. However, based on the record of the prior messages, one can guess that message, like its predecessors, had taken a ridiculously long time to reach Halsey's command. By the time Halsey received Sprague's and Kinkaid's dispatches, too much time had passed for the Third Fleet to help in any significant way. Halsey's carriers and battleships were now too far north to arrive off Samar in time.

One reason for the communications debacle was the divided command structure between MacArthur and Halsey. A consequence of this division of command was that messages had to go through MacArthur's message center on Manus, which was overwhelmed by all sorts of communications.

Later on, Sprague remarked sarcastically about the too-long transmission delays, calling their tardiness "staff work at its best." When Sprague led Taffy 3 out of the rain squall and moved south toward Leyte Gulf, many heroes were made as his small destroyers and destroyer escorts took on the overwhelmingly powerful Japanese force with pitifully small odds for success. These brave men etched into naval history one of the most gallant, bold, and sacrificial episodes in World War II.[3]

Chapter 15: The Valley of the Shadow of Death

K urita's ships now moved closer to Taffy 3 at twice the speed of the American force. Realizing that his beleaguered command could never escape the powerful Japanese gunfire, Sprague had no other options open to him. He had to continue heading south, continue sending his tormenting air attacks against Kurita, and hope that assistance from Halsey or anyone else would arrive soon, or that something else, something unexpected, would happen that would shift the advantage his way.

Within just a few minutes, Kurita's ships closed in on Taffy 3, coming within range of the Americans' smaller caliber guns. Shells from the Japanese guns exploded in the water and drew ever closer to the hapless escort carriers. Every shell splash was nearer than its predecessor. It also seemed that the Japanese gunners' aim increased in accuracy; each shell seemed to be walking across the water's surface toward the *Fanshaw Bay* and the other escort carriers. Giant swirling whirlpools made the water's surface boil and roil as the shells bashed into the water. Meanwhile, jagged, smoking shrapnel ricocheted off the carriers' decks as the huge shells exploded overhead.

Sprague used every resource at his command to execute a combination of tactics to save his ships and keep them from sinking. The Japanese approached Taffy 3 from three sides, leaving the only escape route to the south. However, Sprague was able to keep Kurita's force at bay and away from his command. No tactic, however hopeless or seemingly futile, was left untried, and Sprague somehow managed to avoid disaster while producing the ingredients for a victory.

He took advantage of the shorter distance of his interior lines and moved effectively through the smoke made by his own ships. His carriers zigzagged as Sprague directed them to the place where the latest Japanese shell had exploded in the water in order to reduce the probability of being hit by another shell. His aircraft continued to attack Kurita's ships, even though many of them had no ammunition or bombs to inflict damage. And Sprague used the wind to continue to launch every plane he had.

The desperate situation facing Sprague finally reached the point at which he had to commit his last resource to fend off the charging Japanese.

What happened at this astonishing moment is one of the boldest, most courageous actions in the history of the United States Navy. The audacity of Sprague's maneuver so confused the Japanese that every senior Japanese officer thought they were facing fleet carriers instead of jeep carriers, cruisers instead of destroyers, and destroyers instead of destroyer escorts.

The noted naval historian Samuel Eliot Morison wrote in his volume *Leyte*, chronicling this famous battle, "The most admirable thing about this battle was the way everything we had afloat or airborne went baldheaded for the enemy."[1] No ordinary naval commander would have been able to pull off such a tour de force, to commit such inferior naval resources in such an aggressive way, against such an overwhelmingly superior opposing force, and make it stick. Sprague's bluff proved clearly that he was no ordinary naval commander, and no ordinary person.

Trying to find some way to delay what seemed the inevitable death of his force, Sprague searched "for some trick to delay the kill." Sprague decided that "this was the time for my little group of seven escorts to charge our big tormentors," although this meant he would lose any advantages given to Taffy 3 by the smoke screen that the destroyers and destroyer escorts belched into the sky.

In the next ninety minutes, the men serving in Taffy 3's destroyers and destroyer escorts wrote one of the most gallant, memorable chapters in United States naval history. Sprague ordered his three 2,100-ton Fletcher-class destroyers—the *Heermann, Johnston,* and *Hoel*—and four destroyer escorts—the *Samuel B. Roberts, Dennis, John C. Butler,* and *Raymond*—to attack Kurita's on-charging Center Force at 7:16 A.M., just eighteen minutes after the Japanese opened fire. Outgunned and outmanned, Sprague threw all that he had into the struggle. The series of attacks seemed as if they were two separate actions, but to those who served aboard the ships off Samar Island, the actions by the brave crews aboard these lightly armored, underarmed vessels formed a continuous series of individual or tandem onslaughts that distracted Kurita's attention from the carriers. Dashing out from behind their smoke screen, each American ship attacked so that when Kurita thought one vessel was finished and he could return his focus to the American carriers, another American ship would attack. All of the men who served in Taffy 3 can hold their heads high when they commemorate their incredibly courageous action on October 25, 1944.[2]

Before describing what happened when Taffy 3's screening ships attacked their more powerful adversaries, we should get to know one of the gallant heroes who gave his life that day. This man was the American destroyer *Johnston*'s commanding officer.

Profile of an American Hero

Commander Ernest Edwin Evans was a Cherokee Indian and definitely not a stranger to courageous actions in battle. Born on August 13, 1908, in Pawnee, Oklahoma, Evans enlisted in the United States Navy in 1926. After serving one year in the enlisted ranks, he received an appointment to the Naval Academy in 1927. Commissioned an ensign on June 4, 1931, and promoted to commander on November 1, 1942, his experience on American warships was extensive and varied.

His first assignment was at the Naval Air Station in San Diego, where he remained for one year. He then progressed through a series of assignments on the *Colorado, Roper,* and *Rathburne.* After completing an assignment at the Naval Air Station at Pensacola, Florida, and following six months of service aboard the *Pensacola,* he became an aviation gunnery observer in that cruiser's squadron until April 15, 1937. He then served four years of sea duty on the *Chamount,* the *Cahokia,* and the *Black Hawk.*

About four months before Pearl Harbor, Evans began serving aboard the destroyer *Alden* and was aboard the day the Japanese attacked. On March 14, 1942, he took command of the vessel, remaining at that post until July 7, 1942. At that time, the new Fletcher-class destroyer, the *Johnston,* was nearing completion at the Seattle-Tacoma Shipbuilding Corporation. The new vessel needed a skipper, and Evans received orders to assume that responsibility. He supervised the completion of the ship's construction and took command officially on October 27, 1943. He would remain her captain throughout her short existence.

The *Johnston* immediately went into combat duty, and Evans won the first of what would be many awards for bravery and outstanding service. He received the Bronze Star with Combat "V" for "meritorious achievement as commanding officer of the USS *Johnston* in action against an enemy Japanese submarine on May 16, 1944." The official citation tells what Evans and the rest of his crew did to warrant this high award:

> Participating in a search and attack mission, Commander Evans skillfully maneuvered his ship into position to gain sound contact and delivered a vigorous depth-charge attack. Quickly regaining contact, he again dropped his depth charges, which resulted in a heavy underwater ripple explosion heard five minutes after the last detonation with appearance later of debris and a heavy oil slick in the vicinity as evidence of the probable sinking of the enemy submarine. Commander Evans' persistent tactics and his effective coordination with the assisting ships of the search and attack group were contributing factors in the success of a vital mission and in keeping with the highest traditions of the U.S. Naval Service.[3]

After serving with distinction in some of the Pacific war's most violent actions—Kwajalein, Guam, Bougainville, Peleliu, and Ulithi—the *Johnston* joined Kinkaid's Seventh Fleet and was assigned to Taffy 3's screening force. When Kurita's Center Force appeared on the northern horizon on October 25, Sprague was facing the seemingly impossible task of escaping annihilation, so he sent Evans and the other screening ships into harm's way to do everything possible to protect the relatively helpless, lightly armored, and undergunned escort carriers.[4]

Initial Sacrifice

Evans's naval service experiences matched Cliff Sprague's more than that of any other commanding officer serving in Taffy 3. He, too, could make rapid and, more importantly, correct decisions under highly stressful battle conditions.

It seemed as though the *Johnston*'s crew had been at general quarters for almost all of her two-year life. When Evans ordered the ship into action, that feeling was confirmed once again. Immediately after Sprague ordered his screening ships to attack the oncoming Japanese, the destroyers *Johnston* and *Hoel* were the first to respond to the admiral's orders.

Interestingly, Evans took action six minutes before Sprague's order arrived to attack the oncoming Japanese ships. His destroyer was 18,000 yards from the Japanese when Evans turned toward Kurita's approaching cruisers and battleships, which had been shooting at the carriers. Maneuvering so as to fire at the leading cruiser's flank, Evans ordered his 5-inch guns to open fire at the heavy cruiser *Kumano* when the *Johnston* came within their limited range. The destroyer's small shells hit the Japanese ship's superstructure, exploded, but did no damage. The Japanese cruisers fired their forward guns in retaliation, and soon four or five colored splashes rose around the *Johnston* as she plummeted through the churning sea. At almost that exact instant, Sprague ordered a torpedo attack.

Evans responded by closing the distance to his target, bringing the *Johnston* within torpedo firing range. He fired a ten-torpedo spread from 9,000 yards at the *Kumano*, turned sharply and headed back toward the carriers. The missiles ran "hot, straight, and normal" and soon underwater explosions were heard. At 7:27 A.M., three torpedoes struck the *Kumano*'s stern, exploded, and the cruiser burst into flames.

The *Johnston*'s surviving senior officer, Lt. Robert C. Hagen, later recalled the sequence of events: "Two or possibly three heavy underwater explosions were heard by two officers . . . at the time our torpedoes were scheduled to hit. Upon emerging a minute later from the smoke screen, the leading enemy cruiser was observed to be burning furiously astern."[5]

The damage forced the Japanese ship to slow to 20 knots. Swerving from her original course, she could no longer be part of the battle. She was the flagship of the cruiser division, so the Japanese cruiser division commander transferred his flag to her sister ship, the *Suzuya*, which had been put out of the battle by air attacks in the Sibuyan Sea. Although the *Johnston* now raced away from the Japanese, she and her gallant crew were not finished doing their duty.

The *Johnston* did not escape heavy damage, however. The Japanese guns continued firing at her. Three 14-inch shells smashed into the *Johnston*, followed by three 6-inch shells thirty seconds later, shaking her like "a puppy being smacked by a truck." She lost the after fire room and engine room, all power to the steering column and aft three 5-inch guns, and the usefulness of the gyro compass. The now heavily damaged ship slowed to 17 knots. The radar mast tumbled onto the bridge, killing three officers, while many men died below decks. A massive explosion tore Evans's clothing above the waist and amputated two fingers from his left hand. As all gun stations reported "Aye!" to control commands, he shifted steering control aft so that it could be operated manually with orders from the bridge using phones. The doomed ship passed under the same rain squall that had temporarily sheltered the escort carriers. This added ten minutes to her life, giving her crew time to restore the number 3 and 5 guns for partial fire control with number 4 under manual fire control. She was not out of the fight yet.

Another David Versus Goliath Struggle

As Sprague eluded salvos and the critically wounded Evans tried to remove the *Johnston* from danger, Cmdr. Leon S. Kintberger, the *Hoel's* captain, swerved his destroyer toward one of the many targets facing him. The destroyer's position was on the northeast corner of Sprague's formation, about 7½ miles northeast of where the *Kumano* dropped out of the battle. Kintberger saw a battleship column maneuvering forward to his left and a line of cruisers steaming on his right. Knowing the looming battleships were the most dangerous to Taffy 3, Kintberger ordered his ship to full speed to rapidly close the distance and get within torpedo firing range.

The destroyer accelerated, swerving through 150-foot-tall shell splashes from the battleships' 18-, 16-, and 14-inch guns. Moving at over 30 knots, Kintberger bored in and stayed on course, although a shell wrecked his firing director's platform near the bridge and the ship's radio at 7:25 A.M.

Two minutes later, the *Hoel* daringly came within 9,000 yards and launched five torpedoes from tubes aimed at the *Kongo*, the first Japanese battleship in the line. Its lookouts saw the torpedoes coming, and the big battleship began to swerve and weave to avoid being hit by the approaching torpedoes. Just before Kintberger could launch the remaining five torpedoes, a 14-inch shell penetrated the *Hoel's* hull, exploded in the destroyer's after engine room, destroyed the port engine, and jammed the rudder to a hard right position. Another shell smacked aft, disabling the ship's electrical steering. Kintberger then moved to the wheelhouse aft to manually steer his ship. Steering in a tight circle, the

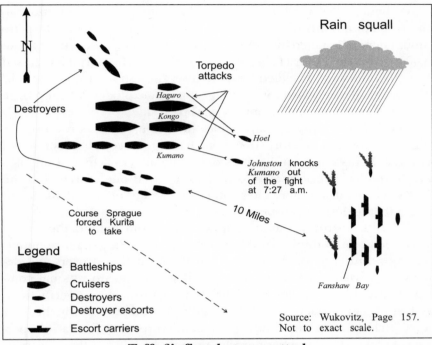

Taffy 3's first destroyer attack

Hoel pointed her forward 5-inch guns at the *Kongo* and kept up a continuous fire at the battleship and other targets of opportunity. Clearly, there were plenty of them.

Although his destroyer was now gravely disabled, Kintberger had more to do. He turned the now almost crippled but still operational destroyer toward the cruisers off his starboard side, pointed the ship's beam at them, placing it in firing position, and launched five more torpedoes.

The *Hoel*'s captain had but one objective—to inflict as much damage on the Japanese ships before his ship could fight no more or she sank. He hoped to give the overpowered escort carriers as much protection from Japanese main battery gunfire as possible while his crippled ship had life. Undaunted by the loss of one engine, her fire control director, fire direction radar, and three of her five guns, the heavily damaged destroyer returned to the ongoing fray hoping to launch all the torpedoes she had left at the *Haguro*.

At about 7:50 A.M., with all radio and telephone communications to the torpedo mounts now gone, the officer on the number 2 torpedo mount manually aimed his torpedoes, selecting a Japanese cruiser about 6,000 yards away. From a firing angle of 50 degrees, five torpedoes hissed from their tubes and headed for the cruiser "hot, straight, and normal." All five missiles smashed into the big ship and exploded, causing large water geysers to shoot up from her starboard side.

Ignoring the seemingly impossible odds against two destroyers drawing near enough to fire torpedoes at such a large force of battleships and cruisers, Evans's and Kintberger's desperate attacks achieved unimaginable results. The *Johnston*'s torpedoes disabled one cruiser, and the *Hoel*'s damaged another. These suicidal assaults impacted Kurita so much that he lost his perspective.

The two destroyers' sudden appearance from behind the smoke screen led him to think that these destroyers were larger, more powerful ships. Kurita mentally transformed these small destroyers and destroyer escorts into cruisers, and, in his judgment, no rational commander would ever recklessly risk his ships against such a powerful force as his. Sprague's tactic of turning Taffy 3 southward from the rain squall's cloud cover and sending his screen directly at Kurita—desperate risks taken by a commander who thought he had less than five minutes to live—confused Kurita into making tenuous evaluations and questionable decisions.

Sprague had a 360-degree view of the situation from the *Fanshaw Bay*'s bridge, but the destroyers' smoke screen and exploding shells kept him from seeing his screening ships. He could see them only when the smoke cleared up somewhat, and then they would disappear again when the smoke blocked his sight. However, Sprague saw clearly that the Japanese salvos had completely encircled his six carriers, and he did not like what he saw.

Being the logical commander he was, Sprague saw it was inevitable that Kurita's faster ships would narrow the distance to his force in a short time. At 7:35 A.M., Sprague, showing his characteristic wry humor, ordered his escort carriers to "open up with peashooter [5-inch gun] on stern" as soon as the Japanese came within range. Sprague knew the single puny 5-inch guns on the escort carriers in no way matched the tremendous firepower now aimed at Taffy 3. He had tried every tool he had to fight his powerful adversary, so he figured why not try the last instrument he had left. If his force was doomed for annihilation, why not go down with all guns blazing? Immediately after giving the order for the carriers to open fire, *St. Lô*'s 5-incher belched smoke and flame at an oncoming target. A crusty navy chief on the *Fanshaw Bay* remarked, "They oughta fire that thing under water—we could use a little jet propulsion right now."

The carriers needed only their main armament to fire back so they could dodge the many salvos now surrounding Taffy 3. Sprague tried to avoid issuing orders for drastic course changes, because these would have reduced speed and given the Japanese an even greater chance of drawing closer. So, he kept Taffy 3's course as straight as possible, asking for only minor course changes. Each carrier's captain kept directing his carrier to the spot of the last fallen shot.

To Sprague and others in Taffy 3, the monstrous shells the Japanese sent toward the *Fanshaw Bay* and the other carriers looked like giant trucks. They screeched through the air, sounding like out-of-control rumbling boxcars, hitting the sea with such force that huge water columns sent deluges of water skyward and soaked the sailors on deck. Sprague followed many shells' paths toward the other carriers and watched as their explosions completely engulfed their intended targets.

Lieutenant Hipchings recalled, "You were in an arena of active noise, like you sat in the middle of a big opera show with sound coming from every side." The machine guns' staccato fire and the slower-paced boom of the carriers' single 5-inch guns expanded the bizarre and deadly crescendo of the battle's sounds. Meanwhile, men scrambled about the *Fanshaw Bay*'s deck and pushed wheelbarrows filled with bombs, rockets, or anything that could explode over the ship's side into the sea. They threw anything overboard that could burn before one of Kurita's shells penetrated the *Fanshaw Bay*'s thin hull.

Sprague's attempts to escape could buy only so much time. Kurita's maneuvers to prevent Taffy 3 from reaching help from the Seventh Fleet's heavy ships began to achieve some success. The Japanese ships were now drawing a box around Taffy 3 on three sides. Two columns of destroyers with a leading cruiser closed the range to Sprague within 10,000 yards on his starboard side. Meanwhile, four heavy cruisers— *Chikuma*, *Tone*, *Haguro*, and *Chokai*—moved into position to prevent any try by Taffy 3 to flee eastward. Kurita's battleships, still pursuing on Sprague's stern, kept firing round after round at the six carriers from distances between 10,000 and 15,000 yards away. Two of Sprague's carriers, the *Gambier Bay* and the *Kalinin Bay*, were in the most vulnerable position, because they were closest to the pursuing Japanese. The *Kalinin Bay*'s chaplain, Elmer E. Bosserman, an avid hunter when back home, saw the situation facing him and his crew and remarked, "I now know what a squirrel feels like sitting up on the limb of a tree."

Sprague kept his carriers in a tight circular formation and turned to a heading of about 220 degrees. The *Kitkun Bay* and the *White Plains* were on the formation's southern side, the *St. Lô* and the *Kalinin Bay* on the northernmost, and the *Gambier Bay* and the *Fanshaw Bay* on the eastern and western sides. Depending upon which Japanese ship column raised the greatest threat, he moved the formation side to side 10 to 20 degrees. The Japanese fire had become more predictable when falling shot seemed to scream over Sprague's carriers once every two seconds.

On board the *Gambier Bay*, Lieutenant Pyzdrowski followed the formation's maneuvers and was impressed by Sprague's ability to get all six

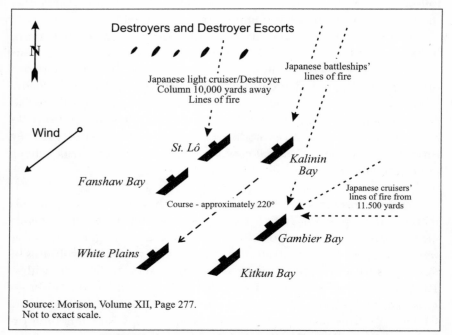

Source: Morison, Volume XII, Page 277.
Not to exact scale.

Taffy 3's increasingly precarious position

escort carriers to move as one, given the shell splashes and extremely loud battle sounds surrounding them. Pyzdrowski remembered later:

> When you see six escorts working in harmony, rather than one drifting on its own, that is an example of leadership. It is hard for one ship to do what's right in the strain of battle, let alone six. Sprague had command of that task unit. These were definitely not helter-skelter movements. Also, Sprague cleverly took advantage of the smoke.

However, the many Japanese shells filling the air finally started to take their toll on the beleaguered little carriers. By 7:50 A.M., several shells had struck the *Fanshaw Bay* and the *Kalinin Bay*, while others exploded so near the other carriers that they shook them to their keels. One 8-inch shell crashed into the *Fanshaw Bay*'s bow, passed through several bulkheads, killed two crewmen, and wounded two others before smashing through the ship's hull. But, fortunately, it did not explode. Amazingly enough, the carrier's paper-thin hull now had many holes in it, and, paradoxically this saved the flagship from utter destruction. It was as if the hull was not there at all when the large caliber Japanese shells ripped through its thin armor like a hot knife through butter, never exploding and never allowed to do their worst.

The first shell that penetrated the *Fanshaw Bay*'s front, according to Hipchings, "sounded like somebody had dropped a whole load of sheet metal. Most of their armor-piercing shells went through us and exploded overboard, sort of like firing a pistol through an empty shoe box. If everyone that hit us exploded, we wouldn't be here today. Pure luck sure helps in battle."

But luck wasn't the only thing working in the Americans' favor. Maintaining his now well-known calm demeanor while under fire, Sprague remained cool and collected as the battle continued its frenzied pace. The Japanese had narrowed the range, and their guns' aim became increasingly more accurate. Still determined to make use of every ship he had to stop the Japanese, Sprague ordered another torpedo assault by his screening vessels. Once again, and after taking a tremendous beating from Japanese shellfire, Evans unhesitatingly reversed the *Johnston*'s course again toward the charging Japanese with Kintberger's *Hoel*, Cmdr. Amos T. Hathaway's *Heermann*, and Commander Copeland's tiny destroyer escort, the *Samuel B. Roberts* joining the fray.

• • •

The *Samuel B. Roberts*'s Copeland pulled no punches when he addressed his crew as to the peril now facing them. Speaking over the destroyer escort's loudspeaker system, he warned his crew they were about to face "a fight against overwhelming odds from which survival could not be expected, during which time we would do what damage we could." This petrifying, bold statement typified the fighting spirit that flowed throughout Sprague's entire harried command caught up in this quixotic conflict.

Copeland's statement had a telling effect on his crew. Lieutenant Everett E. Roberts, the *Samuel B. Roberts*'s executive officer, recalled, "I thought our torpedo attack was hopeless. His announcement over the speaker gave us all cold chills, and one guy became so scared he ran to the back of the ship, which is senseless because you can't hide on an escort."

Copeland first planned to wait for the other destroyers to catch up with him, since their attack was supposed to be coordinated. However, five minutes passed and nothing happened. Copeland, therefore, lined up behind the *Hoel* and the *Johnston* and plunged into his attack on the Japanese cruiser column's starboard side. His little ship plowed through heavy shellfire and churning seas until it closed within 4,000 yards of a heavy cruiser, then launched three torpedoes at 8:00 A.M. Surprised by this new threat, the Japanese cruisers opened fire at the destroyer escort while she vainly tried to fight back with her puny 5-inch guns.

For the next fifty minutes, a desperate fight took place between the little ship and its awesome adversaries. Copeland fought the Japanese cruisers at close range as the *Samuel B. Roberts* darted through the roiling water at top speed, trying to elude Japanese shellfire by slipping in and out of smoke cover, all the while firing torpedoes and 5-inch shells at the cruisers.

Then, throwing caution to the winds, she steamed straight ahead with no idea what might suddenly confront her when she cleared the shield of heavy smoke. As she darted along, she swept so close to the *Heermann* that one of that destroyer's crew recalled, "We could have almost shaken hands with the other crew." Using her two 5-inch guns, her crew fired 608 shells at the Japanese. Despite the severe damage to the *Samuel B. Roberts*, she was not finished as a fighting ship.

The *Hoel*'s luck began to ebb as well. With one engine and three 5-inch guns gone, she tried to leave the battle in a southwesterly direction but could not escape. One of her officers remembered later, "With

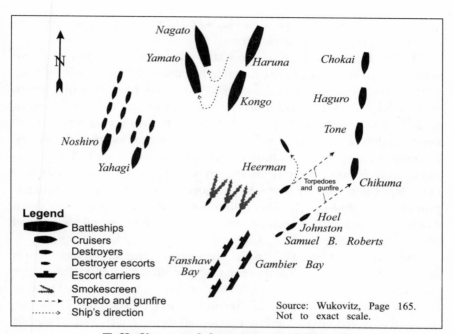

Legend
- Battleships
- Cruisers
- Destroyers
- Destroyer escorts
- Escort carriers
- Smokescreen
- - - - ► Torpedo and gunfire
- ....► Ship's direction

Source: Wukovitz, Page 165.
Not to exact scale.

Taffy 3's second destroyer attack Phase I

our ten 'fish' fired, we decided to get the hell out of there."[6] The other Japanese battleships and cruisers now threatened the *Hoel* from both flanks. Trying to reach the safety of the smoke screen, Kintberger reversed course to put as much distance between his ship and the Japanese as possible. Shells fired from the *Kongo* 8,000 yards to port and from the heavy cruisers 7,000 yards to starboard straddled the destroyer. Making maximum use of what she had left, the *Hoel* increased speed via her one engine, but she could not outrun the more powerful Japanese warships but could only match their speed.

Trying to avoid incoming salvos from every Japanese ship within range of her, the *Hoel* fishtailed through the overwhelming fire beleaguering her on all sides. Her remaining two bow 5-inch guns defiantly spit back as she fired over 500 rounds at her tormentors. More than forty 5-inch, 8-inch and 16-inch shells rocked the gallant ship as she tried to escape. The Japanese ships drew so near the doomed destroyer that her crew could almost see the Japanese sailors on the ships' decks. After an hour and a half of a tormented, ill-fated journey through churning waters, and just when Sprague sent in the rest of his screening ships at 8:30

A.M., an 8-inch shell struck her and knocked out her only remaining, serviceable engine and her generator.

The *Hoel* stopped dead in the water. All engineering spaces below decks filled with water as a fire raged in her number 1 ammunition magazine. Fires engulfed her upper decks from bow to stern while dents, shell holes, blood, and body parts covered her decks. She listed to port, settled by the stern, and at 8:35, knowing his ship was doomed, Kintberger ordered "abandon ship" for all hands. Engineers below deck fixed the engines to reduce the chance of explosions as she sank. The surviving crew dove into the water where they clung to floating rubble and sadly left their ship to her fate as more Japanese shells relentlessly pounded her. At 8:55, the *Hoel* rolled over and disappeared into about 4,000 fathoms. Out of a crew of 353 officers and enlisted men on board the gallant destroyer, only 82 survived.

Commander William D. Thomas, the screen commander, was severely wounded but recovered; Kintberger, who also survived, remembered this gallant, extraordinary action with an appropriate seaman's epitaph: "Fully cognizant of the inevitable result of engaging such vastly superior forces, these men performed their assigned duties coolly and efficiently until their ship was shot from under them."[7]

Near the *Samuel B. Roberts,* the destroyer *Heermann*'s Commander Hathaway heroically and fearlessly inaugurated his own attack on the Japanese. He had to steam through the escort carriers' formation in order to link up with the *Hoel.* Periodic rain squalls and smoke from smoke screens, gunfire, and exploding shells all hung over the water, severely limiting visibility to within a few hundred yards. However, the sprint was almost stillborn for the *Heermann* barely missed colliding with the scarcely visible *Samuel B. Roberts.* With visibility practically nil in the dense, rolling smoke, Hathaway almost collided with the *Hoel,* too.

Now free of the *Hoel* and *Samuel B. Roberts,* the *Heermann* closed the range with the heavy cruiser *Haguro.* Her crew fired seven torpedoes at the Japanese ship at 7:54 A.M., then rapidly steered to port and went after the battleship *Kongo.* A pitched battle between the destroyer and the *Haguro* and the *Kongo* raged for approximately six minutes. The Japanese cruiser dodged the torpedoes and answered with fifteen gunfire salvos; all shells missed the *Heermann.* When two more battleships entered the massive struggle, Hathaway's command boldly kept fighting and gave no quarter.

As the *Heermann*'s torpedoes hurtled toward the Japanese cruiser, Hathaway saw another column of large Japanese ships to the north. These ships were about the same distance (4½ miles) as the Japanese cruisers already under fire. With half her "fish" in the water on their way to the *Haguro*, the destroyer's gunnery officer, Lt. W. W. Meadors, saw the battleship *Kongo* on the port bow with the *Yamato* and the *Nagato* following in the faint distance. Seeing these powerful ships coming nearer to the *Heermann* did not worry Hathaway as he climbed on the exposed fire-control platform to help guide the ship.

He ordered a change of course to 270 degrees and commanded his main 5-inch batteries to open fire at the familiar Japanese battleships' pagoda-shaped superstructures. But the big battleships did not passively stand by. They returned fire and huge yellow splashes advanced across the water toward the *Heermann*. This time their accuracy improved over their previous attempts. But the American destroyer nonetheless nimbly dodged the huge splashes, and the large shells missed their target. Hit only by exploding shell fragments from the near misses, the destroyer fired three torpedoes from 4,400 yards away and changed course to 100 degrees at 20 knots. She headed back to the carrier formation, believing one of her torpedoes had hit one of the battleships.

This extraordinarily one-sided duel between the audacious American destroyer and the ominous Japanese battleships lasted for about eight minutes. But the *Heermann* still was not finished. She changed course again and, at 8:00 A.M., headed for the old battleship *Haruna*. Reflecting the terrible tension of that devil-may-care moment, the *Heermann*'s officer of the deck, Lt. Robert F. Newsome, remembered Hathaway saying, "Buck, what we need is a bugler to sound the charge." The destroyer's 5-inch guns fired many times at the *Haruna* as he moved close enough to the Japanese battleship to launch his last three torpedoes. Weaving his ship through the many shell splashes that surrounded the destroyer, Hathaway said that he needed "a periscope with which to see over the wall of water."[8] At 8:03, out of torpedoes, Hathaway veered 180 degrees and headed for the carriers.

The *Heermann* was a very lucky ship that day. She had escaped the hellish, bitter struggle with only minor damage. Although none of her torpedoes hit their intended targets, some headed directly at the *Yamato*, and in this way the *Heerman* greatly influenced the battle's outcome.

The *Yamato*'s commanding officer, RAdm. Nobuei Morishita, made an independent, albeit grave tactical error when he turned northward in order to try to outrun the *Heerman*'s torpedoes. The best course of action would have been to present a smaller target to the oncoming missiles by turning into the wakes of the oncoming seven torpedoes. But Hathaway's torpedoes moved too fast and rapidly narrowed the distance as the bulky battleship slowly turned, forcing the embarrassed Morishita to increase his speed to the maximum and steam northward, until the *Heerman*'s torpedoes exhausted their fuel. Endeavoring to lend assistance to her compatriot, the battleship *Nagato* turned as well in order to follow the Japanese flagship. After ten minutes on this course, the torpedoes ran out of fuel and sank. However, this tactic took two ships out of the battle, for they had to assume the rear position in the Japanese fleet's disheveled formation.

These ten minutes proved to be one of the most critical periods in the battle, for Kurita's two most powerful ships now headed away from the action, as if these huge battleships had sunk.

Kurita was generally obsessed with keeping the weather gauge, that is, with keeping his leeward side facing the opposing fleet's windward side, on the American carriers. Therefore, instead of heading directly for them, he maintained his course and speed for the fleet as a whole. As a consequence, the distance between him and the Americans lengthened, reducing the accuracy of his ships' gunfire. Shells still fell around the American carriers; but they were not as close as they had been before. The attacking American planes and destroyers had forced Kurita to dodge and weave, and this further contributed to the inaccuracy of his gunfire. In addition, he tried to locate the Americans by radar in order to improve the accuracy of his shooting. However, the type of radar used on his ships had never operated effectively; as a result, his gunfire became even more inaccurate, lacking the normal precision that had been so characteristic of Japanese naval gunfire in the past. Furthermore, Kurita apparently could not reliably assess the results of his attack due to the poor visibility made even more obscure by the American smoke screens.

Later, he would confess that the American smoke screen and air attacks bothered him considerably as he took evasive action. As a result, his ships opened the distance to the American ships. He also could not maintain his ships' formation and therefore could not concentrate maximum firepower. But these were not the only reasons Kurita's attack failed. The daring, bold, innovative, and seemingly hopeless American torpedo attacks had already decided, in fact, the outcome of this most crucial of all battles in the Leyte Gulf struggle.

A Second Bite at the Apple

While performing feats of valor and audacity, Sprague's thirteen ships, their crews, and his airmen could not indefinitely keep Kurita's incomparable strength at bay. When the smoke cleared, Sprague could see what was happening. He noted that Kurita's cruisers were gaining tactical superiority. After absorbing several hits, the *Gambier Bay* now had only one engine left and was 1½ miles northeast of the *Fanshaw Bay*, unable to keep up with the rest of Taffy 3's carriers. Like wolves pursuing straggling reindeer, the Japanese cruiser *Chikuma* and her companions closed in for the kill. Sprague thought the ship "was getting the worst working over" as fourteen shells of all sizes continuously smashed into the nearly defenseless carrier.

The *Gambier Bay*, *Kitkun Bay*, and the *Kalinin Bay* were on Sprague's port side, and therefore nearest to the closing Japanese cruisers approaching from the east. The *Chikuma* and the *Tone* led the way, followed by the *Haguro* and the *Chokai* as the four cruisers tried to cut off Sprague's escape route. Rapidly closing in on Sprague's hammered formation, each Japanese cruiser continuously belched streams of 8- and 5-inch shells at the beleaguered American carriers. Trying to avoid losing all of his carriers, Sprague ordered his screening vessels by radio at 8:26 A.M.: "Intercept heavy cruiser coming in on port quarter."

By this time, Taffy 2's and Taffy 3's aviators had received orders to stop attacking their current targets and to strike instead at the cruisers. But hits from Japanese shells were falling so fast and furiously that Sprague estimated that Taffy 3 could not survive much longer.

Commander Hathaway had reported that the *Heermann* had fired all of its torpedoes, and other ships were reporting similarly discouraging news. Later, Hathaway wrote, "As I listened, it became evident that there wasn't a torpedo among us. Anything we could do from now on would have to be mostly bluff."

The rest of Taffy 3's screening vessels were almost out of torpedoes, too. If they used every single one, the only self-defense would be their puny 5-inch guns, which would merely bounce off the Japanese cruisers' armor. Like sharks smelling blood in the water, the Japanese now moved in to finish off their prey. As the increasingly dire information poured into each ship's radio room, a *White Plains* radioman mumbled with ironic understatement, "The situation is getting a little tense, isn't it?" As ever, though, Sprague kept calm as the crippling circumstances continued. He still had a few moves left in him. He wasn't ready to give up yet. Sprague then sent an order to his screening ships: "Expedite!"

Knowing what this command meant, Hathaway swerved the *Heermann* to confront the Japanese cruisers while trying to maintain an optimistic attitude. By way of a few incisive remarks, he later captured the moment and the situation perfectly:

> We were opposed by a total of thirty-eight 8-inch and about twenty 5-inch guns. Our entire strength on the *Heermann* consisted of five 5-inchers. I had one thing in my favor: a splendid range. Those cruisers made beautiful targets for our little guns at 12,000 yards; we made a difficult target for their big ones.

The other screening ships also understood the meaning of Sprague's order. Acting as one, the *Samuel B. Roberts, Dennis*, and *John C. Butler* immediately veered from their positions on the carriers' port side and stormed straight across the carriers' circular formation to place themselves between Sprague and Kurita. Sprague watched from the *Fanshaw Bay*'s bridge, knowing sadly that some of his men would not survive the battle. However, he had no alternative but to send these brave ships to a daredevil doom.

As Lieutenant Pierson stood on the deck directly above Sprague, he gaped at the tiny destroyers and destroyer escorts heading directly into the jaws of the killing colossus. It was like watching a man on trial for his life who knows the jury is rigged and he faces certain execution. Pierson recalled later, "My heart went out for those guys as they headed straight across into certain death without a second's hesitation." As he focused on one of the smaller destroyer escorts—called DEs—he turned to another officer standing nearby and remarked, "Look at that little DE committing suicide, Mac."[9]

The "Little Wolves" Join In

The *Heermann* and *Johnston* were then joined by their smaller sister screening ships in this second torpedo attack. The smaller vessels, the DEs, had been built primarily to protect convoys from submarine attacks in the North Atlantic. Although the DEs mounted torpedoes, their crews had received no torpedo attack training, but instead had been instructed in the practice of antisubmarine duty and antiaircraft fire. When Admiral Sprague ordered, "Wolves make torpedo attack," the *Samuel B. Roberts*'s skipper, Lieutenant Commander Copeland, replied to the screen commander, Commander Thomas, "Do you want little wolves to go in with wolves?" Thomas's initial response was "negative," but a more reassuring message immediately followed, "Little wolves form up for second attack." These ships had never attacked any ship with torpedoes; but this did not stop them. Unhesitatingly, the *Samuel B. Roberts* followed 3,000 yards behind the larger destroyers.

The other destroyer escorts joined the attack, boring in on the formidable Japanese cruiser column. The *Raymond*'s captain assumed that this torpedo attack order included his ship and accordingly turned her due north and closed the range to the *Haguro*. The Japanese cruiser immediately aimed her 8-inch guns at the little ship, placing a salvo 200 yards astern of the *Raymond*. Fourteen more salvos followed as the DE made 24 knots while the cruiser made 25. It looked like curtains for the *Raymond*.

At this juncture, it was 8:56 A.M. The *Raymond* was only 6,000 yards from the *Haguro* when she launched a three-torpedo spread. The Japanese cruiser had just begun a turn to escape the other torpedoes aimed at her, a movement that caused the *Raymond*'s torpedoes to miss their target. Prudently, the small ship reversed course at high speed as giant water geysers from a barrage of 8-inch shells pursued her.

Another destroyer escort, the *Dennis*, attacked the cruiser column from a northwesterly direction. The *Haguro* spotted her about a mile to the southeast and blasted a three-minute gunfire and torpedo barrage, one the destroyer escort dodged successfully. The *Dennis* then launched a torpedo spread of her own at 8,000 yards, not at the *Haguro*, but at the *Tone* and the *Chokai*, the second and fourth ships in the cruiser column. All missed. At 9:02, the *Dennis* reversed course to 240 degrees as three hits from the Japanese cruiser *Tone* shook the destroyer escort. Ten minutes later, the *Dennis* opened fire with her 5-inch battery at a Japanese cruiser. This cruiser was closing rapidly while being attacked by American aircraft. Despite the goulash of gunfire and torpedoes, the only visible results of this frenetic activity were multitudes of tall columns from shells smacking the water. No ship sustained any damage. There was a lot of sound and fury, but in the end it didn't signify something.

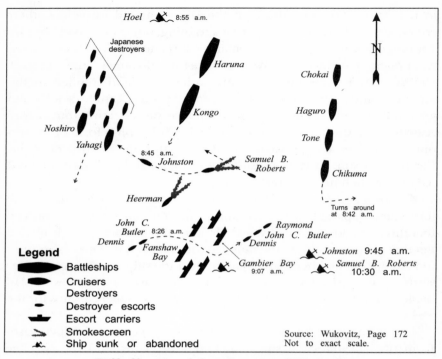

Taffy 3's second destroyer attack-Phase II

The *John C. Butler* had but three torpedoes left, and it was difficult for her to get into an advantageous firing position. Along with the *Dennis*, she steamed through the carrier formation, made smoke, and tried to avoid colliding with the *Heermann, Fanshaw Bay,* and *Johnston*. The leading Japanese cruiser, the *Chikuma*, moved faster than the *John C. Butler*. The little destroyer escort could close the range only if the Japanese cruisers changed course toward the carriers, but the Japanese cruisers did not oblige, so the *John C. Butler* lost her opportunity to fire her torpedoes. She and the *Dennis* exchanged gunfire with the cruisers at ranges between 14,000 and 17,000 yards. The Japanese cruiser did, however, come close to the *Raymond* and shifted fire from the destroyer escort to the escort carrier *Gambier Bay*. The American carrier was not touched.

The *Chikuma* made a complete circle at 8:42 A.M., probably in an effort to avoid bombs falling from attacking aircraft. The *Tone* took the lead, made a course parallel with the American carriers, and fired at the

John C. Butler, Dennis, and *Samuel B. Roberts.* The American ships briskly returned fire. At 8:50, a Japanese shell struck the *Dennis,* passed through her deck, and bored a hole through her port side 3 feet above the waterline, but caused no explosion. Ten minutes later, a second shell knocked out her 40mm gun director and number 1 gun. A broken breech disabled her number 2 gun as well. Sustaining too much damage, the little ship had to drop out of the battle at 9:02, when she changed course to retire behind the *John C. Butler*'s smoke. Huge columns of water surrounded the *John C. Butler* as she executed a rapid right-and-left zigzag. Meanwhile, the *Raymond* still fired at the Japanese.

Unable to inflict more serious damage on the destroyer escorts, the *Tone* shifted her fire toward the carriers. Five or six salvos landed near one, surrounding her with giant splashes close off the port bow. Ten minutes later, the *Tone* fired at the *Fanshaw Bay,* now on the *John C. Butler*'s starboard bow. The destroyer escort had run low on ammunition, so Admiral Sprague ordered her to position herself to provide better smoke cover. Nonetheless, the Japanese main body got a clear view of the leading American carrier's bow, for the smoke from the *John C. Butler* and *Dennis* was the only cover available during this critical moment.

The *Heermann* joined with the *Samuel B. Roberts* and the *Johnston* to form a line giving some protection to Sprague's rear so he would have time to retreat. The *Heermann* and *Samuel B. Roberts* moved in a wide circle, and the *Johnston* made smoke while firing 5-inch broadsides, at the same time coping with a barrage of Japanese gunfire. When the *Johnston* had taken all the punishment she could, the *Heermann* moved into her place and continued the vain, seemingly hopeless task of keeping the Japanese cruisers away from the escort carriers.

Japanese shells screamed continuously overhead and around the *Fanshaw Bay,* their splashes coming ever closer to her and the rest of Taffy 3's ships. The *Samuel B. Roberts*'s Copeland bellowed, "All engines back full!" when one 14-inch shell splashed astern a mere 50 yards away. This abrupt course change nearly buried her stern underwater. Nonetheless, the drastic maneuver temporarily saved the little destroyer escort from being struck by three shells, which snarled overhead, smacking the water 100 yards dead ahead. If she had not stopped her forward progress, they would have sunk her. Nevertheless, despite her hair breadth escape, her luck was just about to run out. When Copeland tried to resume his attack, ordering, "All engines ahead flank," an 8-inch shell followed by two more rocked the *Samuel B. Roberts* to her keel. The remainder of the little ship's life was now numbered in minutes.

While the damage mounted on their ship, the *Samuel B. Roberts*'s number 2 gun crew kept firing defiantly at their tormentors. Copeland recalled later what happened as the life of the *Samuel B. Roberts* was about to end:

> After all power, air, and communications had been lost, and before the word to abandon ship was passed, the crew of No. 2 gun, who as a crew distinguished themselves throughout the entire action, loaded, rammed, and fired six charges entirely by hand, and with the certain knowledge of the hazards involved due to the failure of the gas injection system caused by the air supply having been entirely lost. While attempting to get off the seventh charge in this manner, there was an internal explosion in the gun, killing all but three members of the gun crew, two of whom subsequently died on rafts.

The last time anyone saw Gunner's Mate 3d Class Paul H. Carr, he held the last 5-inch shell in his arms, trying to load it into the number 2 wrecked gun while blood poured from wounds extending from neck to thighs. It is not possible for anyone to survive such injuries; Carr died soon after the explosion.

Sonarman 3d Class Felt recalled, "I heard the whine of shells as they came closer to the ship. That first shell hit, and then an explosion and tremendous shaking, as if a giant had grabbed hold of the ship and given it a good shaking."

The *Samuel B. Roberts*'s forward movement stopped. Copeland glanced quickly about his ship and saw only dead and wounded men strewn all over her decks. Clearly, the brave, defiant ship was finished. At 9:10 A.M., he gave the "abandon ship" order, but it took the crew twenty-five minutes to get off the doomed ship. Copeland insisted that first aid be given to the wounded and placed the injured crew members into rafts. The ill-fated ship leaned over 80 degrees, twisted in the water, and slowly sank by the stern and finally disappeared beneath the waves at 10:15 A.M. The *Samuel B. Roberts* had carried a crew of eight officers and about 170 enlisted men. Of those, three officers and 86 enlisted men perished.

Commander Copeland paid his crew the highest tribute:

> To witness the conduct of the average enlisted man on board this vessel, newly inducted, married, unaccustomed to navy ways and

with an average of less than one year's service, would make any man proud to be an average American. The crew were informed over the loudspeaker system at the beginning of the action of the commanding officer's estimate of the situation; that is, a fight against overwhelming odds from which survival could not be expected, during which time we would do what damage we could. *In the face of this knowledge the men zealously manned their stations wherever they might be, and fought and worked with such calmness, courage, and efficiency that no higher honor could be conceived than to command such a group of men.* [Copeland's emphasis.]

No patriotic American could say any more.[10]

As the valiant *Samuel B. Roberts* sank, the *Johnston* steamed past her to carry out its final, fatal assault. Copeland saw the destroyer speed by to try to stop the Japanese destroyers threatening Sprague's starboard quarter. Later, Copeland wrote that the *Johnston's* captain, Commander Evans, had the same pummeled appearance as his ship. Naked to the waist, he was "covered with blood. His left hand was wrapped in a handkerchief." As the *Johnston* sped by less than 100 feet away, "he turned a little and waved his hand at me. That's the last I saw of him."[11]

A Hero's Last Stand

The flagship *Yamato* issued no orders to the light cruiser *Yahagi* and four destroyers, and they apparently acted on their own and closed the range on the carriers. With the *Hoel* abandoned and the *Samuel B. Roberts* burning, the rest of the American destroyer screen moved to intercept the new threat. This latest Japanese attack would seal the *Johnston's* fate. The Japanese light cruiser and destroyers' commander, RAdm. Masanori Kimura, wrote in his action report: "0850 - Enemy destroyer plunged out of smoke screen on our port bow and opened gunfire and torpedo attack on us. *Yahagi* executed right rudder, making wide evasive turn, at same time ordering destroyers to attack."

The *Johnston* spotted the Japanese destroyers 10,000 yards away and fired at the *Yahagi.* Gradually closing the range to 7,000 yards, several 5-inch shells blasted into the *Johnston.* Boldly, she returned fire, hit the *Yahagi* fourteen times, and tried to cross the Japanese "T." Before the American destroyer could complete this maneuver, Kimura's entire Japanese screening force unexpectedly and inexplicably turned 90 degrees right and rapidly opened the range.

In strict accordance with prevailing naval doctrine, Admiral Kimura ordered his force to make a sharp right turn so that his destroyers could fire their torpedoes, but before they could complete the turn, several of the *Johnston*'s 5-inch shells smashed into the *Yahagi* while several American airplanes strafed the cruiser. However, the *Johnston*'s gunfire had little effect. Lieutenant Hagen remembers that firing 5-inch shells against the more heavily armored Japanese ships "was like bouncing paper wads off a steel helmet." At 9:05 A.M., the cruiser fired its torpedoes, and the Japanese destroyers fired theirs ten minutes later. Kimura wrote in his action report that he thought these torpedoes had hit their targets: "Three enemy carriers and one cruiser were enveloped in black smoke and observed to sink one after another."

It would have been a very sad situation indeed had this been true. Instead, the *Johnston*'s maneuvers had fooled the Japanese admiral into prematurely launching his torpedo attack. The Japanese ships were 10,500 yards astern of the *Kalinin Bay*, which was moving away from the Japanese at about 18 knots and was too far away for torpedoes to reach it.

One gravely damaged destroyer, with all its torpedoes gone and running on one engine, had delayed, bluffed, and confused an entire Japanese cruiser and destroyer squadron into retreating from an inferior force. Evans's courageous defense allowed him to proudly strut on his bridge, triumphantly exclaiming, "Now, I've seen everything!"

It was truly a glorious victory for the *Johnston*. But more fighting was to be done by the *Johnston* before she would meet her end.

Copeland's view of Evans on the *Johnston*'s blood-soaked decks might have been the last time anyone not aboard the *Johnston* saw this brave American naval officer. Making the motions of a swivel-hipped football halfback trying to avoid tacklers for more than thirty minutes, Evans's destroyer battled cruisers to the port and then destroyers to starboard. Lieutenant Hagen described the *Johnston*'s last moments as "a somewhat desperate attempt to keep all of [the Japanese ships] from closing the carrier formation." The Japanese ships now had the surrounded *Johnston* as their only target and spared nothing in their efforts to destroy the single encroacher. They aimed their guns and accurately shot with a withering fire so that the "ship was getting hit with disconcerting frequency throughout this period."

Evans saw the heavy cruiser *Chikuma* trying to administer the coup de grâce to the damaged *Gambier Bay*. Realizing the criticality of the situation, Evans roared at his gunnery officer, "Commence firing on the cruiser, Hagen." Figuring that if he could distract the cruiser's attention to the *Johnston* by firing at it, he would give the escort carrier time to escape. But the Japanese warship kept firing on the *Gambier Bay* until Hathaway's *Heermann* came to the beleaguered escort carrier's aid.

Earning the Medal of Honor

The nettlesome *Johnston* basked in the last minutes of its glory. Much like a pride of lions closing in on its prey, the Japanese cruisers and destroyers were gradually surrounding the destroyer. Lieutenant Hagen, the *Johnston's* senior surviving officer witnessed the last minutes of the *Johnston's* life and recorded her demise:

> We checked fire as the Japanese destroyers retired, turned left, and closed range on the Japanese cruisers. For the next half hour this ship engaged first the cruisers on our port hand and then the destroyers on our starboard hand, alternating between the two groups in a somewhat desperate attempt to keep all of them from closing [on] the carrier formation. The ship was getting hit with disconcerting frequency throughout this period.
>
> At 9:10 A.M., we had taken a hit which knocked out one forward gun and damaged the other. Fires had broken out. One of our 40mm readylockers was hit and the exploding shells were causing as much damage as the Japs. The bridge was rendered untenable by the fires and explosions, and Commander Evans had been forced at 9:20 A.M. to shift his command to the fantail, where he yelled his steering orders through an open hatch at the men who were turning the rudder by hand. . . .
>
> We were now in a position where all the gallantry and guts in the world couldn't save us. There were two cruisers on our port, another dead ahead of us, and several destroyers on our starboard side; the battleships, well astern of us, fortunately had turned coy. We desperately traded shots first with one group and then the other.

As the fusillade of Japanese shells turned into an avalanche, the *Johnston* lost her remaining engine and fire rooms; all intraship communications ceased operations. Her guns stopped firing except for the number four 5-incher, which kept shooting under manual control since all automated fire control had vanished due to the tremendous damage she had sustained. Realizing all hope was lost, Evans ordered all depth charges overboard. And at 9:40 A.M., she was dead in the water.

Five minutes later, Evans sent out the "abandon ship" order, and all hands headed for the life rafts. The *Johnston* sank at 10:10 A.M. As American sailors swam in the water, they saw a Japanese commander standing at attention on his destroyer's bridge, giving a touching hand salute to a gallant foe. With body parts and limbs scattered all over, men moaning and dying in pools of blood that painted her decks red, she still kept firing as she rolled over and sank beneath the waves. The Japanese commander continued saluting. We will never know what actually happened to the *Johnston* in those last confusing, gallant moments because her log went down with her. Only 141 of her complement of 327 survived. Of the 186 lost, 50 were killed by enemy action, 45 died on the rafts, and 92 died in the water. No one ever saw Commander Evans again.[12]

For his bravery, dedication to duty, and demonstration of outstanding command abilities, Evans was posthumously awarded the Congressional Medal of Honor, America's highest military honor. The citation that came with the award reads as follows:

> For conspicuous gallantry and intrepidity at the risk of his life above and beyond the call of duty as Commanding Officer of the USS *Johnston*, in action against major units of the enemy Japanese Fleet during the Battle off Samar on 25 October 1944. The first to lay smoke screen and to open fire as an enemy task force, vastly superior in number, firepower and armor, rapidly approached, Comdr. Evans gallantly diverted the powerful blasts of hostile guns from the lightly armed and armored carriers under his protection, launching the first torpedo attack when the *Johnston* came under straddling shell fire. Undaunted by damage sustained under the terrific volume of fire, he unhesitatingly joined others of his group to provide fire support during subsequent torpedo attacks against the Japanese and, outshooting and outmaneuvering the enemy as he consistently interposed his vessel between the hostile fleet units and our carriers despite the crippling loss of engine power and communications with steering aft, shifted command to the fantail, shouted steering orders through an open hatch to men turning the rudder by hand and battled furiously until the *Johnston*, burning and shuddering from a mortal blow, lay dead in the water after three hours of fierce combat. Seriously wounded early in the en-

gagement, Comdr. Evans, by his indomitable courage and brilliant professional skill, aided materially in turning back the enemy during a critical phase of the action. His valiant fighting spirit throughout his historic battle will endure as an inspiration to all who served with him.[13]

I do not think one can say any more than this in paying the highest tribute to a true naval hero.

Fighting for Survival

Sprague realized the danger to Taffy 3 was far from over as Japanese shells fell nearer their intended targets. Deep below the *Kalinin Bay's* flight deck, water and oil rose rapidly as damage-control teams tried to stem the tide. Meanwhile, Sprague saw three shells strike the *Gambier Bay's* flight deck in quick succession, crash near its port beam, and penetrate near and just below the carrier's waterline. The third shell made a large hole in the hull, causing water to rush into the forward engine room, forcing the *Gambier Bay* to drop out of formation as she slowed to 11 knots.

The captain of the now severely disabled carrier, Walter V. R. Vieweg, recalled, "The Japs really poured it on then and we were being hit with practically every salvo." From 8:10 to 9:10 A.M., thirty Japanese shells struck the little carrier. Absorbing so much damage in such a short time soon doomed the carrier to a watery grave.

Meanwhile, the *Fanshaw Bay's* problems continued unabated. A sequence of shells corkscrewed into her, sounding like two trains in a head-on collision. One shell penetrated under a 40mm gun's barrels and tore off its pointer's (the person responsible for aiming the gun) face, instantly killing him. However, that shell's power to wreak havoc did not stop there. It bounced off the gun shield's top forward edge and broke into pieces that scattered along the deck. The next shell smacked into the flight deck and, like its predecessor, broke into fragments that damaged the catapult track and anchor windlass, killing one man and wounding two others.

One of the wounded men was Sprague's chief petty officer, Harold Moeller, who received his injuries as that shell pierced the wall of Sprague's flag office. Another officer, standing near Sprague and Moeller, later recalled that the shell "clanked through, like a bowling ball bouncing through metal pins." Another shell ripped into the aircraft catapult's track while two others hit the water with a loud splat, exploding on both sides of the escort carrier. These shells' fragments penetrated the hull, causing the carrier to roll from side to side as huge water columns soaked the flagship's decks. However, they did not do as much damage to the little carrier as they could have. Damage control parties quickly controlled the minor flooding and sporadic fires. Their diligent work allowed the *Fanshaw Bay* to keep up with the formation and remain fully operational.

While some wondered how much longer the *Fanshaw Bay*'s luck would hold, another nagging question buzzed through Sprague's nimble mind. By applying brilliant maneuvering and delaying tactics, and being on the receiving end of a few miracles, Taffy 3 had thus far avoided complete annihilation. But time was not on their side, and the way the deck was stacked, their supply of luck was slated to run out. Sprague still had no answers to his pleas for help from Halsey. If the Third Fleet's commander had heard the beleaguered admiral's appeals, Halsey's ships should not be very far away. A puzzled Sprague ranted: "Where was Halsey?"[14]

Chapter 16: A Mystery Looking for a Solution

At Pearl Harbor on the morning of October 25, Nimitz grew ever more alarmed over the Third Fleet's whereabouts. He knew Kurita's Center Force should have exited the San Bernardino Strait's eastern mouth about midnight, and if the Third Fleet had been where Nimitz thought it should be—off the San Bernardino Strait, waiting to pounce when the Japanese came through—messages from Halsey should have been pouring in by now, assuming Halsey had engaged the Japanese. However, the communications channel between Hawaii and the Third Fleet was conspicuously silent.

Nimitz queried his assistant chief of staff, Capt. Bernard L. Austin, as to whether any dispatches had come in from Halsey. Austin informed Nimitz that he had already seen every message received thus far, and not only was there no information about the location of the Third Fleet's carriers, no one knew where Halsey's battleships—Task Force 34—were either. Everyone in Hawaii assumed Halsey's earlier message about forming Lee's battleships into Task Force 34 meant that the fast battleships would be together as a group guarding the San Bernardino Strait. Assuming this was true was one thing, making it true was quite another.

The morning hours passed, and still no one at CINCPAC knew any more about what Halsey was doing than they had earlier. Growing impatient, Nimitz asked Austin twice more for messages from Halsey. Trying to satisfy his superior's need for definitive information, Austin recommended that Nimitz ask Halsey specifically about the location of the battleships. However, the admiral decided against acting on this suggestion, since he reasoned it might be construed by his erratic subordinate as interfering with a fleet commander's tactical decision making. He decided to wait for the situation to become clearer but secretly hoped Halsey had not taken Lee's battleships northward, thus leaving Sprague's lightly armored carriers at the mercy of the powerful Japanese Center Force.

Aboard the *New Jersey*, meanwhile, suggestions poured into the flagship informing Halsey that the Third Fleet was needed elsewhere, and with the arrival of each message, Halsey's anger grew. About 8:30 A.M., twenty minutes after he heard about Oldendorf's victory in the Surigao Strait, two dispatches—Sprague's 7:35 A.M. frantic appeal for help and Kinkaid's message that Japanese ships were within 15 miles of Sprague's Taffy 3—were placed in his hands.

Halsey's reaction to these messages was to wonder how Kinkaid could have allowed Sprague to be surprised in this way. Further, Halsey did not believe Kurita's ships had escaped the notice of Cliff Sprague's search planes. In addition, he assumed that Tom Sprague's eighteen escort carriers had strength enough to hold Kurita at bay until Oldendorf's battleships came up from the south to rescue Cliff Sprague. Hoping these presumptions would prove to be correct, Halsey's anger subsided, and he relaxed a bit.

But his anger stirred again when, eight minutes later, an urgent message from Kinkaid arrived stating: "Situation critical, battleships and fast carrier strike wanted to prevent enemy penetrating Leyte Gulf."

This message perplexed Halsey. How could a fellow commander urge him to send his carrier planes south when a battle with Ozawa's carriers was about to begin? This battle was the one Halsey had prepared for his entire naval career, a once-in-a-lifetime opportunity, and he felt he could allow nothing to prevent him from taking advantage of it.

Attempting to respond to the rapidly changing situation, Halsey ordered VAdm. John S. McCain's Task Group 38.1, now refueling far to the east, to head to Leyte Gulf at top speed. However, if Halsey knew this was an exercise in futility because it was impossible for McCain to reach Leyte Gulf in time, he never confessed this then or any time afterward.

Halsey's actions annoyed two intelligence officers at Nimitz's headquarters. Lt. W. Jasper Holmes read the many messages bouncing between Sprague, Kinkaid, and Halsey and pondered the whereabouts of Task Force 34. He first made the reasonable assumption that it stood off the San Bernardino Strait. However, no clearly worded messages from Halsey made clear that the Third Fleet's battleships indeed were where they should be.

Holmes telephoned his superior, Cmdr. Edwin T. Layton, asking what he thought Halsey had done with the battleships. Layton responded angrily that Halsey must have taken Lee's battleships with him when he ordered the Third Fleet north to go after Ozawa's carriers. When Holmes suggested it was possible Halsey had sent an order to Lee by either signal lamp or flags to stay at the San Bernardino Strait, Layton sneered, "I doubt it," and slammed down the phone.

Aboard the fast carrier *Franklin*, Rear Admiral Davison and his chief of staff, Capt. James S. Russell, held little hope that Cliff Sprague would escape annihilation by Kurita. Russell later explained, "When we got Ziggy's message, we knew he was in a bad spot because we thought Lee should have been detached. Admiral Davison and I almost had the feeling toward Halsey, 'What the hell, we told you so!'"

Lieutenant Robb White, on board Taffy 2's *Natoma Bay*, and a staff member from CINCPAC's public relations office, also watched the extraordinary flow of events off Samar. Reflecting the pessimistic mood of his carrier's crew, he wrote in his notebook that the men "are wishing that aid would come and knowing that it will not... the great and famous Task Force 38 [Halsey] is far to the north. No help is coming."

In piecing together what Cliff Sprague really thought of his abandonment by Halsey, we can find clues in notes written in a draft of an early history of the *Battle of Leyte Gulf* by C. Vann Woodward. Here Sprague far exceeded White's mild sarcasm about Halsey's continuing on his northbound course despite Sprague and Kinkaid's urgent pleas for help when he wrote, "Can you beat it?" Almost filling the entire right margin beside the description of Halsey sending McCain to his aid, Sprague wrote, "McCain's planes didn't get to my area until after noon and the battle was over a good three hours and then they nearly attacked us and were only diverted at the last moment by CIC [Combat Information Center] on the *Fanshaw*." In those remarks, Sprague makes plain his disgust for and anger at what happened on that fateful October 25. Whether he had those feelings on that day, it was quite possible that he was much too busy either to be aware of them or to show them.[1]

End of a Carrier's Life

Two heavy cruisers moved in and closed the distance to the *Fanshaw Bay*. They came within 10,000 yards and fired forty to fifty broadsides at the carrier. Shells whistled over the bridge, smacking the water astern a few yards distant. As they fell close by, Pierson marveled, "They are really pouring it on us, or I should say all around us." Sprague reasoned that Taffy 3's end was near, as there was nothing to stop the cruisers from moving closer and firing at the carriers at point-blank range. Yet for some reason, they kept their distance at 10,000 yards. A puzzled Sprague wrote later, "I never did figure out why they didn't close to 5,000 and polish us off."

The other carriers faced certain destruction as well. Weakly firing his only 5-inch gun, *Kitkun Bay*'s commander, Capt. John P. Whitney, ordered the gun crew to keep the barrage going so her crew's morale wouldn't waver. Whitney believed this act of aggression would encourage them so that "at least we were throwing something at the enemy." The Japanese cruisers and destroyers kept their distance, out of the range of the carrier's 40mm and 20mm guns. Reflecting the helplessness the guns' crews felt, one 40mm battery officer cynically remarked to his men, "It won't be long now, boys. We're sucking them into 40mm range."

However, the *Gambier Bay* did not share in her fellow carriers' fortune. Although the *Johnston* and *Heermann* had managed to divert some of the Japanese cruisers' fire, the little carrier was too heavily damaged to remain afloat. Her speed slowed dramatically as the Japanese ships passed 2,000 yards to her port beam, where they executed the coup de grâce. At 8:50 A.M., Captain Vieweg ordered his crew to abandon ship. Seventeen minutes later, she rolled over on her port side and sank.

After giving his command fifteen minutes of life and watching as his ships and airplanes kept Kurita's powerful force away for almost two hours, Sprague noted, "To me it was a miracle that under such terrific fire for that length of time only one carrier had suffered a crippling hit. Two others had suffered several hits and three others none at all. And all of my six carriers, except the *Gambier Bay*, were able to make their maximum speed." His chief quartermaster, William Morgan, heard Sprague exclaim, "By God, I think we may have a chance."

There were other signs, too, albeit small ones, that Taffy 3 was actually going to survive this ordeal. Airplanes from the *Kitkun Bay* scored hit after hit on the heavy cruiser *Chokai*, and six 5-inch shells from the *White Plains* smacked into the big cruiser. Swerving sharply to starboard, the heavy cruiser moved slowly for 500 yards. Abruptly, a huge explosion engulfed her in smoke and flames, and she sank in five minutes. Sprague's hopes rose on receiving a report that American carrier planes were less than 60 miles away to the southwest, on their way to help. Like much that had been rumored during the confusion and chaos of this dramatic day, this story later proved to be false.

Short-Lived, Blissful Ignorance

Meanwhile, Halsey continued his aggressive pursuit of Ozawa's carriers about 350 miles north of Sprague's position as Taffy 3 fought for its life. Halsey seemed totally oblivious of Sprague's heroic defense off Samar. He had seen a mass of messages from Kinkaid and Sprague that alerted him to the fact that Kurita had steamed through the San Bernardino Strait and was now in position along Samar's eastern coast. However, Halsey knew Kinkaid still had battleships that had thoroughly destroyed Nishimura in the Surigao Strait, as well as aircraft on the escort carriers. It seemed obvious to Halsey that Kinkaid had more than enough strength to handle anything Kurita could throw at the Seventh Fleet.

His reverie was short-lived, however. As more dispatches poured into the *New Jersey*'s communications center, Halsey finally realized the dangerousness of the situation in the south—as if a bucket of cold water had been thrown over his head. A desperate message from Kinkaid in plain English and pleading for help arrived at 9:00 A.M. It got Halsey's attention: "Enemy force attacking our CVES composed of 4 battleships, 8 cruisers, and X other ships. Request Lee proceed top speed cover, Leyte. Request immediate strike by fast carriers."

The shock of the urgent battle going on southward finally sank in when a second dispatch pleading for help arrived twenty-two minutes later. Up to this time, Halsey had hoped that Sprague's escort carriers could hold Kurita at bay until Oldendorf's battleships arrived. However, this message made it clear to Halsey that Oldendorf's battleships did not have enough high-caliber ammunition to take on Kurita's powerful force. Perturbed, Halsey wondered why Kinkaid had waited so long to tell him this important information. Had he known this fact earlier, he might have changed his plan. The mystery of the message's delay disappeared when he saw the dispatch's time: 7:25 A.M., almost two hours earlier.

This latest piece of news stunned Halsey. Nonetheless, it did not deter him from his original mission. The Third Fleet's pursuit of Ozawa continued relentlessly. Halsey's sole answer to Kinkaid's increasingly desperate messages was that McCain's Task Group was now heading toward Leyte. But as far as Lee's battleships and the rest of Mitscher's carrier groups were concerned, they were staying with him, for he was receiving reports that some of his aircraft were now attacking the Japanese carriers. The temptation to inflict a death blow on Japanese naval aviation was far too compelling for him to abandon.

Halsey was like the man whose sleeve was being tugged just as he was focusing on the task in front of him. He said later, "Here I was on the brink of a critical battle, and my kid brother was yelling for help around the corner. There was nothing else I could do, except become angrier." After all, he had Nimitz's order to go after the Japanese carriers if the opportunity presented itself, and nothing had changed his mind or feelings. His tunnel vision, his single-minded purpose, shut out all other factors—including the dire crisis of his brother officers.

A Perpetual Controversy

As time passed that morning, Nimitz's anxiety about what was happening in the Philippines intensified. If Halsey had left Task Force 34 at the San Bernardino Strait, Nimitz thought that an order from Halsey to Lee to attack Kurita would have been issued by now. However, the only order Halsey had sent out that Nimitz was aware of was the one ordering McCain to head for Leyte and to help Kinkaid. Nimitz deduced, therefore, that Lee's battleships must also have gone north with the rest of the Third Fleet. Given all the messages he had read from Kinkaid and Sprague begging for help, Nimitz wondered why Halsey was keeping the battleships with him instead of ordering them southward. As far as Nimitz was concerned, the time had long since passed for Halsey to dispatch Lee's battleships, and the situation had become too critical to continue practicing the nicety of noninterference with his commanders' tactical decisions. Accordingly, he ordered Captain Austin to draft a dispatch asking Halsey the whereabouts of Task Force 34.

What followed, then, is one of the most controversial episodes of the entire Pacific War. Although messages normally were sent in code due to the danger of enemy interception, a standard practice had evolved that included padding the beginning and end of messages in order to make deciphering them more difficult. But in this case, Nimitz wanted his message to be as short and to the point as possible in order to rouse Halsey into ordering Lee's battleships south. So, the message he sent simply asked Halsey, "Where is Task Force 34?" But the message did not, in fact, go out in that format. When transmitted from the Pacific Fleet Headquarters Communications Center, it read as follows: "TURKEY TROTS TO WATER GG WHERE IS RPT WHERE IS TASK FORCE THIRTY-FOUR RR THE WORLD WONDERS."[2]

When the message arrived in the *New Jersey*'s communications center, the decoders became confused over its last three words. The separators between the message itself and the header and trailer words were "RPT" and "RR." Since it seemed obvious to the decoders that "TURKEY TROTS TO WATER" was the header inserted to confuse Japanese decoders, they eliminated it. But the words "THE WORLD WONDERS" which followed the "RR" separator might have come from Tennyson's poem, "The Charge of the Light Brigade." To the *New Jersey* decoders, "the world wonders" might be part of the message. Not wishing to hold back any meaningful information from higher command, they left the trailer phrase in the message, confidently believing they had done the right thing. The decoded message sent to Halsey's flag bridge read: "WHERE IS RPT WHERE IS TASK FORCE THIRTY-FOUR RR THE WORLD WONDERS."

When this message arrived in Halsey's hands shortly after 10:00 A.M., its effect could not have been more dramatic. In keeping with his temperamental nature, his face turned red with anger as he read it. In all the years he had known and respected Nimitz, it seemed inconceivable to him that he would ever receive what seemed to be such a severe reprimand from his superior. He later described in his memoirs what he felt like on reading the apparently inflammatory message:

> I was stunned as if I had been struck in the face. The paper rattled in my hands. I snatched off my cap, threw it on the deck, and shouted something that I am ashamed to remember. Mick Carney [his chief of staff] rushed over and grabbed my arm: "Stop it! What the hell's the matter with you? Pull yourself together!"

Halsey's violent reaction to Nimitz's seemingly abusive, reprimanding message suggests that two trains of thought stirred in Halsey's mind. An intensely ambitious man, Halsey saw the opportunity to destroy the

Japanese carriers as a cardinal achievement, one that would secure for him an illustrious place in America naval history. But Nimitz's message questioned the wisdom of this course. The second train of thought concerned what he owed a brother officer in danger. Individualism and communal obligations conflicted within him, and he felt pulled in two directions by forces of equal strength.

Of course, we will never know what actually went through Halsey's mind when he crumpled up the message and threw his cap vehemently on the deck. One fact is unmistakeningly clear, however, and this was that he was not certain whether he had done the right thing when he ordered the Third Fleet north, taking the battleships with him.

Still seething, Halsey responded slowly to Nimitz's inquiry. Seventy-five minutes passed after the arrival of the dispatch before he ordered his ships south. The Third Fleet was 350 miles from Taffy 3 and would not arrive off Samar until 8:00 A.M. on the 26th. Halsey sent Nimitz a message to that effect. The fact that he took so long to issue the order shows clearly that his heart was not in it. Later, in his memoirs, Halsey mournfully pointed out his deep-felt regrets about what he had to do: "I turned my back on the opportunity I had dreamed of since my days as a cadet."

After the war, Cliff Sprague vehemently disagreed with Halsey when he read the noted naval historian Woodward's account of the Battle off Samar. Next to the passages telling of Halsey's belated decision to turn south, Sprague irately wrote, "Might just as well have stayed there or gone back to Pearl." Zeroing in on the flaw in Halsey's regret about abandoning what the Third Fleet commander thought of as a golden opportunity, Sprague rebutted, "His golden opportunity had been lost the day before," when he abandoned his assigned post of guarding the San Bernardino Strait, thereby letting Kurita slip through with a clear path to the Leyte beaches. As far as Sprague was concerned, it was Halsey's failure to do his duty that left Taffy 3 in a perilous position and, according to Sprague, cost the lives of hundreds of American sailors.

Surprise!

While Halsey was hurling his hat on the deck, the amazing events off Samar became even more bizarre. For more than two hours, Taffy 3 had fought off the Japanese Center Force amid screaming shells, diving aircraft, foul-smelling smoke, and engines strained to the breaking point.

Then, as suddenly as the powerful Japanese ships had appeared on the horizon almost three hours earlier, silence inexplicably fell on the debris-strewn and, in some places, bloody waters off Samar. Unbelievably, the most powerful surface fleet the Japanese had sent into combat since the Battle of Midway ceased firing, turned around, and retreated to the north.

An astonished signalman near Sprague yelled, "Goddamn it, boys, they're getting away." Gaping across the waters at the receding Japanese sterns, the admiral could not believe what he saw. Thinking the Japanese movement might be a ruse, Sprague waited for their next move before receiving confirmation from Taffy 2's and Taffy 3's aircraft that the Japanese ships were indeed heading north. As he watched the phenomenal sight through his binoculars again, he could hardly take in this reversal of fortune.

Yet, one after another, the Japanese ships changed course and left the site of battle. The *Haguro* turned around first, followed by the *Tone*. A third message arrived confirming that the Japanese battleships were heading northeast as well. Final proof confirmed that the battle was over when the *Fanshaw Bay*'s Combat Information Center reported that the entire Japanese fleet was pulling out. Releasing the incredible tensions that had racked him throughout that historic morning, Sprague roared a shout of delight and relief.

Then, he resumed his customary status as commander when he admonished his men, "Stay on your toes and stay alert. We're not out of the woods yet." Later, Sprague wrote, "I could not believe my eyes, but it looked as if the whole Japanese fleet was indeed retiring. However, it took a whole series of reports from circling planes to convince me. And still I could not get the fact to soak into my battle-numbed brain. At best, I had expected to be swimming by this time." At this time of almost certain defeat and annihilation, Sprague had no time to wonder what must have been going through Kurita's mind as he led the Japanese ships north, away from almost certain victory.

Admiral Kurita was a harried, overwrought man. The ferocious American attacks had shaken him to the core. Their aircraft had lit into his ships like hornets defending their nests. Their ships had charged into combat like cyclones, making so much smoke his gunners could not get accurate beads on their carriers. Both his destroyer squadrons had in-

creased speed in order to draw near enough to fire on the carriers. At
8:10 A.M., lookouts on the *Haruna* sighted Taffy 3's carriers, and the battleship opened fire from a range of 36,000 yards. Both the *Kongo* and
the *Yamato* claimed to have sunk a carrier (the *Gambier Bay*) fifteen minutes later.

However, Japanese spotters continuously overestimated the size and
strength of their opposition. They asserted the sunken American ship
was an Essex-class carrier. The Japanese heavy cruiser *Haguro* claimed firing seventy-eight of her shells over a period from 8:42 to 8:52 A.M. at one
American carrier and sinking her. Another carrier, the *Fanshaw Bay*, did
indeed absorb four 8-inch shells and two near misses. Two more carriers, the *Kitkun Bay* and *St. Lô*, had better luck as huge water columns from
many shells surrounded them but damaged nothing.

Despite what actually happened, the Japanese gunners claimed that
they had sunk two light cruisers (they were in actuality the destroyers
Hoel and *Johnston*) and one destroyer (the destroyer escort *Samuel B.
Roberts*) under a rainstorm of overwhelming gunfire.

By 9:00 A.M., Taffy 3's life as an effective fighting unit seemed about
to end. The Americans had fought with everything they had and had no
more to give. They had already lost one escort carrier and three screening vessels, and the other carriers had sustained heavy damage. It appeared that Sprague's command had run out of luck. The Japanese listening station on Formosa had intercepted several American plain
language messages pleading for help. Perhaps another Japanese commander would have seen these events for what they really were—an opportunity to move in closer to the enemy and crush him. But Kurita's
thinking ran along different lines. The fact was that Kurita's tolerance
for punishment was exhausted. He had never fully agreed with the wisdom of the original SHO-1 plan, and now he had to face an American
carrier fleet on which he was unable to inflict the crippling blows needed
for victory. It can be argued that Kurita's lack of full agreement with the
wisdom of the SHO-1 plan shows that he was a better strategist than the
war planners in Tokyo, for the primary weakness in this plan—the lack
of aircraft and trained pilots—meant that Japan could not, and had not
been able since Guadalcanal, to win the war. It could only defer defeat,
and, on an unconscious level, this knowledge could very well have influenced Kurita's decisions.

Furthermore, his Center Force had been torpedoed by submarines in
the Palawan Passage and viciously attacked by American carrier aircraft

in the Sibuyan Sea. And now, off Samar, just when his force was on the verge of a glorious conquest, another American force put up a brilliant defense using bold aircraft attacks, audacious torpedo runs, and incessant gunfire from what seemed to be carriers, cruisers, and destroyers.

Kurita had lost one of his battleships and several cruisers since the submarine attack. He also had been unceremoniously dumped into and fished out of the waters of the Palawan Passage. During the desperate struggle off Samar, the cruiser *Chikuma* lost her rudder in a torpedo attack, and the cruiser *Chokai* lost all engine power when subjected to more torpedo attacks. Before the day's end, both ships would sink. The American torpedo attacks had forced his command to disperse in a variety of directions at once, causing their attacks to become so uncoordinated that any resemblance of attack efficiency vanished altogether.

It seemed that the American force confronting him off the waters of Samar was too tough a nut to crack. In Kurita's mind, no rational naval commander would have so boldly and courageously attacked his powerful force unless those carriers were from Halsey's Third Fleet and surrounded by the new American fast battleships, cruisers, plus a vast fleet of destroyers.

The pleas for help Kurita picked up over the course of the battle had one meaning only to him. Why would the Americans ask for help in plain language unless the forces being called on were near enough to deliver immediate aid? Even though he could not see much of the power backing up his opponent, Kurita reasoned that they must be just over the horizon and a few minutes away. The fact that one of the *Yamato*'s lookouts thought he had seen an American "battleship" at 8:22 A.M. strengthened his assumption that Halsey was not far away. Also, Kurita had already felt the sting of Halsey's carriers in the Sibuyan Sea and seen what damage they could inflict on ships lacking air cover during the battle off the Marianas.

With the loss of Nishimura's Force C and the retreat of Shima's cruisers in the Surigao Strait, coupled with the fact that he had heard nothing from Ozawa, and knowing that the Japanese carriers were merely a shell force with no appreciable aircraft strength, Kurita was fully aware that his Center Force possessed the only ships that the Japanese Empire could use to oppose the American drive to win the war and to lay waste to his homeland. If his Center Force was lost, then the Japanese homeland would be wide open to an invasion and to the unthinkable defeat of the empire.

Fuel was running low, and the Center Force was not reducing its range to the American carriers. Some of his ships, such as the battleship *Nagato*, could steam only at a top speed of 24 knots. If the American carriers, which had an apparent top speed of 30 knots, were to increase their steaming speed to the maximum, his ships would never be able to catch them. Furthermore, there was not enough fuel left to close the distance. Even if he could close the distance, Kurita must have reasoned, Halsey's Third Fleet had too many planes, ships, and too much firepower for even his powerful force. To continue on with his attack, therefore, now seemed to be a hopeless choice, one that would result in the complete and utter devastation of his command.

To make matters worse, he could not speak effectively with the ships in his command because the *Yamato*'s radio telephones had failed. This communication failure meant his fleet could not pool information, and this prevented Kurita from learning just how close his ships actually were to obliterating Taffy 3, or just how close they were to the victory he had so ardently sought when his force left Brunei just seven days ago.

The situation now seemed so futile to Kurita that he could not visualize a clear path to victory. Seeing Kurita's dilemma and realizing the problems confronting his superior, Rear Admiral Koyanagi recommended that Kurita "discontinue this chase. There's still Leyte Gulf to attack." Rejecting Koyanagi's advice, and thoroughly exhausted by the accumulated effects of the last three days' incessant gunfire and air, torpedo, and submarine attacks, Kurita could see only one alternative: he had to preserve what was left of the once magnificent Imperial Fleet and take it out of harm's way.

Whether he was too tired to go on or not, we shall never know. Mystery, in fact, surrounds what it was he feared and why he suffered a loss of will. To this day such matters remain unresolved. Several naval historians later accused Kurita of cowardice. Others have offered softer appraisals of his conduct. Later in this book, I take up of the matter of the aftermath of the Battle of Leyte Gulf. (Here I will offer an analysis of possible motivation leading up to his momentus and critical decision to retreat.)

All we do know is what he did next. In the end, Kurita agreed with Koyanagi that chasing the Americans should cease, but he did not agree to proceed to Leyte Gulf and there fulfill his original mission. Instead, he issued the following unexpected, astonishing order at 9:11 A.M.: "Rendezvous, my course north, speed 20."

After being so near to achieving a magnificent victory, he decided to back away, to retreat. The Center Force thereupon broke off its attacks, reversed course, headed north away from a flabbergasted opponent, and safely left the waters off Samar—never to fight in a naval battle against the American navy again.[3]

Taffy 3's screening force contributed far more to its defense than Sprague had ever imagined possible. In interviews after the war, Kurita conceded that Sprague's ceaseless zigzagging, coupled with the American destroyers and destroyer escorts' audacious torpedo assaults, threw his gunfire's accuracy into utter chaos. While Kurita's spotters had no difficulty pinpointing the Americans' slow torpedoes as they approached his ships, his formation nonetheless was forced, frequently and quickly, to change course in order to avoid being hit. When his force had to break up its attack formations, this reduced its guns' accuracy and frustrated the Japanese gun crews. Kurita also stated during the interviews that the American's plentiful use of smoke "was very serious trouble for us. It was exceedingly well used tactically."

Rear Admiral Koyanagi also said that leaving a battle scene when the adversary is attacking them "is the most difficult of all tactics to execute successfully." He also commended Sprague's maneuvers as "valiant and skillful. The enemy destroyers coordinated perfectly to cover the low speed of the escort carriers, bravely launched torpedoes to intercept us, and embarrassed us with their dense smoke screen." While the Japanese ships frantically tried to avoid the Americans' incessant attacks that caused their ships to be scattered all over the ocean, Koyanagi praised the discipline of Sprague's carriers as they moved as one: "I must admit admiration for the skill of their commanders."[4]

The Japanese perspectives on these attacks are revealing. Admiral Kurita's operations officer, Cmdr. Tonosuke Otani, reported after the war that although the attacks "were almost incessant," not many aircraft were actually involved. Otani adds the following: "The bombers and torpedo planes were very aggressive and skillful and the coordination was impressive; even in comparison with the many experiences of American attacks we had already had, this was the most skillful work of your planes."[5]

Why Did the Japanese Retreat?

The chaotic and gritty fight off Samar lasted just over two hours. Outgunned and outnumbered, six American escort carriers, three destroyers, and four destroyer escorts outfought and outmaneuvered a vastly superior Japanese fleet that had four battleships, six heavy cruisers, and two destroyer divisions, causing them to turn back. Worse yet for the Japanese, five out of six American escort carriers in Taffy 3 escaped unharmed.

When Admiral Kurita ordered his force to break off the action at 9:11 A.M. by issuing the "Rendezvous, my course north, speed 20" message, he intended to re-form his fleet and assess the damage. After that, he intended to fulfill his mission by attacking the landings at Leyte. Nevertheless, as time passed, the destruction of the Leyte landings became a less attractive objective, and though he changed course several times in the process of retreating, eventually, Kurita headed for the San Bernardino Strait.

However, there was nothing of a substantive nature to stop him from lunging past Taffy 3 into Leyte Gulf. Although he had lost three heavy cruisers in the Battle Off Samar, his battleships and the heavy cruisers he had left emerged from the struggle unscathed. The *Yamato* had sustained only minor damage from bombs and 5-inch shells so she could still fight and do considerable damage to any opponent. Some of his destroyers were low on fuel, but this was not, in fact, a problem serious enough to stop the destruction of Taffy 3 and the move to the Leyte beaches. Kurita's force had plenty of armor-piercing ammunition. Clearly he had caught the Americans with their pants down and had embarrassed Admirals Kinkaid and Oldendorf. He still was in firm possession of the tactical advantage after the Battle Off Samar.

So why did he retreat? The explanations given by him and his chief of staff shed light on this question. When Kurita stopped chasing Taffy 3, he believed the Americans were steaming at 30 knots. However, the escort carriers' top speed was, in reality, only 18 knots, while Kurita had the ability to maintain about 24 knots, thus providing a 6-knot speed advantage. The Americans' smoke screen obscured them from Japanese optical range finders, because the Center Force did not have any rangefinding radar with which to overcome the heavy smoke. Also, Kurita's communications with his force were poor. The discovery that two heavy cruisers had gotten within 10,000 yards of the American carriers even surprised his chief of staff at the end of the war.

The Japanese admiral had, in effect, maneuvered without creating any attack plan for more than two hours, in an effort to escape the American air attacks. Late in the evening on the 24th, Kurita had received word that the Americans had destroyed Nishimura's Force C in the Surigao

Strait. Because his lookouts had little training in identifying the newest American ships, his staff thought the American escort carriers were actually some of Halsey's fast Independence-class carriers, that the destroyers were Baltimore-class cruisers, and that a Pennsylvania-class battleship was hiding among the American ships. The *Yamato*'s lookouts thought Taffy 2 was another fast carrier task force.

Other factors also entered into the admiral's evaluations and made him even more cautious. Two of the *Yamato*'s reconnaissance planes dispatched to look over Leyte Gulf had not returned. Kurita had heard nothing from Admiral Ozawa's Northern Force but did receive an obscure message to the effect that an American task force was only 113 miles away. Kurita reasoned that this task force surely must be Halsey's Third Fleet. Admiral Kinkaid's calls for help also reached Kurita. The fact that these were in plain language made him think that a powerful force was on its way. Although a *Nagato* plane had sighted thirty-five transports in Leyte Gulf, he thought these would escape before he could get there, thus depriving him of the victory that Tokyo had ordered.

While Kurita did analyze what he knew, he tried to take into account what he thought he was facing, and here is where he went wrong. The way the Americans attacked clearly suggested to him that he was battling a force of cruisers and destroyers instead of destroyers and destroyer escorts. He believed the American aircraft had assaulted his ships with a ferocity that could only have come from experienced naval aviators who had served aboard Halsey's fast carriers. Of course, Kurita had no way of knowing that these aircrews actually had served only on the small jeep carriers of the Seventh Fleet and had almost no experience attacking warships.

Given this set of facts and assumptions, he assessed both his prospects and probability of success as equally grim. To Kurita, it was better that he save his fleet to fight another day. Just as Taffy 2's planes attacked him, the admiral decided not to attempt any more breakthroughs into Leyte Gulf. At 12:36 P.M., he sent a message to the commander in chief of the Combined Fleet: "First Striking Force has abandoned penetration of Leyte anchorage. Is proceeding north searching for enemy task force. Will engage decisively, then pass through San Bernardino Strait."

The task force mentioned in Kurita's dispatch proved to be a phantom. Thus, a rather inglorious chapter in Japanese naval history ended. His too cautious assessment cost the Japanese their only chance to stop the Americans from taking the Philippines.

Where Does the Blame Fall?

A heated debate has raged among naval historians ever since that fateful October 25 morning. The major question asked is the following: Who was responsible for the Japanese surprise attack on the American escort carriers? Halsey's incorrect estimate that the Japanese Center Force was too badly damaged to be a serious menace set off a chain of wrong assumptions that could have left a devastated, defeated, and mortally wounded American landing force on Leyte Island's beaches. The outcome of the American invasion of the Philippines could then have ended in a disastrous American defeat and prolonged the Pacific War.

After the war, Admiral King examined Admiral Kinkaid's air searches and "regrettably concluded that the Seventh Fleet—despite its excellent performance in other respects—had failed to take the reasonable precaution that would have discovered the approach of the Japanese Center Force." King attributed the surprise appearance of Kurita's Center Force off Samar Island "not only to Halsey's absence in the north but also to Kinkaid's failure to use his own air squadrons for search at the crucial moment."

A closer examination of this assessment yields somewhat different conclusions, however. Kinkaid did indeed order two northern air searches. The first was by escort planes, but this search was launched too late; the second was by PBY-5s, the Black Cat Catalina patrol plane equipped for flying at night. Five planes were selected from their anchored seaplane tender in Hunanagan Bay off Leyte, but only three actually took off, and only one might have been able to spot Kurita.

In the approaching darkness of October 24, the Black Cat Catalina slowly accelerated on the bay's waters, gradually gathering enough speed to lift into the air. Lieutenant (jg) C. B. Sillers heard the throbbing of the two engines above his head as he had so often before. Scattered clouds pockmarked the darkening night sky. Glancing down as the big plane gathered speed, he saw the water's smooth surface, making his job of searching for the Japanese that much easier. His hand rested on the throttles as he examined the air speed dial. The arrow pointed to a place on the dial indicating enough air speed to lift the big plane aloft. He pulled the yolk back toward his stomach; the plane lifted smoothly from the water's surface and became airborne.

The Catalina may be slow, but it was the most stable plane in the United States Navy. Planes such as this one had already proven their usefulness. Catalinas had sighted Japanese ships in the slot off Guadalcanal, and this had given the struggling marines on that jungle-infested island enough time to take cover and allowed the few American ships and planes in the area to intercept the Japanese ships. They had also given Admirals Spruance and Fletcher early warning of the Japanese fleet's approach off Midway. These slow but steady aircraft showed what a valuable resource they were by providing decisively valuable intelligence that resulted in the crucial and strategic American naval victories that forced the Japanese back from their conquests.

Sillers' assignment was clear. He would head north to look for Japanese ships that the Americans had attacked in the Sibuyan Sea. Reports showed that the American planes had inflicted heavy damage on these ships and that these ships were retreating to the west and north. However, prudence dictated that it was better to be safe than sorry.

As all the plane's crews' eyes searched the seas for any sign of ships, no sign of any kind was to be found.

The black plane flew along the strait into the Sibuyan Sea. Samar Island soon appeared out the port window. About one hour later, Kurita's ships would pass through the strait. By this time, the Catalina was nearing its landing zone in Leyte Gulf. Japanese fortunes were picking up. They had missed each other.

So, Admiral King's assessment that partially blamed Kinkaid for not sighting the Japanese Center Force seems too harsh. The element of luck now seems to have played a larger part in the outcome of what happened off Samar than anyone with command responsibility was willing to admit. As in all events of historical importance, the parts that random occurrences play can have just as much influence on a battle's outcome as factors such as relative force strength, command decisions, and fighting courage.

Kinkaid's staff confidently assumed that Halsey would "take care" of the northern sector. Despite these assumptions, some of Kinkaid's people expressed fear that Kurita might be heading south. Admiral Wilkinson was one of those who reasoned in this way, but felt it was not his place to pass his worries up the command chain. After all, Task Force 38's carriers were out there where they were supposed to be. Halsey's forceful sense of duty would never allow him to abandon his post, and the operational plan reinforced this conviction in Wilkinson. In addition, Kinkaid had intercepted some messages convincing him that the Third Fleet was watching the San Bernardino Strait with its powerful battleships and heavy cruisers.

In a dispatch sent at 3:12 P.M. on the 24th, which had the title "Battle Plan," Halsey ordered all Third Fleet task force and group commanders to "engage decisively at long ranges" enemy forces with specific battleships and other heavy forces. Another provision in Halsey's "battle plan" was that Admirals Davison and Bogan's carrier groups would keep their ships clear of any surface action.

Halsey's "battle plan" helped Kinkaid feel confident that Halsey's ships would be where they should be if he needed them. Nevertheless, when Kinkaid intercepted this message, he observed he was not on the addressee list, although Nimitz was.

Yet was this an order or simply a plan for battle? Should Kinkaid have relied on what he assumed was a command when it was actually a plan? Kinkaid believed the word "will" in the phrase "will be" meant Halsey's communiqué was an order, rather than an expression of what was to be part of a plan. Despite these questions, which should have cast doubts on Halsey's intentions, other senior American naval officers agreed with Kinkaid's assessment. Admiral Nimitz in Hawaii and RAdm. C. M. Cooke, deputy chief of naval operations, in Washington, interpreted Halsey's dispatch in the same way as Kinkaid.

Another source of information supporting Kinkaid's estimate of the situation was a "secret, urgent" message sent by Halsey at 10:22 P.M. on October 24, ordering Bogan's and Davison's carrier groups to meet Admiral Sherman's force at midnight, at which time VAdm. Marc Mitscher in the Lexington would take command and attack the Japanese Northern Force. Kinkaid assumed that Task Force 34 (Lee's battleships) had already been formed and separated from Task Force 38. Since, in Halsey's view, this order had never been given, all of the battleships went north with the rest of the Third Fleet.

Several Seventh Fleet staff officers continued to disagree with Kinkaid's interpretation of Halsey's messages. At 4:12 A.M. on October 25, they finally persuaded him to ascertain Third Fleet's intentions. When Kinkaid informed Halsey in a message that disclosed the Surigao Strait victory, he asked the Third Fleet commander whether Task Force 34 was in a position to intercept an enemy attack from the San

Bernardino Strait. More than two hours later, Halsey sent a discouraging answer to Kinkaid's question, that is, Task Force 34 was heading north with the rest of the Third Fleet to attack the Japanese carriers.

Six minutes later, Admiral Kurita's battleships and cruisers had opened fire, and bright, multicolored water geysers from heavy caliber shells surrounded the little ships of Taffy 3. This event dramatically confirmed the fact that no American ships were protecting them and shocked the Seventh Fleet's staff. Admiral Kinkaid's preliminary action report states what was on his mind:

> The first news of this enemy force was received on board the flagship about 0724 when CTU 77.4.3 [Clifton Sprague's command] reported he was under fire by four battleships, eight heavy cruisers, and many destroyers, at a range of 30,000 yards. This was the first indication that the enemy's Center Force had succeeded in passing through San Bernardino Strait. Up to this time, from information available to Commander Seventh Fleet, it was assumed that Third Fleet forces were guarding the San Bernardino Strait position to intercept and destroy any enemy forces attempting to come through.

Pearl Harbor's surprise was as complete as the attack on Taffy 3. Nimitz also wanted to know the location of Task Force 34. At 10:00 A.M. on the 25th, he sent the now infamous "Where is Task Force 34?" message to Halsey.

Should the escort carriers' commanders accept any of the blame for the surprise attack? As we examine the facts, it is apparent that there is no need to assign responsibility to these officers for this fiasco. The dawn search ordered by Kinkaid several hours prior to the battle ended prematurely while the planes were still aloft. Therefore, not a single escort carrier was prepared for Kurita's appearance on the northern horizon. All American eyes in the fleet were looking southward, attempting to destroy any surviving Japanese cripples from the victory in the Surigao Strait.

Cliff Sprague expressed anger about the Seventh Fleet's failure to guard against a northern Japanese attack. The statement he made after the battle reflected the feelings of most of the American sailors involved: "In the absence of any information that this exit was no longer blocked, it was logical to assume that our northern flank could not be exposed without ample warning."

The Seventh Fleet flag officers had placed too much reliance on what they thought Halsey would do. Halsey, in turn, had placed too much trust in the preliminary damage assessments reported by the Third Fleet's carrier pilots during the Sibuyan Sea action on October 24. If only one destroyer had been placed in the San Bernardino Strait, Adm. Thomas Sprague would have had plenty of warning to move his fleet out of the range of Japanese guns.

In summary, Kurita was able to pass through the San Bernardino Strait undetected because of a series of wrong assumptions made by both the Seventh and Third Fleet commanders. Nevertheless, what did these admirals do once the Japanese had revealed themselves and attacked Taffy 3?

The planes that were already performing their current missions were sent to attack the Japanese ships and to relieve Taffy 3's plight. Admiral Kinkaid sent repeated messages to Halsey that show the increasingly frantic nature of the struggle happening between Taffy 3 and the Japanese Center Force.

Message Traffic Between Kinkaid and Halsey—October 25, 1944

Time sent	Received	Message
7:07 A.M.	8:22 A.M.	Japanese capital ships firing at Taffy 3
7:25 A.M.	9:22 A.M.	Oldendorf's battleships running out of ammunition
7:27 A.M.	9:00 A.M.	Request Lee proceed top speed to cover Leyte; request immediate strike by fast carriers
7:39 A.M.	Unknown	Help needed from heavy ships immediately.
8:29 A.M	Unknown	Situation critical, battleships and fast carrier forces wanted to prevent enemy penetrating Leyte Gulf

Halsey's answer to these repeated and increasingly desperate requests for help was that he was already attacking Ozawa's Northern Force. However, he ordered Admiral McCain's carrier group to provide immediate assistance, but since McCain was fueling hundreds of miles to the east, this was a futile gesture. His fast carriers *Hancock*, *Hornet*, and *Wasp* could not have been turned into the wind until 10:30 A.M. in order to launch their aircraft at Kurita's Center Force, 335 miles away. The planes would have taken nearly one and one-half hours to reach their target. By that time, the Battle off Samar was over, and Kurita was steaming northward toward the San Bernardino Strait.

Could Oldendorf's battleships and cruisers have helped? There were persistent rumors that his ships' supplies of armor-piercing ammunition were critically low. These conjectures were partially true. Oldendorf's light cruisers had almost exhausted their armor-piercing shells but had plenty of high explosive ammunition. Although this kind of ammunition was considered ineffective against capital ships, many cruiser skippers thought this was not true. The light cruisers searched for 6-inch armor-piercing ammunition all over the Leyte Gulf area, a search that proved to be in vain. But what about the battleships? The following table shows how many armor-piercing shells per gun these ships had after their annihilation of the Japanese Southern Force.

Number of Armor-piercing Shells in Oldendorf's Battleships

Battleship	Armor-piercing shells per gun
Maryland	More than 24
Tennessee	More than 24
Pennsylvania	More than 24
Mississippi	More than 15
West Virginia	13
California	13

As the table makes clear, there were enough armor-piercing shells to engage the oncoming Japanese ships. However, at 8:00 A.M., Oldendorf's battleships were 65 miles away, and it would take them over three hours steaming at top speed to get within firing range. If the old battleships stopped what they were doing and immediately headed for the battle scene, they would arrive more than two and one-half hours after the Japanese had turned around and fled. If Kurita had pressed into Leyte Gulf, Oldendorf would have had enough armor-piercing ammunition for one more crossing the "T" opportunity, but not enough for a running sea fight.

Still, Oldendorf received an order from Kinkaid at 8:50 A.M. to sail to a point a few miles north of Hibuson Island and stand by. A second order arrived at 9:53 to detach half his force to help the escort carriers. In just a short moment after that order, Kinkaid sent a countermanding order; Kurita's fleet had already left.

In defense of Admiral Kinkaid, his primary responsibility was to protect MacArthur's beachhead, amphibious forces, and the army troops on shore. He had to keep some of his battleships nearby should Admiral Shima's Second Striking Force return. He repeatedly called Halsey for help, showing by this that he believed that Kurita would press the attack to its conclusion and not turn back.

The American-born Japanese propagandist, Tokyo Rose, radioed, "Kinkaid hallooing for help in plain English showed his great anxiety." After the battle was over, Kinkaid remarked, "She didn't know how true that was!"

Never-ending Harassment

Although the Battle off Samar ended after Kurita's force withdrew from the battle, Kurita was not yet free of American attacks as he headed north toward the San Bernardino Strait. American aircraft from the escort carriers under Tommy Sprague and the fleet carriers under McCain continued to exact revenge as they tried to inflict as much damage as they could. Kurita must have thought his ordeal in the waters surrounding the Philippine Islands would never end.

After directing the air attacks on Kurita's ships, Cmdr. Richard L. Fowler of the *Kitkun Bay* landed on the *Manila Bay* on October 25, replenished all his planes with four 500-pound bombs each, and took off at 11:00 A.M. About sixteen Avengers and sixteen fighters from various carriers joined up with him, and a few more planes joined Lt. John R. Dale, the *Kadashan Bay*'s air group commander. A total of thirty-five Avengers and thirty-five Wildcats now sped northward after Kurita while he was steaming in circles deciding what to do next. Following Adm. Felix Stump's order to damage as many ships as possible instead of sinking just a few, the American planes bypassed the *Suzuya*, which would sink at 1:22 P.M. and be the third heavy cruiser in Kurita's fleet lost in this battle.

Fowler spotted the Center Force at 12:20 P.M. about 15 miles off Samar's middle land point. He reported the Japanese fleet's position, course, and speed and followed it until it turned north. Kurita's lookouts also saw the American planes and reported this sighting to the Japanese admiral. The presence of American aircraft was the final factor that convinced him that he had made the correct decision to retire.

Fowler ordered Dale's group to attack from the starboard side while his group would attack from port. Fowler's group dove out of a large cumulus cloud with the Wildcats strafing in advance of the approaching Avengers. When the Japanese ships saw the attacking American planes, they turned hard left, moving their ships into a more advantageous position for the attacking American aircraft. One Avenger dropped a bomb on the *Nagato* that penetrated its bow and exploded in the water. Another bomb hit the heavy cruiser *Tone* and temporarily knocked out her steering gear. While Kurita reported that the American air attack did not inflict much damage, the ships' actual action reports disputed this assertion.

One hour after the Fowler-Dale attack, Kurita would be subjected to a far more ominous danger. An aircraft attack began that had been planned for some time by Vice Admiral McCain's Fast Carrier Group, which was getting within striking range. Halsey had ordered the task group to help the beleaguered Taffies at 8:48 A.M. The American fleet finished fueling and steamed on a course of 245 degrees at 30 knots to reach a place where planes could be launched. The fleet carriers *Wasp*, *Hornet*, and *Hancock*, and the light carriers *Monterey* and *Cowpens* were a far more powerful force than the small escort carriers that had previously attacked the Center Force off Samar.

McCain assigned search duties to the *Hornet*, and she launched six Hellcats between 10:30 and 10:40 A.M. to find Kurita. At the same time, the *Hornet* launched its share of the first strike that included forty-eight Hellcats, thirty-three Helldivers, and nineteen Avengers. It made up one of the longest air carrier strikes in the war in terms of flying time. McCain's radios kept receiving many pleas for help, but no one knew whether the planes could land near Tacloban. Consequently, the aircraft were equipped with wing tanks that could carry enough fuel to return to their home carriers and were loaded with bombs instead of torpedoes to reduce weight.

The American first strike easily found Kurita circling aimlessly in the seas below them. They dove at the *Tone* but inflicted no damage, because the bomb that landed on the cruiser was a dud. The *Hornet* and the *Hancock* launched a smaller second strike and flew for over two hours before they reached the Japanese. In total, 147 sorties flew off McCain's carriers against the Center Force that day. The American pilots optimistically claimed many hits, but this is not supported by Japanese action reports. The cost to the Americans was fourteen planes lost with five pilots and seven crew. A few planes damaged or out of gas landed at Tacloban or found sanctuary on one of the escort carriers. The rest of the aircraft made their way back to their home bases safely and landed between 3:45 and 6:45 P.M.

Rear Admiral Stump's Taffy 2 was not yet finished with Kurita's ships. He launched the last strike of the day, which included twenty-six Avengers, some with torpedoes, and twenty-four Wildcats from the *Natoma Bay*, the *Savo Island*, and other carriers, with instructions to find and attack the Japanese. Following the oil trails left from damaged Japanese ships, they had no difficulty finding Kurita. The aircraft attacked the Japanese with their characteristic aggressiveness and determination. However, they inflicted no appreciable damage because the Japanese had improved their antiaircraft fire.

The Center Force now approached a position of safety in the San Bernardino Strait. They were spotted, however, by a search plane from the *Independence* as they steamed in a single column. All Kurita's ships had survived thus far except for the destroyer *Nowaki*, which had been standing by the heavily damaged heavy cruiser *Chikuma*. These two ships never caught up with their compatriots and met their end in a later action.

As the Americans made several attempts to chase down the Japanese, Kurita's weakened force sustained some heavy damage. American aircraft attacked the light cruiser *Noshiro*, and she eventually sank just before noon on October 26. The heavy cruiser *Kumano*, her bow already blown off by American torpedo attacks off Samar, took a bomb hit that destroyed all its boilers except one. However, she struggled to make 5 knots and eventually managed to escape to Manila Bay. Four American submarines attacked her on November 6 but failed to sink her. She took refuge in Lingayen Gulf, where planes from the *Ticonderoga* sent her to the bottom on November 25.

Kurita retreated from any further action because he wanted to keep his ships as a "fleet in being." His force was no longer capable of any further offensive action but would continue to be a cause of concern by the planners of the Seventh Fleet. None of Kurita's capital ships would see action until April 6, 1945, when the *Yamato*, the remaining behemoth of the once mighty Imperial Fleet, sortied for the last time against American carrier aircraft. The recent history of conflicts between capital ships and aircraft repeated itself. American aircraft again exacted revenge for the destruction of the *Arizona*, *Oklahoma*, *Repulse*, and *Prince of Wales* by sinking the giant battleship. When this great ship disappeared beneath the waves, the fate of large capital ships in further naval warfare was irrevocably sealed. Such ships would never be used in ship-to-ship battles again, and were relegated to bombardment missions of land targets and as support for the landing of troops invading enemy shores.

Kurita's mission ended in failure. His fleet never came close enough to the Leyte landing areas to inflict the destruction hoped for by the Japanese naval war planners. The unconquerable spirit of the American sailors in destroyers and escort carriers had ruined the carefully laid Japanese plans when they gallantly stopped the most powerful Japanese surface fleet ever to sortie since Midway.[6]

Unfortunately and tragically, many of the sailors from Sprague's escort carrier force were never found. After fighting the battle of their lives, most of the unfortunate American sailors who had been thrust into the sea perished without a trace.

The Consequences

The Battle off Samar was over. American bravery, daring, audacity, and just plain luck had saved the men ashore in the American landing force from certain annihilation. In the long history of the United States Navy, this pivotal action would go down in its annals as a supreme example of how an inferior force was able to win a victory against overwhelming odds. Many sailors who fought that St. Crispin's day, officers and enlisted men alike, will remain nameless, but we must never forget that they willingly sacrificed themselves to save their compatriots' lives ashore.

Praise for the American sailors' gallantry has been aptly expressed by Admirals Clifton Sprague and Kinkaid. Sprague expressed his feeling in his action report:

> The failure of the enemy main body and encircling light forces to completely wipe out all vessels of this Task Unit can be attributed to our successful smoke screen, our torpedo counterattack, continuous harassment of enemy by bomb, torpedo, and stressing attacks, timely maneuvers, and the definite partiality of Almighty God.[7]

Admiral Kinkaid acknowledged the heroism of Sprague's command in an afternoon message in which he described the struggle as "a magnificent performance" for which "my admiration knows no bounds. You have carried a load that only fleet carriers could be expected to carry."

However, the outpouring of affection by the *Fanshaw Bay*'s crew meant much more to Sprague than any praise he received from his superiors. Many of these men later credited Sprague's cool demeanor under fire with saving their lives. The calm commands he issued that continuously moved the escort carriers away from the incoming heavy Japanese shells made him beloved among his men. The crew of the *Fanshaw Bay* took up a collection and purchased a silver smoking set that had the following engraved words: Admiral C. A. F. Sprague, From Ship's Company, U. S. S. FANSHAW BAY, Remembering October 25, 1944.

The crew also sent a delegation to the ship's captain, Capt. D. P. Johnson, who requested that the flag that flew atop the escort carrier during the battle be presented to Sprague. It is rare that men warmly honor an admiral. Sprague would later tell his friends, "I was deeply affected I can assure you."[8]

Since the eventful days of the Battle off Samar, a debate has raged attempting to assess the responsibility of the two key commanders. It is my judgment that both Admiral Halsey and Admiral Kinkaid should share the blame in what went wrong. Each thought the other was carrying out his respective mission. Kinkaid assumed Halsey's ships were where he thought they should be—protecting the eastern approaches of San Bernardino Strait. Halsey assumed that (1) his planes had inflicted too much damage on the Center Force in the Battle of the Sibuyan Sea for Kurita to desire to steam through the San Bernardino Strait; (2) Kinkaid had sent out enough search planes to establish where Kurita was; and (3) Oldendorf's battleships were sufficiently powerful to meet and destroy the Center Force if this force should appear off Samar.

Plainly, Kinkaid and Halsey had made incorrect assumptions. The part of the Japanese SHO-1 plan that concerned luring Halsey's powerful fleet to the north had been successful. Halsey did indeed leave the San Bernardino Strait wide open for Kurita to pass through. Perhaps if all American forces had been required to report to a single theater commander, this situation never would have developed. But it did. Only the courage and boldness of the individual task group commanders, the ships' captains, and the individual crew members prevented a Japanese victory in Leyte Gulf. Their thoughts and actions speak for themselves. Their heroism was true to the highest naval tradition and to the greatest valor of which humans are capable.

However, Halsey's Third Fleet made its presence felt. After Halsey decided to go after Ozawa's Northern Force, his fleet relentlessly pursued them, inflicting great damage in the Battle off Cape Engaño, a battle that would, for all intents and purposes, finish the Imperial Fleet as an effective naval force.

Chapter 17: A Tragic Figure

As pilots returned from missions over the Sibuyan Sea on October 24, a flood of contact and damage reports inundated Task Force 38's flag plot. After Mitscher, Burke, and other members of the admiral's staff completed extensive interviews with a great many pilots, they still were unable to form a definitive picture of the situation because of the conflicting reports and damage assessments from the pilots.

Assuming that the Japanese carriers were still out there to the north, Mitscher ordered Burke to make plans to attack Ozawa's carriers that evening, using a surface force of battleships and cruisers that would be detached from the task groups. When daylight dawned on the morning of the 25th, Task Force 38 aircraft could take off to finish whatever ships remained. Mitscher discussed the planned attack in detail with his staff; but he did not forward the plans to Halsey, thinking they might interfere with plans the latter might be making. In retrospect, his staff expressed the nearly unanimous opinion that Mitscher should have kept Halsey informed.

Meanwhile, at 10:24 P.M. on October 24, Halsey sent a message to Admiral Kinkaid, who was then preparing to face Nishimura's Force C and Shima's cruisers advancing up the Surigao Strait. Halsey's message stated that he was moving north with three task groups to attack the Japanese carriers. All task-group commanders of the Third and Seventh Fleets received the same message. The message to the *Lexington* arrived at 10:29 P.M. Another message from Halsey went to Kinkaid stating that the battle line (Task Force 34) would form and continue northward. Kinkaid interpreted this latest dispatch as saying that the fast battleships were remaining behind to cover the San Bernardino Strait. This dispatch proved to be a controversial advisory message, as matters turned out, one that was no more than an expression of Halsey's plan and not an actual order that was issued to the Third Fleet.

When Halsey's message arrived, Mitscher interpreted it as meaning that Halsey had assumed tactical command of Task Force 38 and, thus, that he was relieved of any further command responsibilities. Although Halsey had never issued formal orders effecting a change in command, naval command discipline, in reality, dictated that these messages could not be interpreted in any other way. As Mitscher went to bed that night, realizing that two tactical commanders could never decide a battle's course, he ruminated unhappily that "Admiral Halsey is in command now."

Before Mitscher left the flag plot for some long-deserved rest, Burke, concerned about the whereabouts of the Japanese Center Force, observed, "We'd better see where that fleet is." Gazing steadily at Burke, Mitscher answered, "Yes."

Since the early afternoon of the 24th, Task Force 38's staff worried about Kurita's force because of the returning pilots' contradictory, confusing damage reports on the Japanese heavy ships. Halsey, however, was actually acting on the assumption that these ships had been too heavily damaged to pose a threat to the Seventh Fleet when he decided to send Task Force 38 northward. He regarded the oncoming Northern Force with its still-undamaged Japanese carriers to be a far greater threat to the Leyte beaches and to the American ships off-loading supplies in Leyte Gulf than Kurita's Center Force.

However, a busy Admiral Kinkaid, more concerned about the Japanese Southern Force to the south in the Surigao Strait, did not know that Halsey had ordered *all* of the Third Fleet's carriers and fast battleships away from the eastern exit of the San Bernardino Strait. Based on Halsey's order to form the battleships into a task group, Kinkaid assumed that the fast battleships had been separated in order to protect the Seventh Fleet, while the rest of the Third Fleet had moved northward.

About 10:45 P.M., Halsey's staff received an alarming report from an *Independence* search plane stating that the Japanese Center Force was not as heavily damaged as had been assumed and that it was still moving toward the San Bernardino Strait.

Burke and Cmdr. James Flatlet, Task Force 38's staff operations officer, examined the search-plane's contact report. Knowing Mitscher's health was deteriorating, Burke decided not to wake up the admiral until another report arrived confirming the original sighting. He did not have long to wait. Twenty minutes after the first message arrived, Burke received another message clipped to a dispatch board that not only confirmed the first report, but stated that the Center Force was persistently moving northwest at 12 knots with their bows pointed straight toward the San Bernardino Strait.

As Mitscher slept soundly in his sea cabin, Flatlet examined the chart, made a large X on the San Bernardino Strait, and left the flag plot to wake up Mitscher. To both Burke and Flatlet, the Japanese intentions were clear. They saw the only answer to this impending disaster was to disconnect the fast battleships immediately from the task force and send them rapidly south to the Philippines' soft middle—off Samar.

Flatlet entered Mitscher's sea cabin and shook the admiral awake. Mitscher had been sleeping on his side. Raising himself on one elbow, he tried to shake away the sleep cobwebs. Flatlet exclaimed urgently, "Admiral, we'd better tell Halsey to turn around." Mitscher's eyes widened as Flatlet related the *Independence*'s search plane's report.

"Does Admiral Halsey have that report?" he asked.

"Yes, he does," Flatlet replied ominously.

Resigned to the fact that he was not in tactical command, and doing everything he could to hide his anger over having been unceremoniously removed from the responsibilities he thought were rightfully his, Mitscher declared in his characteristically soft voice, "If he wants my advice, he'll ask for it." And with that, he rolled over, leaving his back toward Flatlet, and fell asleep.

From that moment on, Mitscher relinquished any further responsibility over the command of Task Force 38 until its search planes made contact with Ozawa's Northern Force. For the next few hours, as Halsey pursued the Japanese Northern Force, the exhausted admiral became a bystander in the upcoming action, making no important decisions. Halsey was in charge. Mitscher had neither the will nor the strength to dispute this fact.

When Mitscher left for Ulithi at the end of October to receive a well-deserved respite from the war, Admiral McCain took command of Task Force 38. In writing his final action report while serving as commander of Task Force 38, Mitscher spoke for all the men serving in the task force as well as for himself:

> It is one very nice thing to have the ships, but it is also a very serious responsibility to keep these same ships ready for battle, their crews enthusiastic and ready to fight. Attention is invited to the fact that the ships of Third Fleet 58/38 have been under constant pressure in the tropics for over ten months. Probably ten thousand men had not put a foot on shore during this period. No other force in the world has been subjected to such a period of constant operation without rest or rehabilitation. The spirit of these ships is commendable. However, the reactions of their crews are slowed down. The result is that they are not completely effective against attack.

However, it is important to bear one fact in mind: Mitscher wanted to remain in command of Task Force 58/38. Yet during the short passage to Ulithi, he spent most of the time in his cabin bunk. Realizing that his superior was too tired to continue his work, Burke left orders that the admiral was not be disturbed. Halsey, however, realized it was time to make a change. So, with Nimitz's permission, Halsey relieved Mitscher, and, when the *Lexington* was anchored at Ulithi, Halsey offered his seaplane to fly Mitscher back to Pearl Harbor.

As the late afternoon of October 31 wore down, rumors circulated in the *Lexington* to the effect that Mitscher would be leaving early the next morning. In the early hours of November 1, Mitscher climbed down several decks and walked through the dimly lit hangar deck. Showing an almost reverent respect for their leader, more than a hundred people stood near the after brow. Almost all of the *Lexington*'s Air Group 19 were there, even though they had not gotten a full night's sleep in weeks. The group's commander, Hugh Winters, set his alarm for 3:30 A.M., then awakened the pilots who volunteered to miss a few hours sleep in order to pay their respects. Some were in uniform while others stood in the background dressed in pajamas and bathrobes, quietly waiting.

As Mitscher came into view, he looked around. Surprised, he asked Burke, "What the devil are all these people doing here?" "I don't know, Admiral," Burke replied. Winters answered the admiral's question, "Well, Admiral, they just wanted to be here when you left."

Trying to hold his emotions in check, the admiral moved quickly to the carrier's side, descended the gangway's stairs, and got into his barge.

As he sat in the barge, its engine chugging in the water, the men saw him take out a handkerchief and rub his eyes.[1]

Mitscher would return to command the task force before and during the kamikaze attacks off Okinawa. He lived to see victory over Japan but finally succumbed to the stress of those many months of tense combat conditions. He died on February 1, 1946.[2]

Chapter 18: Cape of Fools

The location of the Japanese carriers puzzled Halsey and his staff. Experience with Japanese naval warfare had shown that when large formations of capital ships were present, the carriers were not far away. But no carriers had been spotted. Neither American submarines nor search planes had found any in the vicinity of the Chinese coast or around the waters in the Singapore-Brunei area. If any Japanese carriers were going to attack the American Philippine operations, Halsey and his staff surmised they were based in, and would have to come southward from the Japanese home islands.

It was Admiral Sherman's responsibility to search the seas for Japanese ships, since his northernmost Task Group was located nearest to the point from where Ozawa's carriers would come. But by late afternoon on the 24th, no search planes had been sent to seek out the Japanese carriers, because Sherman's group had been occupied with the sinking *Princeton*. As afternoon approached and no Japanese carriers had been sighted, Halsey's aviation officer, Douglas Mouton, pounded the charts in the *New Jersey*'s map room exclaiming, "Where in hell *are* those goddamn Nip carriers?"

Just before 5:00 P.M., sighting reports of the carriers finally began arriving into Halsey's flag plot. Halsey's patience had worn thin waiting for them, but answers were not forthcoming because Sherman had not launched search planes until late afternoon. The American scouts finally reported sighting Japanese carriers to the north, divided into two sections. The most-distant section was 180 miles east of Cape Engaño and had at least three carriers, four to six cruisers, and about six destroyers. Nearer by were the two converted battleships, *Ise* and *Hyuga*, which the Japanese had modified to have shortened flight decks to accommodate landing and launching aircraft; the light cruiser *Tama*; and four destroyers.

Meanwhile, the *Princeton* burned furiously in the looming dark, providing a bright navigational beacon for the oncoming Japanese carriers. Mitscher asked for permission to scuttle the doomed light carrier, which Halsey approved. Halsey then sent a message to MacArthur and Nimitz that informed them the Japanese carriers had been found.

With the Japanese carriers sighted, Halsey and his staff set to work to come up with a plan to counter the Japanese attack plan, which was now becoming apparent. The Southern and Center Forces were heading for the Leyte beaches to attack the American amphibious ships, and they planned to converge near the Leyte beaches at dawn on October 25. The Southern Force continued northward, likely to arrive on schedule. The Center Force, which had reversed course, was not likely to arrive in Leyte Gulf before 11:00 A.M.

Halsey's staff judged that Oldendorf's battle line could intercept the Southern Force as it traversed the Surigao Strait. It could destroy the Southern Force at night before the Center Force could arrive. Even though the old American battleships were slower than the modern Japanese ships, Oldendorf was able to set a static defense by using their 14- and 16-inch guns to destroy the Japanese ships when and if Kurita's force came within range.[1]

Meanwhile, the Japanese had set the bait. And what tempting bait it was! The Japanese Northern Force had the only aircraft carriers the Americans would face during the Battle of Leyte Gulf. Halsey had some of his greatest successes in World War II with carriers under his command. After the Pearl Harbor debacle, his ships were the only ones that attacked the Japanese with any success until the Battle of the Coral Sea.

Halsey had established himself as a leading proponent of naval air power and had always felt that his mission was to destroy the Japanese navy. With such tempting targets as Admiral Ozawa's carriers to the north, Halsey made the decision to go after the Japanese carriers. The aftermath of that decision was a resounding Japanese defeat, but, in another sense, it was a hollow victory, for it left the Leyte landing force vulnerable to attack.

• • •

On October 24 at 10:22 P.M., the Third Fleet changed course north-ward. The carrier *Independence*, which had the only planes capable of night reconnaissance, recalled its planes, which had been tracking Kurita's Center Force while still in the Sibuyan Sea, and now the San Bernardino Strait was left unwatched and unguarded. All minds, eyes, radar, search planes, and hearts in the Third Fleet looked hungrily north-ward for Ozawa's carriers—doing exactly what the Japanese had hoped they would do. One year later, Ozawa stated, "My chief concern was to lure your forces farther north. We expected complete destruction."[2] Their expectations were met.

The Americans outgunned and overpowered the approaching Japanese. However, since they were determined to sacrifice themselves, so that Kurita's Center Force and Nishimura's Southern Force could wreak havoc on the Leyte beaches, this was an ironic victory. The American Task Force 38 was a juggernaut of American sea power. Even without McCain's Task Group 38.1 on its way to Ulithi, it had overwhelming advantages over the Japanese Northern Force, as the following tables make clear:

Task Force 38 (as of Oct. 24, 1944)
VAdm. M. A. Mitscher in *Lexington*

Task Group 38.2 RAdm. G. F. Bogan	Task Group 38.3 RAdm. F. C. Sherman	Task Group 38.4 RAdm. R. E. Davison
Fleet Carriers *Intrepid*	**Fleet Carriers** *Essex, Lexington*	**Fleet Carriers** *Enterprise, Franklin*
Light Carriers *Cabot, Independence*	**Light Carriers** *Langley*	**Light Carriers** *San Jacinto, Belleau Wood*
Battleships *Iowa, New Jersey,* *South Dakota*	**Battleships** *Massachusetts*	**Battleships** *Washington, Alabama*
Light Cruisers *Biloxi, Vincennes, Miami*	**Light Cruisers** *Santa Fe, Mobile, Reno*	**Heavy Cruisers** *New Orleans, Wichita*
Destroyers 18	**Destroyers** 10	**Destroyers** 12

Facing the Third Fleet's sixty-four ships, the Japanese Northern Force's twenty-six ships were nowhere near as formidable, but this force was the best the Japanese could muster given its severe losses in the Battle of the Philippine Sea.

Northern Force
Vice Admiral J. Ozawa in *Zuikaku*

Carrier Division 3	**Carrier Division 4**
Fleet carrier *Zuikaku*	Converted battleships *Ise, Hyuga*
Light carriers *Zuiho, Chitose, Chiyoda*	—
Light cruisers *Izuzu, Oyodo*	Light cruiser *Tama*
Five destroyers, two tankers,	Four destroyers
six escort vessels	

Carrier Division 3 carried fifty-two fighters, twenty-eight bombers, thirty-two torpedo-bombers, and four high-level bombers for a total of 116 planes, while Carrier Division 4 had no planes at all.

Halsey faced a number of problems as he prepared his fleet for combat with the Japanese. The first was gathering together his widely scattered task groups. McCain's Task Group 38.1 had been steaming for Ulithi when Halsey recalled it to join the Third Fleet. While steaming toward Leyte Gulf, McCain had received additional orders to help Cliff Sprague. Therefore, McCain would not arrive in time to have any effect on the effort to destroy Ozawa's force. Bogan's Task Group 38.2, which included Halsey's flagship *New Jersey*, was off the San Bernardino Strait with Davison's Group 38.4 to the south. Meanwhile, Sherman's Task Group 38.3 was steaming southeasterly off Luzon Island to the north. Halsey issued orders just after 10:00 P.M. on the 24th for each task group to join him in his quest to destroy Ozawa. Task Groups 38.2, 38.3, and 38.4 would join up at about 11:45 P.M.

Although the Third Fleet did not have its largest task group—McCain's Task Group 38.1—what was left was still a naval force of enormous power. Imagine standing on the bridge of one of these fast carriers and scanning the surrounding horizon with binoculars as ships of every size and type filled your field of vision, almost blotting out the horizon. You would see five Essex-class fast carriers, five light carriers, six battleships, two heavy cruisers, six light cruisers, and forty destroyers, along with hundreds of bombers and fighters.

At 1:00 A.M. on October 25, the light carrier *Independence* held its position on the fleet's weather side. She turned into the wind and launched five radar-equipped aircraft to search a 50-degree northern sector between 320 degrees and 10 degrees from a 350-mile range. Meanwhile, Kurita reassembled his forces after their struggle with American aircraft in the Sibuyan Sea and exited the San Bernardino Strait, heading southward around Samar. Nishimura approached the Surigao Strait sailing north to a tragic destiny.

An Attempt for Halsey to Retrieve His Honor

At 8:00 A.M. on October 25, the first of five air strikes attacked Ozawa's force with Helldiver bombers, fighter planes, and Avenger torpedo planes. The end of what had been the magnificent Imperial Japanese Fleet was fast approaching. That day, the Americans flew 527 sorties with 431 planes. Although the American attacks were hardly any surprise to Ozawa, he was not going to sacrifice his force without vigorously defending it. By this time, the battleships *Ise* and *Hyuga* had rejoined the carriers, supplying the Japanese with a formidable antiaircraft defense. Positioning his ships so as to put up the best antiaircraft fire possible, Ozawa ordered the *Hyuga* to open fire at 8:17 A.M. and the light cruiser *Oyodo* to open fire ten minutes later as the American torpedo-bombers launched torpedoes from almost a point-blank range of between 1,400 and 1,600 yards away and from altitudes between 700 and 1,000 feet.

The experiences of the *Essex*'s Air Group 15 illustrate what had happened during that first strike. Their action report tells the story best:

> Searches were launched at dawn on the 25th to regain contact with the enemy's carriers. In addition to the regular search teams a 4 plane VF [fighter] division on CAP [Combat Air Patrol] over the disposition led by Lieutenant J. J. Collins . . . was diverted to a high-speed search mission. At 0710 just as this fighter search made a turn at the end of its northern leg, the enemy was sighted 18 miles beyond by Lieutenant Collins' wingman, Lieutenant Voorhest. Voorhest directed Collins' attention to the enemy disposition. Lieutenant Collins then reported the contacts, retired, gained altitude, and returned to observe the enemy from 18,000 feet until forced to return to base because of low fuel at 0840 at which time all attacks of Strike I had been completed.

Air Group 15's fourteen fighters, under Cmdr. David McCampbell—the same man who had considerable success the previous day over the Sibuyan Sea—was ordered to search for Japanese ships but found nothing. However, when Collins did locate the Japanese, the strike group was only 50 miles away from Ozawa's fleet. Collins reported this to Mc-

Campbell, who then ordered his fighters to attack. While four of their comrades flew protective cover, ten pilots headed in with each plane carrying a 500-pound bomb. Meanwhile, McCampbell flew high above his group to coordinate their strikes. The ten bomb-carrying fighters went into a steep high-speed dive and dropped their bombs on the destroyer screen, which sent up strong antiaircraft fire, and the pilots strafed as they pulled out.

When one of the northernmost Japanese carriers launched about eighteen to twenty Zero fighters during their first strike, four American fighters counterattacked, shooting down eight and then probably three more Japanese planes. One American fighter took several machine-gun hits and was shot down in flames. The pilot bailed out safely, however, and was rescued by an American destroyer late in the afternoon. The rest of Air Group 15's fighters returned safely to base.

Some of the Japanese fought back vigorously in the air and on the sea. Only one American plane was lost, and the pilot was Lt. Joseph R. Strane. His personal experience provides insight into the skill and dedication of both sides in this conflict.

After bombing and strafing the carriers, Strane saw five or six Zeroes to the left and 9,000 feet above him. As the American dive-bombers retired below him, Strane's team followed to provide cover, then climbed but did not attack the Japanese fighters until the Japanese began their assault.

Just as one Japanese fighter pulled away from its attack, Strane set the plane on fire on his first pass using several machine-gun bursts from below the luckless Japanese pilot. He saw the plane crash into the water. Next, Strane saw his wingman begin a diving turn to the left, and as he rolled over, he saw two Zeroes firing at his companion. Strane continued his dive, moving into an ideal firing position astern and above both Zeroes, and set them on fire by riveting short bursts of machine-gun fire into each one. Both Zeroes splashed into the ocean below. At this time, he saw that his wingman, who was to the left ahead, was recovering from the Zeroes' attack. When he looked to his rear for his section, he did not see any other American planes. However, he did see many Zeroes. Turning toward the nearest one, he fired a short burst that started smoke and flames belching from it. He did not see it crash because shells from another Zero firing from ahead of him struck his plane. Strane tried to roll toward this Japanese plane to get a shot, but he did not quite make it before the Zero flew directly in front of and over him. It was at this time that his engine failed.

His plane began smoking badly and burst into flames. Another Zero then shot at him, scoring several hits on his port side, causing his instrument panel to fall apart. Strane thought about trying to put out the fire in the cockpit so he could ditch, but the fire was too intense to be extinguished; he picked up his microphone, reported his position over his undamaged radio, and got ready to bail out. His parachute's cords and survival raft tangled twice on the cockpit enclosure. He leaped from his plane's wing from an altitude of 2,500 feet. As Strane descended, he saw two Zekes circling, so he delayed pulling his chute's rip cord as late as possible.

However, Strane almost waited too long. When his parachute opened, he made only one swing before hitting the water. Trying to disentangle himself from the parachute's shrouds, he swallowed quite a bit of seawater. Nonetheless, he managed to rid himself of the shrouds, drag out his inflatable raft that had been stored in his aircraft, inflate it, and climb into it. Strane fired three Very cartridges—flares to identify his location—at low-flying search planes throughout the day. However, the bright sun kept the planes from seeing him in the water. He watched as more than 350 planes attacked the Japanese ships. Strane covered himself for protection from the strong sun and slept fitfully. At 4:00 P.M., Strane saw an American ship 9,000 yards away and succeeded in attracting its attention by using his mirror. It picked him up, finding him more than a little relieved at surviving his ordeal. The ship's captain allowed him to watch his compatriots in the air finish sinking the carrier he had attacked. Later that evening, he saw the American surface ships sink a Japanese cruiser.

The American dive-bombers from the *Essex* were just as busy as the carrier's fighter planes. Lieutenant John David Bridgers led fifteen Helldivers as they rendezvoused with McCampbell's fighters and torpedo planes. The *Essex*'s CIC directed them to a point 50 miles north of the carrier, where they orbited at 12,000 feet as air groups from the other American carriers joined them. The communications relay planes radioed a contact report that caused the dive-bombers to climb to 14,500 feet and head for the Japanese fleet. One dive-bomber had to drop out of the formation and return to its base due to engine trouble.

Acting as target coordinator, McCampbell assigned the *Essex*'s group to attack a Chitose-class light carrier in the Japanese fleet. As the

Japanese carrier seemed to be in the process of launching planes, the dive-bombers moved into attack position and began a high-speed approach from the south. Advancing on the Japanese ship with the bright sun in the Japanese gunners' eyes, the pilots accelerated to 240 knots and broke into attack groups from 11,000 feet. The planes these pilots flew were the first to reach and attack the Japanese formation. During their approach, the Japanese threw up heavy antiaircraft fire as many batteries concentrated on the one formation. The American planes dove from the northeast, released twelve bombs at the light carrier, with eight of them observed directly hitting it. As the attack progressed, the Japanese light carrier began a slight turn, then resumed its original course, and made no attempt to evade the oncoming American planes. After completing their attack, the *Essex*'s dive-bombers left the scene, with flames engulfing the carrier, appearing on the verge of sinking.

The *Essex*'s torpedo planes took part in the action. Twelve torpedo planes, led by Lt. Cmdr. V. G. Lambert, each carrying a torpedo, left the *Essex*'s flight deck at 6:15 A.M. to attack a Japanese carrier task force whose reported position was about 250 miles east of northern Luzon. With the dive-bombers leading and the fighters flying cover, the torpedo planes circled for about thirty minutes until they received a report that the Japanese force had been sighted. On his way to the target, and with about 30 miles to go, Lt. (jg) C. G. Hurd noted that the plane's heating system had caught fire, forcing him to jettison his torpedo and return to base.

As the American torpedo planes began their attack, the ships' movements seemed chaotic and disorganized, making it impossible for the American fliers to discern a clear pattern. It seemed that the ships were trying to form a circle. McCampbell ordered the torpedo planes to coordinate their attack with the dive-bombers and fighters on a Japanese light carrier that appeared to be of the Chitose-class type. An attack was planned. The attack was to be on its rear starboard side. The planes descended from 10,000 feet to between 6,000 and 7,000 feet. Upon reaching that altitude, Lambert divided his torpedo-bombers to attack from both sides of the carrier.

When the torpedo-bombers started their attack runs, the American dive-bombers were already attacking with bombs exploding on the carrier's flight deck. The carrier burned so fiercely now that it was no longer operational, so McCampbell ordered the torpedo-bombers to concentrate on the converted battleship *Ise* near to their port side.

However, four pilots had already begun their attack runs on the light carrier when they heard the new orders over the radio. As three pilots attacked from the southwest, the ship made a hard turn to starboard, so they dropped their torpedoes on the ship's starboard side while a fourth plane attacked from the east on the port side.

Lieutenant (jg) M. P. Deputy and Lt. (jg) L. G. Muskin dropped their torpedoes, which ran hot, straight and normal toward the carrier. Lieutenant (jg) J. C. Huggins dropped his also. As he flew over the carrier, his crew looked back and reported two large explosions near the bow. Ensign Kenneth B. Horton dropped his torpedo. Both he and his crewmen saw it run hot and explode on the carrier's aft port side. These assaults finished the carrier, and by the time the strike ended, it sank beneath the waves.

Meanwhile, the other torpedo plane pilots responded to McCampbell's new orders and changed their attack runs in order to strike the battleship *Ise*. Lieutenant (jg) H. D. Jolly dropped his torpedo off the ship's starboard bow and thought he got a hit. Ensign P. J. Ward dropped his torpedo below *Ise*'s number 2 turret and saw two explosions, one of which he thought was his. Directing his aim toward the starboard bow, Lt. (jg) J. Smith dropped his missile and thought he got a hit.

McCampbell ordered the rest of the torpedo-bombers to focus on a Zuiho-class carrier. Lieutenant Charles William H. Sorenson and his wingman, Lt. (jg) L. R. Timberlake, found the new target and dropped their torpedoes, which they believed ran true, exploding on impact. Lieutenant (jg) S. M. Holladay aimed his torpedo at the carrier and thought his also hit and exploded on the carrier's side.

These attacks completed, Air Group 15's torpedo planes climbed and turned toward the *Essex*, flying by a few Japanese fighters that seemed to ignore them. All the torpedo planes returned safely.

This narrative traces in detail the action of one American carrier's air group in order to give a close-up of the action and offensive approach used by the Americans. In fact, the planes from ten carriers attacked Ozawa's force on that day, so if one multiplies the impact achieved by one air group by ten, it is evident these aircraft inflicted a great deal of damage on Ozawa's force.[3]

Returning now to a more general description of the battle, only twelve to fifteen Japanese aircraft flew combat air patrol. Their orders were to not sacrifice themselves needlessly; therefore these planes did not have much impact. However, Ozawa did order the use of brisk, intense anti-aircraft fire, including large-caliber phosphorous shells when the attacking Americans were 10 miles away.

The American planes immediately sank the destroyer *Akitsuki* with several bombs and hit the light carrier *Chitose* with several bomb hits, three below the waterline. This attack finished the carrier, and she rapidly lost way and sank beneath the waves. Another light carrier, the *Zuiho*, changed course into the wind and tried launching the few planes she had on her flight deck. Torpedo planes from the *Essex* and *Lexington* tried to attack the carrier but missed. She did not escape damage during that first wave's attacks, however. A plane from the *Intrepid* dropped a bomb on her, though this did not slow her down.

One torpedo hit the big carrier *Zuikaku*. The hit caused her to lose all communications and to list 6 degrees. Ozawa then transferred his flag to the light cruiser *Oyodo*, because the large carrier's steering mechanism had been damaged, making maneuvering extremely difficult. At least nine Japanese planes crashed into the sea. Now Ozawa had but six planes left. The American attack, however, proceeded according to the Japanese plan by keeping the Third Fleet totally occupied and not interfering with Kurita's Center Force.

The planes for the Americans' second strike were in the air about one hour before the first strike's aircraft returned to their ships. This second strike consisted of sixteen torpedo planes, six bombers, and fourteen fighters and assaulted the Japanese fleet between 9:45 and 10:00 A.M. Meanwhile, at 9:57, Davison's group detected twenty to twenty-five Japanese planes, most likely land-based craft, closing in on Task Force 38. An already aloft, alert American Combat Air Patrol immediately intercepted these planes, and when the inexperienced Japanese pilots saw the approaching American fighters, they turned and fled.

The absence of an effective Japanese combat air patrol allowed the Americans to station aircraft above the battle so they could relay damage reports to attacking aircraft. When planes from one strike returned, they shared their observations with the aircrews of the next phalanx of planes. When the second strike arrived on the scene, the Japanese ships were steaming in all directions, trying to avoid the persistently attacking American aircraft. Dive-bombers from the *Lexington* and *Franklin* closed on the light carrier *Chiyoda*, scoring several direct hits. Flames covered the unfortunate ship, water flooded her compartments, and she developed a pronounced list. Then, at 10:18 A.M., a bomb hit made her dead in the water. The converted battleship *Hyuga* tried towing the carrier away, but by now the third American strike had arrived, preventing further aid. The cruiser *Izuzu* and the destroyer *Maki* tried unsuccessfully to remove the carrier's crew, but the fires were too intense. So, the *Chiyoda* was abandoned with her crew still on board. At 4:30 P.M., American destroyers put her out of her misery.

Lieutenant C. O. Roberts saw from his fuel gauge that he had enough fuel to keep going for a while, so he maneuvered his Wildcat fighter to circle above Ozawa's fleet. After forty-five minutes of flying, Roberts radioed a report about what was happening below. The Japanese fleet was no longer aimlessly turning about but was steaming in a straight line. At this stage of the battle, fourteen Japanese ships remained afloat, which meant there was more work for the Americans to do.

Roberts's information was valuable, and Mitscher ordered the third strike to attack Ozawa's main body 102 miles north of the *Lexington*. Their mission was to cripple the remaining Japanese ships so they could be sunk at leisure by the fast battleships, cruisers, and destroyers. Taking off between 11:45 A.M. and noon, it took about one hour to reach the target area. The strike comprised more than 200 planes and was the largest of the day. Three-quarters of the planes had participated in the first strike. Commander T. Hugh Winters relieved Lieutenant Roberts as target coordinator and directed the incoming attack.

The *Lexington*'s planes attacked the *Zuikaku* while the *Essex*'s planes directed their attention at the *Zuiho*. The *Langley*'s planes split their attacks between the two carriers. Immediately after the attack began, three torpedoes simultaneously hit the *Zuikaku* and exploded. Fires erupted all over her, and she settled in the water. Fires also engulfed the *Zuiho* but her damage control crews managed to bring these under control. Increasing her speed to move as fast as she could go, she tried to escape.

Winters remained behind as some of the American's planes started for home and directed more planes at the *Zuiho*. Approximately forty planes hit and severely damaged her. One pilot shouted excitedly over his radio, "I got a hit on a carrier! I got a hit on a carrier!" As Winters flew over the cripples, he looked directly below and saw the *Zuikaku* roll over and sink. The third strike's attack was the most productive air strike of the day. Not only did all the American planes return undamaged, but the Japanese ships from the crippled group that survived the third strike changed course to escape further damage.

But a fourth strike was on the way, having about the same number of planes as the third. Taking off around 1:15 P.M., it arrived over the Northern Force one and one-half hours later. Duplicating the ferocity of the earlier strikes, its planes attacked the Japanese main body, which was 30 miles ahead of the stragglers. Planes from the *Lexington* and *Langley* thought they had hit the *Ise*, but the converted battleship was a tough target to sink. She put up intense antiaircraft fire; only four near misses came close to her. Twenty-seven planes again attacked the crippled *Zuiho* and sank her at 3:16 P.M.

At 4:10, the American's fifth strike took off, arriving over the target area one hour later. Carrying full bomb and torpedo loads from all five American carriers, all the aircraft attacked the *Ise*, but scored thirty-four near misses. The converted battleship's intense antiaircraft fire and effective evasive maneuvers prevented her tormentors from scoring direct hits.

By 5:00 P.M., the Japanese Northern Force was a scattered, depleted fleet. The *Hyuga* and a light cruiser with a second light cruiser following 20 miles behind were making their best speed of 18 knots northward. The fifth attack inflicted seven near misses on the *Hyuga*, but she had not taken a single direct hit all day. A light cruiser, probably the *Tama*, steamed slowly 20 miles off the *Hyuga*'s port beam and trailed oil. The *Ise*, another light cruiser, and three destroyers were trying to rescue the *Zuiho*'s survivors. Sixty miles to the south, American cruisers shelled the light cruiser *Chiyoda*, and, as noted earlier, she sank at 4:30 P.M. Twelve of Ozawa's seventeen ships were still afloat.

A last and sixth air attack of thirty-six planes took off at 5:10 P.M. and claimed some hits. However, it did not sink any ships. Despite all these attacks, Admiral Ozawa did not have much respect for the American pilots after the third strike. According to his chief of staff, "I saw all this bombing and thought the American pilots were not so good."

A superior American force had attacked an inferior enemy naval force with mixed results. The Americans flew 527 sorties and sank four carriers and a destroyer. The pilots of Taffy 2 and Taffy 3, blow for blow, had inflicted much more damage than the fast carrier pilots. Neither experienced any Japanese air opposition.[5]

What Was Ozawa Doing?

Just as October 24 turned into the 25th, Ozawa sent a message to the Combined Fleet Headquarters about what he understood had happened that day. He knew that Kurita had been severely attacked and knew that the attacks on Kurita would continue. He still was moving as quickly as he could to do his part in carrying out the SHO-1 plan, that is, his fleet and its twenty-nine planes were to be sacrificed to draw Halsey away from Kurita.

Earlier on the 24th, he launched his pathetic air strike and professed in interviews after the war complete ignorance about what happened to the planes. He did not even know whether they actually reached their intended targets. If they had, they were most likely part of the land-based air strike that had attacked Forrest Sherman's group. However, no one knew with any degree of certainty what it was that had actually happened. Ozawa knew that the Americans had been tracking his force when darkness descended at dusk on the 24th. Furthermore, he knew that if the Americans continued to track and pursue him that he would turn his force to make certain that he drew Halsey away from Kurita.

By 4:00 A.M. on October 25, Ozawa received a report stating that Nishimura had penetrated the Surigao Strait. Forty minutes later, another message arrived stating that Nishimura had been annihilated. Almost immediately, confusing and unbelievable reports began arriving from land-based air forces describing many different American formations and locations, which made one thing a certainty: Throughout the SHO operation, the Japanese had no real appreciation of the exact nature of the naval power the Americans had brought to the Philippines. Also, they had no real sense of what they were up against in and around Leyte Gulf.

By 7:20 A.M., Ozawa reported to Imperial Headquarters that the Americans were tracking him and sent up a combat air patrol of about a dozen planes. However, he instructed the pilots to avoid wasting themselves uselessly, and with typical Japanese dedication, the pilots followed this order faithfully.

As the American planes attacked in waves, scoring hits on the *Zuikaku*, *Chitose*, *Zuiho*, and other screening ships, the *Zuikaku's* action report provides important insights into this assault, which was a challenge to the men who had to see it through as sacrificial victims.

Let us look at excerpts from the *Zuikaku's* action report for October 24, 1944, for this ship was also the last fleet carrier the Japanese had and Ozawa's flagship. What follows are excerpts from that report, interspersed with other comments:

> 1:00 A.M.: Zuikaku prepares to make 20 knots on thirty minutes' notice, which means firing and readying her boilers.

[The chances of expending large amounts of scarce fuel increases given this rate of speed.]

5:30 A.M.: The crew goes to action stations.

6:00 A.M.: They prepared to make 24 knots immediately and flank speed on fifteen minutes' notice.

[The battle's cadence accelerates.]

6:13 A.M.: Ozawa launches one bomber and five fighter-bombers launched for attack purposes. [One-third of his available planes.]

6:22 A.M.: The cruiser *Tama* reported seeing planes coming in.

6:25 A.M.: Rice balls and other battle rations passed out to the men at their posts.

[Then they waited.]

7:13 A.M.: *Hyuga* reports aircraft on her radar screen, 170 kilometers away.

7:17 A.M.: The *Zuikaku* launches four additional fighters to fly combat air patrol.

7:34 A.M.: Encouraging news arrives that says Kurita has successfully come through the San Bernardino Strait and is battling three American carriers. Worse news arrives. Says one of his search planes springs an oil leak and has to head for its assigned land base.

[With the loss of this search plane, Ozawa loses another means of tracking the Americans.

After all of their preparation, the Japanese continued to wait. However, their crews went to battle call, and they manned their antiaircraft guns. The Americans drew closer, just 100 kilometers away.]

8:07 A.M.: Ozawa launches another nine fighters.

8:08 A.M.: 130 American planes spotted: Bearing, 160 degrees, Distance, 6,000 meters. Ozawa orders the battle flag showing the rising sun and flared rays raised.

[Ozawa was now about to fulfill his mission of carrying out his sacrificial role in the SHO-1 plan. It was the event for which he had been waiting since he left the home islands with the remnant of Japanese naval aviation under his command.

But these American planes were not the only ones heading for his force. The *Hyuga* reported another American formation on its radar, only 90 kilometers away. In just a few minutes, the Japanese Northern Force felt the full fury of Halsey's overwhelming compulsion for revenge when the Americans attacked.

Suddenly, accurate, heavy antiaircraft fire filled the air as the American planes swooped down from the skies. Meanwhile, Commander McCampbell, circling high above the battle, effectively coordinated the attacks.

The action report continues:]

8:17 A.M.: Eleven Grummans approached on bearing 220 degrees divided into two groups.

8:21 A.M.: Opened fire.

8:24 A.M.: Speed 24 knots.

8:29 A.M.: Enemy aircraft [forty bombers, ten attack planes] making continuous dive-bombing and torpedo attacks. Torpedo track on starboard beam.

8:35 A.M.: Torpedo track on port stern. Bomb hit [250 kilograms] on port side amidships.

8:37 A.M.: Torpedo hit on No. 4 generator room [flooded]. List to port, 29.5 degrees. Secondary switchboard control panel, starboard low voltage switch panel, port switch room. No. 10 power line conduit and No. 8 power line conduit flooded. No. 3 foam pump unusable. Power supply for helm cut. Rudder disabled. Carried out direct steering. Port after engine room flooded and unusable. Impossible to remain in engine room due to heat.

8:40 A.M.: Only starboard No. 2 shaft operable.

8:45 A.M.: List corrected to 6 degrees by speedy flooding of tanks. Helm restored by emergency power.

8:46 A.M.: All [radio] transmitters out of commission.

8:54 A.M.: Fire in upper and lower No. 2 hangars [extinguished]. Eight enemy planes 20 degrees to starboard.

8:54 A.M.: Antiair[craft] action.

8:59 A.M.: Check fire.

9:23 A.M.: Message from *Oyodo* "notify condition of your communications equipment." [It was very serious.]

9:27 A.M.: Stow antiaircraft gear.

[The first wave of American planes had finished their work. If any Japanese sailor thought the battle was over, he was sorely mistaken. Three minutes later, the second wave arrived. Reading the action report, one can gain a sense of the highs and lows of Japanese optimism.]

9:50 A.M.: Ammunition in aft magazine shifted to starboard side. [Then came the second wave of planes.]

9:53 A.M.: Large air formation [about thirty planes] coming in 160 degrees to port. [Fourteen Curtiss carrier-bombers.] Anti-air[craft] action. Full speed ahead.

9:58 A.M.: Open fire. [Ten bombers and six to eight attack planes attacking this ship.] Two torpedo tracks on starboard stem.

10:08 A.M.: Check fire. All enemy planes repulsed.

10:22 A.M.: Unidentified aircraft [One Grumman, One Curtiss] sighted.

10:32 A.M.: Hove to for transfer of flag to *Oyodo*.

10:45 A.M.: Submarine apparently 900 [meters] to starboard.

10:51 A.M.: Commander [Ozawa] transferred to boat.

11:00 A.M.: Flag transferred to the *Oyodo*.

11:02 A.M.: Aircraft spotted through closed gaps. Antiair[craft] action. Full speed ahead. Open fire. All carriers of CarDiv 3 unable to recover planes. Nine planes of direct air cover landed in water.

The same ferocity of action continued for the next four waves of American air assaults. Ozawa's communications aboard the doomed *Zuikaku* were lost, and he had no choice but to transfer his flag to the cruiser *Oyodo*. The destroyer *Hatsuzuki* picked up Lieutenant Kobayashi, the air-cover commander, and at least seven others. The Japanese estimated they had shot down six Grummans and three bombers. Ozawa's spirits lifted when good news came in from the south that Kurita's Center Force had sunk three or four American carriers and one cruiser.[6]

One piece of news omitted from Kurita's dispatch was that he had turned around and changed the Battle of Leyte Gulf's outcome.

A Pursuit on the Surface

At 9:00 A.M., about forty-five minutes prior to the second air strike on the Japanese, Halsey received Kinkaid's plain-language message that Kurita's Center Force was off Samar. Prior to this time, at 8:30, Halsey had received an urgent plea for help from Sprague, and at 8:38, he received one from Kinkaid asking for assistance either on sea or in the air. In response, Halsey issued an order at 8:48 for McCain's task group "to proceed at best possible speed" and attack the Japanese fleet, even though it was not feasible for McCain to arrive at Leyte quickly, because McCain was refueling to the east. Still, Halsey refused to detach Admiral Lee's battleships (Task Force 34) to block Kurita's escape until it was too late.

Nimitz's controversial inquiry about the whereabouts of Task Force 34 arrived on the *New Jersey* shortly after 10:00 A.M. Halsey wanted to keep the battleships with him to pursue and sink any of Ozawa's cripples and the yet undamaged *Ise* and *Hyuga*. The pressure to help the Seventh Fleet increased tremendously. After seventy-five minutes of careful thought, Halsey relented. His action report said: "Although Task Force 34 was within 42 miles of the crippled Northern Force, Commander Third Fleet at 1115 turned back Group 38.2 [plus four battleships] south and dispatched T.G. 34.5, Rear Admiral [Oscar C.] Badger, ahead at high speed to the assistance of the Seventh Fleet Forces."

Halsey had no wish to send his battleships south. He wanted to keep them so they could sink the remnants of Ozawa's sacrificial lambs. But CINCPAC could not be denied, so Halsey sent his ships to help Sprague's beleaguered escort carriers and the endangered landing fleet.

Lee's six battleships steamed at only 20 knots, then slowed to about 12 knots in order to refuel its screening destroyers. However, four of Lee's battleships did not head south but stayed behind with the bulk of the Third Fleet. After finishing refueling, the group then reformed into Task Group 34.5 with only two battleships and pushed southward at 28 knots. Task Group 34.5 thus included Badger's flagship *Iowa*, Halsey's flagship *New Jersey*, three light cruisers, and eight destroyers. Admiral Bogan's Task Group 38.2 and its carriers sailed eastward to provide air cover and supply air support if needed.

Admiral Badger was ordered to appear off the San Bernardino Strait at 1:00 A.M. on October 26, sweep its approaches, continue along Samar's eastern coast, and sink any enemy ships he might encounter. Unfortunately for the Americans, Kurita's Center Force had already escaped when they had passed through the San Bernardino Strait three hours earlier. The only warship left behind from the Center Force was the wounded destroyer *Nowaki*. The Americans sank this unfortunate straggler at 1:10 A.M. Badger's group then continued southward but found only six survivors from the heavy cruiser *Suzuya*.

If the entire Task Force 34 had heeded Kinkaid's first plea for help, and if it had not slowed down to refuel the destroyers, the Americans would have arrived in time to face Kurita's force. What an encounter this would have been! The most modern battleships in the world under Lee's command would have faced off against the best battleships the Japanese had. As America's most experienced battle group commander, Admiral Lee was more than a match for the reluctant, gun-shy Kurita.

But this encounter never took place, so one can only speculate as to how any battle between two surface forces would have played out. The Iowa-class battleships were faster than those in the Japanese force and more competently commanded. Thus, it is quite possible that Lee would have crossed Kurita's "T" and utterly destroyed the Center Force. Compelled to approach the San Bernardino Strait's eastern entrance in single file with the Americans blocking their path—a perfect setup for a crossing the T maneuver—the Japanese would have had no way to escape. Although this would not have altered the overall outcome of the Battle of Leyte Gulf, it would have compensated for Halsey's error in judgment.

However, the ships under Badger's command that did arrive had only two battleships, three light cruisers, and eight destroyers. Although Bogan's carriers were nearby and would have put up a good fight against Kurita's Center Force, it is clear that the Americans would have been outgunned even had they arrived in time. A clear American victory was possible only if Halsey's entire force had arrived in time.

As most of Task Force 34 sailed south, the light cruisers *Santa Fe*, *Mobile*, *Wichita*, *New Orleans* and nine destroyers, under RAdm. Laurence T. DuBose's command, continued north with the carriers, except for Bogan's task group. Commander Winters, flying as air coordinator, flew over the dead-in-the-water *Chiyoda* and spotted DuBose's cruisers on the horizon. He directed the fall of shot as the cruisers opened fire on the doomed Japanese carrier. After thirty minutes of deadly accurate pummeling by the American cruisers and destroyers' guns, she rolled over on her back and slid beneath the waves.

After the *Chiyoda* sank, the American cruisers continued northward. Two night-fighters from the *Essex* coached the approaching ships toward the destroyer *Hatsuzuki* and two smaller destroyers. As the Americans came within 14 miles of the Japanese destroyers, the *Wichita* fired. The *Hatsuzuki* returned fire and increased its speed in order to escape. DuBose observed the Japanese destroyer's movements on the radar screen as the destroyer prepared to deliver a torpedo attack. But DuBose, making use of hard-won experience, ordered his cruisers to execute a set of drastic, evasive maneuvers to avoid the potential threat.

The Americans resumed chasing the Japanese ships at 28 knots and gradually closed the range. DuBose ordered the destroyers *Clarence L. Bronson*, *Cotten*, and *Patterson* ahead to attack the retreating Japanese ships with torpedoes. Several hit the *Hatsuzuki,* causing her to slow. The cruisers meanwhile closed to 6,000 yards, illuminated the doomed destroyer with star shells, and, employing the deliberative motions of an experienced surgeon, they slowly brought the hapless destroyer under fire. After sustaining this calculatingly destructive attack, the *Hatsuzuki* blew up, leaving a circle of rubble floating on the sea.

DuBose, however, nearly became a victim himself. Admiral Ozawa overheard radio transmissions from the *Hatsuzuki* while under siege, so he collected the *Ise, Hyuga,* his light cruiser flagship, the *Oyodo,* and one destroyer, and tried to come to the beleaguered destroyer's aid. But he was too late. The *Hatsuzuki* and her American tormentors were gone. Ozawa continued southward, hoping to engage the American ships with gunfire, but, in the end, he gave up the chase and resumed his northward course. Had these two forces met, the Americans would have faced a more powerful Japanese force of two converted battleships against DuBose's four cruisers. The outcome, at best, would have been uncertain.

Two *Independence* night fighters spotted the Japanese ships steaming north at 22 knots. The ships' position was abeam of the Bashi Channel, which is the northernmost passage between the Philippines and Formosa. Even if DuBose's cruisers had increased their speed to 30 knots, they could not have overtaken the retreating Japanese before dawn. This would have put the pursuing Americans in danger of a land-based Japanese air attack.

DuBose re-formed his force into a circular formation and retired. His ships had not sustained any damage from Japanese gunfire, although the *Santa Fe* had been straddled by the *Hatsuzuki*'s guns. The gallant Japanese destroyer won the admiration and respect of the Americans. Many American sailors thought the *Hatsuzuki* was not a destroyer but a heavy cruiser—the same compliment paid by the Japanese to the American destroyers off Samar.

American Submarines Enter the Fray

Vice Admiral Charles A. Lockwood, Commander Submarines Pacific, received a radio message from Admiral Mitscher ten hours from the time of its dispatch. The Americans' split command structure again caused an overly long communication's delay at the Manus Island decoding station. This dispatch warned that Mitscher would be pursuing the Japanese, and that he expected American pilots to be splashing into the sea. He wanted Lockwood's submarines to pick up any downed pilots before they fell into Japanese hands or perished. Lockwood responded that his submarines would try their best.

Two wolf packs of three submarines each—the *Haddock, Tuna,* and *Halibut* under the Cmdr. J. P. Roach (Roach's Raiders), and the *Pintado, Jallao* and *Atule,* led by Cmdr. B. A. Clarey (Clarey's Crushers)—proceeded from Saipan to the Luzon Strait on the 24th. The next morning they received orders from Admiral Lockwood to sail at maximum speed to a position such that they could sink cripples or pick up downed pilots. By 6:30 P.M. on the 25th, Clarey's Crushers established positions on an east-west line with 20 miles between boats, while Roach's Raiders went to the west with their submarines 15 miles apart.

The *Halibut* slid through the sea on the surface. Its sonar had picked up explosions in the distance and heard radio chatter from American pilots. At 5:42 P.M., the *Ise's* pagoda-like superstructure, a now familiar characteristic of Japanese capital ships, appeared about 31,000 yards away in the bridge lookouts' glasses. The American submarine dove to periscope depth. After its periscope rose, the cruiser *Oyodo,* now Ozawa's flagship, appeared in the scope's glass. The submarine made a classic approach, firing six torpedoes at what the crew thought was the *Ise.* After the torpedoes had run their course, five explosions rumbled in the ocean, followed by the sickening noise of a ship breaking apart. The *Halibut* later surfaced and searched the battle area. A hull was sighted keel-up but could not be identified. Later combat reports credited the *Halibut* with sinking the destroyer *Akitsuki.* Subsequent Japanese reports stated, however, that the *Akitsuki* was sunk by air attacks on October 25. So what had the *Halibut* encountered? No one knows. It remains a mystery to this day.

The *Halibut* continued pursuing the *Ise* and *Hyuga,* both of which had escaped in the darkness. The chase continued, but the Japanese ships were far too fast for the submarine. By 6:00 A.M. on October 26, she gave up the quest and returned to her patrol station off central Formosa.

The *Halibut* was not the only American submarine to pursue the retreating Japanese ships. The *Jallao,* newly built in a Wisconsin shipyard, went into action when her radar scope showed a contact 27,000 yards away. This was the crippled light cruiser *Tama,* which moved at 16 knots and had sustained bomb damage. The submarine closed the range, submerged, and fired seven torpedoes from her bow and stern tubes at the

Japanese ship. As the submarine's skipper viewed the misty moonlit scene through his periscope, the small, three-piped cruiser looked "as big as the Pentagon." Three torpedoes struck the hapless Japanese ship. From the *Pintado*'s bridge, Clarey saw the warship break up into several pieces and sink. The *Tama* was the last Japanese ship lost off Cape Engaño.

What was left of the Japanese Northern Force—the *Ise, Hyuga, Oyodo,* and five destroyers—escaped to the protection of the East China Sea. They had successfully run the gauntlet of the American submarine wolf pack commanded by Cmdr. F. J. Harlfinger in the *Trigger.* She picked up the Japanese ships on her radar and tried to pursue them, but the Japanese ships were too fast. Eventually the Northern Force rendezvoused with the remnants of Admiral Shima's Southern Force escaping from the Surigao Strait, and they sought the safety of Lingga Roads. Their next and last appearance in the war would be to haul gasoline from Singapore to Kure in February 1945.

The Battle's Aftermath

Looking at the Battle off Cape Engaño from a historical perspective, it is evident that the SHO-1 plan succeeded as far as luring Halsey's powerful Third Fleet away from Kurita's Center Force is concerned. The second conclusion one can draw is that the American naval pilots had lost their fighting edge to a certain extent, in that they failed to wipe out the Northern Force. They did sink four carriers—the *Zuikaku, Zuiho, Chitose, Chitose*—and one destroyer, but failed to completely destroy Ozawa's entire force. American submarines, cruisers, and destroyers were responsible for the rest of the Japanese losses—the light cruiser *Tama* and the two destroyers, *Hatsuzuki* and *Nowaki.* The bombing accuracy of the American pilots did not meet the standards their predecessors had set at Midway and the Marianas Turkey Shoot. As for the overwhelming power of the Third Fleet's battleships, it was never used to annihilate the Japanese ships because of Halsey's decision to take Lee's battleships with him to pursue Ozawa.

The third conclusion is that the Japanese had guessed correctly as to what Halsey would do if a tempting target was offered to him. One fleet carrier and three light carriers appeared from the north, and Halsey went after them. While the American admiral had more than once demonstrated extreme bravery and dedication to duty, these very attributes were used against him by the Japanese naval planners. One can only wonder what would have happened if Halsey had been in command at Midway and had acted in an equally impulsive manner. An unknown former cruiser commander named Spruance is the one who made the sound decisions that changed history by stopping the Japanese in their tracks.

The Battle off Cape Engaño was the last major engagement in the Battle of Leyte Gulf. Admiral Ozawa was the only Japanese commander who performed the duty assigned to him and achieved the desired strategic success. But, there is irony in this success in that Ozawa was a leading proponent of carrier warfare after Yamamoto's death. When the Japanese carrier fleet had been decimated in the Battle of the Philippine Sea, and in the Battle off Cape Engaño, it became a mere shadow of its former self. Nonetheless, Ozawa had obeyed orders and willingly given up four carriers so Halsey would be lured out of Kurita's way. Unflinchingly he had faced up to his situation and done his duty. In later years, Ozawa would be judged by his former enemies as among the most able of the Japanese admirals to serve in World War II. He neither ran away from his assignment nor failed to make the most of every opportunity his situation afforded.[7]

It is part of the Leyte Gulf picture that the Japanese began using kamikaze tactics toward the end of this battle. Although the attacks inflicted some damage on the American ships, they did not alter the outcome. This battle tactic would make its force felt later during the invasion of Luzon in Lingayen Gulf and the invasion of Okinawa. To give this new and problematic tactic its just due, one could easily write another book (and perhaps one day I will).

With the conclusion of the Battle off Cape Engaño, the massive naval engagement known as the Battle of Leyte Gulf had ended. Who won? Undoubtedly, it was a decisive American victory despite a number of tactical blunders made by the Americans. How did the Japanese lose? Was their defeat the result of bad planning, bad execution, or both? While many factors influenced the outcome, and there have been many volumes written on the subject, I will offer my analysis in the closing chapter with the help of some distinguished naval analysts and historians.

Chapter 19: The Harsh Prism of Historical Perspective

It is tempting to discuss the aftermath of the Battle of Leyte Gulf in terms of the bravery, sacrifice, heroism, and daring of the American sailors who participated in this historic confrontation. No words can possibly do justice to what transpired over those tumultuous days. I have attempted to describe the heroic feats that unfolded, in context, as they happened. But it is now time to look at some of the tactical errors that took place on the American side, even though the battle produced an American victory.

The Americans used their carrier-based resources to their utmost capacity by inflicting heavy damage on the Japanese warships, although they could have been more effective in the Battle off Cape Engaño. The same cannot be said about the use of superior American naval gunfire, however. Although the Battle of Surigao Strait demonstrated how superior gunfire can defeat a vastly inferior enemy, the Third Fleet's overwhelming firepower embodied in its modern fast battleships was never brought to bear. Halsey's battleships' and cruisers' guns never fired a shot at the inferior Japanese Center Force, except for sinking a few hapless cripples. The Americans had greater gun power in the Third Fleet than was present in the entire Japanese navy. And the Seventh Fleet's gun power was only half-utilized in the Surigao Strait against an opposing force only one-fifth its size. The well-executed torpedo attacks carried out by American destroyers in the Surigao Strait inflicted the heaviest damage to Nishimura's Force C well before the guns of the American battle line ever made a single hit on the outnumbered, outgunned Japanese.

Despite this vast superiority on the American side, the Japanese Center Force was allowed to pass through the San Bernardino Strait undetected. The Center Force, though it was a valuable naval prize, was presumed to be too severely damaged to be dangerous again after it had been attacked by American carrier aircraft in the Sibuyan Sea. But, as usual, combat pilots exaggerated the damage they had inflicted. Tragically, the American commanders believed some of these overly optimistic reports. The Center Force, however, reversed its course in the Sibuyan Sea, entered the seas off Samar, caught the Seventh Fleet by surprise, and almost inflicted a major defeat on the Americans. Luckily for them, a few daring and brave American escort carrier pilots and some equally self-sacrificing and courageous destroyer sailors saved the day.

The Japanese fought bravely. However, their SHO-1 battle plan lacked the flexibility necessary to adapt to changing battle conditions. The plan was too complicated and too difficult to execute because it required three simultaneous operations to be performed perfectly in order for the plan to succeed. It would have taken optimum conditions for the Japanese to pull off the SHO-1 plan. Consider the SHO-1 plan's assumption that Japanese land-based aircraft would fly air cover and protect the Japanese ships from American air attacks. The naval planners in Tokyo had failed to comprehend that many of the Japanese planes on which they were depending had been destroyed by the American carrier air forces during the Formosa Air Battle. The conditions on which the Japanese based their plan could only have existed on a war game table in a naval war college or seminar.

There is no mystery as to why the Japanese lost the Battle of Leyte Gulf. Japanese execution was faulty. Their timing was bad, their torpedo technique was fainthearted and ineffectual, their gunnery was mediocre, their ship identification was horrible, and communications were abominable. The forces that were sent into battle obviously had not been in a major naval battle recently.

The Japanese commanders lacked the flexible thinking needed to adapt to the rapidly changing battle conditions. Admiral Nishimura's force steamed into a certain trap and was uselessly sacrificed. Despite outfoxing Halsey, Admiral Kurita's Center Force never pressed its overwhelming advantage off Samar. Any admiral worth his salt, when confronted by only six escort carriers and a few destroyers, would have formed his battle line, sent it in full force, and pounded the unfortunate American force into oblivion. But Kurita's imagination transformed the opposing ships into behemoths, so he broke off the action, reversed course, and retired after inflicting only minor damage. Had he pressed the attack, his battle line and cruisers could have mercilessly shelled the American landing forces before Halsey's Third Fleet or Oldendorf's battleships could come to the rescue. If the Center Force had faced the Seventh Fleet's older battleships, the outcome would have been uncertain at best. The Japanese battle line was more modern and faster than the American Seventh Fleet's ships. After all, other than crossing the "T" in the Surigao Strait, the older American battleships had been used exclusively for bombarding shore installations in anticipation of an invasion.

Of course, this is sheer speculation. Because of a few brave souls who gave everything they had to save their landing force comrades from almost certain annihilation, the power of the Center Force was never actually tested.

The Americans cannot escape criticism for their actions during this event. The two senior naval commanders, Admirals Kinkaid and Halsey, do not emerge from this battle unscathed and unblemished. Both are culpable as regards what happened to Cliff Sprague off Samar.

Admiral Kinkaid failed to comprehend the meaning of Halsey's messages when he said he was forming Task Force 34. Kinkaid assumed Lee's battleships were going to guard the eastern approaches to the San Bernardino Strait and to prevent the Japanese Center Force from successfully exiting that waterway, and then moving southward toward Leyte Gulf. The way it appears is that Kinkaid wanted to believe that Halsey was doing what Kinkaid thought he should be doing. No one in the Seventh Fleet's senior command staff believed that Halsey would ever abandon his assigned post. However, wishful thinking does not win battles.

The furor over Halsey's and Kinkaid's actions at Leyte Gulf endures even to this day. Kinkaid and the other naval commanders in the Seventh Fleet believed that Halsey behaved in a truly reckless manner when he took the Third Fleet northward after Ozawa. These men have contended that if Halsey had left the Third Fleet where it was, Cliff Sprague's Taffy 3 would not have been left to fend for itself. The overwhelming air and surface power of the Third Fleet would have decimated Kurita and his ships. The Taffies then would merely have joined the battle to make whatever contribution they could.

Of course, Halsey disagreed with these officers' opinions. To justify his position, he cited the paragraph in the original orders Nimitz had given him prior to the battle: "In case opportunity for destruction of major portion of the enemy fleet offers or can be created, such destruction becomes the primary task." Halsey argued that while he had a "major portion of the enemy fleet"—Kurita's Center Force—in front of him, Ozawa's Northern Force with its carriers posed the greater threat because of its presumed aircraft strength.

Until Halsey died in 1959, he continued to dispute the criticisms of his decisions at the Battle of Leyte Gulf by his fellow officers and naval historians, including the Japanese. In 1946 he attempted to shift the blame elsewhere, such as at Kinkaid, in the seventh installment of his memoirs in the *Saturday Evening Post*. In that article he asserted the problems at Leyte Gulf were due to the fact there was no single naval officer in charge. Halsey redirected the blame to Kinkaid when he stated, "I wondered how Kinkaid allowed 'Ziggy' Sprague [to] get caught like this."[1] Halsey wrote that Kinkaid's repeated pleas for help from the fast battleships "surprised me. It was not my job to protect the Seventh Fleet. My job was offensive to strike with the Third Fleet."[2] And so on.

The controversy over whether Halsey made the right decisions at Leyte Gulf continues to this day. Nevertheless, one can safely state that history's verdict on Halsey's behavior at Leyte Gulf has been, to say the least, less than complementary. What he did there should not, however, fully tarnish the contributions he made bringing victory to the Americans in the Pacific War. Today, the criticisms of Halsey have surfaced again in popular media outlets such as The History Channel. But current public opinion is understandably muted since these events occurred more than fifty years ago. Nonetheless, the debate will continue among those who study and analyze naval history.

There is one problem in this drama that both sides have shared. Both commands were divided. Like the Americans, the Japanese had no overall commander in charge. But the fragmentation of the Japanese command structure was even more severe than that of the Americans. Each Japanese force had its own commander, and this commander was allowed to operate independently of the others under the ambiguous guidelines of the SHO-1 plan. Therefore, when Nishimura's vastly weaker Southern Force came northward through the Surigao Strait and ran into the overwhelmingly powerful force consisting of American destroyers and Admiral Oldendorf's battle line, there was nothing he could do but go blindly to his doom with little or no communication with Kurita, Ozawa, and even Shima. When Kurita was under attack by the Taffies off Samar, he was under no obligation nor did he have any orders obliging him to tell either Ozawa or Nishimura about his progress—or lack of it. Also, the Japanese splintered command prevented its naval commanders from asking for air assistance from Japanese land-based airpower, upon which the SHO-1 plan originally depended in order to succeed.

The Japanese command structure was divided five ways. None of the admirals commanding the Japanese naval forces—Kurita, Nishimura, Ozawa, and Shima—and the commander of the Japanese land-based air forces, had any unifying command from which to take orders, except from the Combined Fleet Headquarters in Tokyo. There was no Japanese commander in charge *at the scene of battle.*

The Americans' greatest weakness, however, was its divided command structure at the top. Unlike the Japanese, there were two command divisions: MacArthur's and Nimitz's. Had either commander been in full charge at Leyte, Halsey would not have been allowed to improvise. Before moving the Third Fleet northward and away from its assigned location off the San Bernardino Strait for whatever reason, he would have had to ask his superior's permission. Of course, one must assume that in such a scenario permission would have been refused. Also, the vital communication delays for messages between the Third Fleet and the Seventh Fleet would never have occurred, since all naval commanders would have been included in all message traffic. The American communications station on Manus could have been more adequately staffed to handle the increased message traffic. Thus, the tragically slow message turnaround would have been significantly reduced. Perhaps additional communications stations could have been established so not all messages would have to go through the Manus bottleneck. Therefore, neither Kinkaid nor Halsey would have endured those intolerable delays of one to three hours in receiving messages reporting the Japanese Center Force's attack on Taffy 3.

Which division of command was the worst? Looking at what happened at the Battle of Leyte Gulf, it is clear that the Japanese structure was inferior. The disparity in the way command was divided between the two nations did not solely create Japan's defeat at Leyte Gulf. Other factors were involved as well. Among these were a lack of determination by Kurita to press the issue off Samar, the overwhelming American superiority in ships and experienced naval aircraft crews, and the remarkable ability of the American commanders to adapt their tactics to changing battle conditions.

Aftermath and Historical Significance

The Battle of Leyte Gulf ended on October 26, 1944. The Americans lost one light carrier, two escort carriers (one by naval gunfire, the other from kamikaze attacks), two destroyers, and a destroyer escort. The Japanese lost one battleship, one fleet carrier, three light carriers, six heavy cruisers, four light cruisers, and nine destroyers.

One major lesson again reinforced by the Battle of Leyte Gulf was how helpless a modern fleet is without air cover. Taffy 3 effectively blocked a powerful force of battleships and cruisers by the relentless application of naval airpower. The key event leading to the victory at Leyte Gulf was the October air strikes on Formosa. The earlier destruction of Japanese naval airpower in the Battles of the Philippine Sea in June and Formosa in October, in reality, decided the outcome of the Battle of Leyte Gulf. Had the invasion occurred in December, as originally planned, the Japanese would have had sufficient time to train new Japanese air groups, and the Imperial Navy might have fought more effectively than it did.

After the Battle of Leyte Gulf, Allied naval forces continued to hammer away at Japanese efforts to aid its beleaguered ground troops on Leyte. They maintained air supremacy until American army planes could assume that role. Although the Americans met slight resistance when they first landed on October 20, ground operations on Leyte proved to be more difficult than originally thought. The toughness of Japanese ground forces forced MacArthur to commit 250,000 troops to take the island. By December 1944, the only operations that remained were the mopping up of what was left of Japanese forces on Leyte and the preparation for the Luzon landings. After desperately gambling everything it had at Leyte Gulf, the Japanese navy stopped being an independent fighting force and was banished to an auxiliary role for the rest of the war. Leyte Gulf dealt a death blow to the Imperial Fleet, an event that meant Japan would finally be defeated in the end. After the war, the Japanese chief of naval staff, Adm. Mitsumasa Yonai, said, "Our defeat at Leyte was tantamount to the loss of the Philippines. When you took the Philippines, that was the end of our resources."[3]

After the Battle of Leyte Gulf, Japan ceased to be a naval power.

The Battle of Leyte Gulf was the last naval struggle to include large formations of warships, and there was an air of finality about it. The likelihood of a future conflict such as this one is almost nonexistent. The nature of naval warfare has changed drastically with the arrival of state-sponsored terrorism and the end of the Soviet Union. The United States of America is the only remaining superpower capable of having fleets akin to the ones that faced each other on those dramatic days in October almost fifty-six years ago. Even when the naval power of the Soviet Union was at its zenith, its primary methods of sea warfare were concentrated on potential engagements among submarines, the selective use of naval airpower to quell outbreaks of small wars, and engagements among relatively small groups of naval vessels.

In the broad scheme of naval history, the Battle of Leyte Gulf did not alter the course of the Pacific War in the way that the battles of Midway or the Solomons did, and no naval historian has ever made such a claim. In fact, this tremendous conflict was a continuation of the American overall strategic objective to cripple the Japanese Empire's ability to prosecute the war and force it to surrender. One impact this battle had was the establishment of the Americans as the reigning naval power over the vast Pacific Ocean until the war ended. The Americans' overwhelming dominance after Leyte Gulf brought the Pacific War to a swifter conclusion than would otherwise have been the case.

No matter how anyone looks at this massive battle, the Battle of Leyte Gulf should be emblazoned in our national heritage. The night confrontation in the Surigao Strait exemplified the Americans' perfect timing, supreme organization, and almost perfect execution. Furthermore, there is no peer in American naval warfare to the action off Samar. The glorious defiance of the American destroyers that attacked battleships and cruisers with no regard for their own safety, the valiant pilots, sometimes carrying no ammunition or bombs themselves, who bombed and strafed in the face of vicious Japanese antiaircraft fire, the quick thinking and decision making of Adm. Clifton Sprague, and the courage of them all against overwhelming odds, should indelibly engrave this action in the hearts of those who enjoy reading naval history.

Notes

Prologue: The First Blow

1. *Air Raid, Pearl Harbor. This is no drill!* Map of Pearl Harbor, O.S.B. Map Mania Publishing. Bess Atfield, publisher, 1995.

2. Wukovitz, pp. 49–52.

3. Wukovitz, p. 56.

4. Wukovitz, p. 63

5. Wukovitz. p. 58.

6. Morison, vol. 12, pp. 1–12.

7. Morison, vol. 12, p. 413.

Chapter 1: American Strategy

1. Potter, *Nimitz*, p. 279.

2. Potter, *Nimitz*, pp. 291–292.

3. James, pp. 189–190.

4. Willoughby, p. 233.

5. Willoughby, pp. 232–233.

6. Potter, *Nimitz*, p. 304.

7. Potter, *Nimitz*, p. 315.

8. Cutler, pp. 31–32.

9. Cutler, p. 32.

10. See note 12.

11. See note 12.

12. The content of the preceding part of the conversation that took place between Roosevelt and MacArthur that day in Hawaii has not been

fully chronicled with the exact words. The conversation did occur on July 26, 1944, and is a re-creation using various sources that indicated the subjects covered. These sources include the following: Cutler, pp. 33–34; Morison, vol. 12, pp. 9–10; Manchester (1978), pp. 425–427; Hunt, p. 335; MacArthur, pp. 196–199; Potter, *Nimitz*, pp. 318–319.

13. Potter, *Nimitz*, pp. 315–319.
14. Cutler, p. 33.
15. Cutler, pp. 31–35.
16. Morison, vol. 12, pp. 10–11.
17. Morison, vol. 12, p. 11.
18. Falk, pp. 51–52.
19. Buell, pp. 471–473.
20. Willoughby, pp. 232–234.
21. Morison, vol. 12, pp. 55–61.
22. Potter, *Bull Halsey*, p. 279.
23. Cutler, p. 61.
24. Corbett, p. 261.
25. Morison, vol. 12, p. 59.
26. Cutler, pp. 55–61.

Chapter 2: The Japanese Get Ready

1. Toland, p. 658.
2. Prados, pp. 585–586.
3. Ito, p. 111.
4. Prados, p. 586.
5. To those of us who have been trained to think as Westerners, the Japanese planner shows some confusion here in that he was aware of Japan's inability to meet the American challenge over time. The idea that it was feasible to check the American advance appears to be a hope based on wishful thinking. However, it is essential to try to understand the thinking prevalent in the Japanese government during World War II. Japan had achieved such dramatic success in the first six months of the Pacific War that they seemed to continuously think that these victories would continue unabated. To the Japanese mind, they were so dedicated to the idea that they had proven their invincibility against what they considered to be inferior Western enemies that this sense of remaining undefeated was their destiny. And no power on earth could stop them.
6. Prados, pp. 585–586.
7. The Japanese called their land-based air forces Base Air Forces.
8. Ito, pp. 111–120.

9. Morison, vol. 12, pp. 65–73.

10. Morison, vol. 12, p. 18. Text of that order follows: "General MacArthur will liberate Luzon, starting 20 December, and establish bases there to support later operations. Admiral Nimitz will provide fleet cover and support, occupy one or more positions in the Bonin-Volcano Island group 20 January 1945, and invade the Ryukyus, target date 1 March 1945."

11. Morison, vol. 12, p. 91.

12. Morison, p. 93; Cutler, p. 70.

13. Taylor, page 261.

14. Morison, vol. 12, pp. 86–95.

15. Taylor, p. 254.

16. Taylor, p. 262.

17. Ito, p. 169.

18. Falk, pp. 63–64.

19. Prados, pp. 658–659.

20. Ito, p. 130.

21. Morison, vol. 12, pp. 160–168.

22. Prados, p. 628.

23. Hoyt, p. 2.

24. Prados, p. 629.

25. Wukovits, pp. 122–123; Grove, p. 198.

26. Cutler, pp. 69–71.

27. Cutler, p. 89.

28. Ito, p. 120.

29. Cutler, pp. 91–92.

30. Ito, p. 120.

31. Cutler, pp. 88–93.

32. Hoyt, pp. 49–50.

33. Hoyt, p. 51.

34. Falk, p. 131.

35. Grove, pp. 200–201.

36. Prados, pp. 643–644.

37. Morison, vol. 12, p. 169.

Chapter 3: A Promise Kept

1. Morison, vol. 12, pp. 117–123.

2. Keane, personal recollection in a letter to author, postmarked April 16, 1996.

3. Morison, vol. 12, pp. 123–124.

4. Oldendorf, p. 37.

5. Morison, vol. 12, p. 124.

6. The Battle of Leyte Gulf was the greatest naval conflict since the Battle of Jutland (1916) in all respects—the size of the battle itself and the size of the invasion fleet in terms of the number of ships, which was larger than that for Operation Overlord, the invasion of France on June 6, 1944.

7. Morison, vol. 12, pp. 124–127.

8. Keasler, from his web site.

9. Morison, vol. 12, pp. 127–129.

10. *New York Times*, Oct. 21, 1944.

11. Morison, vol. 12, pp. 130–132.

12. Keasler, from his web site.

13. Morison, vol. 12, pp. 132–136.

Chapter 4: A Historic Event

1. Whan, pp. 132–133.

2. Morison, vol. 12, pp. 130–140.

3. *New York Times*, Oct. 20, 1944.

4. Morison, vol. 12, pp. 141–156.

Chapter 5: Landing the First Punch

1. Prados, p. 636.

2. Hoyt, *Battle of Leyte Gulf*, pp. 60–62.

3. Morison, vol. 12, pp. 169–170.

4. Hoyt, *Battle of Leyte Gulf*, pp. 63–64.

5. Morison, vol. 12, pp. 171–174.

6. Hoyt, *Battle of Leyte Gulf*, pp. 50–68.

7. Hoyt, *Battle of Leyte Gulf*, p. 59.

8. Hoyt, *Battle of Leyte Gulf*, pp. 69–71.

9. Hoyt, *Battle of Leyte Gulf*, p. 63.

10. Hoyt, *Battle of Leyte Gulf*, pp. 72–74.

11. Hoyt, *Battle of Leyte Gulf*, p. 77.

12. Morison, vol. 12, pp. 171–174.

13. Solberg, p. 9.

14. Grove, pp. 85–94.

Chapter 6: The Americans Lose a Great Lady

1. Solberg, p. 102.

2. Morison, vol. 12, p. 179.

3. Morison, vol. 12, pp. 181–182.

4. Morison, vol. 12, pp. 177–183.

Chapter 7: Struggle in the Sibuyan Sea

1. Grove, pp. 68–71.

2. Hoyt, *Battle of Leyte Gulf,* p. 82.

3. Hoyt, *Battle of Leyte Gulf,* pp. 85–100.

4. Hoyt, *Battle of Leyte Gulf,* p. 83.

5. Hoyt, *Battle of Leyte Gulf,* pp. 100–101.

6. Hoyt, *Battle of Leyte Gulf,* p. 106.

7. Morison, vol. 12, pp. 174–176.

8. There were 112 more ships attached to the Third Fleet that did not directly engage in combat operations but supplied indispensable support to Third Fleet operations. These included 11 escort carriers, 18 destroyers, 26 destroyer escorts, 34 oilers, 10 fleet tugs, and 13 ammunition ships, bringing the total number of ships in the Third Fleet to 209. Morison, vol. 12, pp. 424–429.

9. Potter, *Bull Halsey,* pp. 290–291.

10. Morison, vol. 12, pp. 424–428.

11. Hoyt, *Battle of Leyte Gulf,* pp. 121–122.

12. Hoyt, *Battle of Leyte Gulf,* pp. 135–136.

13. Potter, *Bull Halsey,* p. 292.

14. Solberg, pp. 103–104.

15. Hoyt, *Battle of Leyte Gulf,* pp. 110–125.

16. Solberg, p. 106.

17. Potter, *Bull Halsey,* p. 292.

18. Solberg, pp. 106–109.

19. Potter, *Bull Halsey,* pp. 291–293.

Chapter 8: The Japanese Fight Back

1. Cutler, p. 144.

2. Ito, p. 170.

3. Cutler, pp. 144–145.

4. Boyne, pp. 307–309.

5. Cutler, p. 145.

6. Cutler, p. 146.

7. Cutler. p. 148.

8. Hoyt, *Battle of Leyte Gulf,* p. 126.

9. Ito, p. 170.

10. Cutler, pp. 147–151.

11. Hoyt, *Battle of Leyte Gulf,* pp. 126–132.

12. Ito, pp. 170-173.

13. Morison, vol. 12, p. 189.

14. Ito, pp. 170–174.

15. Morison, vol. 12, pp. 183–189.

16. Cutler, B*attle of Leyte Gulf,* p. 144.

17. Hoyt, *Battle of Leyte Gulf,* pp. 130–131.

18. Hoyt, *Battle of Leyte Gulf,* pp. 132–133.

19. *Bushido* is the code of honor and behavior of the Japanese warrior class (samurai) that emphasized courage, loyalty, and self-discipline.

20. Hoyt, *Battle of Leyte Gulf,* pp. 138–139.

21. Cutler, *Battle of Leyte Gulf,* pp. 144–153.

Chapter 9: Making a Deadly Decision

1. Prados, p. 647.

2. Prados, pp. 645–647.

3. Ito, p. 146.

4. Ito, pp. 170–171.

5. Prados, pp. 647–648.

6. Solberg, pp. 76–84.

7. Solberg, p. 115.

8. Potter, *Bull Halsey,* p. 294.

9. Hoyt, *Battle of Leyte Gulf,* pp. 120–121.

10. Hoyt, *Battle of Leyte Gulf,* p. 129.

11. Solberg, pp. 110–113.

12. Hoyt, *Battle of Leyte Gulf,* p. 153.

13. Hoyt, *Battle of Leyte Gulf,* p. 130.

14. Hoyt, *Battle of Leyte Gulf,* pp. 136–137.

15. Solberg, pp. 114–117.

16. Hoyt, *Battle of Leyte Gulf,* pp. 153–154.

17. Potter, *Bull Halsey,* pp. 293, 295–296.

18. Solberg, pp. 117–119; Potter, *Bull Halsey,* pp. 294–295.

19. Potter, *Bull Halsey,* pp. 297–298.

20. Wheeler, p. 399.

21. Potter, *Bull Halsey,* p. 296.

22. Potter, *Bull Halsey,* p. 296.

23. Solberg, pp. 120–126; Hoyt, *Battle of Leyte Gulf,* pp. 155–156.

Chapter 10: Crossing the "T"

1. Falk, p. 154.
2. Dull, p. 62.
3. Ito, pp. 175–177.
4. Prados, pp. 660–661.
5. Morison, vol. 12, pp. 190–191.
6. Hoyt, *Battle of Leyte Gulf,* pp. 109–110.
7. Morison, vol. 12, p. 190.
8. Oldendorf, pp. 40–41.
9. Morison, vol. 12, pp. 199–208.
10. Morison, vol. 12, pp. 414–432.
11. Oldendorf, p. 41.
12. Oldendorf, p. 43.
13. Morison, vol. 12, pp. 208–213.
14. Kent, personal recollections.
15. Morison, vol. 12, p. 213.
16. Cutler, p. 190.
17. Cutler, pp. 189–191.
18. Dye, personal recollections.
19. Morison, vol. 12, pp. 214–215.
20. Kent, personal recollections.
21. Cutler, pp. 191–192.
22. Morison, vol. 12, p. 215.
23. Cutler, p. 192.
24. The rapid changes in the technology of naval warfare and in the way wars after World War II would be fought precluded the future use of torpedo attacks such as those of the Americans in the Surigao Strait. The conflicts after World War II did not include battles between large naval fleets because naval warfare evolved to undersea operations with nuclear-powered submarines. Also, the development of the nuclear-powered supercarrier by the United States made that nation the only one with a large naval fleet that rivaled the power of the fleets that fought in the Pacific Ocean in World War II.
25. Fast, personal recollections.
26. Morison, vol. 12, pp. 217–221.
27. Conley, interview with author, January 27, 1997.
28. Morison, vol. 12, pp. 220–223; interview with Jack Conley, January 27, 1997.
29. Morison, vol. 12, p. 223.

30. Grove, pp. 207–209.

31. Morison, vol. 12, p. 223.

32. Morison, vol. 12, pp. 223–224.

33. Oldendorf, pp. 44–45.

34. Morison, vol. 12, pp. 224–226.

35. Ito, p. 136.

36. Morison, vol. 12, p. 217.

37. Ito, p. 136.

38. Ito, pp. 136–137.

39. Morison, vol. 12, pp. 226–230.

40. Ito, pp. 135–140.

41. Morison, vol. 12, pp. 230–233.

42. Ito, pp. 177–178.

43. Morison, vol. 12, p. 234.

44. Morison, vol. 12, p. 236.

45. Morison, vol. 12, p. 238.

46. Morison, vol. 12, pp. 234–240; Dull, pp. 211–212.

47. Falk, p. 159.

48. Morison, vol. 12, pp. 240–241.

Chapter 11: Band of Brothers

1. Morison, vol. 12, pp. 191–192.

2. Ito, p. 151.

3. Hoyt, *Battle of Leyte Gulf*, pp. 203–205; Ito, pp. 149–151.

Chapter 12: A Morning to Remember

1. Wukovits, pp. 82–110.

2. Morison, vol. 12, pp. 242–245.

3. Wukovits, pp. 123–124.

4. Wukovits, pp. 126–127.

5. Wukovits, pp. 141–142.

6. Youngblood, pp. 154–156.

7. Wukovits, pp. 142–145; Morison, vol. 12, pp. 245–250.

8. Wukovits, p. 146.

9. Wukovits, p. 148.

10. Youngblood, p. 160.

11. Wukovits, pp. 145–152.

12. Prados, p. 666.

13. Wukovits, pp. 152–155.

Chapter 13: Swarming Bees
1. Wukovits, pp. 155–157.
2. Youngblood, p. 163. Although Huxtable was a lieutenant commander, he was commander of one of the aircraft units aboard the *Gambier Bay*. It is the custom in the navy for subordinates within a command to address their commanding officer as "Captain," although that commander may not have that rank.
3. Youngblood, pp. 164–167.
4. Wukovits, p. 155.
5. Youngblood, pp. 163–173.
6. Morison, vol. 12, pp. 285–288.

Chapter 14: Deadly Delays and Unanswered Pleas for Help
1. Prados, p. 680.
2. Prados, p. 682.
3. Wukovits, pp. 157–158; Morison, vol. 12, pp. 293–294.

Chapter 15: The Valley of the Shadow of Death
1. Morison, vol. 12, p. 255.
2. Wukovits, pp. 159–160.
3. Mercer, pp. 2–3.
4. Excerpts from Evans's biography, published by U.S. Navy Office of Information, are reprinted in Mercer, pp. 1–3.
5. Morison, vol. 12, p. 256.
6. Wukovits, pp. 160–166.
7. Morison, vol. 12, pp. 255–262.
8. Wukovits, p. 166.
9. Wukovits, pp. 170–171.
10. Morison, vol. 12, pp. 262–271.
11. Wukovits, pp. 170–175.
12. Morison, vol. 12, pp. 271–276.
13. Citation published by the U.S. Navy Office of Information.
14. Wukovits, pp. 167–168.

Chapter 16: A Mystery Looking for a Solution
1. Wukovits, pp. 168–170.
2. Cutler, p. 251.
3. Prados, pp. 686–687; Wukovits, pp. 169–178.
4. Wukovits, p. 167; Morison, vol. 12, pp. 250–255.
5. Morison, vol. 12, p. 280.

6. Morison, vol. 12, pp. 296–312.

7. Wukovits, pp. 183–184.

8. Wukovits, p. 187.

Chapter 17: A Tragic Figure

1. Taylor, pp. 260–267.

2. Taylor, pp. 339–340.

Chapter 18: Cape of Fools

1. Potter, *Bull Halsey*, p. 294.

2. Morison, vol. 12, p. 318.

3. Hoyt, *Battle of Leyte Gulf*, pp. 315–322.

4. Earlier in the narrative, the American pilots reported attacking a Chitose-class carrier. When attacking a ship from aircraft, the best identification that can be made is to say a ship is in a certain class, because it is impossible to identify uniquely a ship by its name from an airplane flying at high speed from altitudes of thousands of feet. Pilots are trained to identify ships by silhouette, which only identifies all ships of that type or class.

5. Morison, vol. 12, pp. 322–328.

6. Hoyt, *Battle of Leyte Gulf*, pp. 315–325.

7. Morison, vol. 12, pp. 329–336.

Chapter 19: The Harsh Prism of Historical Perspective

1. Potter, *Bull Halsey*, p. 371.

2. Potter, *Bull Halsey*, p. 371.

3. Morison, vol. 12, pp. 337–338.

Bibliography

Primary Sources

Conley, Lt. (jg) Jack, USNR (ret.). Interview conducted by author, January 27, 1997.

Dye, Jessie D. Letter written to author, May 1996.

Fast, Charles. Letter to author, April 24, 1996.

Keane, Patrick. Letter to author, postmarked April 16, 1996.

Keasler, Carlos. From his web site (www.webcom.com/wak/lestweforget/), 1999.

Kent, Cecil M. Personal recollections in a letter to author, July 1996.

Raggie, John. Interview conducted by author, February 8, 1996.

Secondary Sources

Boyne, Walter J. *Clash of Titans: World War II at Sea.* New York: Simon and Schuster, 1995.

Buell, Thomas B. *Master of Sea Power: A Biography of Fleet Admiral Ernest J. King.* Boston: Little, Brown, 1980.

Burke, Colin. *Information and Secrecy: Vannevar Bush, Ultra, and the Other Memex.* Lanham, Maryland: Scarecrow, 1994.

Clark, J. J., with Clark G. Reynolds. *Carrier Admiral.* New York: David McKay, 1967.

Corbett, Sir Julian. *Some Principles of Maritime Strategy.* London: Longmans, Green, 1918.

Cutler, Thomas J. *The Battle of Leyte Gulf: 23–26 October 1944.* New York, HarperCollins, 1994.

Doolittle, James H. *I Could Never Be so Lucky*. New York: Bantam Books, 1994.

Dull, Paul S. *The Imperial Japanese Fleet, 1941–1945*. Annapolis, Maryland: U.S. Naval Institute, 1978.

Falk, Stanley L. *Decision at Leyte*. New York: W. W. Norton, 1966.

Grove, Eric. *Sea Battles: In Close Up*. Volume 2. Annapolis, Maryland: Naval Institute Press, 1993.

Halsey, William F. *Memoirs*. Washington, D.C.: Naval Historical Center, 1947.

Holmes, W. J. *Double-edged Secrets*. Annapolis, Maryland: Naval Institute Press, 1979.

Hoyt, Edwin P. *How They Won the War in the Pacific: Nimitz and His Admirals*. New York: Weybright and Talley, 1970.

———. *The Battle of Leyte Gulf: The Death Knell of the Japanese Fleet*. New York: Weybright and Talley, 1972.

———. *MacArthur's Navy*. New York: Orion Books, 1989.

———. *The Last Kamikaze*. Westport, Connecticut: Praeger, 1993.

Hunt, Frazier. *The Untold Story of Douglas MacArthur*. New York: Devin-Adair Company, 1954.

Interviews with Japanese POWs. Washington, D.C.: Naval Historical Center, 1945–1948.

Ito, Masanori. *The End of the Imperial Japanese Navy*. Tokyo: Orion Press, 1956.

James, D. Clayton. *A Time for Giants*. New York: Franklin Watts, 1987.

Kennedy, David M. "Victory at Sea." *Atlantic Monthly* 23 (March 1999): 51–56, 59, 62–64, 66–68, 70–74, 76.

Koenig, William. *Epic Sea Battles*. Hong Kong: Mandarin Publishers, 1975.

Lewin, Ronald. *The American Magic Codes, Ciphers, and the Defeat of Japan*. New York: Farrar, Straus, 1982.

Lorenzo, Capt. Frank, USN (ret.). Oral recollection. Midway Email Discussion Group, January 11, 1998.

MacArthur, Douglas. *Reminiscences*. New York: McGraw-Hill, 1964.

Manchester, William. *American Caesar*. Hardcover edition. Boston: Little, Brown, 1978. Paperback edition. New York: Bantam, 1978.

Mercer, William E., and Robert Chastain. *The Fighting and Sinking of the USS Johnston as Told by Her Crew*. Johnston/Hoel Association, 1991.

Morison, Samuel E. *History of United States Naval Operations in World War II*. Volumes 3, 5, 8, 12. Boston: Little, Brown, 1984.

Mosley, Leonard. *Marshall: Hero for Our Times*. New York: Hearst Books, 1982.

Navy Office of Information. *Biography of Commander Ernest E. Evans.* Washington, D.C.: Biographies Branch, August 29, 1961.

Nimitz, Adm. Chester. Oral recollections by staff and relatives. Annapolis, Maryland: U.S. Naval Institute, U.S. Naval Academy, 1947–1950.

Oldendorf, Jesse B., as told to Daniel Hawthorne. "The Battle of Surigao Strait." *Blue Book* magazine, March 1949.

O'Toole, G. J. A. *Encyclopedia of American Intelligence and Espionage: From the Revolutionary War to the Present.* New York: Facts on File, 1988.

Potter, E. B. *Nimitz.* Annapolis, Maryland: Naval Institute Press, 1976.

———. *Bull Halsey.* Annapolis, Maryland: Naval Institute Press, 1985.

Prados, John. *Combined Fleet Decoded.* New York, Random House, 1995.

Prange, Gordon W. *Dec. 7, 1941: The Day the Japanese Attacked Pearl Harbor.* New York: McGraw-Hill, 1988.

Rosenheim, Shawn J. *The Cryptographic Imagination.* Baltimore, Maryland: Johns Hopkins, 1997.

Solberg, Carl. *Decision and Dissent: With Halsey at Leyte Gulf.* Annapolis, Maryland: Naval Institute Press, 1995.

Stripp, Alan. *Codebreakers in the Far East.* London: Frank Carr, 1989.

Taylor, Theodore. *The Magnificent Mitscher.* New York: Norton, 1954. Annapolis, Maryland: United States Naval Institute, 1991.

Toland, John. *The Rising Sun.* New York: Random House, 1970.

Whan, Maj. Vorin E., Jr., ed. *A Soldier Speaks: Public Papers and Speeches of General of the Army Douglas MacArthur.* New York: Praeger, 1965.

Wheeler, Gerald E. *Kinkaid of the Seventh Fleet.* Washington, D.C.: Naval Historical Center, 1995.

Willoughby, C. A., and J. Chamberlain. *MacArthur, 1941–1951.* New York: McGraw-Hill, 1954.

Winterbotham, Frederic William. *The Ultra Spy.* London: Macmillan, 1989.

Winton, John. *Ultra in the Pacific: How Breaking Japanese Codes and Ciphers Affected Naval Operations Against Japan.* Annapolis, Maryland: Naval Institute Press, 1993.

Wukovits, John F. *Devotion to Duty.* Annapolis, Maryland: Naval Institute Press, 1995.

Youngblood, William T. *The Little Giants: U.S. Escort Carriers Against Japan.* Annapolis, Maryland: Naval Institute Press, 1987.

Index